SECOND EDITION

Data Science from Scratch
First Principles with Python

Joel Grus

Beijing · Boston · Farnham · Sebastopol · Tokyo

Data Science from Scratch

by Joel Grus

Published by O'Reilly Media, Inc., 1005 Gravenstein Highway North, Sebastopol, CA 95472.

O'Reilly books may be purchased for educational, business, or sales promotional use. Online editions are also available for most titles (*http://oreilly.com*). For more information, contact our corporate/institutional sales department: 800-998-9938 or *corporate@oreilly.com*.

Editor: Michele Cronin
Production Editor: Deborah Baker
Copy Editor: Rachel Monaghan
Proofreader: Rachel Head

Indexer: Judy McConville
Interior Designer: David Futato
Cover Designer: Karen Montgomery
Illustrator: Rebecca Demarest

April 2015:   First Edition
May 2019:   Second Edition

Revision History for the Second Edition
2019-04-10:   First Release

See *http://oreilly.com/catalog/errata.csp?isbn=9781492041139* for release details.

978-1-492-04113-9

[LSI]

Table of Contents

Preface to the Second Edition

I am exceptionally proud of the first edition of *Data Science from Scratch*. It turned out very much the book I wanted it to be. But several years of developments in data science, of progress in the Python ecosystem, and of personal growth as a developer and educator have *changed* what I think a first book in data science should look like.

In life, there are no do-overs. In writing, however, there are second editions.

Accordingly, I've rewritten all the code and examples using Python 3.6 (and many of its newly introduced features, like type annotations). I've woven into the book an emphasis on writing clean code. I've replaced some of the first edition's toy examples with more realistic ones using "real" datasets. I've added new material on topics such as deep learning, statistics, and natural language processing, corresponding to things that today's data scientists are likely to be working with. (I've also removed some material that seems less relevant.) And I've gone over the book with a fine-toothed comb, fixing bugs, rewriting explanations that are less clear than they could be, and freshening up some of the jokes.

The first edition was a great book, and this edition is even better. Enjoy!

Joel Grus
Seattle, WA
2019

Conventions Used in This Book

The following typographical conventions are used in this book:

Italic
>   Indicates new terms, URLs, email addresses, filenames, and file extensions.

Constant width

> Used for program listings, as well as within paragraphs to refer to program elements such as variable or function names, databases, data types, environment variables, statements, and keywords.

Constant width bold

> Shows commands or other text that should be typed literally by the user.

Constant width italic

> Shows text that should be replaced with user-supplied values or by values determined by context.

 This element signifies a tip or suggestion.

 This element signifies a general note.

 This element indicates a warning or caution.

Using Code Examples

Supplemental material (code examples, exercises, etc.) is available for download at *https://github.com/joelgrus/data-science-from-scratch*.

This book is here to help you get your job done. In general, if example code is offered with this book, you may use it in your programs and documentation. You do not need to contact us for permission unless you're reproducing a significant portion of the code. For example, writing a program that uses several chunks of code from this book does not require permission. Selling or distributing a CD-ROM of examples from O'Reilly books does require permission. Answering a question by citing this book and quoting example code does not require permission. Incorporating a significant amount of example code from this book into your product's documentation does require permission.

We appreciate, but do not require, attribution. An attribution usually includes the title, author, publisher, and ISBN. For example: "*Data Science from Scratch*, Second Edition, by Joel Grus (O'Reilly). Copyright 2019 Joel Grus, 978-1-492-04113-9."

If you feel your use of code examples falls outside fair use or the permission given above, feel free to contact us at *permissions@oreilly.com*.

O'Reilly Online Learning

 For almost 40 years, *O'Reilly Media* has provided technology and business training, knowledge, and insight to help companies succeed.

Our unique network of experts and innovators share their knowledge and expertise through books, articles, conferences, and our online learning platform. O'Reilly's online learning platform gives you on-demand access to live training courses, in-depth learning paths, interactive coding environments, and a vast collection of text and video from O'Reilly and 200+ other publishers. For more information, please visit *http://oreilly.com*.

How to Contact Us

Please address comments and questions concerning this book to the publisher:

> O'Reilly Media, Inc.
> 1005 Gravenstein Highway North
> Sebastopol, CA 95472
> 800-998-9938 (in the United States or Canada)
> 707-829-0515 (international or local)
> 707-829-0104 (fax)

We have a web page for this book, where we list errata, examples, and any additional information. You can access this page at *http://bit.ly/data-science-from-scratch-2e*.

To comment or ask technical questions about this book, send email to *bookquestions@oreilly.com*.

For more information about our books, courses, conferences, and news, see our website at *http://www.oreilly.com*.

Find us on Facebook: *http://facebook.com/oreilly*

Follow us on Twitter: *http://twitter.com/oreillymedia*

Watch us on YouTube: *http://www.youtube.com/oreillymedia*

Acknowledgments

First, I would like to thank Mike Loukides for accepting my proposal for this book (and for insisting that I pare it down to a reasonable size). It would have been very easy for him to say, "Who's this person who keeps emailing me sample chapters, and how do I get him to go away?" I'm grateful he didn't. I'd also like to thank my editors, Michele Cronin and Marie Beaugureau, for guiding me through the publishing process and getting the book in a much better state than I ever would have gotten it on my own.

I couldn't have written this book if I'd never learned data science, and I probably wouldn't have learned data science if not for the influence of Dave Hsu, Igor Tatarinov, John Rauser, and the rest of the Farecast gang. (So long ago that it wasn't even called data science at the time!) The good folks at Coursera and DataTau deserve a lot of credit, too.

I am also grateful to my beta readers and reviewers. Jay Fundling found a ton of mistakes and pointed out many unclear explanations, and the book is much better (and much more correct) thanks to him. Debashis Ghosh is a hero for sanity-checking all of my statistics. Andrew Musselman suggested toning down the "people who prefer R to Python are moral reprobates" aspect of the book, which I think ended up being pretty good advice. Trey Causey, Ryan Matthew Balfanz, Loris Mularoni, Núria Pujol, Rob Jefferson, Mary Pat Campbell, Zach Geary, Denise Mauldin, Jimmy O'Donnell, and Wendy Grus also provided invaluable feedback. Thanks to everyone who read the first edition and helped make this a better book. Any errors remaining are of course my responsibility.

I owe a lot to the Twitter #datascience commmunity, for exposing me to a ton of new concepts, introducing me to a lot of great people, and making me feel like enough of an underachiever that I went out and wrote a book to compensate. Special thanks to Trey Causey (again), for (inadvertently) reminding me to include a chapter on linear algebra, and to Sean J. Taylor, for (inadvertently) pointing out a couple of huge gaps in the "Working with Data" chapter.

Above all, I owe immense thanks to Ganga and Madeline. The only thing harder than writing a book is living with someone who's writing a book, and I couldn't have pulled it off without their support.

Preface to the First Edition

Data Science

Data scientist has been called "the sexiest job of the 21st century," (*https://hbr.org/2012/10/data-scientist-the-sexiest-job-of-the-21st-century*) presumably by someone who has never visited a fire station. Nonetheless, data science is a hot and growing field, and it doesn't take a great deal of sleuthing to find analysts breathlessly prognosticating that over the next 10 years, we'll need billions and billions more data scientists than we currently have.

But what is data science? After all, we can't produce data scientists if we don't know what data science is. According to a Venn diagram (*http://drewconway.com/zia/2013/3/26/the-data-science-venn-diagram*) that is somewhat famous in the industry, data science lies at the intersection of:

- Hacking skills
- Math and statistics knowledge
- Substantive expertise

Although I originally intended to write a book covering all three, I quickly realized that a thorough treatment of "substantive expertise" would require tens of thousands of pages. At that point, I decided to focus on the first two. My goal is to help you develop the hacking skills that you'll need to get started doing data science. And my goal is to help you get comfortable with the mathematics and statistics that are at the core of data science.

This is a somewhat heavy aspiration for a book. The best way to learn hacking skills is by hacking on things. By reading this book, you will get a good understanding of the way I hack on things, which may not necessarily be the best way for you to hack on things. You will get a good understanding of some of the tools I use, which will not necessarily be the best tools for you to use. You will get a good understanding of the way I approach data problems, which may not necessarily be the best way for you to approach data problems. The intent (and the hope) is that my examples will inspire you to try things your own way. All the code and data from the book is available on GitHub (*https://github.com/joelgrus/data-science-from-scratch*) to get you started.

Similarly, the best way to learn mathematics is by doing mathematics. This is emphatically not a math book, and for the most part, we won't be "doing mathematics." However, you can't really do data science without *some* understanding of probability and statistics and linear algebra. This means that, where appropriate, we will dive into mathematical equations, mathematical intuition, mathematical axioms, and cartoon versions of big mathematical ideas. I hope that you won't be afraid to dive in with me.

Throughout it all, I also hope to give you a sense that playing with data is fun, because, well, playing with data is fun! (Especially compared to some of the alternatives, like tax preparation or coal mining.)

From Scratch

There are lots and lots of data science libraries, frameworks, modules, and toolkits that efficiently implement the most common (as well as the least common) data science algorithms and techniques. If you become a data scientist, you will become intimately familiar with NumPy, with scikit-learn, with pandas, and with a panoply of other libraries. They are great for doing data science. But they are also a good way to start doing data science without actually understanding data science.

In this book, we will be approaching data science from scratch. That means we'll be building tools and implementing algorithms by hand in order to better understand them. I put a lot of thought into creating implementations and examples that are clear, well commented, and readable. In most cases, the tools we build will be illuminating but impractical. They will work well on small toy datasets but fall over on "web-scale" ones.

Throughout the book, I will point you to libraries you might use to apply these techniques to larger datasets. But we won't be using them here.

There is a healthy debate raging over the best language for learning data science. Many people believe it's the statistical programming language R. (We call those people *wrong*.) A few people suggest Java or Scala. However, in my opinion, Python is the obvious choice.

Python has several features that make it well suited for learning (and doing) data science:

- It's free.
- It's relatively simple to code in (and, in particular, to understand).

- It has lots of useful data science–related libraries.

I am hesitant to call Python my favorite programming language. There are other languages I find more pleasant, better designed, or just more fun to code in. And yet pretty much every time I start a new data science project, I end up using Python. Every time I need to quickly prototype something that just works, I end up using Python. And every time I want to demonstrate data science concepts in a clear, easy-to-understand way, I end up using Python. Accordingly, this book uses Python.

The goal of this book is not to teach you Python. (Although it is nearly certain that by reading this book you will learn some Python.) I'll take you through a chapter-long crash course that highlights the features that are most important for our purposes, but if you know nothing about programming in Python (or about programming at all), then you might want to supplement this book with some sort of "Python for Beginners" tutorial.

The remainder of our introduction to data science will take this same approach—going into detail where going into detail seems crucial or illuminating, at other times leaving details for you to figure out yourself (or look up on Wikipedia).

Over the years, I've trained a number of data scientists. While not all of them have gone on to become world-changing data ninja rockstars, I've left them all better data scientists than I found them. And I've grown to believe that anyone who has some amount of mathematical aptitude and some amount of programming skill has the necessary raw materials to do data science. All she needs is an inquisitive mind, a willingness to work hard, and this book. Hence this book.

## CHAPTER 1

Introduction

"Data! Data! Data!" he cried impatiently. "I can't make bricks without clay."
—Arthur Conan Doyle

The Ascendance of Data

We live in a world that's drowning in data. Websites track every user's every click. Your smartphone is building up a record of your location and speed every second of every day. "Quantified selfers" wear pedometers-on-steroids that are always recording their heart rates, movement habits, diet, and sleep patterns. Smart cars collect driving habits, smart homes collect living habits, and smart marketers collect purchasing habits. The internet itself represents a huge graph of knowledge that contains (among other things) an enormous cross-referenced encyclopedia; domain-specific databases about movies, music, sports results, pinball machines, memes, and cocktails; and too many government statistics (some of them nearly true!) from too many governments to wrap your head around.

Buried in these data are answers to countless questions that no one's ever thought to ask. In this book, we'll learn how to find them.

What Is Data Science?

There's a joke that says a data scientist is someone who knows more statistics than a computer scientist and more computer science than a statistician. (I didn't say it was a good joke.) In fact, some data scientists are—for all practical purposes—statisticians, while others are fairly indistinguishable from software engineers. Some are machine learning experts, while others couldn't machine-learn their way out of kindergarten. Some are PhDs with impressive publication records, while others have never read an academic paper (shame on them, though). In short, pretty much no matter how you define data science, you'll find practitioners for whom the definition is totally, absolutely wrong.

Nonetheless, we won't let that stop us from trying. We'll say that a data scientist is someone who extracts insights from messy data. Today's world is full of people trying to turn data into insight.

For instance, the dating site OkCupid asks its members to answer thousands of questions in order to find the most appropriate matches for them. But it also analyzes these results to figure out innocuous-sounding questions you can ask someone to find out how likely someone is to sleep with you on the first date (*https://theblog.okcu pid.com/the-best-questions-for-a-first-date-dba6adaa9df2*).

Facebook asks you to list your hometown and your current location, ostensibly to make it easier for your friends to find and connect with you. But it also analyzes these locations to identify global migration patterns (*https://www.facebook.com/notes/ facebook-data-science/coordinated-migration/10151930946453859*) and where the fanbases of different football teams live (*https://www.facebook.com/notes/facebook-data-science/nfl-fans-on-facebook/10151298370823859*).

As a large retailer, Target tracks your purchases and interactions, both online and instore. And it uses the data to predictively model (*https://www.nytimes.com/ 2012/02/19/magazine/shopping-habits.html*) which of its customers are pregnant, to better market baby-related purchases to them.

In 2012, the Obama campaign employed dozens of data scientists who data-mined and experimented their way to identifying voters who needed extra attention, choosing optimal donor-specific fundraising appeals and programs, and focusing get-out-the-vote efforts where they were most likely to be useful. And in 2016 the Trump campaign tested a staggering variety of online ads (*https://www.wired.com/2016/11/ facebook-won-trump-election-not-just-fake-news/*) and analyzed the data to find what worked and what didn't.

Now, before you start feeling too jaded: some data scientists also occasionally use their skills for good—using data to make government more effective (*https:// www.marketplace.org/2014/08/22/tech/beyond-ad-clicks-using-big-data-social-good*), to help the homeless (*https://dssg.uchicago.edu/2014/08/20/tracking-the-paths-of-homelessness/*), and to improve public health (*https://plus.google.com/communities/ 109572103057302114737*). But it certainly won't hurt your career if you like figuring out the best way to get people to click on advertisements.

Motivating Hypothetical: DataSciencester

Congratulations! You've just been hired to lead the data science efforts at DataSciencester, *the* social network for data scientists.

When I wrote the first edition of this book, I thought that "a social network for data scientists" was a fun, silly hypothetical. Since then people have actually created social networks for data scientists, and have raised much more money from venture capitalists than I made from my book. Most likely there is a valuable lesson here about silly data science hypotheticals and/or book publishing.

Despite being *for* data scientists, DataSciencester has never actually invested in building its own data science practice. (In fairness, DataSciencester has never really invested in building its product either.) That will be your job! Throughout the book, we'll be learning about data science concepts by solving problems that you encounter at work. Sometimes we'll look at data explicitly supplied by users, sometimes we'll look at data generated through their interactions with the site, and sometimes we'll even look at data from experiments that we'll design.

And because DataSciencester has a strong "not-invented-here" mentality, we'll be building our own tools from scratch. At the end, you'll have a pretty solid understanding of the fundamentals of data science. And you'll be ready to apply your skills at a company with a less shaky premise, or to any other problems that happen to interest you.

Welcome aboard, and good luck! (You're allowed to wear jeans on Fridays, and the bathroom is down the hall on the right.)

Finding Key Connectors

It's your first day on the job at DataSciencester, and the VP of Networking is full of questions about your users. Until now he's had no one to ask, so he's very excited to have you aboard.

In particular, he wants you to identify who the "key connectors" are among data scientists. To this end, he gives you a dump of the entire DataSciencester network. (In real life, people don't typically hand you the data you need. Chapter 9 is devoted to getting data.)

What does this data dump look like? It consists of a list of users, each represented by a dict that contains that user's id (which is a number) and name (which, in one of the great cosmic coincidences, rhymes with the user's id):

```
users = [
    { "id": 0, "name": "Hero" },
    { "id": 1, "name": "Dunn" },
    { "id": 2, "name": "Sue" },
    { "id": 3, "name": "Chi" },
    { "id": 4, "name": "Thor" },
    { "id": 5, "name": "Clive" },
    { "id": 6, "name": "Hicks" },
```

```
    { "id": 7, "name": "Devin" },
    { "id": 8, "name": "Kate" },
    { "id": 9, "name": "Klein" }
]
```

He also gives you the "friendship" data, represented as a list of pairs of IDs:

```
friendship_pairs = [(0, 1), (0, 2), (1, 2), (1, 3), (2, 3), (3, 4),
                    (4, 5), (5, 6), (5, 7), (6, 8), (7, 8), (8, 9)]
```

For example, the tuple (0, 1) indicates that the data scientist with id 0 (Hero) and the data scientist with id 1 (Dunn) are friends. The network is illustrated in Figure 1-1.

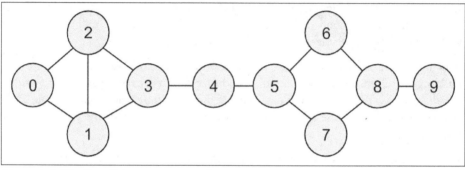

Figure 1-1. The DataSciencester network

Having friendships represented as a list of pairs is not the easiest way to work with them. To find all the friendships for user 1, you have to iterate over every pair looking for pairs containing 1. If you had a lot of pairs, this would take a long time.

Instead, let's create a dict where the keys are user ids and the values are lists of friend ids. (Looking things up in a dict is very fast.)

 Don't get too hung up on the details of the code right now. In Chapter 2, I'll take you through a crash course in Python. For now just try to get the general flavor of what we're doing.

We'll still have to look at every pair to create the dict, but we only have to do that once, and we'll get cheap lookups after that:

```
# Initialize the dict with an empty list for each user id:
friendships = {user["id"]: [] for user in users}

# And loop over the friendship pairs to populate it:
for i, j in friendship_pairs:
```

```
    friendships[i].append(j)  # Add j as a friend of user i
    friendships[j].append(i)  # Add i as a friend of user j
```

Now that we have the friendships in a dict, we can easily ask questions of our graph,
like "What's the average number of connections?"

First we find the *total* number of connections, by summing up the lengths of all the
friends lists:

```
def number_of_friends(user):
    """How many friends does _user_ have?"""
    user_id = user["id"]
    friend_ids = friendships[user_id]
    return len(friend_ids)

total_connections = sum(number_of_friends(user)
                        for user in users)        # 24
```

And then we just divide by the number of users:

```
num_users = len(users)                            # length of the users list
avg_connections = total_connections / num_users   # 24 / 10 == 2.4
```

It's also easy to find the most connected people—they're the people who have the largest numbers of friends.

Since there aren't very many users, we can simply sort them from "most friends" to
"least friends":

```
# Create a list (user_id, number_of_friends).
num_friends_by_id = [(user["id"], number_of_friends(user))
                     for user in users]

num_friends_by_id.sort(                           # Sort the list
        key=lambda id_and_friends: id_and_friends[1],  # by num_friends
        reverse=True)                             # largest to smallest

# Each pair is (user_id, num_friends):
# [(1, 3), (2, 3), (3, 3), (5, 3), (8, 3),
#  (0, 2), (4, 2), (6, 2), (7, 2), (9, 1)]
```

One way to think of what we've done is as a way of identifying people who are somehow central to the network. In fact, what we've just computed is the network metric
degree centrality (Figure 1-2).

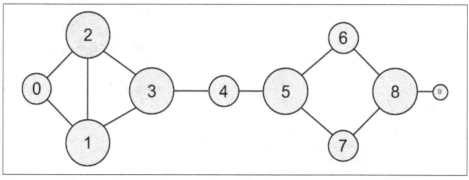

Figure 1-2. The DataSciencester network sized by degree

This has the virtue of being pretty easy to calculate, but it doesn't always give the results you'd want or expect. For example, in the DataSciencester network Thor (id 4) only has two connections, while Dunn (id 1) has three. Yet when we look at the network, it intuitively seems like Thor should be more central. In Chapter 22, we'll investigate networks in more detail, and we'll look at more complex notions of centrality that may or may not accord better with our intuition.

Data Scientists You May Know

While you're still filling out new-hire paperwork, the VP of Fraternization comes by your desk. She wants to encourage more connections among your members, and she asks you to design a "Data Scientists You May Know" suggester.

Your first instinct is to suggest that users might know the friends of their friends. So you write some code to iterate over their friends and collect the friends' friends:

```
def foaf_ids_bad(user):
    """foaf is short for "friend of a friend" """
    return [foaf_id
            for friend_id in friendships[user["id"]]
            for foaf_id in friendships[friend_id]]
```

When we call this on users[0] (Hero), it produces:

```
[0, 2, 3, 0, 1, 3]
```

It includes user 0 twice, since Hero is indeed friends with both of his friends. It includes users 1 and 2, although they are both friends with Hero already. And it includes user 3 twice, as Chi is reachable through two different friends:

```
print(friendships[0])  # [1, 2]
print(friendships[1])  # [0, 2, 3]
print(friendships[2])  # [0, 1, 3]
```

Knowing that people are friends of friends in multiple ways seems like interesting information, so maybe instead we should produce a *count* of mutual friends. And we should probably exclude people already known to the user:

```
from collections import Counter                    # not loaded by default

def friends_of_friends(user):
    user_id = user["id"]
    return Counter(
        foaf_id
        for friend_id in friendships[user_id]      # For each of my friends,
        for foaf_id in friendships[friend_id]      # find their friends
        if foaf_id != user_id                      # who aren't me
        and foaf_id not in friendships[user_id]    # and aren't my friends.
    )


print(friends_of_friends(users[3]))                # Counter({0: 2, 5: 1})
```

This correctly tells Chi (id 3) that she has two mutual friends with Hero (id 0) but only one mutual friend with Clive (id 5).

As a data scientist, you know that you also might enjoy meeting users with similar interests. (This is a good example of the "substantive expertise" aspect of data science.) After asking around, you manage to get your hands on this data, as a list of pairs (user_id, interest):

```
interests = [
    (0, "Hadoop"), (0, "Big Data"), (0, "HBase"), (0, "Java"),
    (0, "Spark"), (0, "Storm"), (0, "Cassandra"),
    (1, "NoSQL"), (1, "MongoDB"), (1, "Cassandra"), (1, "HBase"),
    (1, "Postgres"), (2, "Python"), (2, "scikit-learn"), (2, "scipy"),
    (2, "numpy"), (2, "statsmodels"), (2, "pandas"), (3, "R"), (3, "Python"),
    (3, "statistics"), (3, "regression"), (3, "probability"),
    (4, "machine learning"), (4, "regression"), (4, "decision trees"),
    (4, "libsvm"), (5, "Python"), (5, "R"), (5, "Java"), (5, "C++"),
    (5, "Haskell"), (5, "programming languages"), (6, "statistics"),
    (6, "probability"), (6, "mathematics"), (6, "theory"),
    (7, "machine learning"), (7, "scikit-learn"), (7, "Mahout"),
    (7, "neural networks"), (8, "neural networks"), (8, "deep learning"),
    (8, "Big Data"), (8, "artificial intelligence"), (9, "Hadoop"),
    (9, "Java"), (9, "MapReduce"), (9, "Big Data")
]
```

For example, Hero (id 0) has no friends in common with Klein (id 9), but they share interests in Java and big data.

It's easy to build a function that finds users with a certain interest:

```
def data_scientists_who_like(target_interest):
    """Find the ids of all users who like the target interest."""
    return [user_id
```

```
                    for user_id, user_interest in interests
                    if user_interest == target_interest]
```

This works, but it has to examine the whole list of interests for every search. If we
have a lot of users and interests (or if we just want to do a lot of searches), we're probably better off building an index from interests to users:

```
from collections import defaultdict

# Keys are interests, values are lists of user_ids with that interest
user_ids_by_interest = defaultdict(list)

for user_id, interest in interests:
    user_ids_by_interest[interest].append(user_id)
```

And another from users to interests:

```
# Keys are user_ids, values are lists of interests for that user_id.
interests_by_user_id = defaultdict(list)

for user_id, interest in interests:
    interests_by_user_id[user_id].append(interest)
```

Now it's easy to find who has the most interests in common with a given user:

- Iterate over the user's interests.
- For each interest, iterate over the other users with that interest.
- Keep count of how many times we see each other user.

In code:

```
def most_common_interests_with(user):
    return Counter(
        interested_user_id
        for interest in interests_by_user_id[user["id"]]
        for interested_user_id in user_ids_by_interest[interest]
        if interested_user_id != user["id"]
    )
```

We could then use this to build a richer "Data Scientists You May Know" feature
based on a combination of mutual friends and mutual interests. We'll explore these
kinds of applications in Chapter 23.

Salaries and Experience

Right as you're about to head to lunch, the VP of Public Relations asks if you can provide some fun facts about how much data scientists earn. Salary data is of course sensitive, but he manages to provide you an anonymous dataset containing each user's
salary (in dollars) and tenure as a data scientist (in years):

```
salaries_and_tenures = [(83000, 8.7), (88000, 8.1),
                        (48000, 0.7), (76000, 6),
                        (69000, 6.5), (76000, 7.5),
                        (60000, 2.5), (83000, 10),
                        (48000, 1.9), (63000, 4.2)]
```

The natural first step is to plot the data (which we'll see how to do in Chapter 3). You can see the results in Figure 1-3.

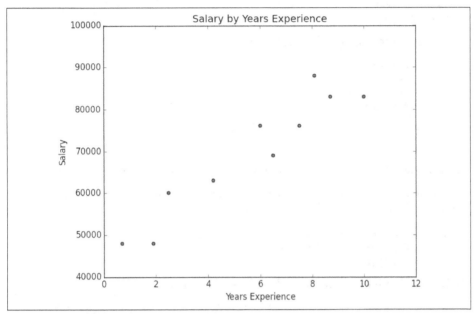

Figure 1-3. Salary by years of experience

It seems clear that people with more experience tend to earn more. How can you turn this into a fun fact? Your first idea is to look at the average salary for each tenure:

```
# Keys are years, values are lists of the salaries for each tenure.
salary_by_tenure = defaultdict(list)

for salary, tenure in salaries_and_tenures:
    salary_by_tenure[tenure].append(salary)

# Keys are years, each value is average salary for that tenure.
average_salary_by_tenure = {
    tenure: sum(salaries) / len(salaries)
    for tenure, salaries in salary_by_tenure.items()
}
```

This turns out to be not particularly useful, as none of the users have the same tenure, which means we're just reporting the individual users' salaries:

```
{0.7: 48000.0,
 1.9: 48000.0,
 2.5: 60000.0,
 4.2: 63000.0,
 6: 76000.0,
 6.5: 69000.0,
 7.5: 76000.0,
 8.1: 88000.0,
 8.7: 83000.0,
 10: 83000.0}
```

It might be more helpful to bucket the tenures:

```
def tenure_bucket(tenure):
    if tenure < 2:
        return "less than two"
    elif tenure < 5:
        return "between two and five"
    else:
        return "more than five"
```

Then we can group together the salaries corresponding to each bucket:

```
# Keys are tenure buckets, values are lists of salaries for that bucket.
salary_by_tenure_bucket = defaultdict(list)

for salary, tenure in salaries_and_tenures:
    bucket = tenure_bucket(tenure)
    salary_by_tenure_bucket[bucket].append(salary)
```

And finally compute the average salary for each group:

```
# Keys are tenure buckets, values are average salary for that bucket.
average_salary_by_bucket = {
  tenure_bucket: sum(salaries) / len(salaries)
  for tenure_bucket, salaries in salary_by_tenure_bucket.items()
}
```

Which is more interesting:

```
{'between two and five': 61500.0,
 'less than two': 48000.0,
 'more than five': 79166.66666666667}
```

And you have your soundbite: "Data scientists with more than five years' experience earn 65% more than data scientists with little or no experience!"

But we chose the buckets in a pretty arbitrary way. What we'd really like is to make some statement about the salary effect—on average—of having an additional year of experience. In addition to making for a snappier fun fact, this allows us to *make predictions* about salaries that we don't know. We'll explore this idea in Chapter 14.

Paid Accounts

When you get back to your desk, the VP of Revenue is waiting for you. She wants to better understand which users pay for accounts and which don't. (She knows their names, but that's not particularly actionable information.)

You notice that there seems to be a correspondence between years of experience and paid accounts:

```
0.7   paid
1.9   unpaid
2.5   paid
4.2   unpaid
6.0   unpaid
6.5   unpaid
7.5   unpaid
8.1   unpaid
8.7   paid
10.0  paid
```

Users with very few and very many years of experience tend to pay; users with average amounts of experience don't. Accordingly, if you wanted to create a model—though this is definitely not enough data to base a model on—you might try to predict "paid" for users with very few and very many years of experience, and "unpaid" for users with middling amounts of experience:

```python
def predict_paid_or_unpaid(years_experience):
    if years_experience < 3.0:
        return "paid"
    elif years_experience < 8.5:
        return "unpaid"
    else:
        return "paid"
```

Of course, we totally eyeballed the cutoffs.

With more data (and more mathematics), we could build a model predicting the likelihood that a user would pay based on his years of experience. We'll investigate this sort of problem in Chapter 16.

Topics of Interest

As you're wrapping up your first day, the VP of Content Strategy asks you for data about what topics users are most interested in, so that she can plan out her blog calendar accordingly. You already have the raw data from the friend-suggester project:

```python
interests = [
    (0, "Hadoop"), (0, "Big Data"), (0, "HBase"), (0, "Java"),
    (0, "Spark"), (0, "Storm"), (0, "Cassandra"),
    (1, "NoSQL"), (1, "MongoDB"), (1, "Cassandra"), (1, "HBase"),
    (1, "Postgres"), (2, "Python"), (2, "scikit-learn"), (2, "scipy"),
```

```
    (2, "numpy"), (2, "statsmodels"), (2, "pandas"), (3, "R"), (3, "Python"),
    (3, "statistics"), (3, "regression"), (3, "probability"),
    (4, "machine learning"), (4, "regression"), (4, "decision trees"),
    (4, "libsvm"), (5, "Python"), (5, "R"), (5, "Java"), (5, "C++"),
    (5, "Haskell"), (5, "programming languages"), (6, "statistics"),
    (6, "probability"), (6, "mathematics"), (6, "theory"),
    (7, "machine learning"), (7, "scikit-learn"), (7, "Mahout"),
    (7, "neural networks"), (8, "neural networks"), (8, "deep learning"),
    (8, "Big Data"), (8, "artificial intelligence"), (9, "Hadoop"),
    (9, "Java"), (9, "MapReduce"), (9, "Big Data")
]
```

One simple (if not particularly exciting) way to find the most popular interests is to count the words:

1. Lowercase each interest (since different users may or may not capitalize their interests).

2. Split it into words.

3. Count the results.

In code:

```
words_and_counts = Counter(word
                           for user, interest in interests
                           for word in interest.lower().split())
```

This makes it easy to list out the words that occur more than once:

```
for word, count in words_and_counts.most_common():
    if count > 1:
        print(word, count)
```

which gives the results you'd expect (unless you expect "scikit-learn" to get split into two words, in which case it doesn't give the results you expect):

```
learning 3
java 3
python 3
big 3
data 3
hbase 2
regression 2
cassandra 2
statistics 2
probability 2
hadoop 2
networks 2
machine 2
neural 2
scikit-learn 2
r 2
```

We'll look at more sophisticated ways to extract topics from data in Chapter 21.

Onward

It's been a successful first day! Exhausted, you slip out of the building before anyone can ask you for anything else. Get a good night's rest, because tomorrow is new employee orientation. (Yes, you went through a full day of work *before* new employee orientation. Take it up with HR.)

## CHAPTER 2

A Crash Course in Python

People are still crazy about Python after twenty-five years, which I find hard to believe.
—Michael Palin

All new employees at DataSciencester are required to go through new employee orientation, the most interesting part of which is a crash course in Python.

This is not a comprehensive Python tutorial but instead is intended to highlight the parts of the language that will be most important to us (some of which are often not the focus of Python tutorials). If you have never used Python before, you probably want to supplement this with some sort of beginner tutorial.

The Zen of Python

Python has a somewhat Zen description of its design principles (*http://legacy.python.org/dev/peps/pep-0020/*), which you can also find inside the Python interpreter itself by typing "import this."

One of the most discussed of these is:

There should be one—and preferably only one—obvious way to do it.

Code written in accordance with this "obvious" way (which may not be obvious at all to a newcomer) is often described as "Pythonic." Although this is not a book about Python, we will occasionally contrast Pythonic and non-Pythonic ways of accomplishing the same things, and we will generally favor Pythonic solutions to our problems.

Several others touch on aesthetics:

Beautiful is better than ugly. Explicit is better than implicit. Simple is better than complex.

and represent ideals that we will strive for in our code.

Getting Python

 As instructions about how to install things can change, while printed books cannot, up-to-date instructions on how to install Python can be found in the book's GitHub repo (*https://github.com/ joelgrus/data-science-from-scratch/blob/master/INSTALL.md*).

If the ones printed here don't work for you, check those.

You can download Python from Python.org (*https://www.python.org/*). But if you don't already have Python, I recommend instead installing the Anaconda (*https:// www.anaconda.com/download/*) distribution, which already includes most of the libraries that you need to do data science.

When I wrote the first version of *Data Science from Scratch*, Python 2.7 was still the preferred version of most data scientists. Accordingly, the first edition of the book was based on Python 2.7.

In the last several years, however, pretty much everyone who counts has migrated to Python 3. Recent versions of Python have many features that make it easier to write clean code, and we'll be taking ample advantage of features that are only available in Python 3.6 or later. This means that you should get Python 3.6 or later. (In addition, many useful libraries are ending support for Python 2.7, which is another reason to switch.)

Virtual Environments

Starting in the next chapter, we'll be using the matplotlib library to generate plots and charts. This library is not a core part of Python; you have to install it yourself. Every data science project you do will require some combination of external libraries, sometimes with specific versions that differ from the specific versions you used for other projects. If you were to have a single Python installation, these libraries would conflict and cause you all sorts of problems.

The standard solution is to use *virtual environments*, which are sandboxed Python environments that maintain their own versions of Python libraries (and, depending on how you set up the environment, of Python itself).

I recommended you install the Anaconda Python distribution, so in this section I'm going to explain how Anaconda's environments work. If you are not using Anaconda, you can either use the built-in venv (*https://docs.python.org/3/library/venv.html*) module or install virtualenv (*https://virtualenv.pypa.io/en/latest/*). In which case you should follow their instructions instead.

To create an (Anaconda) virtual environment, you just do the following:

```
# create a Python 3.6 environment named "dsfs"
conda create -n dsfs python=3.6
```

Follow the prompts, and you'll have a virtual environment called "dsfs," with the instructions:

```
#
# To activate this environment, use:
# > source activate dsfs
#
# To deactivate an active environment, use:
# > source deactivate
#
```

As indicated, you then activate the environment using:

```
source activate dsfs
```

at which point your command prompt should change to indicate the active environment. On my MacBook the prompt now looks like:

```
(dsfs) ip-10-0-0-198:~ joelg$
```

As long as this environment is active, any libraries you install will be installed only in the dsfs environment. Once you finish this book and go on to your own projects, you should create your own environments for them.

Now that you have your environment, it's worth installing IPython (*http://ipython.org/*), which is a full-featured Python shell:

```
python -m pip install ipython
```

 Anaconda comes with its own package manager, conda, but you can also just use the standard Python package manager pip, which is what we'll be doing.

The rest of this book will assume that you have created and activated such a Python 3.6 virtual environment (although you can call it whatever you want), and later chapters may rely on the libraries that I told you to install in earlier chapters.

As a matter of good discipline, you should always work in a virtual environment, and never using the "base" Python installation.

Whitespace Formatting

Many languages use curly braces to delimit blocks of code. Python uses indentation:

```
# The pound sign marks the start of a comment. Python itself
# ignores the comments, but they're helpful for anyone reading the code.
for i in [1, 2, 3, 4, 5]:
    print(i)                        # first line in "for i" block
    for j in [1, 2, 3, 4, 5]:
        print(j)                    # first line in "for j" block
        print(i + j)                # last line in "for j" block
    print(i)                        # last line in "for i" block
print("done looping")
```

This makes Python code very readable, but it also means that you have to be very careful with your formatting.

 Programmers will often argue over whether to use tabs or spaces for indentation. For many languages it doesn't matter that much; however, Python considers tabs and spaces different indentation and will not be able to run your code if you mix the two. When writing Python you should always use spaces, never tabs. (If you write code in an editor you can configure it so that the Tab key just inserts spaces.)

Whitespace is ignored inside parentheses and brackets, which can be helpful for long-winded computations:

```
long_winded_computation = (1 + 2 + 3 + 4 + 5 + 6 + 7 + 8 + 9 + 10 + 11 + 12 +
                           13 + 14 + 15 + 16 + 17 + 18 + 19 + 20)
```

and for making code easier to read:

```
list_of_lists = [[1, 2, 3], [4, 5, 6], [7, 8, 9]]

easier_to_read_list_of_lists = [[1, 2, 3],
                                [4, 5, 6],
                                [7, 8, 9]]
```

You can also use a backslash to indicate that a statement continues onto the next line, although we'll rarely do this:

```
two_plus_three = 2 + \
                 3
```

One consequence of whitespace formatting is that it can be hard to copy and paste code into the Python shell. For example, if you tried to paste the code:

```
for i in [1, 2, 3, 4, 5]:

    # notice the blank line
    print(i)
```

into the ordinary Python shell, you would receive the complaint:

```
IndentationError: expected an indented block
```

because the interpreter thinks the blank line signals the end of the for loop's block.

IPython has a magic function called %paste, which correctly pastes whatever is on your clipboard, whitespace and all. This alone is a good reason to use IPython.

Modules

Certain features of Python are not loaded by default. These include both features that are included as part of the language as well as third-party features that you download yourself. In order to use these features, you'll need to import the modules that contain them.

One approach is to simply import the module itself:

```
import re
my_regex = re.compile("[0-9]+", re.I)
```

Here, re is the module containing functions and constants for working with regular expressions. After this type of import you must prefix those functions with re. in order to access them.

If you already had a different re in your code, you could use an alias:

```
import re as regex
my_regex = regex.compile("[0-9]+", regex.I)
```

You might also do this if your module has an unwieldy name or if you're going to be typing it a lot. For example, a standard convention when visualizing data with matplotlib is:

```
import matplotlib.pyplot as plt

plt.plot(...)
```

If you need a few specific values from a module, you can import them explicitly and use them without qualification:

```
from collections import defaultdict, Counter
lookup = defaultdict(int)
my_counter = Counter()
```

If you were a bad person, you could import the entire contents of a module into your namespace, which might inadvertently overwrite variables you've already defined:

```
match = 10
from re import *      # uh oh, re has a match function
print(match)          # "<function match at 0x10281e6a8>"
```

However, since you are not a bad person, you won't ever do this.

Functions

A function is a rule for taking zero or more inputs and returning a corresponding output. In Python, we typically define functions using `def`:

```python
def double(x):
    """
    This is where you put an optional docstring that explains what the
    function does. For example, this function multiplies its input by 2.
    """
    return x * 2
```

Python functions are *first-class*, which means that we can assign them to variables and pass them into functions just like any other arguments:

```python
def apply_to_one(f):
    """Calls the function f with 1 as its argument"""
    return f(1)

my_double = double              # refers to the previously defined function
x = apply_to_one(my_double)     # equals 2
```

It is also easy to create short anonymous functions, or *lambdas*:

```python
y = apply_to_one(lambda x: x + 4)       # equals 5
```

You can assign lambdas to variables, although most people will tell you that you should just use `def` instead:

```python
another_double = lambda x: 2 * x        # don't do this

def another_double(x):
    """Do this instead"""
    return 2 * x
```

Function parameters can also be given default arguments, which only need to be specified when you want a value other than the default:

```python
def my_print(message = "my default message"):
    print(message)

my_print("hello")    # prints 'hello'
my_print()           # prints 'my default message'
```

It is sometimes useful to specify arguments by name:

```python
def full_name(first = "What's-his-name", last = "Something"):
    return first + " " + last

full_name("Joel", "Grus")     # "Joel Grus"
full_name("Joel")             # "Joel Something"
full_name(last="Grus")        # "What's-his-name Grus"
```

We will be creating many, many functions.

Strings

Strings can be delimited by single or double quotation marks (but the quotes have to match):

```
single_quoted_string = 'data science'
double_quoted_string = "data science"
```

Python uses backslashes to encode special characters. For example:

```
tab_string = "\t"        # represents the tab character
len(tab_string)          # is 1
```

If you want backslashes as backslashes (which you might in Windows directory names or in regular expressions), you can create *raw* strings using r"":

```
not_tab_string = r"\t"   # represents the characters '\' and 't'
len(not_tab_string)      # is 2
```

You can create multiline strings using three double quotes:

```
multi_line_string = """This is the first line.
and this is the second line
and this is the third line"""
```

A new feature in Python 3.6 is the *f-string*, which provides a simple way to substitute values into strings. For example, if we had the first name and last name given separately:

```
first_name = "Joel"
last_name = "Grus"
```

we might want to combine them into a full name. There are multiple ways to construct such a full_name string:

```
full_name1 = first_name + " " + last_name                # string addition
full_name2 = "{0} {1}".format(first_name, last_name)  # string.format
```

but the f-string way is much less unwieldy:

```
full_name3 = f"{first_name} {last_name}"
```

and we'll prefer it throughout the book.

Exceptions

When something goes wrong, Python raises an *exception*. Unhandled, exceptions will cause your program to crash. You can handle them using try and except:

```
try:
    print(0 / 0)
except ZeroDivisionError:
    print("cannot divide by zero")
```

Although in many languages exceptions are considered bad, in Python there is no shame in using them to make your code cleaner, and we will sometimes do so.

Lists

Probably the most fundamental data structure in Python is the *list*, which is simply an ordered collection (it is similar to what in other languages might be called an *array*, but with some added functionality):

```
integer_list = [1, 2, 3]
heterogeneous_list = ["string", 0.1, True]
list_of_lists = [integer_list, heterogeneous_list, []]

list_length = len(integer_list)    # equals 3
list_sum    = sum(integer_list)    # equals 6
```

You can get or set the *n*th element of a list with square brackets:

```
x = [0, 1, 2, 3, 4, 5, 6, 7, 8, 9]

zero = x[0]      # equals 0, lists are 0-indexed
one = x[1]       # equals 1
nine = x[-1]     # equals 9, 'Pythonic' for last element
eight = x[-2]    # equals 8, 'Pythonic' for next-to-last element
x[0] = -1        # now x is [-1, 1, 2, 3, ..., 9]
```

You can also use square brackets to *slice* lists. The slice i:j means all elements from i (inclusive) to j (not inclusive). If you leave off the start of the slice, you'll slice from the beginning of the list, and if you leave of the end of the slice, you'll slice until the end of the list:

```
first_three = x[:3]                    # [-1, 1, 2]
three_to_end = x[3:]                   # [3, 4, ..., 9]
one_to_four = x[1:5]                   # [1, 2, 3, 4]
last_three = x[-3:]                    # [7, 8, 9]
without_first_and_last = x[1:-1]       # [1, 2, ..., 8]
copy_of_x = x[:]                       # [-1, 1, 2, ..., 9]
```

You can similarly slice strings and other "sequential" types.

A slice can take a third argument to indicate its *stride*, which can be negative:

```
every_third = x[::3]                   # [-1, 3, 6, 9]
five_to_three = x[5:2:-1]              # [5, 4, 3]
```

Python has an in operator to check for list membership:

```
1 in [1, 2, 3]    # True
0 in [1, 2, 3]    # False
```

This check involves examining the elements of the list one at a time, which means that you probably shouldn't use it unless you know your list is pretty small (or unless you don't care how long the check takes).

It is easy to concatenate lists together. If you want to modify a list in place, you can use extend to add items from another collection:

```
x = [1, 2, 3]
x.extend([4, 5, 6])     # x is now [1, 2, 3, 4, 5, 6]
```

If you don't want to modify x, you can use list addition:

```
x = [1, 2, 3]
y = x + [4, 5, 6]       # y is [1, 2, 3, 4, 5, 6]; x is unchanged
```

More frequently we will append to lists one item at a time:

```
x = [1, 2, 3]
x.append(0)         # x is now [1, 2, 3, 0]
y = x[-1]           # equals 0
z = len(x)          # equals 4
```

It's often convenient to *unpack* lists when you know how many elements they contain:

```
x, y = [1, 2]    # now x is 1, y is 2
```

although you will get a ValueError if you don't have the same number of elements on both sides.

A common idiom is to use an underscore for a value you're going to throw away:

```
_, y = [1, 2]     # now y == 2, didn't care about the first element
```

Tuples

Tuples are lists' immutable cousins. Pretty much anything you can do to a list that doesn't involve modifying it, you can do to a tuple. You specify a tuple by using parentheses (or nothing) instead of square brackets:

```
my_list = [1, 2]
my_tuple = (1, 2)
other_tuple = 3, 4
my_list[1] = 3      # my_list is now [1, 3]

try:
    my_tuple[1] = 3
except TypeError:
    print("cannot modify a tuple")
```

Tuples are a convenient way to return multiple values from functions:

```
def sum_and_product(x, y):
    return (x + y), (x * y)
```

```
sp = sum_and_product(2, 3)     # sp is (5, 6)
s, p = sum_and_product(5, 10)  # s is 15, p is 50
```

Tuples (and lists) can also be used for *multiple assignment*:

```
x, y = 1, 2     # now x is 1, y is 2
x, y = y, x     # Pythonic way to swap variables; now x is 2, y is 1
```

Dictionaries

Another fundamental data structure is a dictionary, which associates *values* with *keys* and allows you to quickly retrieve the value corresponding to a given key:

```
empty_dict = {}                        # Pythonic
empty_dict2 = dict()                   # less Pythonic
grades = {"Joel": 80, "Tim": 95}       # dictionary literal
```

You can look up the value for a key using square brackets:

```
joels_grade = grades["Joel"]           # equals 80
```

But you'll get a KeyError if you ask for a key that's not in the dictionary:

```
try:
    kates_grade = grades["Kate"]
except KeyError:
    print("no grade for Kate!")
```

You can check for the existence of a key using in:

```
joel_has_grade = "Joel" in grades      # True
kate_has_grade = "Kate" in grades      # False
```

This membership check is fast even for large dictionaries.

Dictionaries have a get method that returns a default value (instead of raising an exception) when you look up a key that's not in the dictionary:

```
joels_grade = grades.get("Joel", 0)    # equals 80
kates_grade = grades.get("Kate", 0)    # equals 0
no_ones_grade = grades.get("No One")   # default is None
```

You can assign key/value pairs using the same square brackets:

```
grades["Tim"] = 99                     # replaces the old value
grades["Kate"] = 100                   # adds a third entry
num_students = len(grades)             # equals 3
```

As you saw in Chapter 1, you can use dictionaries to represent structured data:

```
tweet = {
    "user" : "joelgrus",
    "text" : "Data Science is Awesome",
    "retweet_count" : 100,
```

```
        "hashtags" : ["#data", "#science", "#datascience", "#awesome", "#yolo"]
    }
```

although we'll soon see a better approach.

Besides looking for specific keys, we can look at all of them:

```
tweet_keys   = tweet.keys()    # iterable for the keys
tweet_values = tweet.values()  # iterable for the values
tweet_items  = tweet.items()   # iterable for the (key, value) tuples

"user" in tweet_keys           # True, but not Pythonic
"user" in tweet               # Pythonic way of checking for keys
"joelgrus" in tweet_values    # True (slow but the only way to check)
```

Dictionary keys must be "hashable"; in particular, you cannot use lists as keys. If you need a multipart key, you should probably use a tuple or figure out a way to turn the key into a string.

defaultdict

Imagine that you're trying to count the words in a document. An obvious approach is to create a dictionary in which the keys are words and the values are counts. As you check each word, you can increment its count if it's already in the dictionary and add it to the dictionary if it's not:

```
word_counts = {}
for word in document:
    if word in word_counts:
        word_counts[word] += 1
    else:
        word_counts[word] = 1
```

You could also use the "forgiveness is better than permission" approach and just handle the exception from trying to look up a missing key:

```
word_counts = {}
for word in document:
    try:
        word_counts[word] += 1
    except KeyError:
        word_counts[word] = 1
```

A third approach is to use get, which behaves gracefully for missing keys:

```
word_counts = {}
for word in document:
    previous_count = word_counts.get(word, 0)
    word_counts[word] = previous_count + 1
```

Every one of these is slightly unwieldy, which is why defaultdict is useful. A defaultdict is like a regular dictionary, except that when you try to look up a key it doesn't contain, it first adds a value for it using a zero-argument function you provided when you created it. In order to use `defaultdicts`, you have to import them from `collections`:

```
from collections import defaultdict

word_counts = defaultdict(int)          # int() produces 0
for word in document:
    word_counts[word] += 1
```

They can also be useful with `list` or `dict`, or even your own functions:

```
dd_list = defaultdict(list)             # list() produces an empty list
dd_list[2].append(1)                    # now dd_list contains {2: [1]}

dd_dict = defaultdict(dict)             # dict() produces an empty dict
dd_dict["Joel"]["City"] = "Seattle"     # {"Joel" : {"City": Seattle"}}

dd_pair = defaultdict(lambda: [0, 0])
dd_pair[2][1] = 1                       # now dd_pair contains {2: [0, 1]}
```

These will be useful when we're using dictionaries to "collect" results by some key and don't want to have to check every time to see if the key exists yet.

Counters

A `Counter` turns a sequence of values into a `defaultdict(int)`-like object mapping keys to counts:

```
from collections import Counter
c = Counter([0, 1, 2, 0])               # c is (basically) {0: 2, 1: 1, 2: 1}
```

This gives us a very simple way to solve our `word_counts` problem:

```
# recall, document is a list of words
word_counts = Counter(document)
```

A `Counter` instance has a `most_common` method that is frequently useful:

```
# print the 10 most common words and their counts
for word, count in word_counts.most_common(10):
    print(word, count)
```

Sets

Another useful data structure is set, which represents a collection of *distinct* elements. You can define a set by listing its elements between curly braces:

```
primes_below_10 = {2, 3, 5, 7}
```

However, that doesn't work for empty sets, as {} already means "empty dict." In that case you'll need to use set() itself:

```
s = set()
s.add(1)        # s is now {1}
s.add(2)        # s is now {1, 2}
s.add(2)        # s is still {1, 2}
x = len(s)      # equals 2
y = 2 in s      # equals True
z = 3 in s      # equals False
```

We'll use sets for two main reasons. The first is that `in` is a very fast operation on sets. If we have a large collection of items that we want to use for a membership test, a set is more appropriate than a list:

```
stopwords_list = ["a", "an", "at"] + hundreds_of_other_words + ["yet", "you"]

"zip" in stopwords_list      # False, but have to check every element

stopwords_set = set(stopwords_list)
"zip" in stopwords_set       # very fast to check
```

The second reason is to find the *distinct* items in a collection:

```
item_list = [1, 2, 3, 1, 2, 3]
num_items = len(item_list)                  # 6
item_set = set(item_list)                   # {1, 2, 3}
num_distinct_items = len(item_set)          # 3
distinct_item_list = list(item_set)         # [1, 2, 3]
```

We'll use sets less frequently than dictionaries and lists.

Control Flow

As in most programming languages, you can perform an action conditionally using `if`:

```
if 1 > 2:
    message = "if only 1 were greater than two..."
elif 1 > 3:
    message = "elif stands for 'else if'"
else:
    message = "when all else fails use else (if you want to)"
```

You can also write a *ternary* if-then-else on one line, which we will do occasionally:

```
parity = "even" if x % 2 == 0 else "odd"
```

Python has a `while` loop:

```
x = 0
while x < 10:
    print(f"{x} is less than 10")
    x += 1
```

although more often we'll use `for` and `in`:

```
# range(10) is the numbers 0, 1, ..., 9
for x in range(10):
    print(f"{x} is less than 10")
```

If you need more complex logic, you can use `continue` and `break`:

```
for x in range(10):
    if x == 3:
        continue  # go immediately to the next iteration
    if x == 5:
        break      # quit the loop entirely
    print(x)
```

This will print 0, 1, 2, and 4.

Truthiness

Booleans in Python work as in most other languages, except that they're capitalized:

```
one_is_less_than_two = 1 < 2          # equals True
true_equals_false = True == False      # equals False
```

Python uses the value `None` to indicate a nonexistent value. It is similar to other languages' `null`:

```
x = None
assert x == None, "this is the not the Pythonic way to check for None"
assert x is None, "this is the Pythonic way to check for None"
```

Python lets you use any value where it expects a Boolean. The following are all "falsy":

- `False`
- `None`
- `[]` (an empty `list`)
- `{}` (an empty `dict`)
- `""`
- `set()`
- `0`
- `0.0`

Pretty much anything else gets treated as `True`. This allows you to easily use `if` statements to test for empty lists, empty strings, empty dictionaries, and so on. It also sometimes causes tricky bugs if you're not expecting this behavior:

```
s = some_function_that_returns_a_string()
if s:
```

```
        first_char = s[0]
    else:
        first_char = ""
```

A shorter (but possibly more confusing) way of doing the same is:

```
first_char = s and s[0]
```

since and returns its second value when the first is "truthy," and the first value when it's not. Similarly, if x is either a number or possibly None:

```
safe_x = x or 0
```

is definitely a number, although:

```
safe_x = x if x is not None else 0
```

is possibly more readable.

Python has an all function, which takes an iterable and returns True precisely when every element is truthy, and an any function, which returns True when at least one element is truthy:

```
all([True, 1, {3}])    # True, all are truthy
all([True, 1, {}])     # False, {} is falsy
any([True, 1, {}])     # True, True is truthy
all([])                # True, no falsy elements in the list
any([])                # False, no truthy elements in the list
```

Sorting

Every Python list has a sort method that sorts it in place. If you don't want to mess up your list, you can use the sorted function, which returns a new list:

```
x = [4, 1, 2, 3]
y = sorted(x)     # y is [1, 2, 3, 4], x is unchanged
x.sort()          # now x is [1, 2, 3, 4]
```

By default, sort (and sorted) sort a list from smallest to largest based on naively comparing the elements to one another.

If you want elements sorted from largest to smallest, you can specify a reverse=True parameter. And instead of comparing the elements themselves, you can compare the results of a function that you specify with key:

```
# sort the list by absolute value from largest to smallest
x = sorted([-4, 1, -2, 3], key=abs, reverse=True)  # is [-4, 3, -2, 1]

# sort the words and counts from highest count to lowest
wc = sorted(word_counts.items(),
            key=lambda word_and_count: word_and_count[1],
            reverse=True)
```

List Comprehensions

Frequently, you'll want to transform a list into another list by choosing only certain elements, by transforming elements, or both. The Pythonic way to do this is with *list comprehensions*:

```
even_numbers = [x for x in range(5) if x % 2 == 0]   # [0, 2, 4]
squares      = [x * x for x in range(5)]              # [0, 1, 4, 9, 16]
even_squares = [x * x for x in even_numbers]          # [0, 4, 16]
```

You can similarly turn lists into dictionaries or sets:

```
square_dict = {x: x * x for x in range(5)}   # {0: 0, 1: 1, 2: 4, 3: 9, 4: 16}
square_set  = {x * x for x in [1, -1]}        # {1}
```

If you don't need the value from the list, it's common to use an underscore as the variable:

```
zeros = [0 for _ in even_numbers]      # has the same length as even_numbers
```

A list comprehension can include multiple `for`s:

```
pairs = [(x, y)
         for x in range(10)
         for y in range(10)]    # 100 pairs (0,0) (0,1) ... (9,8), (9,9)
```

and later `for`s can use the results of earlier ones:

```
increasing_pairs = [(x, y)                       # only pairs with x < y,
                    for x in range(10)           # range(lo, hi) equals
                    for y in range(x + 1, 10)]   # [lo, lo + 1, ..., hi - 1]
```

We will use list comprehensions a lot.

Automated Testing and assert

As data scientists, we'll be writing a lot of code. How can we be confident our code is correct? One way is with *types* (discussed shortly), but another way is with *automated tests*.

There are elaborate frameworks for writing and running tests, but in this book we'll restrict ourselves to using `assert` statements, which will cause your code to raise an `AssertionError` if your specified condition is not truthy:

```
assert 1 + 1 == 2
assert 1 + 1 == 2, "1 + 1 should equal 2 but didn't"
```

As you can see in the second case, you can optionally add a message to be printed if the assertion fails.

It's not particularly interesting to assert that $1 + 1 = 2$. What's more interesting is to assert that functions you write are doing what you expect them to:

```
def smallest_item(xs):
    return min(xs)

assert smallest_item([10, 20, 5, 40]) == 5
assert smallest_item([1, 0, -1, 2]) == -1
```

Throughout the book we'll be using `assert` in this way. It is a good practice, and I strongly encourage you to make liberal use of it in your own code. (If you look at the book's code on GitHub, you will see that it contains many, many more `assert` statements than are printed in the book. This helps *me* be confident that the code I've written for you is correct.)

Another less common use is to assert things about inputs to functions:

```
def smallest_item(xs):
    assert xs, "empty list has no smallest item"
    return min(xs)
```

We'll occasionally do this, but more often we'll use `assert` to check that our code is correct.

Object-Oriented Programming

Like many languages, Python allows you to define *classes* that encapsulate data and the functions that operate on them. We'll use them sometimes to make our code cleaner and simpler. It's probably simplest to explain them by constructing a heavily annotated example.

Here we'll construct a class representing a "counting clicker," the sort that is used at the door to track how many people have shown up for the "advanced topics in data science" meetup.

It maintains a `count`, can be `clicked` to increment the count, allows you to `read_count`, and can be `reset` back to zero. (In real life one of these rolls over from 9999 to 0000, but we won't bother with that.)

To define a class, you use the `class` keyword and a PascalCase name:

```
class CountingClicker:
    """A class can/should have a docstring, just like a function"""
```

A class contains zero or more *member* functions. By convention, each takes a first parameter, `self`, that refers to the particular class instance.

Normally, a class has a constructor, named `__init__`. It takes whatever parameters you need to construct an instance of your class and does whatever setup you need:

```
def __init__(self, count = 0):
    self.count = count
```

Although the constructor has a funny name, we construct instances of the clicker using just the class name:

```
clicker1 = CountingClicker()           # initialized to 0
clicker2 = CountingClicker(100)        # starts with count=100
clicker3 = CountingClicker(count=100)  # more explicit way of doing the same
```

Notice that the __init__ method name starts and ends with double underscores. These "magic" methods are sometimes called "dunder" methods (double-UNDERscore, get it?) and represent "special" behaviors.

 Class methods whose names start with an underscore are—by convention—considered "private," and users of the class are not supposed to directly call them. However, Python will not *stop* users from calling them.

Another such method is __repr__, which produces the string representation of a class instance:

```
def __repr__(self):
    return f"CountingClicker(count={self.count})"
```

And finally we need to implement the *public API* of our class:

```
def click(self, num_times = 1):
    """Click the clicker some number of times."""
    self.count += num_times

def read(self):
    return self.count

def reset(self):
    self.count = 0
```

Having defined it, let's use assert to write some test cases for our clicker:

```
clicker = CountingClicker()
assert clicker.read() == 0, "clicker should start with count 0"
clicker.click()
clicker.click()
assert clicker.read() == 2, "after two clicks, clicker should have count 2"
clicker.reset()
assert clicker.read() == 0, "after reset, clicker should be back to 0"
```

Writing tests like these help us be confident that our code is working the way it's designed to, and that it remains doing so whenever we make changes to it.

We'll also occasionally create *subclasses* that *inherit* some of their functionality from a parent class. For example, we could create a non-reset-able clicker by using CountingClicker as the base class and overriding the reset method to do nothing:

```
# A subclass inherits all the behavior of its parent class.
class NoResetClicker(CountingClicker):
    # This class has all the same methods as CountingClicker

    # Except that it has a reset method that does nothing.
    def reset(self):
        pass

clicker2 = NoResetClicker()
assert clicker2.read() == 0
clicker2.click()
assert clicker2.read() == 1
clicker2.reset()
assert clicker2.read() == 1, "reset shouldn't do anything"
```

Iterables and Generators

One nice thing about a list is that you can retrieve specific elements by their indices. But you don't always need this! A list of a billion numbers takes up a lot of memory. If you only want the elements one at a time, there's no good reason to keep them all around. If you only end up needing the first several elements, generating the entire billion is hugely wasteful.

Often all we need is to iterate over the collection using for and in. In this case we can create *generators*, which can be iterated over just like lists but generate their values lazily on demand.

One way to create generators is with functions and the yield operator:

```
def generate_range(n):
    i = 0
    while i < n:
        yield i   # every call to yield produces a value of the generator
        i += 1
```

The following loop will consume the yielded values one at a time until none are left:

```
for i in generate_range(10):
    print(f"i: {i}")
```

(In fact, range is itself lazy, so there's no point in doing this.)

With a generator, you can even create an infinite sequence:

```
def natural_numbers():
    """returns 1, 2, 3, ..."""
    n = 1
    while True:
        yield n
        n += 1
```

although you probably shouldn't iterate over it without using some kind of break logic.

 The flip side of laziness is that you can only iterate through a generator once. If you need to iterate through something multiple times, you'll need to either re-create the generator each time or use a list. If generating the values is expensive, that might be a good reason to use a list instead.

A second way to create generators is by using for comprehensions wrapped in parentheses:

```
evens_below_20 = (i for i in generate_range(20) if i % 2 == 0)
```

Such a "generator comprehension" doesn't do any work until you iterate over it (using for or next). We can use this to build up elaborate data-processing pipelines:

```
# None of these computations *does* anything until we iterate
data = natural_numbers()
evens = (x for x in data if x % 2 == 0)
even_squares = (x ** 2 for x in evens)
even_squares_ending_in_six = (x for x in even_squares if x % 10 == 6)
# and so on
```

Not infrequently, when we're iterating over a list or a generator we'll want not just the values but also their indices. For this common case Python provides an enumerate function, which turns values into pairs (index, value):

```
names = ["Alice", "Bob", "Charlie", "Debbie"]

# not Pythonic
for i in range(len(names)):
    print(f"name {i} is {names[i]}")

# also not Pythonic
i = 0
for name in names:
    print(f"name {i} is {names[i]}")
    i += 1

# Pythonic
for i, name in enumerate(names):
    print(f"name {i} is {name}")
```

We'll use this a lot.

Randomness

As we learn data science, we will frequently need to generate random numbers, which we can do with the `random` module:

```
import random
random.seed(10)  # this ensures we get the same results every time

four_uniform_randoms = [random.random() for _ in range(4)]

# [0.5714025946899135,    # random.random() produces numbers
#  0.4288890546751146,    # uniformly between 0 and 1.
#  0.5780913011344704,    # It's the random function we'll use
#  0.20609823213950174]   # most often.
```

The `random` module actually produces *pseudorandom* (that is, deterministic) numbers based on an internal state that you can set with `random.seed` if you want to get reproducible results:

```
random.seed(10)          # set the seed to 10
print(random.random())   # 0.57140259469
random.seed(10)          # reset the seed to 10
print(random.random())   # 0.57140259469 again
```

We'll sometimes use `random.randrange`, which takes either one or two arguments and returns an element chosen randomly from the corresponding range:

```
random.randrange(10)     # choose randomly from range(10) = [0, 1, ..., 9]
random.randrange(3, 6)   # choose randomly from range(3, 6) = [3, 4, 5]
```

There are a few more methods that we'll sometimes find convenient. For example, `random.shuffle` randomly reorders the elements of a list:

```
up_to_ten = [1, 2, 3, 4, 5, 6, 7, 8, 9, 10]
random.shuffle(up_to_ten)
print(up_to_ten)
# [7, 2, 6, 8, 9, 4, 10, 1, 3, 5]   (your results will probably be different)
```

If you need to randomly pick one element from a list, you can use `random.choice`:

```
my_best_friend = random.choice(["Alice", "Bob", "Charlie"])     # "Bob" for me
```

And if you need to randomly choose a sample of elements without replacement (i.e., with no duplicates), you can use `random.sample`:

```
lottery_numbers = range(60)
winning_numbers = random.sample(lottery_numbers, 6)  # [16, 36, 10, 6, 25, 9]
```

To choose a sample of elements *with* replacement (i.e., allowing duplicates), you can just make multiple calls to `random.choice`:

```
four_with_replacement = [random.choice(range(10)) for _ in range(4)]
print(four_with_replacement) # [9, 4, 4, 2]
```

Regular Expressions

Regular expressions provide a way of searching text. They are incredibly useful, but also fairly complicated—so much so that there are entire books written about them. We will get into their details the few times we encounter them; here are a few examples of how to use them in Python:

```
import re

re_examples = [                              # All of these are True, because
    not re.match("a", "cat"),                #   'cat' doesn't start with 'a'
    re.search("a", "cat"),                   #   'cat' has an 'a' in it
    not re.search("c", "dog"),               #   'dog' doesn't have a 'c' in it.
    3 == len(re.split("[ab]", "carbs")),     #   Split on a or b to ['c','r','s'].
    "R-D-" == re.sub("[0-9]", "-", "R2D2")   #   Replace digits with dashes.
    ]

assert all(re_examples), "all the regex examples should be True"
```

One important thing to note is that `re.match` checks whether the *beginning* of a string matches a regular expression, while `re.search` checks whether *any part* of a string matches a regular expression. At some point you will mix these two up and it will cause you grief.

The official documentation (*https://docs.python.org/3/library/re.html*) goes into much more detail.

Functional Programming

 The first edition of this book introduced the Python functions `partial`, `map`, `reduce`, and `filter` at this point. On my journey toward enlightenment I have realized that these functions are best avoided, and their uses in the book have been replaced with list comprehensions, `for` loops, and other, more Pythonic constructs.

zip and Argument Unpacking

Often we will need to *zip* two or more iterables together. The `zip` function transforms multiple iterables into a single iterable of tuples of corresponding function:

```
list1 = ['a', 'b', 'c']
list2 = [1, 2, 3]

# zip is lazy, so you have to do something like the following
[pair for pair in zip(list1, list2)]    # is [('a', 1), ('b', 2), ('c', 3)]
```

If the lists are different lengths, `zip` stops as soon as the first list ends.

You can also "unzip" a list using a strange trick:

```
pairs = [('a', 1), ('b', 2), ('c', 3)]
letters, numbers = zip(*pairs)
```

The asterisk (*) performs *argument unpacking*, which uses the elements of `pairs` as individual arguments to `zip`. It ends up the same as if you'd called:

```
letters, numbers = zip(('a', 1), ('b', 2), ('c', 3))
```

You can use argument unpacking with any function:

```
def add(a, b): return a + b

add(1, 2)        # returns 3
try:
    add([1, 2])
except TypeError:
    print("add expects two inputs")
add(*[1, 2])     # returns 3
```

It is rare that we'll find this useful, but when we do it's a neat trick.

args and kwargs

Let's say we want to create a higher-order function that takes as input some function f and returns a new function that for any input returns twice the value of f:

```
def doubler(f):
    # Here we define a new function that keeps a reference to f
    def g(x):
        return 2 * f(x)

    # And return that new function
    return g
```

This works in some cases:

```
def f1(x):
    return x + 1

g = doubler(f1)
assert g(3) == 8,  "(3 + 1) * 2 should equal 8"
assert g(-1) == 0, "(-1 + 1) * 2 should equal 0"
```

However, it doesn't work with functions that take more than a single argument:

```
def f2(x, y):
    return x + y

g = doubler(f2)
try:
    g(1, 2)
```

```
except TypeError:
    print("as defined, g only takes one argument")
```

What we need is a way to specify a function that takes arbitrary arguments. We can do this with argument unpacking and a little bit of magic:

```
def magic(*args, **kwargs):
    print("unnamed args:", args)
    print("keyword args:", kwargs)

magic(1, 2, key="word", key2="word2")

# prints
#  unnamed args: (1, 2)
#  keyword args: {'key': 'word', 'key2': 'word2'}
```

That is, when we define a function like this, `args` is a tuple of its unnamed arguments and `kwargs` is a `dict` of its named arguments. It works the other way too, if you want to use a `list` (or `tuple`) and `dict` to *supply* arguments to a function:

```
def other_way_magic(x, y, z):
    return x + y + z

x_y_list = [1, 2]
z_dict = {"z": 3}
assert other_way_magic(*x_y_list, **z_dict) == 6, "1 + 2 + 3 should be 6"
```

You could do all sorts of strange tricks with this; we will only use it to produce higher-order functions whose inputs can accept arbitrary arguments:

```
def doubler_correct(f):
    """works no matter what kind of inputs f expects"""
    def g(*args, **kwargs):
        """whatever arguments g is supplied, pass them through to f"""
        return 2 * f(*args, **kwargs)
    return g

g = doubler_correct(f2)
assert g(1, 2) == 6, "doubler should work now"
```

As a general rule, your code will be more correct and more readable if you are explicit about what sorts of arguments your functions require; accordingly, we will use `args` and `kwargs` only when we have no other option.

Type Annotations

Python is a *dynamically typed* language. That means that it in general it doesn't care about the types of objects we use, as long as we use them in valid ways:

```
def add(a, b):
    return a + b
```

```
assert add(10, 5) == 15,                "+ is valid for numbers"
assert add([1, 2], [3]) == [1, 2, 3],   "+ is valid for lists"
assert add("hi ", "there") == "hi there", "+ is valid for strings"

try:
    add(10, "five")
except TypeError:
    print("cannot add an int to a string")
```

whereas in a *statically typed* language our functions and objects would have specific types:

```
def add(a: int, b: int) -> int:
    return a + b

add(10, 5)            # you'd like this to be OK
add("hi ", "there")   # you'd like this to be not OK
```

In fact, recent versions of Python do (sort of) have this functionality. The preceding version of add with the int type annotations is valid Python 3.6!

However, these type annotations don't actually *do* anything. You can still use the annotated add function to add strings, and the call to add(10, "five") will still raise the exact same TypeError.

That said, there are still (at least) four good reasons to use type annotations in your Python code:

- Types are an important form of documentation. This is doubly true in a book that is using code to teach you theoretical and mathematical concepts. Compare the following two function stubs:

  ```
  def dot_product(x, y): ...

  # we have not yet defined Vector, but imagine we had
  def dot_product(x: Vector, y: Vector) -> float: ...
  ```

  I find the second one exceedingly more informative; hopefully you do too. (At this point I have gotten so used to type hinting that I now find untyped Python difficult to read.)

- There are external tools (the most popular is mypy) that will read your code, inspect the type annotations, and let you know about type errors *before you ever run your code*. For example, if you ran mypy over a file containing add("hi ", "there"), it would warn you:

  ```
  error: Argument 1 to "add" has incompatible type "str"; expected "int"
  ```

  Like assert testing, this is a good way to find mistakes in your code before you ever run it. The narrative in the book will not involve such a type checker; how-

Type Annotations | 39

ever, behind the scenes I will be running one, which will help ensure *that the book itself is correct.*

- Having to think about the types in your code forces you to design cleaner functions and interfaces:

```python
from typing import Union

def secretly_ugly_function(value, operation): ...

def ugly_function(value: int,
                  operation: Union[str, int, float, bool]) -> int:
    ...
```

Here we have a function whose `operation` parameter is allowed to be a `string`, or an `int`, or a `float`, or a `bool`. It is highly likely that this function is fragile and difficult to use, but it becomes far more clear when the types are made explicit. Doing so, then, will force us to design in a less clunky way, for which our users will thank us.

- Using types allows your editor to help you with things like autocomplete (Figure 2-1) and to get angry at type errors.

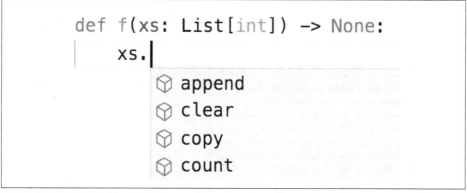

Figure 2-1. VSCode, but likely your editor does the same

Sometimes people insist that type hints may be valuable on large projects but are not worth the time for small ones. However, since type hints take almost no additional time to type and allow your editor to save you time, I maintain that they actually allow you to write code more quickly, even for small projects.

For all these reasons, all of the code in the remainder of the book will use type annotations. I expect that some readers will be put off by the use of type annotations; however, I suspect by the end of the book they will have changed their minds.

How to Write Type Annotations

As we've seen, for built-in types like `int` and `bool` and `float`, you just use the type itself as the annotation. What if you had (say) a `list`?

```
def total(xs: list) -> float:
    return sum(total)
```

This isn't wrong, but the type is not specific enough. It's clear we really want `xs` to be a `list` of `floats`, not (say) a `list` of strings.

The `typing` module provides a number of parameterized types that we can use to do just this:

```
from typing import List  # note capital L

def total(xs: List[float]) -> float:
    return sum(total)
```

Up until now we've only specified annotations for function parameters and return types. For variables themselves it's usually obvious what the type is:

```
# This is how to type-annotate variables when you define them.
# But this is unnecessary; it's "obvious" x is an int.
x: int = 5
```

However, sometimes it's not obvious:

```
values = []         # what's my type?
best_so_far = None  # what's my type?
```

In such cases we will supply inline type hints:

```
from typing import Optional

values: List[int] = []
best_so_far: Optional[float] = None  # allowed to be either a float or None
```

The `typing` module contains many other types, only a few of which we'll ever use:

```
# the type annotations in this snippet are all unnecessary
from typing import Dict, Iterable, Tuple

# keys are strings, values are ints
counts: Dict[str, int] = {'data': 1, 'science': 2}

# lists and generators are both iterable
if lazy:
    evens: Iterable[int] = (x for x in range(10) if x % 2 == 0)
else:
    evens = [0, 2, 4, 6, 8]

# tuples specify a type for each element
triple: Tuple[int, float, int] = (10, 2.3, 5)
```

Finally, since Python has first-class functions, we need a type to represent those as well. Here's a pretty contrived example:

```
from typing import Callable

# The type hint says that repeater is a function that takes
# two arguments, a string and an int, and returns a string.
def twice(repeater: Callable[[str, int], str], s: str) -> str:
    return repeater(s, 2)

def comma_repeater(s: str, n: int) -> str:
    n_copies = [s for _ in range(n)]
    return ', '.join(n_copies)

assert twice(comma_repeater, "type hints") == "type hints, type hints"
```

As type annotations are just Python objects, we can assign them to variables to make them easier to refer to:

```
Number = int
Numbers = List[Number]

def total(xs: Numbers) -> Number:
    return sum(xs)
```

By the time you get to the end of the book, you'll be quite familiar with reading and writing type annotations, and I hope you'll use them in your code.

Welcome to DataSciencester!

This concludes new employee orientation. Oh, and also: try not to embezzle anything.

For Further Exploration

- There is no shortage of Python tutorials in the world. The official one (*https:// docs.python.org/3/tutorial/*) is not a bad place to start.

- The official IPython tutorial (*http://ipython.readthedocs.io/en/stable/interactive/ index.html*) will help you get started with IPython, if you decide to use it. Please use it.

- The mypy documentation (*https://mypy.readthedocs.io/en/stable/*) will tell you more than you ever wanted to know about Python type annotations and type checking.

## CHAPTER 3

Visualizing Data

I believe that visualization is one of the most powerful means of achieving personal goals.
—Harvey Mackay

A fundamental part of the data scientist's toolkit is data visualization. Although it is very easy to create visualizations, it's much harder to produce *good* ones.

There are two primary uses for data visualization:

- To *explore* data
- To *communicate* data

In this chapter, we will concentrate on building the skills that you'll need to start exploring your own data and to produce the visualizations we'll be using throughout the rest of the book. Like most of our chapter topics, data visualization is a rich field of study that deserves its own book. Nonetheless, I'll try to give you a sense of what makes for a good visualization and what doesn't.

matplotlib

A wide variety of tools exist for visualizing data. We will be using the matplotlib library (*http://matplotlib.org/*), which is widely used (although sort of showing its age). If you are interested in producing elaborate interactive visualizations for the web, it is likely not the right choice, but for simple bar charts, line charts, and scatterplots, it works pretty well.

As mentioned earlier, matplotlib is not part of the core Python library. With your virtual environment activated (to set one up, go back to "Virtual Environments" on page 16 and follow the instructions), install it using this command:

```
python -m pip install matplotlib
```

We will be using the `matplotlib.pyplot` module. In its simplest use, `pyplot` main-tains an internal state in which you build up a visualization step by step. Once you're done, you can save it with `savefig` or display it with `show`.

For example, making simple plots (like Figure 3-1) is pretty simple:

```
from matplotlib import pyplot as plt

years = [1950, 1960, 1970, 1980, 1990, 2000, 2010]
gdp = [300.2, 543.3, 1075.9, 2862.5, 5979.6, 10289.7, 14958.3]

# create a line chart, years on x-axis, gdp on y-axis
plt.plot(years, gdp, color='green', marker='o', linestyle='solid')

# add a title
plt.title("Nominal GDP")

# add a label to the y-axis
plt.ylabel("Billions of $")
plt.show()
```

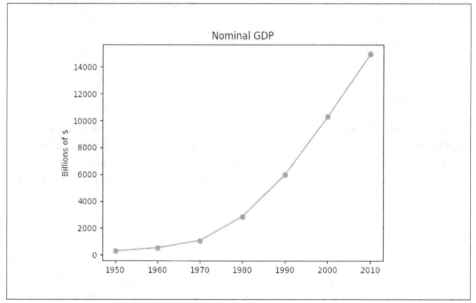

Figure 3-1. A simple line chart

Making plots that look publication-quality good is more complicated and beyond the scope of this chapter. There are many ways you can customize your charts with, for example, axis labels, line styles, and point markers. Rather than attempt a comprehensive treatment of these options, we'll just use (and call attention to) some of them in our examples.

 Although we won't be using much of this functionality, matplotlib is capable of producing complicated plots within plots, sophisticated formatting, and interactive visualizations. Check out its documentation (*https://matplotlib.org*) if you want to go deeper than we do in this book.

Bar Charts

A bar chart is a good choice when you want to show how some quantity varies among some *discrete* set of items. For instance, Figure 3-2 shows how many Academy Awards were won by each of a variety of movies:

```
movies = ["Annie Hall", "Ben-Hur", "Casablanca", "Gandhi", "West Side Story"]
num_oscars = [5, 11, 3, 8, 10]

# plot bars with left x-coordinates [0, 1, 2, 3, 4], heights [num_oscars]
plt.bar(range(len(movies)), num_oscars)

plt.title("My Favorite Movies")     # add a title
plt.ylabel("# of Academy Awards")   # label the y-axis

# label x-axis with movie names at bar centers
plt.xticks(range(len(movies)), movies)

plt.show()
```

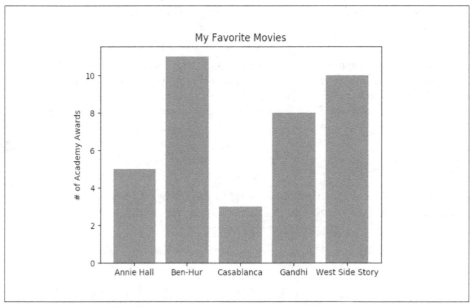

Figure 3-2. A simple bar chart

A bar chart can also be a good choice for plotting histograms of bucketed numeric values, as in Figure 3-3, in order to visually explore how the values are *distributed*:

```
from collections import Counter
grades = [83, 95, 91, 87, 70, 0, 85, 82, 100, 67, 73, 77, 0]

# Bucket grades by decile, but put 100 in with the 90s
histogram = Counter(min(grade // 10 * 10, 90) for grade in grades)

plt.bar([x + 5 for x in histogram.keys()],   # Shift bars right by 5
        histogram.values(),                    # Give each bar its correct height
        10,                                     # Give each bar a width of 10
        edgecolor=(0, 0, 0))                    # Black edges for each bar

plt.axis([-5, 105, 0, 5])                       # x-axis from -5 to 105,
                                                # y-axis from 0 to 5

plt.xticks([10 * i for i in range(11)])        # x-axis labels at 0, 10, ..., 100
plt.xlabel("Decile")
plt.ylabel("# of Students")
plt.title("Distribution of Exam 1 Grades")
plt.show()
```

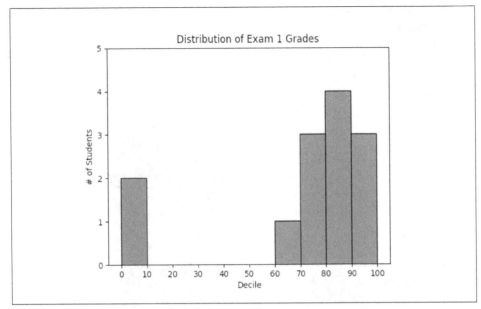

Figure 3-3. Using a bar chart for a histogram

The third argument to plt.bar specifies the bar width. Here we chose a width of 10, to fill the entire decile. We also shifted the bars right by 5, so that, for example, the "10" bar (which corresponds to the decile 10–20) would have its center at 15 and hence occupy the correct range. We also added a black edge to each bar to make them visually distinct.

The call to plt.axis indicates that we want the x-axis to range from –5 to 105 (just to leave a little space on the left and right), and that the y-axis should range from 0 to 5. And the call to plt.xticks puts x-axis labels at 0, 10, 20, ..., 100.

Be judicious when using plt.axis. When creating bar charts it is considered especially bad form for your y-axis not to start at 0, since this is an easy way to mislead people (Figure 3-4):

```
mentions = [500, 505]
years = [2017, 2018]

plt.bar(years, mentions, 0.8)
plt.xticks(years)
plt.ylabel("# of times I heard someone say 'data science'")

# if you don't do this, matplotlib will label the x-axis 0, 1
# and then add a +2.013e3 off in the corner (bad matplotlib!)
plt.ticklabel_format(useOffset=False)

# misleading y-axis only shows the part above 500
```

```
plt.axis([2016.5, 2018.5, 499, 506])
plt.title("Look at the 'Huge' Increase!")
plt.show()
```

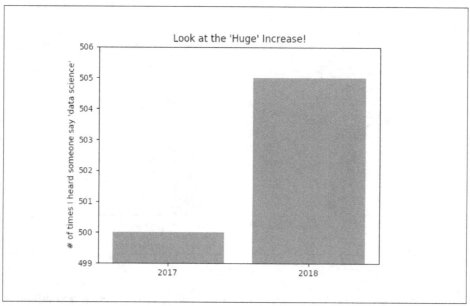

Figure 3-4. A chart with a misleading y-axis

In Figure 3-5, we use more sensible axes, and it looks far less impressive:

```
plt.axis([2016.5, 2018.5, 0, 550])
plt.title("Not So Huge Anymore")
plt.show()
```

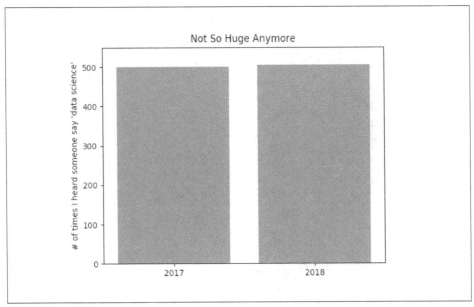

Figure 3-5. The same chart with a nonmisleading y-axis

Line Charts

As we saw already, we can make line charts using `plt.plot`. These are a good choice for showing *trends*, as illustrated in Figure 3-6:

```
variance     = [1, 2, 4, 8, 16, 32, 64, 128, 256]
bias_squared = [256, 128, 64, 32, 16, 8, 4, 2, 1]
total_error  = [x + y for x, y in zip(variance, bias_squared)]
xs = [i for i, _ in enumerate(variance)]

# We can make multiple calls to plt.plot
# to show multiple series on the same chart
plt.plot(xs, variance,     'g-',  label='variance')    # green solid line
plt.plot(xs, bias_squared, 'r-.', label='bias^2')      # red dot-dashed line
plt.plot(xs, total_error,  'b:',  label='total error') # blue dotted line

# Because we've assigned labels to each series,
# we can get a legend for free (loc=9 means "top center")
plt.legend(loc=9)
plt.xlabel("model complexity")
plt.xticks([])
plt.title("The Bias-Variance Tradeoff")
plt.show()
```

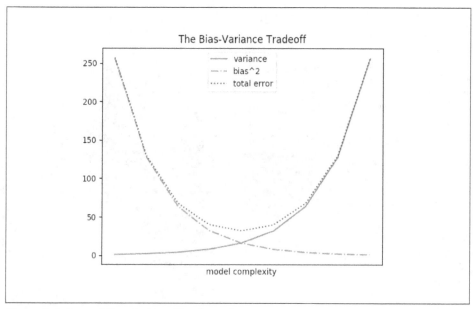

Figure 3-6. Several line charts with a legend

Scatterplots

A scatterplot is the right choice for visualizing the relationship between two paired sets of data. For example, Figure 3-7 illustrates the relationship between the number of friends your users have and the number of minutes they spend on the site every day:

```
friends = [ 70,  65,  72,  63,  71,  64,  60,  64,  67]
minutes = [175, 170, 205, 120, 220, 130, 105, 145, 190]
labels =  ['a', 'b', 'c', 'd', 'e', 'f', 'g', 'h', 'i']

plt.scatter(friends, minutes)

# label each point
for label, friend_count, minute_count in zip(labels, friends, minutes):
    plt.annotate(label,
        xy=(friend_count, minute_count), # Put the label with its point
        xytext=(5, -5),                  # but slightly offset
        textcoords='offset points')

plt.title("Daily Minutes vs. Number of Friends")
plt.xlabel("# of friends")
plt.ylabel("daily minutes spent on the site")
plt.show()
```

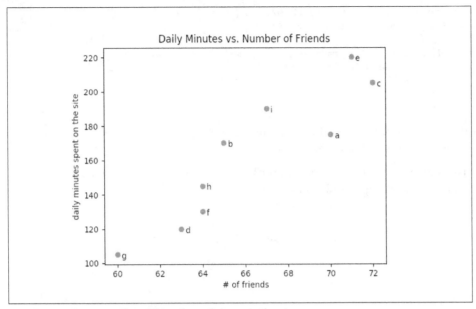

Figure 3-7. A scatterplot of friends and time on the site

If you're scattering comparable variables, you might get a misleading picture if you let matplotlib choose the scale, as in Figure 3-8.

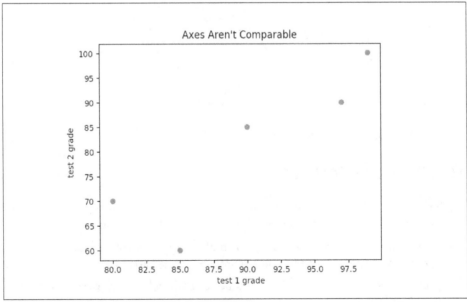

Figure 3-8. A scatterplot with uncomparable axes

```
test_1_grades = [ 99, 90, 85, 97, 80]
test_2_grades = [100, 85, 60, 90, 70]

plt.scatter(test_1_grades, test_2_grades)
plt.title("Axes Aren't Comparable")
plt.xlabel("test 1 grade")
plt.ylabel("test 2 grade")
plt.show()
```

If we include a call to `plt.axis("equal")`, the plot (Figure 3-9) more accurately shows that most of the variation occurs on test 2.

That's enough to get you started doing visualization. We'll learn much more about visualization throughout the book.

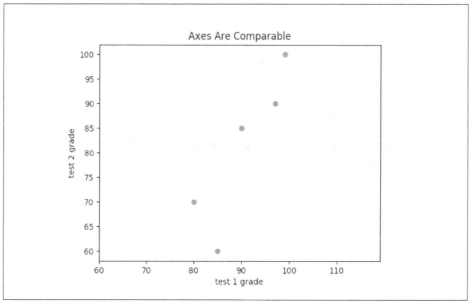

Figure 3-9. The same scatterplot with equal axes

For Further Exploration

- The matplotlib Gallery (*https://matplotlib.org/gallery.html*) will give you a good idea of the sorts of things you can do with matplotlib (and how to do them).
- seaborn (*https://seaborn.pydata.org/*) is built on top of matplotlib and allows you to easily produce prettier (and more complex) visualizations.
- Altair (*https://altair-viz.github.io/*) is a newer Python library for creating declarative visualizations.

- D3.js (*http://d3js.org*) is a JavaScript library for producing sophisticated interactive visualizations for the web. Although it is not in Python, it is widely used, and it is well worth your while to be familiar with it.

- Bokeh (*http://bokeh.pydata.org*) is a library that brings D3-style visualizations into Python.

## CHAPTER 4

Linear Algebra

Is there anything more useless or less useful than algebra?
—Billy Connolly

Linear algebra is the branch of mathematics that deals with *vector spaces*. Although I can't hope to teach you linear algebra in a brief chapter, it underpins a large number of data science concepts and techniques, which means I owe it to you to at least try. What we learn in this chapter we'll use heavily throughout the rest of the book.

Vectors

Abstractly, *vectors* are objects that can be added together to form new vectors and that can be multiplied by *scalars* (i.e., numbers), also to form new vectors.

Concretely (for us), vectors are points in some finite-dimensional space. Although you might not think of your data as vectors, they are often a useful way to represent numeric data.

For example, if you have the heights, weights, and ages of a large number of people, you can treat your data as three-dimensional vectors [height, weight, age]. If you're teaching a class with four exams, you can treat student grades as four-dimensional vectors [exam1, exam2, exam3, exam4].

The simplest from-scratch approach is to represent vectors as lists of numbers. A list of three numbers corresponds to a vector in three-dimensional space, and vice versa.

We'll accomplish this with a type alias that says a Vector is just a list of floats:

```
from typing import List

Vector = List[float]
```

```
height_weight_age = [70,  # inches,
                     170, # pounds,
                     40 ] # years

grades = [95,   # exam1
          80,   # exam2
          75,   # exam3
          62 ]  # exam4
```

We'll also want to perform *arithmetic* on vectors. Because Python `lists` aren't vectors (and hence provide no facilities for vector arithmetic), we'll need to build these arithmetic tools ourselves. So let's start with that.

To begin with, we'll frequently need to add two vectors. Vectors add *componentwise*. This means that if two vectors v and w are the same length, their sum is just the vector whose first element is `v[0] + w[0]`, whose second element is `v[1] + w[1]`, and so on. (If they're not the same length, then we're not allowed to add them.)

For example, adding the vectors `[1, 2]` and `[2, 1]` results in `[1 + 2, 2 + 1]` or `[3, 3]`, as shown in Figure 4-1.

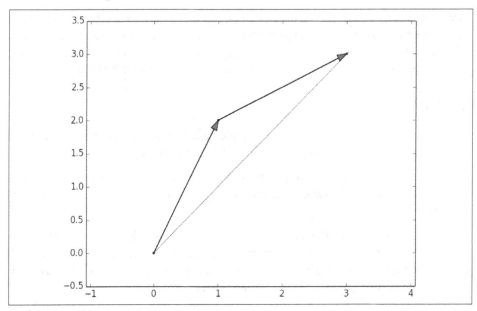

Figure 4-1. Adding two vectors

We can easily implement this by `zip`-ing the vectors together and using a list comprehension to add the corresponding elements:

```
def add(v: Vector, w: Vector) -> Vector:
    """Adds corresponding elements"""
    assert len(v) == len(w), "vectors must be the same length"
```

```
    return [v_i + w_i for v_i, w_i in zip(v, w)]

assert add([1, 2, 3], [4, 5, 6]) == [5, 7, 9]
```

Similarly, to subtract two vectors we just subtract the corresponding elements:

```
def subtract(v: Vector, w: Vector) -> Vector:
    """Subtracts corresponding elements"""
    assert len(v) == len(w), "vectors must be the same length"

    return [v_i - w_i for v_i, w_i in zip(v, w)]

assert subtract([5, 7, 9], [4, 5, 6]) == [1, 2, 3]
```

We'll also sometimes want to componentwise sum a list of vectors—that is, create a new vector whose first element is the sum of all the first elements, whose second element is the sum of all the second elements, and so on:

```
def vector_sum(vectors: List[Vector]) -> Vector:
    """Sums all corresponding elements"""
    # Check that vectors is not empty
    assert vectors, "no vectors provided!"

    # Check the vectors are all the same size
    num_elements = len(vectors[0])
    assert all(len(v) == num_elements for v in vectors), "different sizes!"

    # the i-th element of the result is the sum of every vector[i]
    return [sum(vector[i] for vector in vectors)
            for i in range(num_elements)]

assert vector_sum([[1, 2], [3, 4], [5, 6], [7, 8]]) == [16, 20]
```

We'll also need to be able to multiply a vector by a scalar, which we do simply by multiplying each element of the vector by that number:

```
def scalar_multiply(c: float, v: Vector) -> Vector:
    """Multiplies every element by c"""
    return [c * v_i for v_i in v]

assert scalar_multiply(2, [1, 2, 3]) == [2, 4, 6]
```

This allows us to compute the componentwise means of a list of (same-sized) vectors:

```
def vector_mean(vectors: List[Vector]) -> Vector:
    """Computes the element-wise average"""
    n = len(vectors)
    return scalar_multiply(1/n, vector_sum(vectors))

assert vector_mean([[1, 2], [3, 4], [5, 6]]) == [3, 4]
```

A less obvious tool is the *dot product*. The dot product of two vectors is the sum of their componentwise products:

```
def dot(v: Vector, w: Vector) -> float:
    """Computes v_1 * w_1 + ... + v_n * w_n"""
    assert len(v) == len(w), "vectors must be same length"

    return sum(v_i * w_i for v_i, w_i in zip(v, w))

assert dot([1, 2, 3], [4, 5, 6]) == 32  # 1 * 4 + 2 * 5 + 3 * 6
```

If w has magnitude 1, the dot product measures how far the vector v extends in the w direction. For example, if w = [1, 0], then dot(v, w) is just the first component of v. Another way of saying this is that it's the length of the vector you'd get if you *projected* v onto w (Figure 4-2).

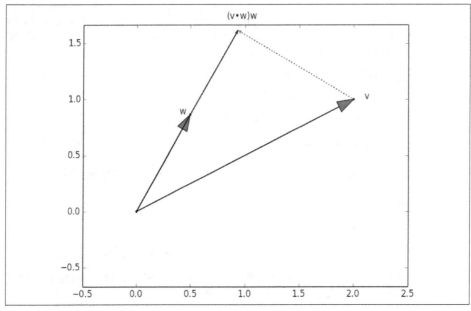

Figure 4-2. The dot product as vector projection

Using this, it's easy to compute a vector's *sum of squares*:

```
def sum_of_squares(v: Vector) -> float:
    """Returns v_1 * v_1 + ... + v_n * v_n"""
    return dot(v, v)

assert sum_of_squares([1, 2, 3]) == 14  # 1 * 1 + 2 * 2 + 3 * 3
```

which we can use to compute its *magnitude* (or length):

```
import math

def magnitude(v: Vector) -> float:
    """Returns the magnitude (or length) of v"""
    return math.sqrt(sum_of_squares(v))  # math.sqrt is square root function
```

```
assert magnitude([3, 4]) == 5
```

We now have all the pieces we need to compute the distance between two vectors, defined as:

$$\sqrt{(v_1 - w_1)^2 + \ldots + (v_n - w_n)^2}$$

In code:

```
def squared_distance(v: Vector, w: Vector) -> float:
    """Computes (v_1 - w_1) ** 2 + ... + (v_n - w_n) ** 2"""
    return sum_of_squares(subtract(v, w))

def distance(v: Vector, w: Vector) -> float:
    """Computes the distance between v and w"""
    return math.sqrt(squared_distance(v, w))
```

This is possibly clearer if we write it as (the equivalent):

```
def distance(v: Vector, w: Vector) -> float:
    return magnitude(subtract(v, w))
```

That should be plenty to get us started. We'll be using these functions heavily throughout the book.

Using lists as vectors is great for exposition but terrible for performance.

In production code, you would want to use the NumPy library, which includes a high-performance array class with all sorts of arithmetic operations included.

Matrices

A *matrix* is a two-dimensional collection of numbers. We will represent matrices as lists of lists, with each inner list having the same size and representing a *row* of the matrix. If A is a matrix, then A[i][j] is the element in the *i*th row and the *j*th column. Per mathematical convention, we will frequently use capital letters to represent matrices. For example:

```
# Another type alias
Matrix = List[List[float]]

A = [[1, 2, 3],    # A has 2 rows and 3 columns
     [4, 5, 6]]

B = [[1, 2],       # B has 3 rows and 2 columns
```

```
        [3, 4],
        [5, 6]]
```

 In mathematics, you would usually name the first row of the matrix "row 1" and the first column "column 1." Because we're representing matrices with Python lists, which are zero-indexed, we'll call the first row of a matrix "row 0" and the first column "column 0."

Given this list-of-lists representation, the matrix A has len(A) rows and len(A[0]) columns, which we consider its shape:

```python
from typing import Tuple

def shape(A: Matrix) -> Tuple[int, int]:
    """Returns (# of rows of A, # of columns of A)"""
    num_rows = len(A)
    num_cols = len(A[0]) if A else 0   # number of elements in first row
    return num_rows, num_cols

assert shape([[1, 2, 3], [4, 5, 6]]) == (2, 3)  # 2 rows, 3 columns
```

If a matrix has n rows and k columns, we will refer to it as an $n \times k$ *matrix*. We can (and sometimes will) think of each row of an $n \times k$ matrix as a vector of length k, and each column as a vector of length n:

```python
def get_row(A: Matrix, i: int) -> Vector:
    """Returns the i-th row of A (as a Vector)"""
    return A[i]             # A[i] is already the ith row

def get_column(A: Matrix, j: int) -> Vector:
    """Returns the j-th column of A (as a Vector)"""
    return [A_i[j]          # jth element of row A_i
            for A_i in A]   # for each row A_i
```

We'll also want to be able to create a matrix given its shape and a function for generating its elements. We can do this using a nested list comprehension:

```python
from typing import Callable

def make_matrix(num_rows: int,
                num_cols: int,
                entry_fn: Callable[[int, int], float]) -> Matrix:
    """
    Returns a num_rows x num_cols matrix
    whose (i,j)-th entry is entry_fn(i, j)
    """
    return [[entry_fn(i, j)            # given i, create a list
             for j in range(num_cols)] #   [entry_fn(i, 0), ... ]
            for i in range(num_rows)]  # create one list for each i
```

Given this function, you could make a 5 × 5 *identity matrix* (with 1s on the diagonal and 0s elsewhere) like so:

```python
def identity_matrix(n: int) -> Matrix:
    """Returns the n x n identity matrix"""
    return make_matrix(n, n, lambda i, j: 1 if i == j else 0)

assert identity_matrix(5) == [[1, 0, 0, 0, 0],
                              [0, 1, 0, 0, 0],
                              [0, 0, 1, 0, 0],
                              [0, 0, 0, 1, 0],
                              [0, 0, 0, 0, 1]]
```

Matrices will be important to us for several reasons.

First, we can use a matrix to represent a dataset consisting of multiple vectors, simply by considering each vector as a row of the matrix. For example, if you had the heights, weights, and ages of 1,000 people, you could put them in a 1,000 × 3 matrix:

```python
data = [[70, 170, 40],
        [65, 120, 26],
        [77, 250, 19],
        # ....
       ]
```

Second, as we'll see later, we can use an $n \times k$ matrix to represent a linear function that maps k-dimensional vectors to n-dimensional vectors. Several of our techniques and concepts will involve such functions.

Third, matrices can be used to represent binary relationships. In Chapter 1, we represented the edges of a network as a collection of pairs (i, j). An alternative representation would be to create a matrix A such that A[i][j] is 1 if nodes i and j are connected and 0 otherwise.

Recall that before we had:

```python
friendships = [(0, 1), (0, 2), (1, 2), (1, 3), (2, 3), (3, 4),
               (4, 5), (5, 6), (5, 7), (6, 8), (7, 8), (8, 9)]
```

We could also represent this as:

```python
#             user 0  1  2  3  4  5  6  7  8  9
#
friend_matrix = [[0, 1, 1, 0, 0, 0, 0, 0, 0, 0],  # user 0
                 [1, 0, 1, 1, 0, 0, 0, 0, 0, 0],  # user 1
                 [1, 1, 0, 1, 0, 0, 0, 0, 0, 0],  # user 2
                 [0, 1, 1, 0, 1, 0, 0, 0, 0, 0],  # user 3
                 [0, 0, 0, 1, 0, 1, 0, 0, 0, 0],  # user 4
                 [0, 0, 0, 0, 1, 0, 1, 1, 0, 0],  # user 5
                 [0, 0, 0, 0, 0, 1, 0, 0, 1, 0],  # user 6
                 [0, 0, 0, 0, 0, 1, 0, 0, 1, 0],  # user 7
                 [0, 0, 0, 0, 0, 0, 1, 1, 0, 1],  # user 8
                 [0, 0, 0, 0, 0, 0, 0, 0, 1, 0]]  # user 9
```

If there are very few connections, this is a much more inefficient representation, since you end up having to store a lot of zeros. However, with the matrix representation it is much quicker to check whether two nodes are connected—you just have to do a matrix lookup instead of (potentially) inspecting every edge:

```
assert friend_matrix[0][2] == 1, "0 and 2 are friends"
assert friend_matrix[0][8] == 0, "0 and 8 are not friends"
```

Similarly, to find a node's connections, you only need to inspect the column (or the row) corresponding to that node:

```
# only need to look at one row
friends_of_five = [i
                   for i, is_friend in enumerate(friend_matrix[5])
                   if is_friend]
```

With a small graph you could just add a list of connections to each node object to speed up this process; but for a large, evolving graph that would probably be too expensive and difficult to maintain.

We'll revisit matrices throughout the book.

For Further Exploration

- Linear algebra is widely used by data scientists (frequently implicitly, and not infrequently by people who don't understand it). It wouldn't be a bad idea to read a textbook. You can find several freely available online:

    — *Linear Algebra* (*http://joshua.smcvt.edu/linearalgebra/*), by Jim Hefferon (Saint Michael's College)

    — *Linear Algebra* (*https://www.math.ucdavis.edu/~linear/linear-guest.pdf*), by David Cherney, Tom Denton, Rohit Thomas, and Andrew Waldron (UC Davis)

    — If you are feeling adventurous, *Linear Algebra Done Wrong* (*https://www.math.brown.edu/~treil/papers/LADW/LADW_2017-09-04.pdf*), by Sergei Treil (Brown University), is a more advanced introduction.

- All of the machinery we built in this chapter you get for free if you use NumPy (*http://www.numpy.org*). (You get a lot more too, including much better performance.)

## CHAPTER 5

Statistics

Facts are stubborn, but statistics are more pliable.
—Mark Twain

Statistics refers to the mathematics and techniques with which we understand data. It is a rich, enormous field, more suited to a shelf (or room) in a library than a chapter in a book, and so our discussion will necessarily not be a deep one. Instead, I'll try to teach you just enough to be dangerous, and pique your interest just enough that you'll go off and learn more.

Describing a Single Set of Data

Through a combination of word of mouth and luck, DataSciencester has grown to dozens of members, and the VP of Fundraising asks you for some sort of description of how many friends your members have that he can include in his elevator pitches.

Using techniques from Chapter 1, you are easily able to produce this data. But now you are faced with the problem of how to *describe* it.

One obvious description of any dataset is simply the data itself:

```
num_friends = [100, 49, 41, 40, 25,
               # ... and lots more
              ]
```

For a small enough dataset, this might even be the best description. But for a larger dataset, this is unwieldy and probably opaque. (Imagine staring at a list of 1 million numbers.) For that reason, we use statistics to distill and communicate relevant features of our data.

As a first approach, you put the friend counts into a histogram using `Counter` and `plt.bar` (Figure 5-1):

```
from collections import Counter
import matplotlib.pyplot as plt

friend_counts = Counter(num_friends)
xs = range(101)                          # largest value is 100
ys = [friend_counts[x] for x in xs]      # height is just # of friends
plt.bar(xs, ys)
plt.axis([0, 101, 0, 25])
plt.title("Histogram of Friend Counts")
plt.xlabel("# of friends")
plt.ylabel("# of people")
plt.show()
```

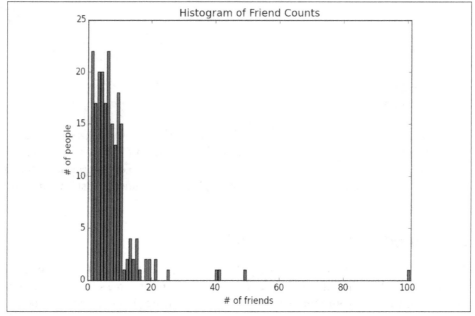

Figure 5-1. A histogram of friend counts

Unfortunately, this chart is still too difficult to slip into conversations. So you start
generating some statistics. Probably the simplest statistic is the number of data points:

```
num_points = len(num_friends)           # 204
```

You're probably also interested in the largest and smallest values:

```
largest_value = max(num_friends)        # 100
smallest_value = min(num_friends)       # 1
```

which are just special cases of wanting to know the values in specific positions:

```
sorted_values = sorted(num_friends)
smallest_value = sorted_values[0]       # 1
```

```
second_smallest_value = sorted_values[1]    # 1
second_largest_value = sorted_values[-2]    # 49
```

But we're only getting started.

Central Tendencies

Usually, we'll want some notion of where our data is centered. Most commonly we'll use the *mean* (or average), which is just the sum of the data divided by its count:

```
def mean(xs: List[float]) -> float:
    return sum(xs) / len(xs)

mean(num_friends)    # 7.333333
```

If you have two data points, the mean is simply the point halfway between them. As you add more points, the mean shifts around, but it always depends on the value of every point. For example, if you have 10 data points, and you increase the value of any of them by 1, you increase the mean by 0.1.

We'll also sometimes be interested in the *median*, which is the middle-most value (if the number of data points is odd) or the average of the two middle-most values (if the number of data points is even).

For instance, if we have five data points in a sorted vector x, the median is x[5 // 2] or x[2]. If we have six data points, we want the average of x[2] (the third point) and x[3] (the fourth point).

Notice that—unlike the mean—the median doesn't fully depend on every value in your data. For example, if you make the largest point larger (or the smallest point smaller), the middle points remain unchanged, which means so does the median.

We'll write different functions for the even and odd cases and combine them:

```
# The underscores indicate that these are "private" functions, as they're
# intended to be called by our median function but not by other people
# using our statistics library.
def _median_odd(xs: List[float]) -> float:
    """If len(xs) is odd, the median is the middle element"""
    return sorted(xs)[len(xs) // 2]

def _median_even(xs: List[float]) -> float:
    """If len(xs) is even, it's the average of the middle two elements"""
    sorted_xs = sorted(xs)
    hi_midpoint = len(xs) // 2  # e.g. length 4 => hi_midpoint 2
    return (sorted_xs[hi_midpoint - 1] + sorted_xs[hi_midpoint]) / 2

def median(v: List[float]) -> float:
    """Finds the 'middle-most' value of v"""
    return _median_even(v) if len(v) % 2 == 0 else _median_odd(v)
```

```
assert median([1, 10, 2, 9, 5]) == 5
assert median([1, 9, 2, 10]) == (2 + 9) / 2
```

And now we can compute the median number of friends:

```
print(median(num_friends))  # 6
```

Clearly, the mean is simpler to compute, and it varies smoothly as our data changes. If we have *n* data points and one of them increases by some small amount *e*, then necessarily the mean will increase by *e* / *n*. (This makes the mean amenable to all sorts of calculus tricks.) In order to find the median, however, we have to sort our data. And changing one of our data points by a small amount *e* might increase the median by *e*, by some number less than *e*, or not at all (depending on the rest of the data).

 There are, in fact, nonobvious tricks to efficiently compute medians (*http://en.wikipedia.org/wiki/Quickselect*) without sorting the data. However, they are beyond the scope of this book, so *we* have to sort the data.

At the same time, the mean is very sensitive to outliers in our data. If our friendliest user had 200 friends (instead of 100), then the mean would rise to 7.82, while the median would stay the same. If outliers are likely to be bad data (or otherwise unrepresentative of whatever phenomenon we're trying to understand), then the mean can sometimes give us a misleading picture. For example, the story is often told that in the mid-1980s, the major at the University of North Carolina with the highest average starting salary was geography, mostly because of NBA star (and outlier) Michael Jordan.

A generalization of the median is the *quantile*, which represents the value under which a certain percentile of the data lies (the median represents the value under which 50% of the data lies):

```
def quantile(xs: List[float], p: float) -> float:
    """Returns the pth-percentile value in x"""
    p_index = int(p * len(xs))
    return sorted(xs)[p_index]

assert quantile(num_friends, 0.10) == 1
assert quantile(num_friends, 0.25) == 3
assert quantile(num_friends, 0.75) == 9
assert quantile(num_friends, 0.90) == 13
```

Less commonly you might want to look at the *mode*, or most common value(s):

```
def mode(x: List[float]) -> List[float]:
    """Returns a list, since there might be more than one mode"""
    counts = Counter(x)
    max_count = max(counts.values())
    return [x_i for x_i, count in counts.items()
```

```
        if count == max_count]

    assert set(mode(num_friends)) == {1, 6}
```

But most frequently we'll just use the mean.

Dispersion

Dispersion refers to measures of how spread out our data is. Typically they're statistics for which values near zero signify *not spread out at all* and for which large values (whatever that means) signify *very spread out*. For instance, a very simple measure is the *range*, which is just the difference between the largest and smallest elements:

```
# "range" already means something in Python, so we'll use a different name
def data_range(xs: List[float]) -> float:
    return max(xs) - min(xs)

assert data_range(num_friends) == 99
```

The range is zero precisely when the max and min are equal, which can only happen if the elements of x are all the same, which means the data is as undispersed as possible. Conversely, if the range is large, then the max is much larger than the min and the data is more spread out.

Like the median, the range doesn't really depend on the whole dataset. A dataset whose points are all either 0 or 100 has the same range as a dataset whose values are 0, 100, and lots of 50s. But it seems like the first dataset "should" be more spread out.

A more complex measure of dispersion is the *variance*, which is computed as:

```
from scratch.linear_algebra import sum_of_squares

def de_mean(xs: List[float]) -> List[float]:
    """Translate xs by subtracting its mean (so the result has mean 0)"""
    x_bar = mean(xs)
    return [x - x_bar for x in xs]

def variance(xs: List[float]) -> float:
    """Almost the average squared deviation from the mean"""
    assert len(xs) >= 2, "variance requires at least two elements"

    n = len(xs)
    deviations = de_mean(xs)
    return sum_of_squares(deviations) / (n - 1)

assert 81.54 < variance(num_friends) < 81.55
```

This looks like it is almost the average squared deviation from the mean, except that we're dividing by n - 1 instead of n. In fact, when we're dealing with a sample from a larger population, x_bar is only an *estimate* of the actual mean, which means that on average (x_i - x_bar) ** 2 is an underestimate of x_i's squared deviation from the mean, which is why we divide by n - 1 instead of n. See Wikipedia (*https://en.wikipedia.org/wiki/Unbiased_estimation_of_standard_deviation*).

Now, whatever units our data is in (e.g., "friends"), all of our measures of central tendency are in that same unit. The range will similarly be in that same unit. The variance, on the other hand, has units that are the *square* of the original units (e.g., "friends squared"). As it can be hard to make sense of these, we often look instead at the *standard deviation*:

```
import math

def standard_deviation(xs: List[float]) -> float:
    """The standard deviation is the square root of the variance"""
    return math.sqrt(variance(xs))

assert 9.02 < standard_deviation(num_friends) < 9.04
```

Both the range and the standard deviation have the same outlier problem that we saw earlier for the mean. Using the same example, if our friendliest user had instead 200 friends, the standard deviation would be 14.89—more than 60% higher!

A more robust alternative computes the difference between the 75th percentile value and the 25th percentile value:

```
def interquartile_range(xs: List[float]) -> float:
    """Returns the difference between the 75%-ile and the 25%-ile"""
    return quantile(xs, 0.75) - quantile(xs, 0.25)

assert interquartile_range(num_friends) == 6
```

which is quite plainly unaffected by a small number of outliers.

Correlation

DataSciencester's VP of Growth has a theory that the amount of time people spend on the site is related to the number of friends they have on the site (she's not a VP for nothing), and she's asked you to verify this.

After digging through traffic logs, you've come up with a list called daily_minutes that shows how many minutes per day each user spends on DataSciencester, and you've ordered it so that its elements correspond to the elements of our previous num_friends list. We'd like to investigate the relationship between these two metrics.

We'll first look at *covariance*, the paired analogue of variance. Whereas variance measures how a single variable deviates from its mean, covariance measures how two variables vary in tandem from their means:

```
from scratch.linear_algebra import dot

def covariance(xs: List[float], ys: List[float]) -> float:
    assert len(xs) == len(ys), "xs and ys must have same number of elements"

    return dot(de_mean(xs), de_mean(ys)) / (len(xs) - 1)

assert 22.42 < covariance(num_friends, daily_minutes) < 22.43
assert 22.42 / 60 < covariance(num_friends, daily_hours) < 22.43 / 60
```

Recall that dot sums up the products of corresponding pairs of elements. When corresponding elements of x and y are either both above their means or both below their means, a positive number enters the sum. When one is above its mean and the other below, a negative number enters the sum. Accordingly, a "large" positive covariance means that x tends to be large when y is large and small when y is small. A "large" negative covariance means the opposite—that x tends to be small when y is large and vice versa. A covariance close to zero means that no such relationship exists.

Nonetheless, this number can be hard to interpret, for a couple of reasons:

- Its units are the product of the inputs' units (e.g., friend-minutes-per-day), which can be hard to make sense of. (What's a "friend-minute-per-day"?)
- If each user had twice as many friends (but the same number of minutes), the covariance would be twice as large. But in a sense, the variables would be just as interrelated. Said differently, it's hard to say what counts as a "large" covariance.

For this reason, it's more common to look at the *correlation*, which divides out the standard deviations of both variables:

```
def correlation(xs: List[float], ys: List[float]) -> float:
    """Measures how much xs and ys vary in tandem about their means"""
    stdev_x = standard_deviation(xs)
    stdev_y = standard_deviation(ys)
    if stdev_x > 0 and stdev_y > 0:
        return covariance(xs, ys) / stdev_x / stdev_y
    else:
        return 0    # if no variation, correlation is zero

assert 0.24 < correlation(num_friends, daily_minutes) < 0.25
assert 0.24 < correlation(num_friends, daily_hours) < 0.25
```

The correlation is unitless and always lies between –1 (perfect anticorrelation) and 1 (perfect correlation). A number like 0.25 represents a relatively weak positive correlation.

However, one thing we neglected to do was examine our data. Check out Figure 5-2.

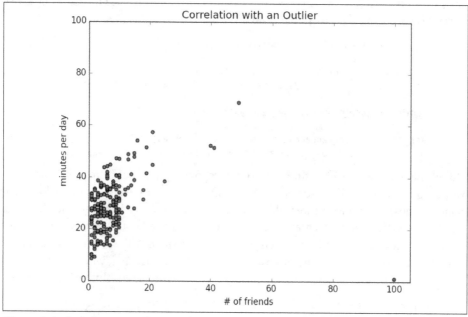

Figure 5-2. Correlation with an outlier

The person with 100 friends (who spends only 1 minute per day on the site) is a huge outlier, and correlation can be very sensitive to outliers. What happens if we ignore him?

```
outlier = num_friends.index(100)    # index of outlier

num_friends_good = [x
                    for i, x in enumerate(num_friends)
                    if i != outlier]

daily_minutes_good = [x
                      for i, x in enumerate(daily_minutes)
                      if i != outlier]

daily_hours_good = [dm / 60 for dm in daily_minutes_good]

assert 0.57 < correlation(num_friends_good, daily_minutes_good) < 0.58
assert 0.57 < correlation(num_friends_good, daily_hours_good) < 0.58
```

Without the outlier, there is a much stronger correlation (Figure 5-3).

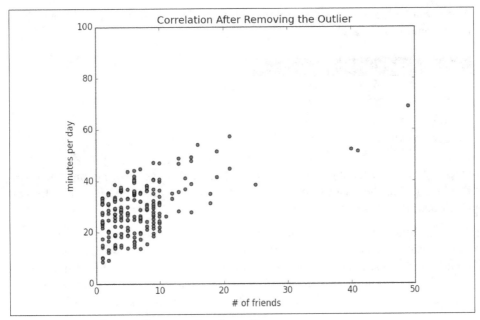

Figure 5-3. Correlation after removing the outlier

You investigate further and discover that the outlier was actually an internal *test* account that no one ever bothered to remove. So you feel justified in excluding it.

Simpson's Paradox

One not uncommon surprise when analyzing data is *Simpson's paradox*, in which correlations can be misleading when *confounding* variables are ignored.

For example, imagine that you can identify all of your members as either East Coast data scientists or West Coast data scientists. You decide to examine which coast's data scientists are friendlier:

Coast	# of members	Avg. # of friends
West Coast	101	8.2
East Coast	103	6.5

It certainly looks like the West Coast data scientists are friendlier than the East Coast data scientists. Your coworkers advance all sorts of theories as to why this might be: maybe it's the sun, or the coffee, or the organic produce, or the laid-back Pacific vibe?

But when playing with the data, you discover something very strange. If you look only at people with PhDs, the East Coast data scientists have more friends on average.

And if you look only at people without PhDs, the East Coast data scientists also have more friends on average!

Coast	Degree	# of members	Avg. # of friends
West Coast	PhD	35	3.1
East Coast	PhD	70	3.2
West Coast	No PhD	66	10.9
East Coast	No PhD	33	13.4

Once you account for the users' degrees, the correlation goes in the opposite direction! Bucketing the data as East Coast/West Coast disguised the fact that the East Coast data scientists skew much more heavily toward PhD types.

This phenomenon crops up in the real world with some regularity. The key issue is that correlation is measuring the relationship between your two variables *all else being equal*. If your dataclasses are assigned at random, as they might be in a well-designed experiment, "all else being equal" might not be a terrible assumption. But when there is a deeper pattern to class assignments, "all else being equal" can be an awful assumption.

The only real way to avoid this is by *knowing your data* and by doing what you can to make sure you've checked for possible confounding factors. Obviously, this is not always possible. If you didn't have data on the educational attainment of these 200 data scientists, you might simply conclude that there was something inherently more sociable about the West Coast.

Some Other Correlational Caveats

A correlation of zero indicates that there is no linear relationship between the two variables. However, there may be other sorts of relationships. For example, if:

```
x = [-2, -1, 0, 1, 2]
y = [ 2,  1, 0, 1, 2]
```

then x and y have zero correlation. But they certainly have a relationship—each element of y equals the absolute value of the corresponding element of x. What they don't have is a relationship in which knowing how x_i compares to mean(x) gives us information about how y_i compares to mean(y). That is the sort of relationship that correlation looks for.

In addition, correlation tells you nothing about how large the relationship is. The variables:

```
x = [-2, -1, 0, 1, 2]
y = [99.98, 99.99, 100, 100.01, 100.02]
```

are perfectly correlated, but (depending on what you're measuring) it's quite possible that this relationship isn't all that interesting.

Correlation and Causation

You have probably heard at some point that "correlation is not causation," most likely from someone looking at data that posed a challenge to parts of his worldview that he was reluctant to question. Nonetheless, this is an important point—if x and y are strongly correlated, that might mean that x causes y, that y causes x, that each causes the other, that some third factor causes both, or nothing at all.

Consider the relationship between num_friends and daily_minutes. It's possible that having more friends on the site *causes* DataSciencester users to spend more time on the site. This might be the case if each friend posts a certain amount of content each day, which means that the more friends you have, the more time it takes to stay current with their updates.

However, it's also possible that the more time users spend arguing in the DataSciencester forums, the more they encounter and befriend like-minded people. That is, spending more time on the site *causes* users to have more friends.

A third possibility is that the users who are most passionate about data science spend more time on the site (because they find it more interesting) and more actively collect data science friends (because they don't want to associate with anyone else).

One way to feel more confident about causality is by conducting randomized trials. If you can randomly split your users into two groups with similar demographics and give one of the groups a slightly different experience, then you can often feel pretty good that the different experiences are causing the different outcomes.

For instance, if you don't mind being angrily accused of *https://www.nytimes.com/ 2014/06/30/technology/facebook-tinkers-with-users-emotions-in-news-feed-experiment-stirring-outcry.html?r=0[experimenting on your users], you could randomly choose a subset of your users and show them content from only a fraction of their friends. If this subset subsequently spent less time on the site, this would give you some confidence that having more friends _causes more time to be spent on the site.*

For Further Exploration

- SciPy (*https://www.scipy.org/*), pandas (*http://pandas.pydata.org*), and StatsModels (*http://www.statsmodels.org/*) all come with a wide variety of statistical functions.

- Statistics is *important*. (Or maybe statistics *are* important?) If you want to be a better data scientist, it would be a good idea to read a statistics textbook. Many are freely available online, including:

  — *Introductory Statistics* (*https://open.umn.edu/opentextbooks/textbooks/introductory-statistics*), by Douglas Shafer and Zhiyi Zhang (Saylor Foundation)

  — *OnlineStatBook* (*http://onlinestatbook.com/*), by David Lane (Rice University)

  — *Introductory Statistics* (*https://openstax.org/details/introductory-statistics*), by OpenStax (OpenStax College)

## CHAPTER 6

Probability

The laws of probability, so true in general, so fallacious in particular.
—Edward Gibbon

It is hard to do data science without some sort of understanding of *probability* and its mathematics. As with our treatment of statistics in Chapter 5, we'll wave our hands a lot and elide many of the technicalities.

For our purposes you should think of probability as a way of quantifying the uncertainty associated with *events* chosen from some *universe* of events. Rather than getting technical about what these terms mean, think of rolling a die. The universe consists of all possible outcomes. And any subset of these outcomes is an event; for example, "the die rolls a 1" or "the die rolls an even number."

Notationally, we write $P(E)$ to mean "the probability of the event E."

We'll use probability theory to build models. We'll use probability theory to evaluate models. We'll use probability theory all over the place.

One could, were one so inclined, get really deep into the philosophy of what probability theory *means*. (This is best done over beers.) We won't be doing that.

Dependence and Independence

Roughly speaking, we say that two events E and F are *dependent* if knowing something about whether E happens gives us information about whether F happens (and vice versa). Otherwise, they are *independent*.

For instance, if we flip a fair coin twice, knowing whether the first flip is heads gives us no information about whether the second flip is heads. These events are independent. On the other hand, knowing whether the first flip is heads certainly gives us information about whether both flips are tails. (If the first flip is heads, then definitely it's not the case that both flips are tails.) These two events are dependent.

Mathematically, we say that two events E and F are independent if the probability that they both happen is the product of the probabilities that each one happens:

$$P(E, F) = P(E)P(F)$$

In the example, the probability of "first flip heads" is 1/2, and the probability of "both flips tails" is 1/4, but the probability of "first flip heads *and* both flips tails" is 0.

Conditional Probability

When two events E and F are independent, then by definition we have:

$$P(E, F) = P(E)P(F)$$

If they are not necessarily independent (and if the probability of F is not zero), then we define the probability of E "conditional on F" as:

$$P(E|F) = P(E, F)/P(F)$$

You should think of this as the probability that E happens, given that we know that F happens.

We often rewrite this as:

$$P(E, F) = P(E|F)P(F)$$

When E and F are independent, you can check that this gives:

$$P(E|F) = P(E)$$

which is the mathematical way of expressing that knowing F occurred gives us no additional information about whether E occurred.

One common tricky example involves a family with two (unknown) children. If we assume that:

- Each child is equally likely to be a boy or a girl.
- The gender of the second child is independent of the gender of the first child.

Then the event "no girls" has probability 1/4, the event "one girl, one boy" has probability 1/2, and the event "two girls" has probability 1/4.

Now we can ask what is the probability of the event "both children are girls" (B) conditional on the event "the older child is a girl" (G)? Using the definition of conditional probability:

$$P(B\mid G) = P(B, G)/P(G) = P(B)/P(G) = 1/2$$

since the event B and G ("both children are girls *and* the older child is a girl") is just the event B. (Once you know that both children are girls, it's necessarily true that the older child is a girl.)

Most likely this result accords with your intuition.

We could also ask about the probability of the event "both children are girls" conditional on the event "at least one of the children is a girl" (L). Surprisingly, the answer is different from before!

As before, the event B and L ("both children are girls *and* at least one of the children is a girl") is just the event B. This means we have:

$$P(B\mid L) = P(B, L)/P(L) = P(B)/P(L) = 1/3$$

How can this be the case? Well, if all you know is that at least one of the children is a girl, then it is twice as likely that the family has one boy and one girl than that it has both girls.

We can check this by "generating" a lot of families:

```python
import enum, random

# An Enum is a typed set of enumerated values. We can use them
# to make our code more descriptive and readable.
class Kid(enum.Enum):
    BOY = 0
    GIRL = 1

def random_kid() -> Kid:
    return random.choice([Kid.BOY, Kid.GIRL])

both_girls = 0
older_girl = 0
either_girl = 0

random.seed(0)

for _ in range(10000):
    younger = random_kid()
```

```
older = random_kid()
if older == Kid.GIRL:
    older_girl += 1
if older == Kid.GIRL and younger == Kid.GIRL:
    both_girls += 1
if older == Kid.GIRL or younger == Kid.GIRL:
    either_girl += 1

print("P(both | older):", both_girls / older_girl)      # 0.514 ~ 1/2
print("P(both | either): ", both_girls / either_girl)   # 0.342 ~ 1/3
```

Bayes's Theorem

One of the data scientist's best friends is Bayes's theorem, which is a way of "reversing" conditional probabilities. Let's say we need to know the probability of some event E conditional on some other event F occurring. But we only have information about the probability of F conditional on E occurring. Using the definition of conditional probability twice tells us that:

$$P(E|F) = P(E, F)/P(F) = P(F|E)P(E)/P(F)$$

The event F can be split into the two mutually exclusive events "F and E" and "F and not E." If we write $\neg E$ for "not E" (i.e., "E doesn't happen"), then:

$$P(F) = P(F, E) + P(F, \neg E)$$

so that:

$$P(E|F) = P(F|E)P(E)/[P(F|E)P(E) + P(F|\neg E)P(\neg E)]$$

which is how Bayes's theorem is often stated.

This theorem often gets used to demonstrate why data scientists are smarter than doctors. Imagine a certain disease that affects 1 in every 10,000 people. And imagine that there is a test for this disease that gives the correct result ("diseased" if you have the disease, "nondiseased" if you don't) 99% of the time.

What does a positive test mean? Let's use T for the event "your test is positive" and D for the event "you have the disease." Then Bayes's theorem says that the probability that you have the disease, conditional on testing positive, is:

$$P(D|T) = P(T|D)P(D)/[P(T|D)P(D) + P(T|\neg D)P(\neg D)]$$

Here we know that $P(T|D)$, the probability that someone with the disease tests positive, is 0.99. $P(D)$, the probability that any given person has the disease, is 1/10,000 =

0.0001. $P(T \mid \neg D)$, the probability that someone without the disease tests positive, is 0.01. And $P(\neg D)$, the probability that any given person doesn't have the disease, is 0.9999. If you substitute these numbers into Bayes's theorem, you find:

$$P(D \mid T) = 0.98\,\%$$

That is, less than 1% of the people who test positive actually have the disease.

 This assumes that people take the test more or less at random. If only people with certain symptoms take the test, we would instead have to condition on the event "positive test *and* symptoms" and the number would likely be a lot higher.

A more intuitive way to see this is to imagine a population of 1 million people. You'd expect 100 of them to have the disease, and 99 of those 100 to test positive. On the other hand, you'd expect 999,900 of them not to have the disease, and 9,999 of those to test positive. That means you'd expect only 99 out of (99 + 9999) positive testers to actually have the disease.

Random Variables

A *random variable* is a variable whose possible values have an associated probability distribution. A very simple random variable equals 1 if a coin flip turns up heads and 0 if the flip turns up tails. A more complicated one might measure the number of heads you observe when flipping a coin 10 times or a value picked from range(10) where each number is equally likely.

The associated distribution gives the probabilities that the variable realizes each of its possible values. The coin flip variable equals 0 with probability 0.5 and 1 with probability 0.5. The range(10) variable has a distribution that assigns probability 0.1 to each of the numbers from 0 to 9.

We will sometimes talk about the *expected value* of a random variable, which is the average of its values weighted by their probabilities. The coin flip variable has an expected value of 1/2 (= 0 * 1/2 + 1 * 1/2), and the range(10) variable has an expected value of 4.5.

Random variables can be *conditioned* on events just as other events can. Going back to the two-child example from "Conditional Probability" on page 76, if X is the random variable representing the number of girls, X equals 0 with probability 1/4, 1 with probability 1/2, and 2 with probability 1/4.

We can define a new random variable Y that gives the number of girls conditional on at least one of the children being a girl. Then Y equals 1 with probability 2/3 and 2 with probability 1/3. And a variable Z that's the number of girls conditional on the older child being a girl equals 1 with probability 1/2 and 2 with probability 1/2.

For the most part, we will be using random variables *implicitly* in what we do without calling special attention to them. But if you look deeply you'll see them.

Continuous Distributions

A coin flip corresponds to a *discrete distribution*—one that associates positive probability with discrete outcomes. Often we'll want to model distributions across a continuum of outcomes. (For our purposes, these outcomes will always be real numbers, although that's not always the case in real life.) For example, the *uniform distribution* puts *equal weight* on all the numbers between 0 and 1.

Because there are infinitely many numbers between 0 and 1, this means that the weight it assigns to individual points must necessarily be zero. For this reason, we represent a continuous distribution with a *probability density function* (PDF) such that the probability of seeing a value in a certain interval equals the integral of the density function over the interval.

If your integral calculus is rusty, a simpler way of understanding this is that if a distribution has density function f, then the probability of seeing a value between x and $x + h$ is approximately $h * f(x)$ if h is small.

The density function for the uniform distribution is just:

```python
def uniform_pdf(x: float) -> float:
    return 1 if 0 <= x < 1 else 0
```

The probability that a random variable following that distribution is between 0.2 and 0.3 is 1/10, as you'd expect. Python's `random.random` is a (pseudo)random variable with a uniform density.

We will often be more interested in the *cumulative distribution function* (CDF), which gives the probability that a random variable is less than or equal to a certain value. It's not hard to create the CDF for the uniform distribution (Figure 6-1):

```python
def uniform_cdf(x: float) -> float:
    """Returns the probability that a uniform random variable is <= x"""
    if x < 0:   return 0    # uniform random is never less than 0
    elif x < 1: return x    # e.g. P(X <= 0.4) = 0.4
    else:       return 1    # uniform random is always less than 1
```

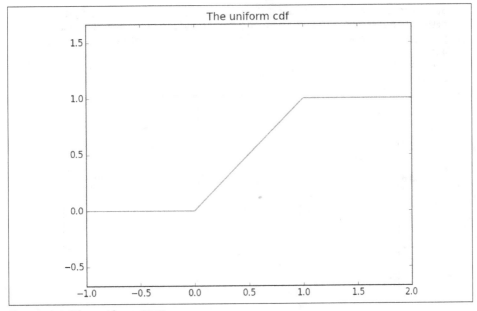

Figure 6-1. The uniform CDF

The Normal Distribution

The normal distribution is the classic bell curve–shaped distribution and is completely determined by two parameters: its mean μ (mu) and its standard deviation σ (sigma). The mean indicates where the bell is centered, and the standard deviation how "wide" it is.

It has the PDF:

$$f(x|\mu, \sigma) = \frac{1}{\sqrt{2\pi}\sigma} \exp\left(-\frac{(x-\mu)^2}{2\sigma^2}\right)$$

which we can implement as:

```
import math
SQRT_TWO_PI = math.sqrt(2 * math.pi)

def normal_pdf(x: float, mu: float = 0, sigma: float = 1) -> float:
    return (math.exp(-(x-mu) ** 2 / 2 / sigma ** 2) / (SQRT_TWO_PI * sigma))
```

In Figure 6-2, we plot some of these PDFs to see what they look like:

```
import matplotlib.pyplot as plt
xs = [x / 10.0 for x in range(-50, 50)]
plt.plot(xs,[normal_pdf(x,sigma=1) for x in xs],'-',label='mu=0,sigma=1')
```

```
plt.plot(xs,[normal_pdf(x,sigma=2) for x in xs],'--',label='mu=0,sigma=2')
plt.plot(xs,[normal_pdf(x,sigma=0.5) for x in xs],':',label='mu=0,sigma=0.5')
plt.plot(xs,[normal_pdf(x,mu=-1)    for x in xs],'-.',label='mu=-1,sigma=1')
plt.legend()
plt.title("Various Normal pdfs")
plt.show()
```

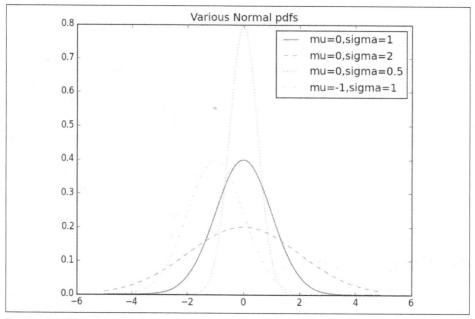

Figure 6-2. Various normal PDFs

When $\mu = 0$ and $\sigma = 1$, it's called the *standard normal distribution*. If Z is a standard normal random variable, then it turns out that:

$$X = \sigma Z + \mu$$

is also normal but with mean μ and standard deviation σ. Conversely, if X is a normal random variable with mean μ and standard deviation σ,

$$Z = (X - \mu)/\sigma$$

is a standard normal variable.

The CDF for the normal distribution cannot be written in an "elementary" manner, but we can write it using Python's `math.erf` error function (*http://en.wikipedia.org/wiki/Error_function*):

```
def normal_cdf(x: float, mu: float = 0, sigma: float = 1) -> float:
    return (1 + math.erf((x - mu) / math.sqrt(2) / sigma)) / 2
```

Again, in Figure 6-3, we plot a few CDFs:

```
xs = [x / 10.0 for x in range(-50, 50)]
plt.plot(xs,[normal_cdf(x,sigma=1) for x in xs],'-',label='mu=0,sigma=1')
plt.plot(xs,[normal_cdf(x,sigma=2) for x in xs],'--',label='mu=0,sigma=2')
plt.plot(xs,[normal_cdf(x,sigma=0.5) for x in xs],':',label='mu=0,sigma=0.5')
plt.plot(xs,[normal_cdf(x,mu=-1) for x in xs],'-.',label='mu=-1,sigma=1')
plt.legend(loc=4) # bottom right
plt.title("Various Normal cdfs")
plt.show()
```

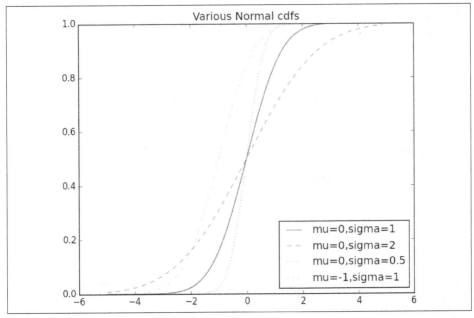

Figure 6-3. Various normal CDFs

Sometimes we'll need to invert normal_cdf to find the value corresponding to a specified probability. There's no simple way to compute its inverse, but normal_cdf is continuous and strictly increasing, so we can use a *binary search* (*http://en.wikipe dia.org/wiki/Binary_search_algorithm*):

```
def inverse_normal_cdf(p: float,
                       mu: float = 0,
                       sigma: float = 1,
                       tolerance: float = 0.00001) -> float:
    """Find approximate inverse using binary search"""

    # if not standard, compute standard and rescale
    if mu != 0 or sigma != 1:
```

```
                return mu + sigma * inverse_normal_cdf(p, tolerance=tolerance)

        low_z = -10.0                    # normal_cdf(-10) is (very close to) 0
        hi_z  =  10.0                    # normal_cdf(10)  is (very close to) 1
        while hi_z - low_z > tolerance:
            mid_z = (low_z + hi_z) / 2    # Consider the midpoint
            mid_p = normal_cdf(mid_z)     # and the CDF's value there
            if mid_p < p:
                low_z = mid_z             # Midpoint too low, search above it
            else:
                hi_z = mid_z              # Midpoint too high, search below it

        return mid_z
```

The function repeatedly bisects intervals until it narrows in on a Z that's close enough to the desired probability.

The Central Limit Theorem

One reason the normal distribution is so useful is the *central limit theorem*, which says (in essence) that a random variable defined as the average of a large number of independent and identically distributed random variables is itself approximately normally distributed.

In particular, if $x_1, ..., x_n$ are random variables with mean μ and standard deviation σ, and if n is large, then:

$$\frac{1}{n}\left(x_1 + ... + x_n\right)$$

is approximately normally distributed with mean μ and standard deviation $\sigma/\sqrt{n}$. Equivalently (but often more usefully),

$$\frac{\left(x_1 + ... + x_n\right) - \mu n}{\sigma\sqrt{n}}$$

is approximately normally distributed with mean 0 and standard deviation 1.

An easy way to illustrate this is by looking at *binomial* random variables, which have two parameters n and p. A Binomial(n,p) random variable is simply the sum of n independent Bernoulli(p) random variables, each of which equals 1 with probability p and 0 with probability $1 - p$:

```
def bernoulli_trial(p: float) -> int:
    """Returns 1 with probability p and 0 with probability 1-p"""
    return 1 if random.random() < p else 0
```

```
def binomial(n: int, p: float) -> int:
    """Returns the sum of n bernoulli(p) trials"""
    return sum(bernoulli_trial(p) for _ in range(n))
```

The mean of a Bernoulli(p) variable is p, and its standard deviation is $\sqrt{p(1-p)}$. The central limit theorem says that as n gets large, a Binomial(n,p) variable is approximately a normal random variable with mean $\mu = np$ and standard deviation $\sigma = \sqrt{np(1-p)}$. If we plot both, you can easily see the resemblance:

```
from collections import Counter

def binomial_histogram(p: float, n: int, num_points: int) -> None:
    """Picks points from a Binomial(n, p) and plots their histogram"""
    data = [binomial(n, p) for _ in range(num_points)]

    # use a bar chart to show the actual binomial samples
    histogram = Counter(data)
    plt.bar([x - 0.4 for x in histogram.keys()],
            [v / num_points for v in histogram.values()],
            0.8,
            color='0.75')

    mu = p * n
    sigma = math.sqrt(n * p * (1 - p))

    # use a line chart to show the normal approximation
    xs = range(min(data), max(data) + 1)
    ys = [normal_cdf(i + 0.5, mu, sigma) - normal_cdf(i - 0.5, mu, sigma)
          for i in xs]
    plt.plot(xs,ys)
    plt.title("Binomial Distribution vs. Normal Approximation")
    plt.show()
```

For example, when you call make_hist(0.75, 100, 10000), you get the graph in Figure 6-4.

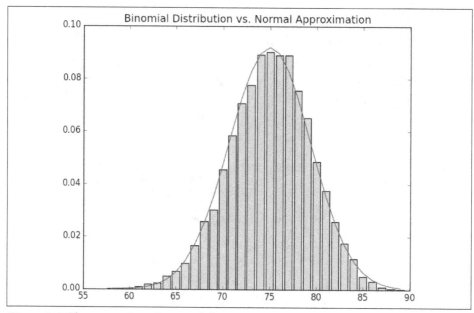

Figure 6-4. The output from binomial_histogram

The moral of this approximation is that if you want to know the probability that (say) a fair coin turns up more than 60 heads in 100 flips, you can estimate it as the probability that a Normal(50,5) is greater than 60, which is easier than computing the Binomial(100,0.5) CDF. (Although in most applications you'd probably be using statistical software that would gladly compute whatever probabilities you want.)

For Further Exploration

- scipy.stats (*https://docs.scipy.org/doc/scipy/reference/stats.html*) contains PDF and CDF functions for most of the popular probability distributions.

- Remember how, at the end of Chapter 5, I said that it would be a good idea to study a statistics textbook? It would also be a good idea to study a probability textbook. The best one I know that's available online is *Introduction to Probability* (*http://www.dartmouth.edu/~chance/teaching_aids/books_articles/probabil ity_book/book.html*), by Charles M. Grinstead and J. Laurie Snell (American Mathematical Society).

## CHAPTER 7

Hypothesis and Inference

It is the mark of a truly intelligent person to be moved by statistics.
—George Bernard Shaw

What will we do with all this statistics and probability theory? The *science* part of data science frequently involves forming and testing *hypotheses* about our data and the processes that generate it.

Statistical Hypothesis Testing

Often, as data scientists, we'll want to test whether a certain hypothesis is likely to be true. For our purposes, hypotheses are assertions like "this coin is fair" or "data scientists prefer Python to R" or "people are more likely to navigate away from the page without ever reading the content if we pop up an irritating interstitial advertisement with a tiny, hard-to-find close button" that can be translated into statistics about data. Under various assumptions, those statistics can be thought of as observations of random variables from known distributions, which allows us to make statements about how likely those assumptions are to hold.

In the classical setup, we have a *null hypothesis*, H_0, that represents some default position, and some alternative hypothesis, H_1, that we'd like to compare it with. We use statistics to decide whether we can reject H_0 as false or not. This will probably make more sense with an example.

Example: Flipping a Coin

Imagine we have a coin and we want to test whether it's fair. We'll make the assumption that the coin has some probability p of landing heads, and so our null hypothesis is that the coin is fair—that is, that $p = 0.5$. We'll test this against the alternative hypothesis $p \neq 0.5$.

In particular, our test will involve flipping the coin some number, n, times and counting the number of heads, X. Each coin flip is a Bernoulli trial, which means that X is a Binomial(n,p) random variable, which (as we saw in Chapter 6) we can approximate using the normal distribution:

```python
from typing import Tuple
import math

def normal_approximation_to_binomial(n: int, p: float) -> Tuple[float, float]:
    """Returns mu and sigma corresponding to a Binomial(n, p)"""
    mu = p * n
    sigma = math.sqrt(p * (1 - p) * n)
    return mu, sigma
```

Whenever a random variable follows a normal distribution, we can use `normal_cdf` to figure out the probability that its realized value lies within or outside a particular interval:

```python
from scratch.probability import normal_cdf

# The normal cdf _is_ the probability the variable is below a threshold
normal_probability_below = normal_cdf

# It's above the threshold if it's not below the threshold
def normal_probability_above(lo: float,
                             mu: float = 0,
                             sigma: float = 1) -> float:
    """The probability that an N(mu, sigma) is greater than lo."""
    return 1 - normal_cdf(lo, mu, sigma)

# It's between if it's less than hi, but not less than lo
def normal_probability_between(lo: float,
                               hi: float,
                               mu: float = 0,
                               sigma: float = 1) -> float:
    """The probability that an N(mu, sigma) is between lo and hi."""
    return normal_cdf(hi, mu, sigma) - normal_cdf(lo, mu, sigma)

# It's outside if it's not between
def normal_probability_outside(lo: float,
                               hi: float,
                               mu: float = 0,
                               sigma: float = 1) -> float:
    """The probability that an N(mu, sigma) is not between lo and hi."""
    return 1 - normal_probability_between(lo, hi, mu, sigma)
```

We can also do the reverse—find either the nontail region or the (symmetric) interval around the mean that accounts for a certain level of likelihood. For example, if we want to find an interval centered at the mean and containing 60% probability, then we find the cutoffs where the upper and lower tails each contain 20% of the probability (leaving 60%):

```
from scratch.probability import inverse_normal_cdf

def normal_upper_bound(probability: float,
                       mu: float = 0,
                       sigma: float = 1) -> float:
    """Returns the z for which P(Z <= z) = probability"""
    return inverse_normal_cdf(probability, mu, sigma)

def normal_lower_bound(probability: float,
                       mu: float = 0,
                       sigma: float = 1) -> float:
    """Returns the z for which P(Z >= z) = probability"""
    return inverse_normal_cdf(1 - probability, mu, sigma)

def normal_two_sided_bounds(probability: float,
                            mu: float = 0,
                            sigma: float = 1) -> Tuple[float, float]:
    """
    Returns the symmetric (about the mean) bounds
    that contain the specified probability
    """
    tail_probability = (1 - probability) / 2

    # upper bound should have tail_probability above it
    upper_bound = normal_lower_bound(tail_probability, mu, sigma)

    # lower bound should have tail_probability below it
    lower_bound = normal_upper_bound(tail_probability, mu, sigma)

    return lower_bound, upper_bound
```

In particular, let's say that we choose to flip the coin $n = 1{,}000$ times. If our hypothesis of fairness is true, X should be distributed approximately normally with mean 500 and standard deviation 15.8:

```
mu_0, sigma_0 = normal_approximation_to_binomial(1000, 0.5)
```

We need to make a decision about *significance*—how willing we are to make a *type 1 error* ("false positive"), in which we reject H_0 even though it's true. For reasons lost to the annals of history, this willingness is often set at 5% or 1%. Let's choose 5%.

Consider the test that rejects H_0 if X falls outside the bounds given by:

```
# (469, 531)
lower_bound, upper_bound = normal_two_sided_bounds(0.95, mu_0, sigma_0)
```

Assuming p really equals 0.5 (i.e., H_0 is true), there is just a 5% chance we observe an X that lies outside this interval, which is the exact significance we wanted. Said differently, if H_0 is true, then, approximately 19 times out of 20, this test will give the correct result.

We are also often interested in the *power* of a test, which is the probability of not making a *type 2 error* ("false negative"), in which we fail to reject H_0 even though it's false. In order to measure this, we have to specify what exactly H_0 being false *means*. (Knowing merely that p is *not* 0.5 doesn't give us a ton of information about the distribution of X.) In particular, let's check what happens if p is really 0.55, so that the coin is slightly biased toward heads.

In that case, we can calculate the power of the test with:

```
# 95% bounds based on assumption p is 0.5
lo, hi = normal_two_sided_bounds(0.95, mu_0, sigma_0)

# actual mu and sigma based on p = 0.55
mu_1, sigma_1 = normal_approximation_to_binomial(1000, 0.55)

# a type 2 error means we fail to reject the null hypothesis,
# which will happen when X is still in our original interval
type_2_probability = normal_probability_between(lo, hi, mu_1, sigma_1)
power = 1 - type_2_probability        # 0.887
```

Imagine instead that our null hypothesis was that the coin is not biased toward heads, or that $p \leq 0.5$. In that case we want a *one-sided test* that rejects the null hypothesis when X is much larger than 500 but not when X is smaller than 500. So, a 5% significance test involves using `normal_probability_below` to find the cutoff below which 95% of the probability lies:

```
hi = normal_upper_bound(0.95, mu_0, sigma_0)
# is 526 (< 531, since we need more probability in the upper tail)

type_2_probability = normal_probability_below(hi, mu_1, sigma_1)
power = 1 - type_2_probability        # 0.936
```

This is a more powerful test, since it no longer rejects H_0 when X is below 469 (which is very unlikely to happen if H_1 is true) and instead rejects H_0 when X is between 526 and 531 (which is somewhat likely to happen if H_1 is true).

p-Values

An alternative way of thinking about the preceding test involves *p-values*. Instead of choosing bounds based on some probability cutoff, we compute the probability—assuming H_0 is true—that we would see a value at least as extreme as the one we actually observed.

For our two-sided test of whether the coin is fair, we compute:

```
def two_sided_p_value(x: float, mu: float = 0, sigma: float = 1) -> float:
    """
    How likely are we to see a value at least as extreme as x (in either
    direction) if our values are from an N(mu, sigma)?
    """
    if x >= mu:
        # x is greater than the mean, so the tail is everything greater than x
        return 2 * normal_probability_above(x, mu, sigma)
    else:
        # x is less than the mean, so the tail is everything less than x
        return 2 * normal_probability_below(x, mu, sigma)
```

If we were to see 530 heads, we would compute:

```
two_sided_p_value(529.5, mu_0, sigma_0)    # 0.062
```

 Why did we use a value of 529.5 rather than using 530? This is what's called a *continuity correction* (*http://en.wikipedia.org/wiki/Continuity_correction*). It reflects the fact that normal_probability_between(529.5, 530.5, mu_0, sigma_0) is a better estimate of the probability of seeing 530 heads than normal_probability_between(530, 531, mu_0, sigma_0) is.

Correspondingly, normal_probability_above(529.5, mu_0, sigma_0) is a better estimate of the probability of seeing at least 530 heads. You may have noticed that we also used this in the code that produced Figure 6-4.

One way to convince yourself that this is a sensible estimate is with a simulation:

```
import random

extreme_value_count = 0
for _ in range(1000):
    num_heads = sum(1 if random.random() < 0.5 else 0    # Count # of heads
                    for _ in range(1000))                # in 1000 flips,
    if num_heads >= 530 or num_heads <= 470:             # and count how often
        extreme_value_count += 1                         # the # is 'extreme'

# p-value was 0.062 => ~62 extreme values out of 1000
assert 59 < extreme_value_count < 65, f"{extreme_value_count}"
```

Since the *p*-value is greater than our 5% significance, we don't reject the null. If we instead saw 532 heads, the *p*-value would be:

```
two_sided_p_value(531.5, mu_0, sigma_0)    # 0.0463
```

which is smaller than the 5% significance, which means we would reject the null. It's the exact same test as before. It's just a different way of approaching the statistics.

Similarly, we would have:

```
upper_p_value = normal_probability_above
lower_p_value = normal_probability_below
```

For our one-sided test, if we saw 525 heads we would compute:

```
upper_p_value(524.5, mu_0, sigma_0) # 0.061
```

which means we wouldn't reject the null. If we saw 527 heads, the computation would be:

```
upper_p_value(526.5, mu_0, sigma_0) # 0.047
```

and we would reject the null.

 Make sure your data is roughly normally distributed before using `normal_probability_above` to compute p-values. The annals of bad data science are filled with examples of people opining that the chance of some observed event occurring at random is one in a million, when what they really mean is "the chance, assuming the data is distributed normally," which is fairly meaningless if the data isn't.

There are various statistical tests for normality, but even plotting the data is a good start.

Confidence Intervals

We've been testing hypotheses about the value of the heads probability p, which is a *parameter* of the unknown "heads" distribution. When this is the case, a third approach is to construct a *confidence interval* around the observed value of the parameter.

For example, we can estimate the probability of the unfair coin by looking at the average value of the Bernoulli variables corresponding to each flip—1 if heads, 0 if tails. If we observe 525 heads out of 1,000 flips, then we estimate p equals 0.525.

How *confident* can we be about this estimate? Well, if we knew the exact value of p, the central limit theorem (recall "The Central Limit Theorem" on page 84) tells us that the average of those Bernoulli variables should be approximately normal, with mean p and standard deviation:

```
math.sqrt(p * (1 - p) / 1000)
```

Here we don't know p, so instead we use our estimate:

```
p_hat = 525 / 1000
mu = p_hat
sigma = math.sqrt(p_hat * (1 - p_hat) / 1000)    # 0.0158
```

This is not entirely justified, but people seem to do it anyway. Using the normal approximation, we conclude that we are "95% confident" that the following interval contains the true parameter p:

```
normal_two_sided_bounds(0.95, mu, sigma)        # [0.4940, 0.5560]
```

 This is a statement about the *interval*, not about p. You should understand it as the assertion that if you were to repeat the experiment many times, 95% of the time the "true" parameter (which is the same every time) would lie within the observed confidence interval (which might be different every time).

In particular, we do not conclude that the coin is unfair, since 0.5 falls within our confidence interval.

If instead we'd seen 540 heads, then we'd have:

```
p_hat = 540 / 1000
mu = p_hat
sigma = math.sqrt(p_hat * (1 - p_hat) / 1000) # 0.0158
normal_two_sided_bounds(0.95, mu, sigma) # [0.5091, 0.5709]
```

Here, "fair coin" doesn't lie in the confidence interval. (The "fair coin" hypothesis doesn't pass a test that you'd expect it to pass 95% of the time if it were true.)

p-Hacking

A procedure that erroneously rejects the null hypothesis only 5% of the time will—by definition—5% of the time erroneously reject the null hypothesis:

```
from typing import List

def run_experiment() -> List[bool]:
    """Flips a fair coin 1000 times, True = heads, False = tails"""
    return [random.random() < 0.5 for _ in range(1000)]

def reject_fairness(experiment: List[bool]) -> bool:
    """Using the 5% significance levels"""
    num_heads = len([flip for flip in experiment if flip])
    return num_heads < 469 or num_heads > 531

random.seed(0)
experiments = [run_experiment() for _ in range(1000)]
num_rejections = len([experiment
                      for experiment in experiments
                      if reject_fairness(experiment)])

assert num_rejections == 46
```

What this means is that if you're setting out to find "significant" results, you usually can. Test enough hypotheses against your dataset, and one of them will almost certainly appear significant. Remove the right outliers, and you can probably get your *p*-value below 0.05. (We did something vaguely similar in "Correlation" on page 68; did you notice?)

This is sometimes called *p-hacking* (*https://www.nature.com/news/scientific-method-statistical-errors-1.14700*) and is in some ways a consequence of the "inference from *p*-values framework." A good article criticizing this approach is "The Earth Is Round" (*http://www.iro.umontreal.ca/~dift3913/cours/papers/cohen1994_The_earth_is_round.pdf*), by Jacob Cohen.

If you want to do good *science*, you should determine your hypotheses before looking at the data, you should clean your data without the hypotheses in mind, and you should keep in mind that *p*-values are not substitutes for common sense. (An alternative approach is discussed in "Bayesian Inference" on page 95.)

Example: Running an A/B Test

One of your primary responsibilities at DataSciencester is experience optimization, which is a euphemism for trying to get people to click on advertisements. One of your advertisers has developed a new energy drink targeted at data scientists, and the VP of Advertisements wants your help choosing between advertisement A ("tastes great!") and advertisement B ("less bias!").

Being a *scientist*, you decide to run an *experiment* by randomly showing site visitors one of the two advertisements and tracking how many people click on each one.

If 990 out of 1,000 A-viewers click their ad, while only 10 out of 1,000 B-viewers click their ad, you can be pretty confident that A is the better ad. But what if the differences are not so stark? Here's where you'd use statistical inference.

Let's say that N_A people see ad A, and that n_A of them click it. We can think of each ad view as a Bernoulli trial where p_A is the probability that someone clicks ad A. Then (if N_A is large, which it is here) we know that n_A/N_A is approximately a normal random variable with mean p_A and standard deviation $\sigma_A = \sqrt{p_A(1 - p_A)/N_A}$.

Similarly, n_B/N_B is approximately a normal random variable with mean p_B and standard deviation $\sigma_B = \sqrt{p_B(1 - p_B)/N_B}$. We can express this in code as:

```
def estimated_parameters(N: int, n: int) -> Tuple[float, float]:
    p = n / N
    sigma = math.sqrt(p * (1 - p) / N)
    return p, sigma
```

If we assume those two normals are independent (which seems reasonable, since the individual Bernoulli trials ought to be), then their difference should also be normal with mean $p_B - p_A$ and standard deviation $\sqrt{\sigma_A^2 + \sigma_B^2}$.

 This is sort of cheating. The math only works out exactly like this if you *know* the standard deviations. Here we're estimating them from the data, which means that we really should be using a *t*-distribution. But for large enough datasets, it's close enough that it doesn't make much of a difference.

This means we can test the *null hypothesis* that p_A and p_B are the same (that is, that $p_A - p_B$ is 0) by using the statistic:

```
def a_b_test_statistic(N_A: int, n_A: int, N_B: int, n_B: int) -> float:
    p_A, sigma_A = estimated_parameters(N_A, n_A)
    p_B, sigma_B = estimated_parameters(N_B, n_B)
    return (p_B - p_A) / math.sqrt(sigma_A ** 2 + sigma_B ** 2)
```

which should approximately be a standard normal.

For example, if "tastes great" gets 200 clicks out of 1,000 views and "less bias" gets 180 clicks out of 1,000 views, the statistic equals:

```
z = a_b_test_statistic(1000, 200, 1000, 180)    # -1.14
```

The probability of seeing such a large difference if the means were actually equal would be:

```
two_sided_p_value(z)                     # 0.254
```

which is large enough that we can't conclude there's much of a difference. On the other hand, if "less bias" only got 150 clicks, we'd have:

```
z = a_b_test_statistic(1000, 200, 1000, 150)    # -2.94
two_sided_p_value(z)                            # 0.003
```

which means there's only a 0.003 probability we'd see such a large difference if the ads were equally effective.

Bayesian Inference

The procedures we've looked at have involved making probability statements about our *tests*: e.g., "There's only a 3% chance you'd observe such an extreme statistic if our null hypothesis were true."

An alternative approach to inference involves treating the unknown parameters themselves as random variables. The analyst (that's you) starts with a *prior distribution* for the parameters and then uses the observed data and Bayes's theorem to get an updated *posterior distribution* for the parameters. Rather than making probability judgments about the tests, you make probability judgments about the parameters.

For example, when the unknown parameter is a probability (as in our coin-flipping example), we often use a prior from the *Beta distribution*, which puts all its probability between 0 and 1:

```
def B(alpha: float, beta: float) -> float:
    """A normalizing constant so that the total probability is 1"""
    return math.gamma(alpha) * math.gamma(beta) / math.gamma(alpha + beta)

def beta_pdf(x: float, alpha: float, beta: float) -> float:
    if x <= 0 or x >= 1:          # no weight outside of [0, 1]
        return 0
    return x ** (alpha - 1) * (1 - x) ** (beta - 1) / B(alpha, beta)
```

Generally speaking, this distribution centers its weight at:

```
alpha / (alpha + beta)
```

and the larger `alpha` and `beta` are, the "tighter" the distribution is.

For example, if `alpha` and `beta` are both 1, it's just the uniform distribution (centered at 0.5, very dispersed). If `alpha` is much larger than `beta`, most of the weight is near 1. And if `alpha` is much smaller than `beta`, most of the weight is near 0. Figure 7-1 shows several different Beta distributions.

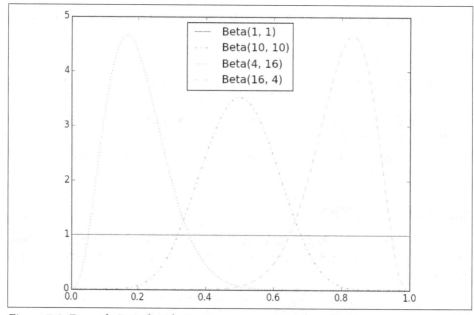

Figure 7-1. Example Beta distributions

Say we assume a prior distribution on p. Maybe we don't want to take a stand on whether the coin is fair, and we choose `alpha` and `beta` to both equal 1. Or maybe we have a strong belief that the coin lands heads 55% of the time, and we choose `alpha` equals 55, `beta` equals 45.

Then we flip our coin a bunch of times and see h heads and t tails. Bayes's theorem (and some mathematics too tedious for us to go through here) tells us that the posterior distribution for p is again a Beta distribution, but with parameters `alpha + h` and `beta + t`.

It is no coincidence that the posterior distribution was again a Beta distribution. The number of heads is given by a Binomial distribution, and the Beta is the *conjugate prior* (*http://www.johndcook.com/blog/conjugate_prior_diagram/*) to the Binomial distribution. This means that whenever you update a Beta prior using observations from the corresponding binomial, you will get back a Beta posterior.

Let's say you flip the coin 10 times and see only 3 heads. If you started with the uniform prior (in some sense refusing to take a stand about the coin's fairness), your posterior distribution would be a Beta(4, 8), centered around 0.33. Since you considered all probabilities equally likely, your best guess is close to the observed probability.

If you started with a Beta(20, 20) (expressing a belief that the coin was roughly fair), your posterior distribution would be a Beta(23, 27), centered around 0.46, indicating a revised belief that maybe the coin is slightly biased toward tails.

And if you started with a Beta(30, 10) (expressing a belief that the coin was biased to flip 75% heads), your posterior distribution would be a Beta(33, 17), centered around 0.66. In that case you'd still believe in a heads bias, but less strongly than you did initially. These three different posteriors are plotted in Figure 7-2.

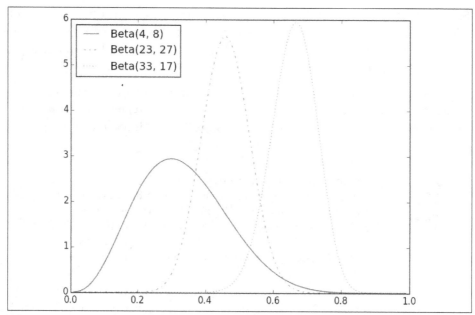

Figure 7-2. Posteriors arising from different priors

If you flipped the coin more and more times, the prior would matter less and less until eventually you'd have (nearly) the same posterior distribution no matter which prior you started with.

For example, no matter how biased you initially thought the coin was, it would be hard to maintain that belief after seeing 1,000 heads out of 2,000 flips (unless you are a lunatic who picks something like a Beta(1000000,1) prior).

What's interesting is that this allows us to make probability statements about hypotheses: "Based on the prior and the observed data, there is only a 5% likelihood the coin's heads probability is between 49% and 51%." This is philosophically very different from a statement like "If the coin were fair, we would expect to observe data so extreme only 5% of the time."

Using Bayesian inference to test hypotheses is considered somewhat controversial—in part because the mathematics can get somewhat complicated, and in part because of the subjective nature of choosing a prior. We won't use it any further in this book, but it's good to know about.

For Further Exploration

- We've barely scratched the surface of what you should know about statistical inference. The books recommended at the end of Chapter 5 go into a lot more detail.
- Coursera offers a Data Analysis and Statistical Inference (*https://www.coursera.org/course/statistics*) course that covers many of these topics.

## CHAPTER 8

Gradient Descent

Those who boast of their descent, brag on what they owe to others.
—Seneca

Frequently when doing data science, we'll be trying to the find the best model for a certain situation. And usually "best" will mean something like "minimizes the error of its predictions" or "maximizes the likelihood of the data." In other words, it will represent the solution to some sort of optimization problem.

This means we'll need to solve a number of optimization problems. And in particular, we'll need to solve them from scratch. Our approach will be a technique called *gradient descent*, which lends itself pretty well to a from-scratch treatment. You might not find it super-exciting in and of itself, but it will enable us to do exciting things throughout the book, so bear with me.

The Idea Behind Gradient Descent

Suppose we have some function f that takes as input a vector of real numbers and outputs a single real number. One simple such function is:

```
from scratch.linear_algebra import Vector, dot

def sum_of_squares(v: Vector) -> float:
    """Computes the sum of squared elements in v"""
    return dot(v, v)
```

We'll frequently need to maximize or minimize such functions. That is, we need to find the input v that produces the largest (or smallest) possible value.

For functions like ours, the *gradient* (if you remember your calculus, this is the vector of partial derivatives) gives the input direction in which the function most quickly increases. (If you don't remember your calculus, take my word for it or look it up on the internet.)

Accordingly, one approach to maximizing a function is to pick a random starting point, compute the gradient, take a small step in the direction of the gradient (i.e., the direction that causes the function to increase the most), and repeat with the new starting point. Similarly, you can try to minimize a function by taking small steps in the *opposite* direction, as shown in Figure 8-1.

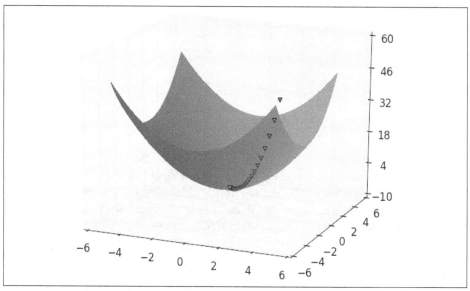

Figure 8-1. Finding a minimum using gradient descent

 If a function has a unique global minimum, this procedure is likely to find it. If a function has multiple (local) minima, this procedure might "find" the wrong one of them, in which case you might rerun the procedure from different starting points. If a function has no minimum, then it's possible the procedure might go on forever.

Estimating the Gradient

If f is a function of one variable, its derivative at a point x measures how f(x) changes when we make a very small change to x. The derivative is defined as the limit of the difference quotients:

```
from typing import Callable

def difference_quotient(f: Callable[[float], float],
                        x: float,
```

```
                   h: float) -> float:
    return (f(x + h) - f(x)) / h
```

as h approaches zero.

(Many a would-be calculus student has been stymied by the mathematical definition of limit, which is beautiful but can seem somewhat forbidding. Here we'll cheat and simply say that "limit" means what you think it means.)

The derivative is the slope of the tangent line at $(x, f(x))$, while the difference quotient is the slope of the not-quite-tangent line that runs through $(x + h, f(x + h))$. As h gets smaller and smaller, the not-quite-tangent line gets closer and closer to the tangent line (Figure 8-2).

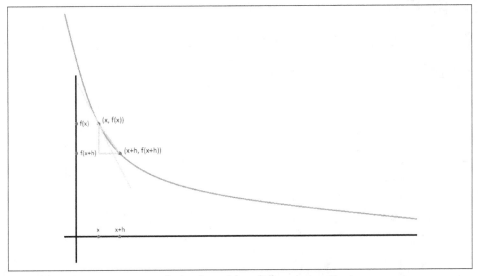

Figure 8-2. Approximating a derivative with a difference quotient

For many functions it's easy to exactly calculate derivatives. For example, the square function:

```
def square(x: float) -> float:
    return x * x
```

has the derivative:

```
def derivative(x: float) -> float:
    return 2 * x
```

which is easy for us to check by explicitly computing the difference quotient and taking the limit. (Doing so requires nothing more than high school algebra.)

What if you couldn't (or didn't want to) find the gradient? Although we can't take limits in Python, we can estimate derivatives by evaluating the difference quotient for a very small e. Figure 8-3 shows the results of one such estimation:

```
xs = range(-10, 11)
actuals = [derivative(x) for x in xs]
estimates = [difference_quotient(square, x, h=0.001) for x in xs]

# plot to show they're basically the same
import matplotlib.pyplot as plt
plt.title("Actual Derivatives vs. Estimates")
plt.plot(xs, actuals, 'rx', label='Actual')      # red  x
plt.plot(xs, estimates, 'b+', label='Estimate')   # blue +
plt.legend(loc=9)
plt.show()
```

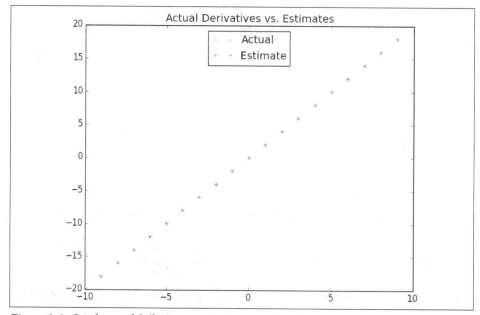

Figure 8-3. Goodness of difference quotient approximation

When f is a function of many variables, it has multiple *partial derivatives*, each indicating how f changes when we make small changes in just one of the input variables.

We calculate its *i*th partial derivative by treating it as a function of just its *i*th variable, holding the other variables fixed:

```
def partial_difference_quotient(f: Callable[[Vector], float],
                                v: Vector,
                                i: int,
                                h: float) -> float:
    """Returns the i-th partial difference quotient of f at v"""
```

```
w = [v_j + (h if j == i else 0)      # add h to just the ith element of v
     for j, v_j in enumerate(v)]

return (f(w) - f(v)) / h
```

after which we can estimate the gradient the same way:

```
def estimate_gradient(f: Callable[[Vector], float],
                      v: Vector,
                      h: float = 0.0001):
    return [partial_difference_quotient(f, v, i, h)
            for i in range(len(v))]
```

 A major drawback to this "estimate using difference quotients" approach is that it's computationally expensive. If v has length *n*, estimate_gradient has to evaluate f on 2*n* different inputs. If you're repeatedly estimating gradients, you're doing a whole lot of extra work. In everything we do, we'll use math to calculate our gradient functions explicitly.

Using the Gradient

It's easy to see that the sum_of_squares function is smallest when its input v is a vector of zeros. But imagine we didn't know that. Let's use gradients to find the minimum among all three-dimensional vectors. We'll just pick a random starting point and then take tiny steps in the opposite direction of the gradient until we reach a point where the gradient is very small:

```
import random
from scratch.linear_algebra import distance, add, scalar_multiply

def gradient_step(v: Vector, gradient: Vector, step_size: float) -> Vector:
    """Moves `step_size` in the `gradient` direction from `v`"""
    assert len(v) == len(gradient)
    step = scalar_multiply(step_size, gradient)
    return add(v, step)

def sum_of_squares_gradient(v: Vector) -> Vector:
    return [2 * v_i for v_i in v]

# pick a random starting point
v = [random.uniform(-10, 10) for i in range(3)]

for epoch in range(1000):
    grad = sum_of_squares_gradient(v)    # compute the gradient at v
    v = gradient_step(v, grad, -0.01)    # take a negative gradient step
    print(epoch, v)

assert distance(v, [0, 0, 0]) < 0.001    # v should be close to 0
```

If you run this, you'll find that it always ends up with a v that's very close to [0,0,0]. The more epochs you run it for, the closer it will get.

Choosing the Right Step Size

Although the rationale for moving against the gradient is clear, how far to move is not. Indeed, choosing the right step size is more of an art than a science. Popular options include:

- Using a fixed step size
- Gradually shrinking the step size over time
- At each step, choosing the step size that minimizes the value of the objective function

The last approach sounds great but is, in practice, a costly computation. To keep things simple, we'll mostly just use a fixed step size. The step size that "works" depends on the problem—too small, and your gradient descent will take forever; too big, and you'll take giant steps that might make the function you care about get larger or even be undefined. So we'll need to experiment.

Using Gradient Descent to Fit Models

In this book, we'll be using gradient descent to fit parameterized models to data. In the usual case, we'll have some dataset and some (hypothesized) model for the data that depends (in a differentiable way) on one or more parameters. We'll also have a *loss* function that measures how well the model fits our data. (Smaller is better.)

If we think of our data as being fixed, then our loss function tells us how good or bad any particular model parameters are. This means we can use gradient descent to find the model parameters that make the loss as small as possible. Let's look at a simple example:

```
# x ranges from -50 to 49, y is always 20 * x + 5
inputs = [(x, 20 * x + 5) for x in range(-50, 50)]
```

In this case we *know* the parameters of the linear relationship between x and y, but imagine we'd like to learn them from the data. We'll use gradient descent to find the slope and intercept that minimize the average squared error.

We'll start off with a function that determines the gradient based on the error from a single data point:

```
def linear_gradient(x: float, y: float, theta: Vector) -> Vector:
    slope, intercept = theta
    predicted = slope * x + intercept    # The prediction of the model.
    error = (predicted - y)              # error is (predicted - actual).
```

```
squared_error = error ** 2        # We'll minimize squared error
grad = [2 * error * x, 2 * error]  # using its gradient.
return grad
```

Let's think about what that gradient means. Imagine for some x our prediction is too large. In that case the error is positive. The second gradient term, 2 * error, is positive, which reflects the fact that small increases in the intercept will make the (already too large) prediction even larger, which will cause the squared error (for this x) to get even bigger.

The first gradient term, 2 * error * x, has the same sign as x. Sure enough, if x is positive, small increases in the slope will again make the prediction (and hence the error) larger. If x is negative, though, small increases in the slope will make the prediction (and hence the error) smaller.

Now, that computation was for a single data point. For the whole dataset we'll look at the *mean squared error*. And the gradient of the mean squared error is just the mean of the individual gradients.

So, here's what we're going to do:

1. Start with a random value for theta.
2. Compute the mean of the gradients.
3. Adjust theta in that direction.
4. Repeat.

After a lot of *epochs* (what we call each pass through the dataset), we should learn something like the correct parameters:

```
from scratch.linear_algebra import vector_mean

# Start with random values for slope and intercept
theta = [random.uniform(-1, 1), random.uniform(-1, 1)]

learning_rate = 0.001

for epoch in range(5000):
    # Compute the mean of the gradients
    grad = vector_mean([linear_gradient(x, y, theta) for x, y in inputs])
    # Take a step in that direction
    theta = gradient_step(theta, grad, -learning_rate)
    print(epoch, theta)

slope, intercept = theta
assert 19.9 < slope < 20.1,   "slope should be about 20"
assert 4.9 < intercept < 5.1, "intercept should be about 5"
```

Minibatch and Stochastic Gradient Descent

One drawback of the preceding approach is that we had to evaluate the gradients on the entire dataset before we could take a gradient step and update our parameters. In this case it was fine, because our dataset was only 100 pairs and the gradient computation was cheap.

Your models, however, will frequently have large datasets and expensive gradient computations. In that case you'll want to take gradient steps more often.

We can do this using a technique called *minibatch gradient descent,* in which we compute the gradient (and take a gradient step) based on a "minibatch" sampled from the larger dataset:

```
from typing import TypeVar, List, Iterator

T = TypeVar('T')  # this allows us to type "generic" functions

def minibatches(dataset: List[T],
                batch_size: int,
                shuffle: bool = True) -> Iterator[List[T]]:
    """Generates `batch_size`-sized minibatches from the dataset"""
    # start indexes 0, batch_size, 2 * batch_size, ...
    batch_starts = [start for start in range(0, len(dataset), batch_size)]

    if shuffle: random.shuffle(batch_starts)  # shuffle the batches

    for start in batch_starts:
        end = start + batch_size
        yield dataset[start:end]
```

> The TypeVar(T) allows us to create a "generic" function. It says that our dataset can be a list of any single type—strs, ints, lists, whatever—but whatever that type is, the outputs will be batches of it.

Now we can solve our problem again using minibatches:

```
theta = [random.uniform(-1, 1), random.uniform(-1, 1)]

for epoch in range(1000):
    for batch in minibatches(inputs, batch_size=20):
        grad = vector_mean([linear_gradient(x, y, theta) for x, y in batch])
        theta = gradient_step(theta, grad, -learning_rate)
    print(epoch, theta)

slope, intercept = theta
assert 19.9 < slope < 20.1,    "slope should be about 20"
assert 4.9 < intercept < 5.1, "intercept should be about 5"
```

Another variation is *stochastic gradient descent*, in which you take gradient steps based on one training example at a time:

```
theta = [random.uniform(-1, 1), random.uniform(-1, 1)]

for epoch in range(100):
    for x, y in inputs:
        grad = linear_gradient(x, y, theta)
        theta = gradient_step(theta, grad, -learning_rate)
    print(epoch, theta)

slope, intercept = theta
assert 19.9 < slope < 20.1,   "slope should be about 20"
assert 4.9 < intercept < 5.1, "intercept should be about 5"
```

On this problem, stochastic gradient descent finds the optimal parameters in a much smaller number of epochs. But there are always tradeoffs. Basing gradient steps on small minibatches (or on single data points) allows you to take more of them, but the gradient for a single point might lie in a very different direction from the gradient for the dataset as a whole.

In addition, if we weren't doing our linear algebra from scratch, there would be performance gains from "vectorizing" our computations across batches rather than computing the gradient one point at a time.

Throughout the book, we'll play around to find optimal batch sizes and step sizes.

The terminology for the various flavors of gradient descent is not uniform. The "compute the gradient for the whole dataset" approach is often called *batch gradient descent*, and some people say *stochastic gradient descent* when referring to the minibatch version (of which the one-point-at-a-time version is a special case).

For Further Exploration

- Keep reading! We'll be using gradient descent to solve problems throughout the rest of the book.

- At this point, you're undoubtedly sick of me recommending that you read textbooks. If it's any consolation, *Active Calculus 1.0* (*https://scholarworks.gvsu.edu/books/10/*), by Matthew Boelkins, David Austin, and Steven Schlicker (Grand Valley State University Libraries), seems nicer than the calculus textbooks I learned from.

- Sebastian Ruder has an epic blog post (*http://ruder.io/optimizing-gradient-descent/index.html*) comparing gradient descent and its many variants.

## CHAPTER 9

Getting Data

To write it, it took three months; to conceive it, three minutes; to collect the data in it, all my life.
　　　—F. Scott Fitzgerald

In order to be a data scientist you need data. In fact, as a data scientist you will spend an embarrassingly large fraction of your time acquiring, cleaning, and transforming data. In a pinch, you can always type the data in yourself (or if you have minions, make them do it), but usually this is not a good use of your time. In this chapter, we'll look at different ways of getting data into Python and into the right formats.

stdin and stdout

If you run your Python scripts at the command line, you can *pipe* data through them using `sys.stdin` and `sys.stdout`. For example, here is a script that reads in lines of text and spits back out the ones that match a regular expression:

```
# egrep.py
import sys, re

# sys.argv is the list of command-line arguments
# sys.argv[0] is the name of the program itself
# sys.argv[1] will be the regex specified at the command line
regex = sys.argv[1]

# for every line passed into the script
for line in sys.stdin:
    # if it matches the regex, write it to stdout
    if re.search(regex, line):
        sys.stdout.write(line)
```

And here's one that counts the lines it receives and then writes out the count:

```
# line_count.py
import sys

count = 0
for line in sys.stdin:
    count += 1

# print goes to sys.stdout
print(count)
```

You could then use these to count how many lines of a file contain numbers. In Windows, you'd use:

```
type SomeFile.txt | python egrep.py "[0-9]" | python line_count.py
```

whereas in a Unix system you'd use:

```
cat SomeFile.txt | python egrep.py "[0-9]" | python line_count.py
```

The | is the pipe character, which means "use the output of the left command as the input of the right command." You can build pretty elaborate data-processing pipelines this way.

If you are using Windows, you can probably leave out the `python` part of this command:

```
type SomeFile.txt | egrep.py "[0-9]" | line_count.py
```

If you are on a Unix system, doing so requires a couple more steps (*https://stackoverflow.com/questions/15587877/run-a-python-script-in-terminal-without-the-python-command*). First add a "shebang" as the first line of your script `#!/usr/bin/env python`. Then, at the command line, use `chmod x egrep.py++` to make the file executable.

Similarly, here's a script that counts the words in its input and writes out the most common ones:

```
# most_common_words.py
import sys
from collections import Counter

# pass in number of words as first argument
try:
    num_words = int(sys.argv[1])
except:
    print("usage: most_common_words.py num_words")
    sys.exit(1)    # nonzero exit code indicates error

counter = Counter(word.lower()                      # lowercase words
                  for line in sys.stdin
                  for word in line.strip().split()) # split on spaces
```

```
                    if word)                          # skip empty 'words'

    for word, count in counter.most_common(num_words):
        sys.stdout.write(str(count))
        sys.stdout.write("\t")
        sys.stdout.write(word)
        sys.stdout.write("\n")
```

after which you could do something like:

```
$ cat the_bible.txt | python most_common_words.py 10
36397   the
30031   and
20163   of
7154    to
6484    in
5856    that
5421    he
5226    his
5060    unto
4297    shall
```

(If you are using Windows, then use type instead of cat.)

 If you are a seasoned Unix programmer, you are probably familiar with a wide variety of command-line tools (for example, egrep) that are built into your operating system and are preferable to building your own from scratch. Still, it's good to know you can if you need to.

Reading Files

You can also explicitly read from and write to files directly in your code. Python makes working with files pretty simple.

The Basics of Text Files

The first step to working with a text file is to obtain a *file object* using open:

```
# 'r' means read-only, it's assumed if you leave it out
file_for_reading = open('reading_file.txt', 'r')
file_for_reading2 = open('reading_file.txt')

# 'w' is write -- will destroy the file if it already exists!
file_for_writing = open('writing_file.txt', 'w')

# 'a' is append -- for adding to the end of the file
file_for_appending = open('appending_file.txt', 'a')
```

```
# don't forget to close your files when you're done
file_for_writing.close()
```

Because it is easy to forget to close your files, you should always use them in a with block, at the end of which they will be closed automatically:

```
with open(filename) as f:
    data = function_that_gets_data_from(f)

# at this point f has already been closed, so don't try to use it
process(data)
```

If you need to read a whole text file, you can just iterate over the lines of the file using for:

```
starts_with_hash = 0

with open('input.txt') as f:
    for line in f:                      # look at each line in the file
        if re.match("^#",line):         # use a regex to see if it starts with '#'
            starts_with_hash += 1       # if it does, add 1 to the count
```

Every line you get this way ends in a newline character, so you'll often want to strip it before doing anything with it.

For example, imagine you have a file full of email addresses, one per line, and you need to generate a histogram of the domains. The rules for correctly extracting domains are somewhat subtle—see, e.g., the Public Suffix List (*https://publicsuffix.org*)—but a good first approximation is to just take the parts of the email addresses that come after the @ (this gives the wrong answer for email addresses like *joel@mail.datasciencester.com*, but for the purposes of this example we're willing to live with that):

```
def get_domain(email_address: str) -> str:
    """Split on '@' and return the last piece"""
    return email_address.lower().split("@")[-1]

# a couple of tests
assert get_domain('joelgrus@gmail.com') == 'gmail.com'
assert get_domain('joel@m.datasciencester.com') == 'm.datasciencester.com'

from collections import Counter

with open('email_addresses.txt', 'r') as f:
    domain_counts = Counter(get_domain(line.strip())
                            for line in f
                            if "@" in line)
```

Delimited Files

The hypothetical email addresses file we just processed had one address per line. More frequently you'll work with files with lots of data on each line. These files are very often either *comma-separated* or *tab-separated*: each line has several fields, with a comma or a tab indicating where one field ends and the next field starts.

This starts to get complicated when you have fields with commas and tabs and newlines in them (which you inevitably will). For this reason, you should never try to parse them yourself. Instead, you should use Python's csv module (or the pandas library, or some other library that's designed to read comma-separated or tab-delimited files).

Never parse a comma-separated file yourself. You will screw up the edge cases!

If your file has no headers (which means you probably want each row as a list, and which places the burden on you to know what's in each column), you can use csv.reader to iterate over the rows, each of which will be an appropriately split list.

For example, if we had a tab-delimited file of stock prices:

```
6/20/2014   AAPL    90.91
6/20/2014   MSFT    41.68
6/20/2014   FB  64.5
6/19/2014   AAPL    91.86
6/19/2014   MSFT    41.51
6/19/2014   FB  64.34
```

we could process them with:

```python
import csv

with open('tab_delimited_stock_prices.txt') as f:
    tab_reader = csv.reader(f, delimiter='\t')
    for row in tab_reader:
        date = row[0]
        symbol = row[1]
        closing_price = float(row[2])
        process(date, symbol, closing_price)
```

If your file has headers:

```
date:symbol:closing_price
6/20/2014:AAPL:90.91
6/20/2014:MSFT:41.68
6/20/2014:FB:64.5
```

you can either skip the header row with an initial call to `reader.next`, or get each row as a `dict` (with the headers as keys) by using `csv.DictReader`:

```
with open('colon_delimited_stock_prices.txt') as f:
    colon_reader = csv.DictReader(f, delimiter=':')
    for dict_row in colon_reader:
        date = dict_row["date"]
        symbol = dict_row["symbol"]
        closing_price = float(dict_row["closing_price"])
        process(date, symbol, closing_price)
```

Even if your file doesn't have headers, you can still use `DictReader` by passing it the keys as a `fieldnames` parameter.

You can similarly write out delimited data using `csv.writer`:

```
todays_prices = {'AAPL': 90.91, 'MSFT': 41.68, 'FB': 64.5 }

with open('comma_delimited_stock_prices.txt', 'w') as f:
    csv_writer = csv.writer(f, delimiter=',')
    for stock, price in todays_prices.items():
        csv_writer.writerow([stock, price])
```

`csv.writer` will do the right thing if your fields themselves have commas in them. Your own hand-rolled writer probably won't. For example, if you attempt:

```
results = [["test1", "success", "Monday"],
           ["test2", "success, kind of", "Tuesday"],
           ["test3", "failure, kind of", "Wednesday"],
           ["test4", "failure, utter", "Thursday"]]

# don't do this!
with open('bad_csv.txt', 'w') as f:
    for row in results:
        f.write(",".join(map(str, row))) # might have too many commas in it!
        f.write("\n")                    # row might have newlines as well!
```

You will end up with a *.csv* file that looks like this:

```
test1,success,Monday
test2,success, kind of,Tuesday
test3,failure, kind of,Wednesday
test4,failure, utter,Thursday
```

and that no one will ever be able to make sense of.

Scraping the Web

Another way to get data is by scraping it from web pages. Fetching web pages, it turns out, is pretty easy; getting meaningful structured information out of them less so.

HTML and the Parsing Thereof

Pages on the web are written in HTML, in which text is (ideally) marked up into elements and their attributes:

```
<html>
  <head>
    <title>A web page</title>
  </head>
  <body>
    <p id="author">Joel Grus</p>
    <p id="subject">Data Science</p>
  </body>
</html>
```

In a perfect world, where all web pages were marked up semantically for our benefit, we would be able to extract data using rules like "find the `<p>` element whose `id` is `subject` and return the text it contains." In the actual world, HTML is not generally well formed, let alone annotated. This means we'll need help making sense of it.

To get data out of HTML, we will use the Beautiful Soup library (*http://www.crummy.com/software/BeautifulSoup/*), which builds a tree out of the various elements on a web page and provides a simple interface for accessing them. As I write this, the latest version is Beautiful Soup 4.6.0, which is what we'll be using. We'll also be using the Requests library (*http://docs.python-requests.org/en/latest/*), which is a much nicer way of making HTTP requests than anything that's built into Python.

Python's built-in HTML parser is not that lenient, which means that it doesn't always cope well with HTML that's not perfectly formed. For that reason, we'll also install the `html5lib` parser.

Making sure you're in the correct virtual environment, install the libraries:

```
python -m pip install beautifulsoup4 requests html5lib
```

To use Beautiful Soup, we pass a string containing HTML into the `BeautifulSoup` function. In our examples, this will be the result of a call to `requests.get`:

```
from bs4 import BeautifulSoup
import requests

# I put the relevant HTML file on GitHub. In order to fit
# the URL in the book I had to split it across two lines.
# Recall that whitespace-separated strings get concatenated.
url = ("https://raw.githubusercontent.com/"
       "joelgrus/data/master/getting-data.html")
html = requests.get(url).text
soup = BeautifulSoup(html, 'html5lib')
```

after which we can get pretty far using a few simple methods.

We'll typically work with Tag objects, which correspond to the tags representing the structure of an HTML page.

For example, to find the first <p> tag (and its contents), you can use:

```
first_paragraph = soup.find('p')        # or just soup.p
```

You can get the text contents of a Tag using its text property:

```
first_paragraph_text = soup.p.text
first_paragraph_words = soup.p.text.split()
```

And you can extract a tag's attributes by treating it like a dict:

```
first_paragraph_id = soup.p['id']       # raises KeyError if no 'id'
first_paragraph_id2 = soup.p.get('id')  # returns None if no 'id'
```

You can get multiple tags at once as follows:

```
all_paragraphs = soup.find_all('p')  # or just soup('p')
paragraphs_with_ids = [p for p in soup('p') if p.get('id')]
```

Frequently, you'll want to find tags with a specific class:

```
important_paragraphs = soup('p', {'class' : 'important'})
important_paragraphs2 = soup('p', 'important')
important_paragraphs3 = [p for p in soup('p')
                         if 'important' in p.get('class', [])]
```

And you can combine these methods to implement more elaborate logic. For example, if you want to find every <span> element that is contained inside a <div> element, you could do this:

```
# Warning: will return the same <span> multiple times
# if it sits inside multiple <div>s.
# Be more clever if that's the case.
spans_inside_divs = [span
                     for div in soup('div')     # for each <div> on the page
                     for span in div('span')]   # find each <span> inside it
```

Just this handful of features will allow us to do quite a lot. If you end up needing to do more complicated things (or if you're just curious), check the documentation (*https://www.crummy.com/software/BeautifulSoup/bs4/doc/*).

Of course, the important data won't typically be labeled as class="important". You'll need to carefully inspect the source HTML, reason through your selection logic, and worry about edge cases to make sure your data is correct. Let's look at an example.

Example: Keeping Tabs on Congress

The VP of Policy at DataSciencester is worried about potential regulation of the data science industry and asks you to quantify what Congress is saying on the topic. In particular, he wants you to find all the representatives who have press releases about "data."

At the time of publication, there is a page with links to all of the representatives' websites at *https://www.house.gov/representatives*.

And if you "view source," all of the links to the websites look like:

```
<td>
  <a href="https://jayapal.house.gov">Jayapal, Pramila</a>
</td>
```

Let's start by collecting all of the URLs linked to from that page:

```python
from bs4 import BeautifulSoup
import requests

url = "https://www.house.gov/representatives"
text = requests.get(url).text
soup = BeautifulSoup(text, "html5lib")

all_urls = [a['href']
            for a in soup('a')
            if a.has_attr('href')]

print(len(all_urls))  # 965 for me, way too many
```

This returns way too many URLs. If you look at them, the ones we want start with either *http://* or *https://*, have some kind of name, and end with either *.house.gov* or *.house.gov/*.

This is a good place to use a regular expression:

```python
import re

# Must start with http:// or https://
# Must end with .house.gov or .house.gov/
regex = r"^https?://.*\.house\.gov/?$"

# Let's write some tests!
assert re.match(regex, "http://joel.house.gov")
assert re.match(regex, "https://joel.house.gov")
assert re.match(regex, "http://joel.house.gov/")
assert re.match(regex, "https://joel.house.gov/")
assert not re.match(regex, "joel.house.gov")
assert not re.match(regex, "http://joel.house.com")
assert not re.match(regex, "https://joel.house.gov/biography")

# And now apply
good_urls = [url for url in all_urls if re.match(regex, url)]

print(len(good_urls))  # still 862 for me
```

That's still way too many, as there are only 435 representatives. If you look at the list, there are a lot of duplicates. Let's use **set** to get rid of them:

```
good_urls = list(set(good_urls))

print(len(good_urls))  # only 431 for me
```

There are always a couple of House seats empty, or maybe there's a representative without a website. In any case, this is good enough. When we look at the sites, most of them have a link to press releases. For example:

```
html = requests.get('https://jayapal.house.gov').text
soup = BeautifulSoup(html, 'html5lib')

# Use a set because the links might appear multiple times.
links = {a['href'] for a in soup('a') if 'press releases' in a.text.lower()}

print(links) # {'/media/press-releases'}
```

Notice that this is a relative link, which means we need to remember the originating site. Let's do some scraping:

```
from typing import Dict, Set

press_releases: Dict[str, Set[str]] = {}

for house_url in good_urls:
    html = requests.get(house_url).text
    soup = BeautifulSoup(html, 'html5lib')
    pr_links = {a['href'] for a in soup('a') if 'press releases'
                                               in a.text.lower()}
    print(f"{house_url}: {pr_links}")
    press_releases[house_url] = pr_links
```

 Normally it is impolite to scrape a site freely like this. Most sites will have a *robots.txt* file that indicates how frequently you may scrape the site (and which paths you're not supposed to scrape), but since it's Congress we don't need to be particularly polite.

If you watch these as they scroll by, you'll see a lot of */media/press-releases* and *media-center/press-releases*, as well as various other addresses. One of these URLs is *https://jayapal.house.gov/media/press-releases*.

Remember that our goal is to find out which congresspeople have press releases mentioning "data." We'll write a slightly more general function that checks whether a page of press releases mentions any given term.

If you visit the site and view the source, it seems like there's a snippet from each press release inside a <p> tag, so we'll use that as our first attempt:

```
def paragraph_mentions(text: str, keyword: str) -> bool:
    """
    Returns True if a <p> inside the text mentions {keyword}
    """
    soup = BeautifulSoup(text, 'html5lib')
    paragraphs = [p.get_text() for p in soup('p')]

    return any(keyword.lower() in paragraph.lower()
               for paragraph in paragraphs)
```

Let's write a quick test for it:

```
text = """<body><h1>Facebook</h1><p>Twitter</p>"""
assert paragraph_mentions(text, "twitter")         # is inside a <p>
assert not paragraph_mentions(text, "facebook")    # not inside a <p>
```

At last we're ready to find the relevant congresspeople and give their names to the VP:

```
for house_url, pr_links in press_releases.items():
    for pr_link in pr_links:
        url = f"{house_url}/{pr_link}"
        text = requests.get(url).text

        if paragraph_mentions(text, 'data'):
            print(f"{house_url}")
            break  # done with this house_url
```

When I run this I get a list of about 20 representatives. Your results will probably be different.

If you look at the various "press releases" pages, most of them are paginated with only 5 or 10 press releases per page. This means that we only retrieved the few most recent press releases for each congressperson. A more thorough solution would have iterated over the pages and retrieved the full text of each press release.

Using APIs

Many websites and web services provide *application programming interfaces* (APIs), which allow you to explicitly request data in a structured format. This saves you the trouble of having to scrape them!

JSON and XML

Because HTTP is a protocol for transferring *text*, the data you request through a web API needs to be *serialized* into a string format. Often this serialization uses *JavaScript Object Notation* (JSON). JavaScript objects look quite similar to Python dicts, which makes their string representations easy to interpret:

```
{ "title" : "Data Science Book",
  "author" : "Joel Grus",
  "publicationYear" : 2019,
  "topics" : [ "data", "science", "data science"] }
```

We can parse JSON using Python's `json` module. In particular, we will use its `loads` function, which deserializes a string representing a JSON object into a Python object:

```
import json
serialized = """{ "title" : "Data Science Book",
                  "author" : "Joel Grus",
                  "publicationYear" : 2019,
                  "topics" : [ "data", "science", "data science"] }"""

# parse the JSON to create a Python dict
deserialized = json.loads(serialized)
assert deserialized["publicationYear"] == 2019
assert "data science" in deserialized["topics"]
```

Sometimes an API provider hates you and provides only responses in XML:

```
<Book>
  <Title>Data Science Book</Title>
  <Author>Joel Grus</Author>
  <PublicationYear>2014</PublicationYear>
  <Topics>
    <Topic>data</Topic>
    <Topic>science</Topic>
    <Topic>data science</Topic>
  </Topics>
</Book>
```

You can use Beautiful Soup to get data from XML similarly to how we used it to get data from HTML; check its documentation for details.

Using an Unauthenticated API

Most APIs these days require that you first authenticate yourself before you can use them. While we don't begrudge them this policy, it creates a lot of extra boilerplate that muddies up our exposition. Accordingly, we'll start by taking a look at GitHub's API (*http://developer.github.com/v3/*), with which you can do some simple things unauthenticated:

```
import requests, json

github_user = "joelgrus"
endpoint = f"https://api.github.com/users/{github_user}/repos"

repos = json.loads(requests.get(endpoint).text)
```

At this point `repos` is a `list` of Python `dicts`, each representing a public repository in my GitHub account. (Feel free to substitute your username and get your GitHub repository data instead. You do have a GitHub account, right?)

We can use this to figure out which months and days of the week I'm most likely to create a repository. The only issue is that the dates in the response are strings:

```
"created_at": "2013-07-05T02:02:28Z"
```

Python doesn't come with a great date parser, so we'll need to install one:

```
python -m pip install python-dateutil
```

from which you'll probably only ever need the `dateutil.parser.parse` function:

```
from collections import Counter
from dateutil.parser import parse

dates = [parse(repo["created_at"]) for repo in repos]
month_counts = Counter(date.month for date in dates)
weekday_counts = Counter(date.weekday() for date in dates)
```

Similarly, you can get the languages of my last five repositories:

```
last_5_repositories = sorted(repos,
                             key=lambda r: r["pushed_at"],
                             reverse=True)[:5]

last_5_languages = [repo["language"]
                    for repo in last_5_repositories]
```

Typically we won't be working with APIs at this low "make the requests and parse the responses ourselves" level. One of the benefits of using Python is that someone has already built a library for pretty much any API you're interested in accessing. When they're done well, these libraries can save you a lot of the trouble of figuring out the hairier details of API access. (When they're not done well, or when it turns out they're based on defunct versions of the corresponding APIs, they can cause you enormous headaches.)

Nonetheless, you'll occasionally have to roll your own API access library (or, more likely, debug why someone else's isn't working), so it's good to know some of the details.

Finding APIs

If you need data from a specific site, look for a "developers" or "API" section of the site for details, and try searching the web for "python <sitename> api" to find a library.

There are libraries for the Yelp API, for the Instagram API, for the Spotify API, and so on.

If you're looking for a list of APIs that have Python wrappers, there's a nice one from Real Python on GitHub (*https://github.com/realpython/list-of-python-api-wrappers*).

And if you can't find what you need, there's always scraping, the last refuge of the data scientist.

Example: Using the Twitter APIs

Twitter is a fantastic source of data to work with. You can use it to get real-time news. You can use it to measure reactions to current events. You can use it to find links related to specific topics. You can use it for pretty much anything you can imagine, just as long as you can get access to its data. And you can get access to its data through its APIs.

To interact with the Twitter APIs, we'll be using the Twython library (*https://github.com/ryanmcgrath/twython*) (`python -m pip install twython`). There are quite a few Python Twitter libraries out there, but this is the one that I've had the most success working with. You are encouraged to explore the others as well!

Getting Credentials

In order to use Twitter's APIs, you need to get some credentials (for which you need a Twitter account, which you should have anyway so that you can be part of the lively and friendly Twitter #datascience community).

Like all instructions that relate to websites that I don't control, these may become obsolete at some point but will hopefully work for a while. (Although they have already changed multiple times since I originally started writing this book, so good luck!)

Here are the steps:

1. Go to *https://developer.twitter.com/*.

2. If you are not signed in, click "Sign in" and enter your Twitter username and password.

3. Click Apply to apply for a developer account.

4. Request access for your own personal use.

5. Fill out the application. It requires 300 words (really) on why you need access, so to get over the limit you could tell them about this book and how much you're enjoying it.

6. Wait some indefinite amount of time.

7. If you know someone who works at Twitter, email them and ask them if they can expedite your application. Otherwise, keep waiting.

8. Once you get approved, go back to developer.twitter.com (*https://developer.twit ter.com/*), find the "Apps" section, and click "Create an app."

9. Fill out all the required fields (again, if you need extra characters for the description, you could talk about this book and how edifying you're finding it).

10. Click CREATE.

Now your app should have a "Keys and tokens" tab with a "Consumer API keys" section that lists an "API key" and an "API secret key." Take note of those keys; you'll need them. (Also, keep them secret! They're like passwords.)

 Don't share the keys, don't publish them in your book, and don't check them into your public GitHub repository. One simple solution is to store them in a *credentials.json* file that doesn't get checked in, and to have your code use `json.loads` to retrieve them. Another solution is to store them in environment variables and use `os.environ` to retrieve them.

Using Twython

The trickiest part of using the Twitter API is authenticating yourself. (Indeed, this is the trickiest part of using a lot of APIs.) API providers want to make sure that you're authorized to access their data and that you don't exceed their usage limits. They also want to know who's accessing their data.

Authentication is kind of a pain. There is a simple way, OAuth 2, that suffices when you just want to do simple searches. And there is a complex way, OAuth 1, that's required when you want to perform actions (e.g., tweeting) or (in particular for us) connect to the Twitter stream.

So we're stuck with the more complicated way, which we'll try to automate as much as we can.

First, you need your API key and API secret key (sometimes known as the consumer key and consumer secret, respectively). I'll be getting mine from environment variables, but feel free to substitute in yours however you wish:

```
import os

# Feel free to plug your key and secret in directly
CONSUMER_KEY = os.environ.get("TWITTER_CONSUMER_KEY")
CONSUMER_SECRET = os.environ.get("TWITTER_CONSUMER_SECRET")
```

Now we can instantiate the client:

```
import webbrowser
from twython import Twython

# Get a temporary client to retrieve an authentication URL
temp_client = Twython(CONSUMER_KEY, CONSUMER_SECRET)
temp_creds = temp_client.get_authentication_tokens()
url = temp_creds['auth_url']

# Now visit that URL to authorize the application and get a PIN
print(f"go visit {url} and get the PIN code and paste it below")
webbrowser.open(url)
PIN_CODE = input("please enter the PIN code: ")

# Now we use that PIN_CODE to get the actual tokens
auth_client = Twython(CONSUMER_KEY,
                      CONSUMER_SECRET,
                      temp_creds['oauth_token'],
                      temp_creds['oauth_token_secret'])
final_step = auth_client.get_authorized_tokens(PIN_CODE)
ACCESS_TOKEN = final_step['oauth_token']
ACCESS_TOKEN_SECRET = final_step['oauth_token_secret']

# And get a new Twython instance using them.
twitter = Twython(CONSUMER_KEY,
                  CONSUMER_SECRET,
                  ACCESS_TOKEN,
                  ACCESS_TOKEN_SECRET)
```

 At this point you may want to consider saving the ACCESS_TOKEN
and ACCESS_TOKEN_SECRET somewhere safe, so that next time you
don't have to go through this rigmarole.

Once we have an authenticated Twython instance, we can start performing searches:

```
# Search for tweets containing the phrase "data science"
for status in twitter.search(q='"data science"')["statuses"]:
    user = status["user"]["screen_name"]
    text = status["text"]
    print(f"{user}: {text}\n")
```

If you run this, you should get some tweets back like:

```
haithemnyc: Data scientists with the technical savvy &amp; analytical chops to
derive meaning from big data are in demand. http://t.co/HsF9Q0dShP

RPubsRecent: Data Science http://t.co/6hcHUz2PHM

spleonard1: Using #dplyr in #R to work through a procrastinated assignment for
@rdpeng in @coursera data science specialization. So easy and Awesome.
```

This isn't that interesting, largely because the Twitter Search API just shows you whatever handful of recent results it feels like. When you're doing data science, more often you want a lot of tweets. This is where the Streaming API (*https://developer.twit ter.com/en/docs/tutorials/consuming-streaming-data*) is useful. It allows you to connect to (a sample of) the great Twitter firehose. To use it, you'll need to authenticate using your access tokens.

In order to access the Streaming API with Twython, we need to define a class that inherits from TwythonStreamer and that overrides its on_success method, and possibly its on_error method:

```
from twython import TwythonStreamer

# Appending data to a global variable is pretty poor form
# but it makes the example much simpler
tweets = []

class MyStreamer(TwythonStreamer):
    def on_success(self, data):
        """
        What do we do when Twitter sends us data?
        Here data will be a Python dict representing a tweet.
        """
        # We only want to collect English-language tweets
        if data.get('lang') == 'en':
            tweets.append(data)
            print(f"received tweet #{len(tweets)}")

        # Stop when we've collected enough
        if len(tweets) >= 100:
            self.disconnect()

    def on_error(self, status_code, data):
        print(status_code, data)
        self.disconnect()
```

MyStreamer will connect to the Twitter stream and wait for Twitter to feed it data. Each time it receives some data (here, a tweet represented as a Python object), it passes it to the on_success method, which appends it to our tweets list if its language is English, and then disconnects the streamer after it's collected 1,000 tweets.

All that's left is to initialize it and start it running:

```
stream = MyStreamer(CONSUMER_KEY, CONSUMER_SECRET,
                    ACCESS_TOKEN, ACCESS_TOKEN_SECRET)

# starts consuming public statuses that contain the keyword 'data'
stream.statuses.filter(track='data')

# if instead we wanted to start consuming a sample of *all* public statuses
# stream.statuses.sample()
```

This will run until it collects 100 tweets (or until it encounters an error) and stop, at which point you can start analyzing those tweets. For instance, you could find the most common hashtags with:

```
top_hashtags = Counter(hashtag['text'].lower()
                       for tweet in tweets
                       for hashtag in tweet["entities"]["hashtags"])

print(top_hashtags.most_common(5))
```

Each tweet contains a lot of data. You can either poke around yourself or dig through the Twitter API documentation (*https://developer.twitter.com/en/docs/tweets/data-dictionary/overview/tweet-object*).

 In a non-toy project, you probably wouldn't want to rely on an in-memory list for storing the tweets. Instead you'd want to save them to a file or a database, so that you'd have them permanently.

For Further Exploration

- pandas (*http://pandas.pydata.org/*) is the primary library that data science types use for working with—and, in particular, importing—data.
- Scrapy (*http://scrapy.org/*) is a full-featured library for building complicated web scrapers that do things like follow unknown links.
- Kaggle (*https://www.kaggle.com/datasets*) hosts a large collection of datasets.

## CHAPTER 10

Working with Data

Experts often possess more data than judgment.
—Colin Powell

Working with data is both an art and a science. We've mostly been talking about the science part, but in this chapter we'll look at some of the art.

Exploring Your Data

After you've identified the questions you're trying to answer and have gotten your hands on some data, you might be tempted to dive in and immediately start building models and getting answers. But you should resist this urge. Your first step should be to *explore* your data.

Exploring One-Dimensional Data

The simplest case is when you have a one-dimensional dataset, which is just a collection of numbers. For example, these could be the daily average number of minutes each user spends on your site, the number of times each of a collection of data science tutorial videos was watched, or the number of pages of each of the data science books in your data science library.

An obvious first step is to compute a few summary statistics. You'd like to know how many data points you have, the smallest, the largest, the mean, and the standard deviation.

But even these don't necessarily give you a great understanding. A good next step is to create a histogram, in which you group your data into discrete *buckets* and count how many points fall into each bucket:

```
from typing import List, Dict
from collections import Counter
import math

import matplotlib.pyplot as plt

def bucketize(point: float, bucket_size: float) -> float:
    """Floor the point to the next lower multiple of bucket_size"""
    return bucket_size * math.floor(point / bucket_size)

def make_histogram(points: List[float], bucket_size: float) -> Dict[float, int]:
    """Buckets the points and counts how many in each bucket"""
    return Counter(bucketize(point, bucket_size) for point in points)

def plot_histogram(points: List[float], bucket_size: float, title: str = ""):
    histogram = make_histogram(points, bucket_size)
    plt.bar(histogram.keys(), histogram.values(), width=bucket_size)
    plt.title(title)
```

For example, consider the two following sets of data:

```
import random
from scratch.probability import inverse_normal_cdf

random.seed(0)

# uniform between -100 and 100
uniform = [200 * random.random() - 100 for _ in range(10000)]

# normal distribution with mean 0, standard deviation 57
normal = [57 * inverse_normal_cdf(random.random())
          for _ in range(10000)]
```

Both have means close to 0 and standard deviations close to 58. However, they have very different distributions. Figure 10-1 shows the distribution of uniform:

```
plot_histogram(uniform, 10, "Uniform Histogram")
```

while Figure 10-2 shows the distribution of normal:

```
plot_histogram(normal, 10, "Normal Histogram")
```

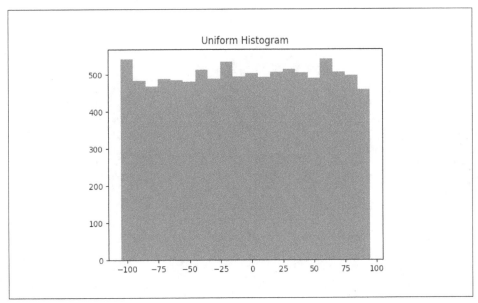

Figure 10-1. Histogram of uniform

In this case the two distributions have a pretty different max and min, but even know-ing that wouldn't have been sufficient to understand *how* they differed.

Two Dimensions

Now imagine you have a dataset with two dimensions. Maybe in addition to daily minutes you have years of data science experience. Of course you'd want to under-stand each dimension individually. But you probably also want to scatter the data.

For example, consider another fake dataset:

```
def random_normal() -> float:
    """Returns a random draw from a standard normal distribution"""
    return inverse_normal_cdf(random.random())

xs = [random_normal() for _ in range(1000)]
ys1 = [ x + random_normal() / 2 for x in xs]
ys2 = [-x + random_normal() / 2 for x in xs]
```

If you were to run plot_histogram on ys1 and ys2, you'd get similar-looking plots (indeed, both are normally distributed with the same mean and standard deviation).

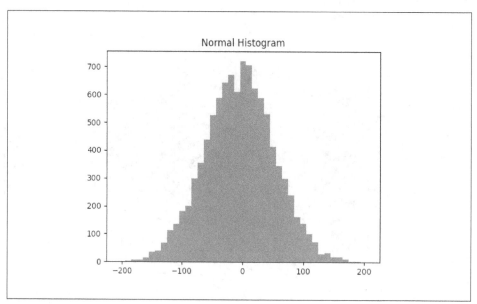

Figure 10-2. Histogram of normal

But each has a very different joint distribution with xs, as shown in Figure 10-3:

```python
plt.scatter(xs, ys1, marker='.', color='black', label='ys1')
plt.scatter(xs, ys2, marker='.', color='gray',  label='ys2')
plt.xlabel('xs')
plt.ylabel('ys')
plt.legend(loc=9)
plt.title("Very Different Joint Distributions")
plt.show()
```

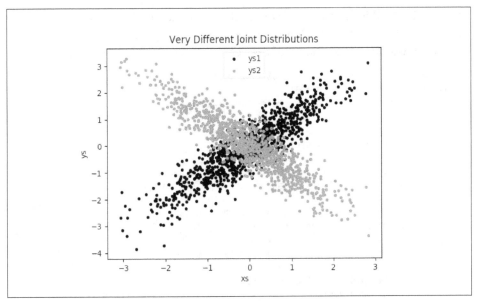

Figure 10-3. Scattering two different ys

This difference would also be apparent if you looked at the correlations:

```
from scratch.statistics import correlation

print(correlation(xs, ys1))      # about 0.9
print(correlation(xs, ys2))      # about -0.9
```

Many Dimensions

With many dimensions, you'd like to know how all the dimensions relate to one another. A simple approach is to look at the *correlation matrix*, in which the entry in row i and column j is the correlation between the ith dimension and the jth dimension of the data:

```
from scratch.linear_algebra import Matrix, Vector, make_matrix

def correlation_matrix(data: List[Vector]) -> Matrix:
    """
    Returns the len(data) x len(data) matrix whose (i, j)-th entry
    is the correlation between data[i] and data[j]
    """
    def correlation_ij(i: int, j: int) -> float:
        return correlation(data[i], data[j])

    return make_matrix(len(data), len(data), correlation_ij)
```

A more visual approach (if you don't have too many dimensions) is to make a *scatterplot matrix* (Figure 10-4) showing all the pairwise scatterplots. To do that we'll use plt.subplots, which allows us to create subplots of our chart. We give it the number of rows and the number of columns, and it returns a figure object (which we won't use) and a two-dimensional array of axes objects (each of which we'll plot to):

```
# corr_data is a list of four 100-d vectors
num_vectors = len(corr_data)
fig, ax = plt.subplots(num_vectors, num_vectors)

for i in range(num_vectors):
    for j in range(num_vectors):

        # Scatter column_j on the x-axis vs. column_i on the y-axis
        if i != j: ax[i][j].scatter(corr_data[j], corr_data[i])

        # unless i == j, in which case show the series name
        else: ax[i][j].annotate("series " + str(i), (0.5, 0.5),
                                xycoords='axes fraction',
                                ha="center", va="center")

        # Then hide axis labels except left and bottom charts
        if i < num_vectors - 1: ax[i][j].xaxis.set_visible(False)
        if j > 0: ax[i][j].yaxis.set_visible(False)

# Fix the bottom-right and top-left axis labels, which are wrong because
# their charts only have text in them
ax[-1][-1].set_xlim(ax[0][-1].get_xlim())
ax[0][0].set_ylim(ax[0][1].get_ylim())

plt.show()
```

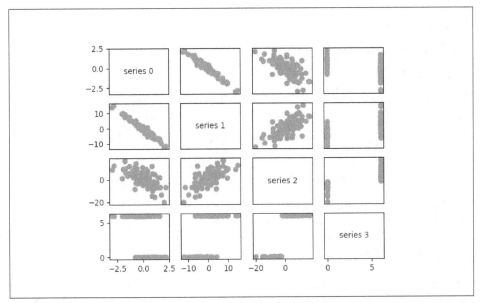

Figure 10-4. Scatterplot matrix

Looking at the scatterplots, you can see that series 1 is very negatively correlated with series 0, series 2 is positively correlated with series 1, and series 3 only takes on the values 0 and 6, with 0 corresponding to small values of series 2 and 6 corresponding to large values.

This is a quick way to get a rough sense of which of your variables are correlated (unless you spend hours tweaking matplotlib to display things exactly the way you want them to, in which case it's not a quick way).

Using NamedTuples

One common way of representing data is using `dicts`:

```
import datetime

stock_price = {'closing_price': 102.06,
               'date': datetime.date(2014, 8, 29),
               'symbol': 'AAPL'}
```

There are several reasons why this is less than ideal, however. This is a slightly inefficient representation (a `dict` involves some overhead), so that if you have a lot of stock prices they'll take up more memory than they have to. For the most part, this is a minor consideration.

A larger issue is that accessing things by `dict` key is error-prone. The following code will run without error and just do the wrong thing:

```
# oops, typo
stock_price['cosing_price'] = 103.06
```

Finally, while we can type-annotate uniform dictionaries:

```
prices: Dict[datetime.date, float] = {}
```

there's no helpful way to annotate dictionaries-as-data that have lots of different value types. So we also lose the power of type hints.

As an alternative, Python includes a `namedtuple` class, which is like a `tuple` but with named slots:

```
from collections import namedtuple

StockPrice = namedtuple('StockPrice', ['symbol', 'date', 'closing_price'])
price = StockPrice('MSFT', datetime.date(2018, 12, 14), 106.03)

assert price.symbol == 'MSFT'
assert price.closing_price == 106.03
```

Like regular `tuples`, `namedtuples` are immutable, which means that you can't modify their values once they're created. Occasionally this will get in our way, but mostly that's a good thing.

You'll notice that we still haven't solved the type annotation issue. We do that by using the typed variant, `NamedTuple`:

```
from typing import NamedTuple

class StockPrice(NamedTuple):
    symbol: str
    date: datetime.date
    closing_price: float

    def is_high_tech(self) -> bool:
        """It's a class, so we can add methods too"""
        return self.symbol in ['MSFT', 'GOOG', 'FB', 'AMZN', 'AAPL']

price = StockPrice('MSFT', datetime.date(2018, 12, 14), 106.03)

assert price.symbol == 'MSFT'
assert price.closing_price == 106.03
assert price.is_high_tech()
```

And now your editor can help you out, as shown in Figure 10-5.

```
if stock_price.clo
                              closing_price
```

Figure 10-5. Helpful editor

 Very few people use NamedTuple in this way. But they should!

Dataclasses

Dataclasses are (sort of) a mutable version of NamedTuple. (I say "sort of" because NamedTuples represent their data compactly as tuples, whereas dataclasses are regular Python classes that simply generate some methods for you automatically.)

 Dataclasses are new in Python 3.7. If you're using an older version, this section won't work for you.

The syntax is very similar to NamedTuple. But instead of inheriting from a base class, we use a decorator:

```python
from dataclasses import dataclass

@dataclass
class StockPrice2:
    symbol: str
    date: datetime.date
    closing_price: float

    def is_high_tech(self) -> bool:
        """It's a class, so we can add methods too"""
        return self.symbol in ['MSFT', 'GOOG', 'FB', 'AMZN', 'AAPL']

price2 = StockPrice2('MSFT', datetime.date(2018, 12, 14), 106.03)

assert price2.symbol == 'MSFT'
assert price2.closing_price == 106.03
assert price2.is_high_tech()
```

As mentioned, the big difference is that we can modify a dataclass instance's values:

```
# stock split
price2.closing_price /= 2
assert price2.closing_price == 51.03
```

If we tried to modify a field of the NamedTuple version, we'd get an AttributeError.

This also leaves us susceptible to the kind of errors we were hoping to avoid by not using dicts:

```
# It's a regular class, so add new fields however you like!
price2.cosing_price = 75  # oops
```

We won't be using dataclasses, but you may encounter them out in the wild.

Cleaning and Munging

Real-world data is *dirty*. Often you'll have to do some work on it before you can use it. We saw examples of this in Chapter 9. We have to convert strings to floats or ints before we can use them. We have to check for missing values and outliers and bad data.

Previously, we did that right before using the data:

```
closing_price = float(row[2])
```

But it's probably less error-prone to do the parsing in a function that we can test:

```
from dateutil.parser import parse

def parse_row(row: List[str]) -> StockPrice:
    symbol, date, closing_price = row
    return StockPrice(symbol=symbol,
                      date=parse(date).date(),
                      closing_price=float(closing_price))

# Now test our function
stock = parse_row(["MSFT", "2018-12-14", "106.03"])

assert stock.symbol == "MSFT"
assert stock.date == datetime.date(2018, 12, 14)
assert stock.closing_price == 106.03
```

What if there's bad data? A "float" value that doesn't actually represent a number? Maybe you'd rather get a None than crash your program?

```
from typing import Optional
import re

def try_parse_row(row: List[str]) -> Optional[StockPrice]:
    symbol, date_, closing_price_ = row
```

```
    # Stock symbol should be all capital letters
    if not re.match(r"^[A-Z]+$", symbol):
        return None

    try:
        date = parse(date_).date()
    except ValueError:
        return None

    try:
        closing_price = float(closing_price_)
    except ValueError:
        return None

    return StockPrice(symbol, date, closing_price)

# Should return None for errors
assert try_parse_row(["MSFT0", "2018-12-14", "106.03"]) is None
assert try_parse_row(["MSFT", "2018-12--14", "106.03"]) is None
assert try_parse_row(["MSFT", "2018-12-14", "x"]) is None

# But should return same as before if data is good
assert try_parse_row(["MSFT", "2018-12-14", "106.03"]) == stock
```

For example, if we have comma-delimited stock prices with bad data:

```
AAPL,6/20/2014,90.91
MSFT,6/20/2014,41.68
FB,6/20/3014,64.5
AAPL,6/19/2014,91.86
MSFT,6/19/2014,n/a
FB,6/19/2014,64.34
```

we can now read and return only the valid rows:

```
import csv

data: List[StockPrice] = []

with open("comma_delimited_stock_prices.csv") as f:
    reader = csv.reader(f)
    for row in reader:
        maybe_stock = try_parse_row(row)
        if maybe_stock is None:
            print(f"skipping invalid row: {row}")
        else:
            data.append(maybe_stock)
```

and decide what we want to do about the invalid ones. Generally speaking, the three options are to get rid of them, to go back to the source and try to fix the bad/missing data, or to do nothing and cross our fingers. If there's one bad row out of millions, it's probably okay to ignore it. But if half your rows have bad data, that's something you need to fix.

A good next step is to check for outliers, using techniques from "Exploring Your Data" on page 129 or by ad hoc investigating. For example, did you notice that one of the dates in the stocks file had the year 3014? That won't (necessarily) give you an error, but it's quite plainly wrong, and you'll get screwy results if you don't catch it. Real-world datasets have missing decimal points, extra zeros, typographical errors, and countless other problems that it's your job to catch. (Maybe it's not officially your job, but who else is going to do it?)

Manipulating Data

One of the most important skills of a data scientist is *manipulating data*. It's more of a general approach than a specific technique, so we'll just work through a handful of examples to give you the flavor of it.

Imagine we have a bunch of stock price data that looks like this:

```
data = [
    StockPrice(symbol='MSFT',
               date=datetime.date(2018, 12, 24),
               closing_price=106.03),
    # ...
]
```

Let's start asking questions about this data. Along the way we'll try to notice patterns in what we're doing and abstract out some tools to make the manipulation easier.

For instance, suppose we want to know the highest-ever closing price for AAPL. Let's break this down into concrete steps:

1. Restrict ourselves to AAPL rows.

2. Grab the `closing_price` from each row.

3. Take the `max` of those prices.

We can do all three at once using a comprehension:

```
max_aapl_price = max(stock_price.closing_price
                     for stock_price in data
                     if stock_price.symbol == "AAPL")
```

More generally, we might want to know the highest-ever closing price for each stock in our dataset. One way to do this is:

1. Create a `dict` to keep track of highest prices (we'll use a `defaultdict` that returns minus infinity for missing values, since any price will be greater than that).

2. Iterate over our data, updating it.

Here's the code:

```
from collections import defaultdict

max_prices: Dict[str, float] = defaultdict(lambda: float('-inf'))

for sp in data:
    symbol, closing_price = sp.symbol, sp.closing_price
    if closing_price > max_prices[symbol]:
        max_prices[symbol] = closing_price
```

We can now start to ask more complicated things, like what are the largest and smallest one-day percent changes in our dataset. The percent change is `price_today / price_yesterday - 1`, which means we need some way of associating today's price and yesterday's price. One approach is to group the prices by symbol, and then, within each group:

1. Order the prices by date.

2. Use `zip` to get (previous, current) pairs.

3. Turn the pairs into new "percent change" rows.

Let's start by grouping the prices by symbol:

```
from typing import List
from collections import defaultdict

# Collect the prices by symbol
prices: Dict[str, List[StockPrice]] = defaultdict(list)

for sp in data:
    prices[sp.symbol].append(sp)
```

Since the prices are tuples, they'll get sorted by their fields in order: first by symbol, then by date, then by price. This means that if we have some prices all with the same symbol, `sort` will sort them by date (and then by price, which does nothing, since we only have one per date), which is what we want.

```
# Order the prices by date
prices = {symbol: sorted(symbol_prices)
          for symbol, symbol_prices in prices.items()}
```

which we can use to compute a sequence of day-over-day changes:

```
def pct_change(yesterday: StockPrice, today: StockPrice) -> float:
    return today.closing_price / yesterday.closing_price - 1

class DailyChange(NamedTuple):
    symbol: str
    date: datetime.date
    pct_change: float

def day_over_day_changes(prices: List[StockPrice]) -> List[DailyChange]:
    """
```

```
    Assumes prices are for one stock and are in order
    """
    return [DailyChange(symbol=today.symbol,
                        date=today.date,
                        pct_change=pct_change(yesterday, today))
            for yesterday, today in zip(prices, prices[1:])]
```

and then collect them all:

```
all_changes = [change
               for symbol_prices in prices.values()
               for change in day_over_day_changes(symbol_prices)]
```

At which point it's easy to find the largest and smallest:

```
max_change = max(all_changes, key=lambda change: change.pct_change)
# see e.g. http://news.cnet.com/2100-1001-202143.html
assert max_change.symbol == 'AAPL'
assert max_change.date == datetime.date(1997, 8, 6)
assert 0.33 < max_change.pct_change < 0.34

min_change = min(all_changes, key=lambda change: change.pct_change)
# see e.g. http://money.cnn.com/2000/09/29/markets/techwrap/
assert min_change.symbol == 'AAPL'
assert min_change.date == datetime.date(2000, 9, 29)
assert -0.52 < min_change.pct_change < -0.51
```

We can now use this new `all_changes` dataset to find which month is the best to
invest in tech stocks. We'll just look at the average daily change by month:

```
changes_by_month: List[DailyChange] = {month: [] for month in range(1, 13)}

for change in all_changes:
    changes_by_month[change.date.month].append(change)

avg_daily_change = {
    month: sum(change.pct_change for change in changes) / len(changes)
    for month, changes in changes_by_month.items()
}

# October is the best month
assert avg_daily_change[10] == max(avg_daily_change.values())
```

We'll be doing these sorts of manipulations throughout the book, usually without
calling too much explicit attention to them.

Rescaling

Many techniques are sensitive to the *scale* of your data. For example, imagine that you
have a dataset consisting of the heights and weights of hundreds of data scientists,
and that you are trying to identify *clusters* of body sizes.

Intuitively, we'd like clusters to represent points near each other, which means that we need some notion of distance between points. We already have a Euclidean `distance` function, so a natural approach might be to treat (height, weight) pairs as points in two-dimensional space. Consider the people listed in Table 10-1.

Table 10-1. Heights and weights

Person	Height (inches)	Height (centimeters)	Weight (pounds)
A	63	160	150
B	67	170.2	160
C	70	177.8	171

If we measure height in inches, then B's nearest neighbor is A:

```
from scratch.linear_algebra import distance

a_to_b = distance([63, 150], [67, 160])      # 10.77
a_to_c = distance([63, 150], [70, 171])      # 22.14
b_to_c = distance([67, 160], [70, 171])      # 11.40
```

However, if we measure height in centimeters, then B's nearest neighbor is instead C:

```
a_to_b = distance([160, 150], [170.2, 160])      # 14.28
a_to_c = distance([160, 150], [177.8, 171])      # 27.53
b_to_c = distance([170.2, 160], [177.8, 171])  # 13.37
```

Obviously it's a problem if changing units can change results like this. For this reason, when dimensions aren't comparable with one another, we will sometimes *rescale* our data so that each dimension has mean 0 and standard deviation 1. This effectively gets rid of the units, converting each dimension to "standard deviations from the mean."

To start with, we'll need to compute the `mean` and the `standard_deviation` for each position:

```
from typing import Tuple

from scratch.linear_algebra import vector_mean
from scratch.statistics import standard_deviation

def scale(data: List[Vector]) -> Tuple[Vector, Vector]:
    """returns the mean and standard deviation for each position"""
    dim = len(data[0])

    means = vector_mean(data)
    stdevs = [standard_deviation([vector[i] for vector in data])
              for i in range(dim)]

    return means, stdevs
```

```
vectors = [[-3, -1, 1], [-1, 0, 1], [1, 1, 1]]
means, stdevs = scale(vectors)
assert means == [-1, 0, 1]
assert stdevs == [2, 1, 0]
```

We can then use them to create a new dataset:

```
def rescale(data: List[Vector]) -> List[Vector]:
    """
    Rescales the input data so that each position has
    mean 0 and standard deviation 1. (Leaves a position
    as is if its standard deviation is 0.)
    """
    dim = len(data[0])
    means, stdevs = scale(data)

    # Make a copy of each vector
    rescaled = [v[:] for v in data]

    for v in rescaled:
        for i in range(dim):
            if stdevs[i] > 0:
                v[i] = (v[i] - means[i]) / stdevs[i]

    return rescaled
```

Of course, let's write a test to conform that `rescale` does what we think it should:

```
means, stdevs = scale(rescale(vectors))
assert means == [0, 0, 1]
assert stdevs == [1, 1, 0]
```

As always, you need to use your judgment. If you were to take a huge dataset of heights and weights and filter it down to only the people with heights between 69.5 inches and 70.5 inches, it's quite likely (depending on the question you're trying to answer) that the variation remaining is simply *noise*, and you might not want to put its standard deviation on equal footing with other dimensions' deviations.

An Aside: tqdm

Frequently we'll end up doing computations that take a long time. When you're doing such work, you'd like to know that you're making progress and how long you should expect to wait.

One way of doing this is with the `tqdm` library, which generates custom progress bars. We'll use it some throughout the rest of the book, so let's take this chance to learn how it works.

To start with, you'll need to install it:

```
python -m pip install tqdm
```

There are only a few features you need to know about. The first is that an iterable wrapped in tqdm.tqdm will produce a progress bar:

```
import tqdm

for i in tqdm.tqdm(range(100)):
    # do something slow
    _ = [random.random() for _ in range(1000000)]
```

which produces an output that looks like this:

```
56%|███████████|                    | 56/100 [00:08<00:06,  6.49it/s]
```

In particular, it shows you what fraction of your loop is done (though it can't do this if you use a generator), how long it's been running, and how long it expects to run.

In this case (where we are just wrapping a call to range) you can just use tqdm.trange.

You can also set the description of the progress bar while it's running. To do that, you need to capture the tqdm iterator in a with statement:

```
from typing import List

def primes_up_to(n: int) -> List[int]:
    primes = [2]

    with tqdm.trange(3, n) as t:
        for i in t:
            # i is prime if no smaller prime divides it
            i_is_prime = not any(i % p == 0 for p in primes)
            if i_is_prime:
                primes.append(i)

            t.set_description(f"{len(primes)} primes")

    return primes

my_primes = primes_up_to(100_000)
```

This adds a description like the following, with a counter that updates as new primes are discovered:

```
5116 primes:  50%|██████|              | 49529/99997 [00:03<00:03, 15905.90it/s]
```

Using tqdm will occasionally make your code flaky—sometimes the screen redraws poorly, and sometimes the loop will simply hang. And if you accidentally wrap a tqdm loop inside another tqdm loop, strange things might happen. Typically its benefits outweigh these downsides, though, so we'll try to use it whenever we have slow-running computations.

Dimensionality Reduction

Sometimes the "actual" (or useful) dimensions of the data might not correspond to the dimensions we have. For example, consider the dataset pictured in Figure 10-6.

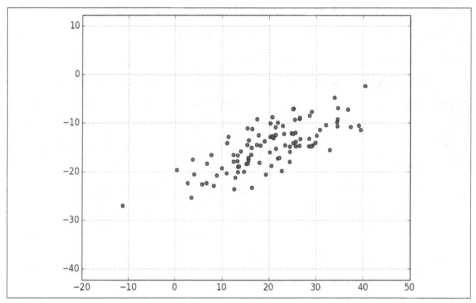

Figure 10-6. Data with the "wrong" axes

Most of the variation in the data seems to be along a single dimension that doesn't correspond to either the x-axis or the y-axis.

When this is the case, we can use a technique called *principal component analysis* (PCA) to extract one or more dimensions that capture as much of the variation in the data as possible.

 In practice, you wouldn't use this technique on such a low-dimensional dataset. Dimensionality reduction is mostly useful when your dataset has a large number of dimensions and you want to find a small subset that captures most of the variation. Unfortunately, that case is difficult to illustrate in a two-dimensional book format.

As a first step, we'll need to translate the data so that each dimension has mean 0:

```
from scratch.linear_algebra import subtract

def de_mean(data: List[Vector]) -> List[Vector]:
    """Recenters the data to have mean 0 in every dimension"""
```

```
    mean = vector_mean(data)
    return [subtract(vector, mean) for vector in data]
```

(If we don't do this, our techniques are likely to identify the mean itself rather than the variation in the data.)

Figure 10-7 shows the example data after de-meaning.

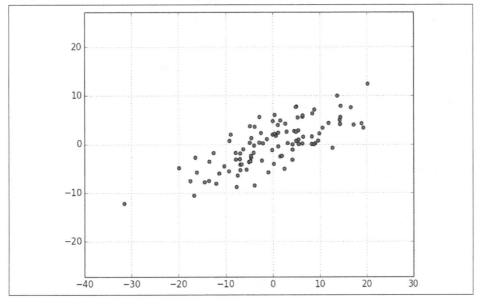

Figure 10-7. Data after de-meaning

Now, given a de-meaned matrix *X*, we can ask which is the direction that captures the greatest variance in the data.

Specifically, given a direction d (a vector of magnitude 1), each row x in the matrix extends dot(x, d) in the d direction. And every nonzero vector w determines a direction if we rescale it to have magnitude 1:

```
from scratch.linear_algebra import magnitude

def direction(w: Vector) -> Vector:
    mag = magnitude(w)
    return [w_i / mag for w_i in w]
```

Therefore, given a nonzero vector w, we can compute the variance of our dataset in the direction determined by w:

```
from scratch.linear_algebra import dot

def directional_variance(data: List[Vector], w: Vector) -> float:
    """
    Returns the variance of x in the direction of w
```

```
    """
    w_dir = direction(w)
    return sum(dot(v, w_dir) ** 2 for v in data)
```

We'd like to find the direction that maximizes this variance. We can do this using gradient descent, as soon as we have the gradient function:

```
def directional_variance_gradient(data: List[Vector], w: Vector) -> Vector:
    """
    The gradient of directional variance with respect to w
    """
    w_dir = direction(w)
    return [sum(2 * dot(v, w_dir) * v[i] for v in data)
            for i in range(len(w))]
```

And now the first principal component that we have is just the direction that maximizes the directional_variance function:

```
from scratch.gradient_descent import gradient_step

def first_principal_component(data: List[Vector],
                              n: int = 100,
                              step_size: float = 0.1) -> Vector:
    # Start with a random guess
    guess = [1.0 for _ in data[0]]

    with tqdm.trange(n) as t:
        for _ in t:
            dv = directional_variance(data, guess)
            gradient = directional_variance_gradient(data, guess)
            guess = gradient_step(guess, gradient, step_size)
            t.set_description(f"dv: {dv:.3f}")

    return direction(guess)
```

On the de-meaned dataset, this returns the direction [0.924, 0.383], which does appear to capture the primary axis along which our data varies (Figure 10-8).

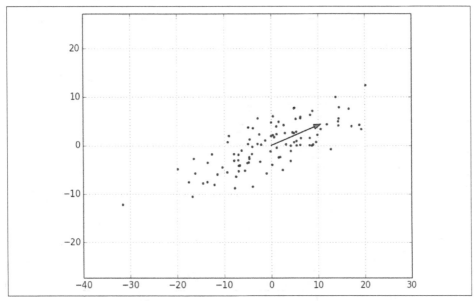

Figure 10-8. First principal component

Once we've found the direction that's the first principal component, we can project our data onto it to find the values of that component:

```
from scratch.linear_algebra import scalar_multiply

def project(v: Vector, w: Vector) -> Vector:
    """return the projection of v onto the direction w"""
    projection_length = dot(v, w)
    return scalar_multiply(projection_length, w)
```

If we want to find further components, we first remove the projections from the data:

```
from scratch.linear_algebra import subtract

def remove_projection_from_vector(v: Vector, w: Vector) -> Vector:
    """projects v onto w and subtracts the result from v"""
    return subtract(v, project(v, w))

def remove_projection(data: List[Vector], w: Vector) -> List[Vector]:
    return [remove_projection_from_vector(v, w) for v in data]
```

Because this example dataset is only two-dimensional, after we remove the first component, what's left will be effectively one-dimensional (Figure 10-9).

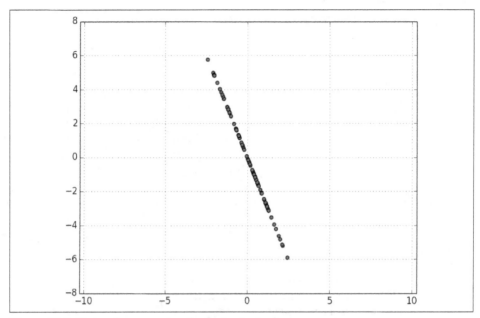

Figure 10-9. Data after removing the first principal component

At that point, we can find the next principal component by repeating the process on the result of remove_projection (Figure 10-10).

On a higher-dimensional dataset, we can iteratively find as many components as we want:

```
def pca(data: List[Vector], num_components: int) -> List[Vector]:
    components: List[Vector] = []
    for _ in range(num_components):
        component = first_principal_component(data)
        components.append(component)
        data = remove_projection(data, component)

    return components
```

We can then *transform* our data into the lower-dimensional space spanned by the components:

```
def transform_vector(v: Vector, components: List[Vector]) -> Vector:
    return [dot(v, w) for w in components]

def transform(data: List[Vector], components: List[Vector]) -> List[Vector]:
    return [transform_vector(v, components) for v in data]
```

This technique is valuable for a couple of reasons. First, it can help us clean our data by eliminating noise dimensions and consolidating highly correlated dimensions.

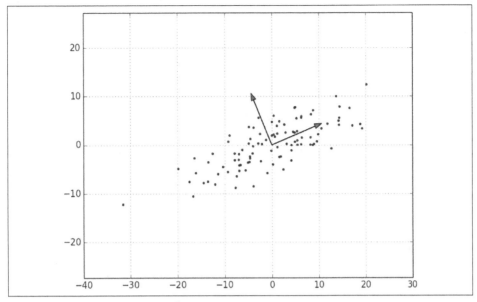

Figure 10-10. First two principal components

Second, after extracting a low-dimensional representation of our data, we can use a variety of techniques that don't work as well on high-dimensional data. We'll see examples of such techniques throughout the book.

At the same time, while this technique can help you build better models, it can also make those models harder to interpret. It's easy to understand conclusions like "every extra year of experience adds an average of $10k in salary." It's much harder to make sense of "every increase of 0.1 in the third principal component adds an average of $10k in salary."

For Further Exploration

- As mentioned at the end of Chapter 9, pandas (*http://pandas.pydata.org/*) is probably the primary Python tool for cleaning, munging, manipulating, and working with data. All the examples we did by hand in this chapter could be done much more simply using pandas. *Python for Data Analysis* (O'Reilly), by Wes McKinney, is probably the best way to learn pandas.

- scikit-learn has a wide variety of matrix decomposition (*https://scikit-learn.org/stable/modules/classes.html#module-sklearn.decomposition*) functions, including PCA.

## CHAPTER 11

Machine Learning

I am always ready to learn although I do not always like being taught.
—Winston Churchill

Many people imagine that data science is mostly machine learning and that data scientists mostly build and train and tweak machine learning models all day long. (Then again, many of those people don't actually know what machine learning *is*.) In fact, data science is mostly turning business problems into data problems and collecting data and understanding data and cleaning data and formatting data, after which machine learning is almost an afterthought. Even so, it's an interesting and essential afterthought that you pretty much have to know about in order to do data science.

Modeling

Before we can talk about machine learning, we need to talk about *models*.

What is a model? It's simply a specification of a mathematical (or probabilistic) relationship that exists between different variables.

For instance, if you're trying to raise money for your social networking site, you might build a *business model* (likely in a spreadsheet) that takes inputs like "number of users," "ad revenue per user," and "number of employees" and outputs your annual profit for the next several years. A cookbook recipe entails a model that relates inputs like "number of eaters" and "hungriness" to quantities of ingredients needed. And if you've ever watched poker on television, you know that each player's "win probability" is estimated in real time based on a model that takes into account the cards that have been revealed so far and the distribution of cards in the deck.

The business model is probably based on simple mathematical relationships: profit is revenue minus expenses, revenue is units sold times average price, and so on. The recipe model is probably based on trial and error—someone went in a kitchen and tried different combinations of ingredients until they found one they liked. And the poker model is based on probability theory, the rules of poker, and some reasonably innocuous assumptions about the random process by which cards are dealt.

What Is Machine Learning?

Everyone has her own exact definition, but we'll use *machine learning* to refer to creating and using models that are *learned from data*. In other contexts this might be called *predictive modeling* or *data mining*, but we will stick with machine learning. Typically, our goal will be to use existing data to develop models that we can use to *predict* various outcomes for new data, such as:

- Whether an email message is spam or not
- Whether a credit card transaction is fraudulent
- Which advertisement a shopper is most likely to click on
- Which football team is going to win the Super Bowl

We'll look at both *supervised* models (in which there is a set of data labeled with the correct answers to learn from) and *unsupervised* models (in which there are no such labels). There are various other types, like *semisupervised* (in which only some of the data are labeled), *online* (in which the model needs to continuously adjust to newly arriving data), and *reinforcement* (in which, after making a series of predictions, the model gets a signal indicating how well it did) that we won't cover in this book.

Now, in even the simplest situation there are entire universes of models that might describe the relationship we're interested in. In most cases we will ourselves choose a *parameterized* family of models and then use data to learn parameters that are in some way optimal.

For instance, we might assume that a person's height is (roughly) a linear function of his weight and then use data to learn what that linear function is. Or we might assume that a decision tree is a good way to diagnose what diseases our patients have and then use data to learn the "optimal" such tree. Throughout the rest of the book, we'll be investigating different families of models that we can learn.

But before we can do that, we need to better understand the fundamentals of machine learning. For the rest of the chapter, we'll discuss some of those basic concepts, before we move on to the models themselves.

Overfitting and Underfitting

A common danger in machine learning is *overfitting*—producing a model that performs well on the data you train it on but generalizes poorly to any new data. This could involve learning *noise* in the data. Or it could involve learning to identify specific inputs rather than whatever factors are actually predictive for the desired output.

The other side of this is *underfitting*—producing a model that doesn't perform well even on the training data, although typically when this happens you decide your model isn't good enough and keep looking for a better one.

In Figure 11-1, I've fit three polynomials to a sample of data. (Don't worry about how; we'll get to that in later chapters.)

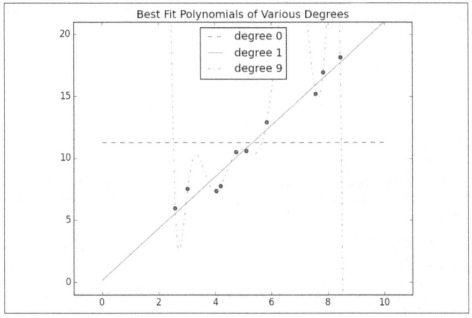

Figure 11-1. Overfitting and underfitting

The horizontal line shows the best fit degree 0 (i.e., constant) polynomial. It severely *underfits* the training data. The best fit degree 9 (i.e., 10-parameter) polynomial goes through every training data point exactly, but it very severely *overfits*; if we were to pick a few more data points, it would quite likely miss them by a lot. And the degree 1 line strikes a nice balance; it's pretty close to every point, and—if these data are representative—the line will likely be close to new data points as well.

Clearly, models that are too complex lead to overfitting and don't generalize well beyond the data they were trained on. So how do we make sure our models aren't too complex? The most fundamental approach involves using different data to train the model and to test the model.

The simplest way to do this is to split the dataset, so that (for example) two-thirds of it is used to train the model, after which we measure the model's performance on the remaining third:

```python
import random
from typing import TypeVar, List, Tuple
X = TypeVar('X')  # generic type to represent a data point

def split_data(data: List[X], prob: float) -> Tuple[List[X], List[X]]:
    """Split data into fractions [prob, 1 - prob]"""
    data = data[:]                  # Make a shallow copy
    random.shuffle(data)            # because shuffle modifies the list.
    cut = int(len(data) * prob)     # Use prob to find a cutoff
    return data[:cut], data[cut:]   # and split the shuffled list there.

data = [n for n in range(1000)]
train, test = split_data(data, 0.75)

# The proportions should be correct
assert len(train) == 750
assert len(test) == 250

# And the original data should be preserved (in some order)
assert sorted(train + test) == data
```

Often, we'll have paired input variables and output variables. In that case, we need to make sure to put corresponding values together in either the training data or the test data:

```python
Y = TypeVar('Y')  # generic type to represent output variables

def train_test_split(xs: List[X],
                     ys: List[Y],
                     test_pct: float) -> Tuple[List[X], List[X], List[Y],
                                                                    List[Y]]:
    # Generate the indices and split them
    idxs = [i for i in range(len(xs))]
    train_idxs, test_idxs = split_data(idxs, 1 - test_pct)

    return ([xs[i] for i in train_idxs],   # x_train
            [xs[i] for i in test_idxs],    # x_test
            [ys[i] for i in train_idxs],   # y_train
            [ys[i] for i in test_idxs])    # y_test
```

As always, we want to make sure our code works right:

```python
xs = [x for x in range(1000)]   # xs are 1 ... 1000
ys = [2 * x for x in xs]        # each y_i is twice x_i
x_train, x_test, y_train, y_test = train_test_split(xs, ys, 0.25)
```

```
# Check that the proportions are correct
assert len(x_train) == len(y_train) == 750
assert len(x_test) == len(y_test) == 250

# Check that the corresponding data points are paired correctly
assert all(y == 2 * x for x, y in zip(x_train, y_train))
assert all(y == 2 * x for x, y in zip(x_test, y_test))
```

After which you can do something like:

```
model = SomeKindOfModel()
x_train, x_test, y_train, y_test = train_test_split(xs, ys, 0.33)
model.train(x_train, y_train)
performance = model.test(x_test, y_test)
```

If the model was overfit to the training data, then it will hopefully perform really poorly on the (completely separate) test data. Said differently, if it performs well on the test data, then you can be more confident that it's *fitting* rather than *overfitting*.

However, there are a couple of ways this can go wrong.

The first is if there are common patterns in the test and training data that wouldn't generalize to a larger dataset.

For example, imagine that your dataset consists of user activity, with one row per user per week. In such a case, most users will appear in both the training data and the test data, and certain models might learn to *identify* users rather than discover relationships involving *attributes*. This isn't a huge worry, although it did happen to me once.

A bigger problem is if you use the test/train split not just to judge a model but also to *choose* from among many models. In that case, although each individual model may not be overfit, "choosing a model that performs best on the test set" is a meta-training that makes the test set function as a second training set. (Of course the model that performed best on the test set is going to perform well on the test set.)

In such a situation, you should split the data into three parts: a training set for building models, a *validation* set for choosing among trained models, and a test set for judging the final model.

Correctness

When I'm not doing data science, I dabble in medicine. And in my spare time I've come up with a cheap, noninvasive test that can be given to a newborn baby that predicts—with greater than 98% accuracy—whether the newborn will ever develop leukemia. My lawyer has convinced me the test is unpatentable, so I'll share with you the details here: predict leukemia if and only if the baby is named Luke (which sounds sort of like "leukemia").

As we'll see, this test is indeed more than 98% accurate. Nonetheless, it's an incredibly stupid test, and a good illustration of why we don't typically use "accuracy" to measure how good a (binary classification) model is.

Imagine building a model to make a *binary* judgment. Is this email spam? Should we hire this candidate? Is this air traveler secretly a terrorist?

Given a set of labeled data and such a predictive model, every data point lies in one of four categories:

True positive
"This message is spam, and we correctly predicted spam."

False positive (Type 1 error)
"This message is not spam, but we predicted spam."

False negative (Type 2 error)
"This message is spam, but we predicted not spam."

True negative
"This message is not spam, and we correctly predicted not spam."

We often represent these as counts in a *confusion matrix*:

	Spam	Not spam
Predict "spam"	True positive	False positive
Predict "not spam"	False negative	True negative

Let's see how my leukemia test fits into this framework. These days approximately 5 babies out of 1,000 are named Luke (*https://www.babycenter.com/baby-names-luke-2918.htm*). And the lifetime prevalence of leukemia is about 1.4%, or 14 out of every 1,000 people (*https://seer.cancer.gov/statfacts/html/leuks.html*).

If we believe these two factors are independent and apply my "Luke is for leukemia" test to 1 million people, we'd expect to see a confusion matrix like:

	Leukemia	No leukemia	Total
"Luke"	70	4,930	5,000
Not "Luke"	13,930	981,070	995,000
Total	14,000	986,000	1,000,000

We can then use these to compute various statistics about model performance. For example, *accuracy* is defined as the fraction of correct predictions:

```
def accuracy(tp: int, fp: int, fn: int, tn: int) -> float:
    correct = tp + tn
    total = tp + fp + fn + tn
```

```
    return correct / total

assert accuracy(70, 4930, 13930, 981070) == 0.98114
```

That seems like a pretty impressive number. But clearly this is not a good test, which means that we probably shouldn't put a lot of credence in raw accuracy.

It's common to look at the combination of *precision* and *recall*. Precision measures how accurate our *positive* predictions were:

```
def precision(tp: int, fp: int, fn: int, tn: int) -> float:
    return tp / (tp + fp)

assert precision(70, 4930, 13930, 981070) == 0.014
```

And recall measures what fraction of the positives our model identified:

```
def recall(tp: int, fp: int, fn: int, tn: int) -> float:
    return tp / (tp + fn)

assert recall(70, 4930, 13930, 981070) == 0.005
```

These are both terrible numbers, reflecting that this is a terrible model.

Sometimes precision and recall are combined into the *F1 score*, which is defined as:

```
def f1_score(tp: int, fp: int, fn: int, tn: int) -> float:
    p = precision(tp, fp, fn, tn)
    r = recall(tp, fp, fn, tn)

    return 2 * p * r / (p + r)
```

This is the *harmonic mean* (*http://en.wikipedia.org/wiki/Harmonic_mean*) of precision and recall and necessarily lies between them.

Usually the choice of a model involves a tradeoff between precision and recall. A model that predicts "yes" when it's even a little bit confident will probably have a high recall but a low precision; a model that predicts "yes" only when it's extremely confident is likely to have a low recall and a high precision.

Alternatively, you can think of this as a tradeoff between false positives and false negatives. Saying "yes" too often will give you lots of false positives; saying "no" too often will give you lots of false negatives.

Imagine that there were 10 risk factors for leukemia, and that the more of them you had the more likely you were to develop leukemia. In that case you can imagine a continuum of tests: "predict leukemia if at least one risk factor," "predict leukemia if at least two risk factors," and so on. As you increase the threshold, you increase the test's precision (since people with more risk factors are more likely to develop the disease), and you decrease the test's recall (since fewer and fewer of the eventual disease-sufferers will meet the threshold). In cases like this, choosing the right threshold is a matter of finding the right tradeoff.

The Bias-Variance Tradeoff

Another way of thinking about the overfitting problem is as a tradeoff between bias and variance.

Both are measures of what would happen if you were to retrain your model many times on different sets of training data (from the same larger population).

For example, the degree 0 model in "Overfitting and Underfitting" on page 155 will make a lot of mistakes for pretty much any training set (drawn from the same population), which means that it has a high *bias*. However, any two randomly chosen training sets should give pretty similar models (since any two randomly chosen training sets should have pretty similar average values). So we say that it has a low *variance*. High bias and low variance typically correspond to underfitting.

On the other hand, the degree 9 model fit the training set perfectly. It has very low bias but very high variance (since any two training sets would likely give rise to very different models). This corresponds to overfitting.

Thinking about model problems this way can help you figure out what to do when your model doesn't work so well.

If your model has high bias (which means it performs poorly even on your training data), one thing to try is adding more features. Going from the degree 0 model in "Overfitting and Underfitting" on page 155 to the degree 1 model was a big improvement.

If your model has high variance, you can similarly *remove* features. But another solution is to obtain more data (if you can).

In Figure 11-2, we fit a degree 9 polynomial to different size samples. The model fit based on 10 data points is all over the place, as we saw before. If we instead train on 100 data points, there's much less overfitting. And the model trained from 1,000 data points looks very similar to the degree 1 model. Holding model complexity constant, the more data you have, the harder it is to overfit. On the other hand, more data won't help with bias. If your model doesn't use enough features to capture regularities in the data, throwing more data at it won't help.

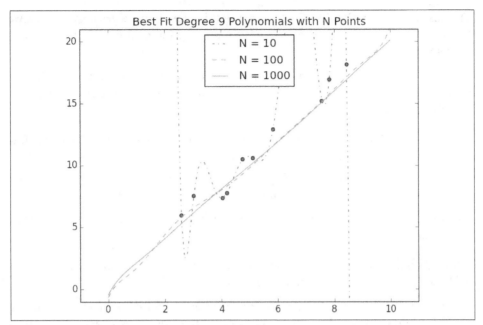

Figure 11-2. Reducing variance with more data

Feature Extraction and Selection

As has been mentioned, when your data doesn't have enough features, your model is likely to underfit. And when your data has too many features, it's easy to overfit. But what are features, and where do they come from?

Features are whatever inputs we provide to our model.

In the simplest case, features are simply given to you. If you want to predict someone's salary based on her years of experience, then years of experience is the only feature you have. (Although, as we saw in "Overfitting and Underfitting" on page 155, you might also consider adding years of experience squared, cubed, and so on if that helps you build a better model.)

Things become more interesting as your data becomes more complicated. Imagine trying to build a spam filter to predict whether an email is junk or not. Most models won't know what to do with a raw email, which is just a collection of text. You'll have to extract features. For example:

- Does the email contain the word *Viagra*?
- How many times does the letter *d* appear?
- What was the domain of the sender?

The answer to a question like the first question here is simply a yes or no, which we typically encode as a 1 or 0. The second is a number. And the third is a choice from a discrete set of options.

Pretty much always, we'll extract features from our data that fall into one of these three categories. What's more, the types of features we have constrain the types of models we can use.

- The Naive Bayes classifier we'll build in Chapter 13 is suited to yes-or-no features, like the first one in the preceding list.
- Regression models, which we'll study in Chapters 14 and 16, require numeric features (which could include dummy variables that are 0s and 1s).
- And decision trees, which we'll look at in Chapter 17, can deal with numeric or categorical data.

Although in the spam filter example we looked for ways to create features, sometimes we'll instead look for ways to remove features.

For example, your inputs might be vectors of several hundred numbers. Depending on the situation, it might be appropriate to distill these down to a handful of important dimensions (as in "Dimensionality Reduction" on page 146) and use only that small number of features. Or it might be appropriate to use a technique (like regularization, which we'll look at in "Regularization" on page 200) that penalizes models the more features they use.

How do we choose features? That's where a combination of *experience* and *domain expertise* comes into play. If you've received lots of emails, then you probably have a sense that the presence of certain words might be a good indicator of spamminess. And you might also get the sense that the number of *d*s is likely not a good indicator of spamminess. But in general you'll have to try different things, which is part of the fun.

For Further Exploration

- Keep reading! The next several chapters are about different families of machine learning models.

- The Coursera Machine Learning (*https://www.coursera.org/course/ml*) course is the original MOOC and is a good place to get a deeper understanding of the basics of machine learning.

- *The Elements of Statistical Learning*, by Jerome H. Friedman, Robert Tibshirani, and Trevor Hastie (Springer), is a somewhat canonical textbook that can be downloaded online for free (*http://stanford.io/1ycOXbo*). But be warned: it's *very* mathy.

k-Nearest Neighbors

If you want to annoy your neighbors, tell the truth about them.
—Pietro Aretino

Imagine that you're trying to predict how I'm going to vote in the next presidential election. If you know nothing else about me (and if you have the data), one sensible approach is to look at how my *neighbors* are planning to vote. Living in Seattle, as I do, my neighbors are invariably planning to vote for the Democratic candidate, which suggests that "Democratic candidate" is a good guess for me as well.

Now imagine you know more about me than just geography—perhaps you know my age, my income, how many kids I have, and so on. To the extent my behavior is influenced (or characterized) by those things, looking just at my neighbors who are close to me among all those dimensions seems likely to be an even better predictor than looking at all my neighbors. This is the idea behind *nearest neighbors classification*.

The Model

Nearest neighbors is one of the simplest predictive models there is. It makes no mathematical assumptions, and it doesn't require any sort of heavy machinery. The only things it requires are:

- Some notion of distance
- An assumption that points that are close to one another are similar

Most of the techniques we'll see in this book look at the dataset as a whole in order to learn patterns in the data. Nearest neighbors, on the other hand, quite consciously neglects a lot of information, since the prediction for each new point depends only on the handful of points closest to it.

What's more, nearest neighbors is probably not going to help you understand the drivers of whatever phenomenon you're looking at. Predicting my votes based on my neighbors' votes doesn't tell you much about what causes me to vote the way I do, whereas some alternative model that predicted my vote based on (say) my income and marital status very well might.

In the general situation, we have some data points and we have a corresponding set of labels. The labels could be True and False, indicating whether each input satisfies some condition like "is spam?" or "is poisonous?" or "would be enjoyable to watch?" Or they could be categories, like movie ratings (G, PG, PG-13, R, NC-17). Or they could be the names of presidential candidates. Or they could be favorite programming languages.

In our case, the data points will be vectors, which means that we can use the distance function from Chapter 4.

Let's say we've picked a number k like 3 or 5. Then, when we want to classify some new data point, we find the k nearest labeled points and let them vote on the new output.

To do this, we'll need a function that counts votes. One possibility is:

```
from typing import List
from collections import Counter

def raw_majority_vote(labels: List[str]) -> str:
    votes = Counter(labels)
    winner, _ = votes.most_common(1)[0]
    return winner

assert raw_majority_vote(['a', 'b', 'c', 'b']) == 'b'
```

But this doesn't do anything intelligent with ties. For example, imagine we're rating movies and the five nearest movies are rated G, G, PG, PG, and R. Then G has two votes and PG also has two votes. In that case, we have several options:

- Pick one of the winners at random.
- Weight the votes by distance and pick the weighted winner.
- Reduce k until we find a unique winner.

We'll implement the third:

```
def majority_vote(labels: List[str]) -> str:
    """Assumes that labels are ordered from nearest to farthest."""
    vote_counts = Counter(labels)
    winner, winner_count = vote_counts.most_common(1)[0]
    num_winners = len([count
                       for count in vote_counts.values()
                       if count == winner_count])
```

```
        if num_winners == 1:
            return winner                    # unique winner, so return it
        else:
            return majority_vote(labels[:-1]) # try again without the farthest

    # Tie, so look at first 4, then 'b'
    assert majority_vote(['a', 'b', 'c', 'b', 'a']) == 'b'
```

This approach is sure to work eventually, since in the worst case we go all the way down to just one label, at which point that one label wins.

With this function it's easy to create a classifier:

```
from typing import NamedTuple
from scratch.linear_algebra import Vector, distance

class LabeledPoint(NamedTuple):
    point: Vector
    label: str

def knn_classify(k: int,
                 labeled_points: List[LabeledPoint],
                 new_point: Vector) -> str:

    # Order the labeled points from nearest to farthest.
    by_distance = sorted(labeled_points,
                         key=lambda lp: distance(lp.point, new_point))

    # Find the labels for the k closest
    k_nearest_labels = [lp.label for lp in by_distance[:k]]

    # and let them vote.
    return majority_vote(k_nearest_labels)
```

Let's take a look at how this works.

Example: The Iris Dataset

The *Iris* dataset is a staple of machine learning. It contains a bunch of measurements for 150 flowers representing three species of iris. For each flower we have its petal length, petal width, sepal length, and sepal width, as well as its species. You can download it from *https://archive.ics.uci.edu/ml/datasets/iris*:

```
import requests

data = requests.get(
  "https://archive.ics.uci.edu/ml/machine-learning-databases/iris/iris.data"
)

with open('iris.dat', 'w') as f:
    f.write(data.text)
```

The data is comma-separated, with fields:

```
sepal_length, sepal_width, petal_length, petal_width, class
```

For example, the first row looks like:

```
5.1,3.5,1.4,0.2,Iris-setosa
```

In this section we'll try to build a model that can predict the class (that is, the species) from the first four measurements.

To start with, let's load and explore the data. Our nearest neighbors function expects a LabeledPoint, so let's represent our data that way:

```python
from typing import Dict
import csv
from collections import defaultdict

def parse_iris_row(row: List[str]) -> LabeledPoint:
    """
    sepal_length, sepal_width, petal_length, petal_width, class
    """
    measurements = [float(value) for value in row[:-1]]
    # class is e.g. "Iris-virginica"; we just want "virginica"
    label = row[-1].split("-")[-1]

    return LabeledPoint(measurements, label)

with open('iris.data') as f:
    reader = csv.reader(f)
    iris_data = [parse_iris_row(row) for row in reader]

# We'll also group just the points by species/label so we can plot them
points_by_species: Dict[str, List[Vector]] = defaultdict(list)
for iris in iris_data:
    points_by_species[iris.label].append(iris.point)
```

We'd like to plot the measurements so we can see how they vary by species. Unfortunately, they are four-dimensional, which makes them tricky to plot. One thing we can do is look at the scatterplots for each of the six pairs of measurements (Figure 12-1). I won't explain all the details, but it's a nice illustration of more complicated things you can do with matplotlib, so it's worth studying:

```python
from matplotlib import pyplot as plt
metrics = ['sepal length', 'sepal width', 'petal length', 'petal width']
pairs = [(i, j) for i in range(4) for j in range(4) if i < j]
marks = ['+', '.', 'x']  # we have 3 classes, so 3 markers

fig, ax = plt.subplots(2, 3)

for row in range(2):
    for col in range(3):
        i, j = pairs[3 * row + col]
```

```
ax[row][col].set_title(f"{metrics[i]} vs {metrics[j]}", fontsize=8)
ax[row][col].set_xticks([])
ax[row][col].set_yticks([])

for mark, (species, points) in zip(marks, points_by_species.items()):
    xs = [point[i] for point in points]
    ys = [point[j] for point in points]
    ax[row][col].scatter(xs, ys, marker=mark, label=species)

ax[-1][-1].legend(loc='lower right', prop={'size': 6})
plt.show()
```

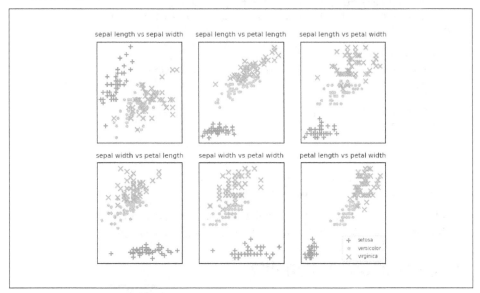

Figure 12-1. Iris scatterplots

If you look at those plots, it seems like the measurements really do cluster by species. For example, looking at sepal length and sepal width alone, you probably couldn't distinguish between *versicolor* and *virginica*. But once you add petal length and width into the mix, it seems like you should be able to predict the species based on the nearest neighbors.

To start with, let's split the data into a test set and a training set:

```
import random
from scratch.machine_learning import split_data

random.seed(12)
iris_train, iris_test = split_data(iris_data, 0.70)
assert len(iris_train) == 0.7 * 150
assert len(iris_test) == 0.3 * 150
```

The training set will be the "neighbors" that we'll use to classify the points in the test set. We just need to choose a value for k, the number of neighbors who get to vote. Too small (think $k = 1$), and we let outliers have too much influence; too large (think $k = 105$), and we just predict the most common class in the dataset.

In a real application (and with more data), we might create a separate validation set and use it to choose k. Here we'll just use $k = 5$:

```
from typing import Tuple

# track how many times we see (predicted, actual)
confusion_matrix: Dict[Tuple[str, str], int] = defaultdict(int)
num_correct = 0

for iris in iris_test:
    predicted = knn_classify(5, iris_train, iris.point)
    actual = iris.label

    if predicted == actual:
        num_correct += 1

    confusion_matrix[(predicted, actual)] += 1

pct_correct = num_correct / len(iris_test)
print(pct_correct, confusion_matrix)
```

On this simple dataset, the model predicts almost perfectly. There's one *versicolor* for which it predicts *virginica*, but otherwise it gets things exactly right.

The Curse of Dimensionality

The k-nearest neighbors algorithm runs into trouble in higher dimensions thanks to the "curse of dimensionality," which boils down to the fact that high-dimensional spaces are *vast*. Points in high-dimensional spaces tend not to be close to one another at all. One way to see this is by randomly generating pairs of points in the d-dimensional "unit cube" in a variety of dimensions, and calculating the distances between them.

Generating random points should be second nature by now:

```
def random_point(dim: int) -> Vector:
    return [random.random() for _ in range(dim)]
```

as is writing a function to generate the distances:

```
def random_distances(dim: int, num_pairs: int) -> List[float]:
    return [distance(random_point(dim), random_point(dim))
            for _ in range(num_pairs)]
```

For every dimension from 1 to 100, we'll compute 10,000 distances and use those to compute the average distance between points and the minimum distance between points in each dimension (Figure 12-2):

```
import tqdm
dimensions = range(1, 101)

avg_distances = []
min_distances = []

random.seed(0)
for dim in tqdm.tqdm(dimensions, desc="Curse of Dimensionality"):
    distances = random_distances(dim, 10000)      # 10,000 random pairs
    avg_distances.append(sum(distances) / 10000)  # track the average
    min_distances.append(min(distances))          # track the minimum
```

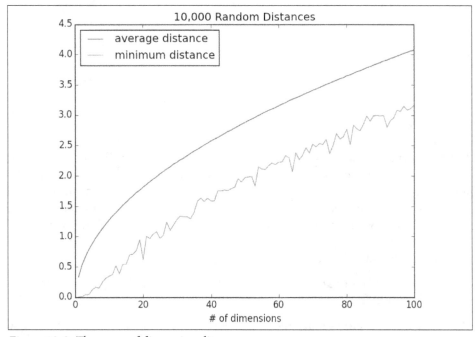

Figure 12-2. The curse of dimensionality

As the number of dimensions increases, the average distance between points increases. But what's more problematic is the ratio between the closest distance and the average distance (Figure 12-3):

```
min_avg_ratio = [min_dist / avg_dist
                 for min_dist, avg_dist in zip(min_distances, avg_distances)]
```

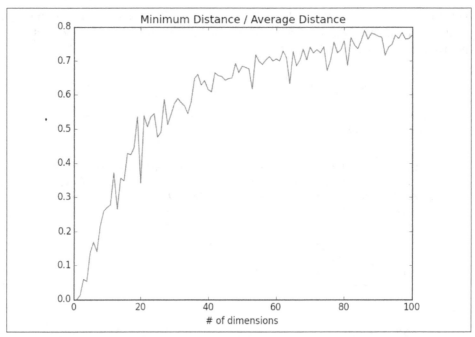

Figure 12-3. The curse of dimensionality again

In low-dimensional datasets, the closest points tend to be much closer than average. But two points are close only if they're close in every dimension, and every extra dimension—even if just noise—is another opportunity for each point to be farther away from every other point. When you have a lot of dimensions, it's likely that the closest points aren't much closer than average, so two points being close doesn't mean very much (unless there's a lot of structure in your data that makes it behave as if it were much lower-dimensional).

A different way of thinking about the problem involves the sparsity of higher-dimensional spaces.

If you pick 50 random numbers between 0 and 1, you'll probably get a pretty good sample of the unit interval (Figure 12-4).

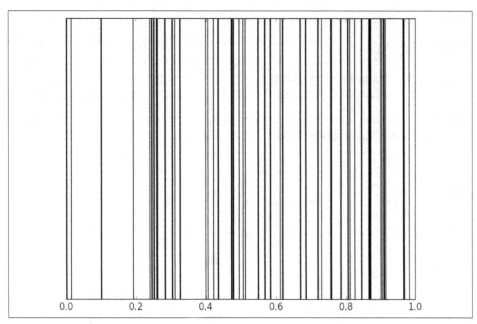

Figure 12-4. Fifty random points in one dimension

If you pick 50 random points in the unit square, you'll get less coverage (Figure 12-5).

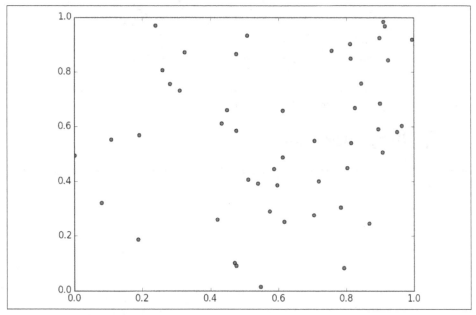

Figure 12-5. Fifty random points in two dimensions

And in three dimensions, less still (Figure 12-6).

matplotlib doesn't graph four dimensions well, so that's as far as we'll go, but you can see already that there are starting to be large empty spaces with no points near them. In more dimensions—unless you get exponentially more data—those large empty spaces represent regions far from all the points you want to use in your predictions.

So if you're trying to use nearest neighbors in higher dimensions, it's probably a good idea to do some kind of dimensionality reduction first.

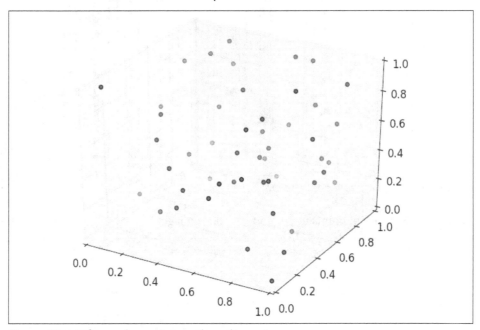

Figure 12-6. Fifty random points in three dimensions

For Further Exploration

scikit-learn has many nearest neighbor (*https://scikit-learn.org/stable/modules/neigh bors.html*) models.

## CHAPTER 13

Naive Bayes

It is well for the heart to be naive and for the mind not to be.
—Anatole France

A social network isn't much good if people can't network. Accordingly, DataSciences-ter has a popular feature that allows members to send messages to other members. And while most members are responsible citizens who send only well-received "how's it going?" messages, a few miscreants persistently spam other members about get-rich schemes, no-prescription-required pharmaceuticals, and for-profit data science credentialing programs. Your users have begun to complain, and so the VP of Messaging has asked you to use data science to figure out a way to filter out these spam messages.

A Really Dumb Spam Filter

Imagine a "universe" that consists of receiving a message chosen randomly from all possible messages. Let S be the event "the message is spam" and B be the event "the message contains the word *bitcoin*." Bayes's theorem tells us that the probability that the message is spam conditional on containing the word *bitcoin* is:

$$P(S|B) = [P(B|S)P(S)]/[P(B|S)P(S) + P(B|\neg S)P(\neg S)]$$

The numerator is the probability that a message is spam *and* contains *bitcoin*, while the denominator is just the probability that a message contains *bitcoin*. Hence, you can think of this calculation as simply representing the proportion of *bitcoin* messages that are spam.

If we have a large collection of messages we know are spam, and a large collection of messages we know are not spam, then we can easily estimate $P(B|S)$ and $P(B|\neg S)$. If we further assume that any message is equally likely to be spam or not spam (so that $P(S) = P(\neg S) = 0.5$), then:

$$P(S|B) = P(B|S)/[P(B|S) + P(B|\neg S)]$$

For example, if 50% of spam messages have the word *bitcoin*, but only 1% of nonspam messages do, then the probability that any given *bitcoin*-containing email is spam is:

$$0.5/(0.5 + 0.01) = 98\%$$

A More Sophisticated Spam Filter

Imagine now that we have a vocabulary of many words, w_1 ..., w_n. To move this into the realm of probability theory, we'll write X_i for the event "a message contains the word w_i." Also imagine that (through some unspecified-at-this-point process) we've come up with an estimate $P(X_i|S)$ for the probability that a spam message contains the ith word, and a similar estimate $P(X_i|\neg S)$ for the probability that a nonspam message contains the ith word.

The key to Naive Bayes is making the (big) assumption that the presences (or absences) of each word are independent of one another, conditional on a message being spam or not. Intuitively, this assumption means that knowing whether a certain spam message contains the word *bitcoin* gives you no information about whether that same message contains the word *rolex*. In math terms, this means that:

$$P\big(X_1 = x_1, \ldots, X_n = x_n | S\big) = P\big(X_1 = x_1 | S\big) \times \cdots \times P\big(X_n = x_n | S\big)$$

This is an extreme assumption. (There's a reason the technique has *naive* in its name.) Imagine that our vocabulary consists *only* of the words *bitcoin* and *rolex*, and that half of all spam messages are for "earn bitcoin" and that the other half are for "authentic rolex." In this case, the Naive Bayes estimate that a spam message contains both *bitcoin* and *rolex* is:

$$P\big(X_1 = 1, X_2 = 1 | S\big) = P\big(X_1 = 1 | S\big)P\big(X_2 = 1 | S\big) = .5 \times .5 = .25$$

since we've assumed away the knowledge that *bitcoin* and *rolex* actually never occur together. Despite the unrealisticness of this assumption, this model often performs well and has historically been used in actual spam filters.

The same Bayes's theorem reasoning we used for our "bitcoin-only" spam filter tells us that we can calculate the probability a message is spam using the equation:

$$P(S \mid X = x) = P(X = x \mid S) / [P(X = x \mid S) + P(X = x \mid \neg S)]$$

The Naive Bayes assumption allows us to compute each of the probabilities on the right simply by multiplying together the individual probability estimates for each vocabulary word.

In practice, you usually want to avoid multiplying lots of probabilities together, to prevent a problem called *underflow*, in which computers don't deal well with floating-point numbers that are too close to 0. Recalling from algebra that $\log (ab) = \log a + \log b$ and that $\exp (\log x) = x$, we usually compute $p_1 * \cdots * p_n$ as the equivalent (but floating-point-friendlier):

$$\exp \left(\log (p_1) + \cdots + \log (p_n) \right)$$

The only challenge left is coming up with estimates for $P(X_i \mid S)$ and $P(X_i \mid \neg S)$, the probabilities that a spam message (or nonspam message) contains the word w_i. If we have a fair number of "training" messages labeled as spam and not spam, an obvious first try is to estimate $P(X_i \mid S)$ simply as the fraction of spam messages containing the word w_i.

This causes a big problem, though. Imagine that in our training set the vocabulary word *data* only occurs in nonspam messages. Then we'd estimate $P(\text{data} \mid S) = 0$. The result is that our Naive Bayes classifier would always assign spam probability 0 to *any* message containing the word *data*, even a message like "data on free bitcoin and authentic rolex watches." To avoid this problem, we usually use some kind of smoothing.

In particular, we'll choose a *pseudocount—k*—and estimate the probability of seeing the *i*th word in a spam message as:

$$P(X_i \mid S) = (k + \text{number of spams containing } w_i) / (2k + \text{number of spams})$$

We do similarly for $P(X_i \mid \neg S)$. That is, when computing the spam probabilities for the *i*th word, we assume we also saw k additional nonspams containing the word and k additional nonspams not containing the word.

For example, if *data* occurs in 0/98 spam messages, and if k is 1, we estimate $P(\text{data} \mid S)$ as $1/100 = 0.01$, which allows our classifier to still assign some nonzero spam probability to messages that contain the word *data*.

Implementation

Now we have all the pieces we need to build our classifier. First, let's create a simple function to tokenize messages into distinct words. We'll first convert each message to lowercase, then use `re.findall` to extract "words" consisting of letters, numbers, and apostrophes. Finally, we'll use `set` to get just the distinct words:

```
from typing import Set
import re

def tokenize(text: str) -> Set[str]:
    text = text.lower()                        # Convert to lowercase,
    all_words = re.findall("[a-z0-9']+", text) # extract the words, and
    return set(all_words)                      # remove duplicates.

assert tokenize("Data Science is science") == {"data", "science", "is"}
```

We'll also define a type for our training data:

```
from typing import NamedTuple

class Message(NamedTuple):
    text: str
    is_spam: bool
```

As our classifier needs to keep track of tokens, counts, and labels from the training data, we'll make it a class. Following convention, we refer to nonspam emails as *ham* emails.

The constructor will take just one parameter, the pseudocount to use when computing probabilities. It also initializes an empty set of tokens, counters to track how often each token is seen in spam messages and ham messages, and counts of how many spam and ham messages it was trained on:

```
from typing import List, Tuple, Dict, Iterable
import math
from collections import defaultdict

class NaiveBayesClassifier:
    def __init__(self, k: float = 0.5) -> None:
        self.k = k  # smoothing factor

        self.tokens: Set[str] = set()
        self.token_spam_counts: Dict[str, int] = defaultdict(int)
        self.token_ham_counts: Dict[str, int] = defaultdict(int)
        self.spam_messages = self.ham_messages = 0
```

Next, we'll give it a method to train it on a bunch of messages. First, we increment the `spam_messages` and `ham_messages` counts. Then we tokenize each message text, and for each token we increment the `token_spam_counts` or `token_ham_counts` based on the message type:

```
def train(self, messages: Iterable[Message]) -> None:
    for message in messages:
        # Increment message counts
        if message.is_spam:
            self.spam_messages += 1
        else:
            self.ham_messages += 1

        # Increment word counts
        for token in tokenize(message.text):
            self.tokens.add(token)
            if message.is_spam:
                self.token_spam_counts[token] += 1
            else:
                self.token_ham_counts[token] += 1
```

Ultimately we'll want to predict P(spam | token). As we saw earlier, to apply Bayes's theorem we need to know P(token | spam) and P(token | ham) for each token in the vocabulary. So we'll create a "private" helper function to compute those:

```
def _probabilities(self, token: str) -> Tuple[float, float]:
    """returns P(token | spam) and P(token | ham)"""
    spam = self.token_spam_counts[token]
    ham = self.token_ham_counts[token]

    p_token_spam = (spam + self.k) / (self.spam_messages + 2 * self.k)
    p_token_ham = (ham + self.k) / (self.ham_messages + 2 * self.k)

    return p_token_spam, p_token_ham
```

Finally, we're ready to write our `predict` method. As mentioned earlier, rather than multiplying together lots of small probabilities, we'll instead sum up the log probabilities:

```
def predict(self, text: str) -> float:
    text_tokens = tokenize(text)
    log_prob_if_spam = log_prob_if_ham = 0.0

    # Iterate through each word in our vocabulary
    for token in self.tokens:
        prob_if_spam, prob_if_ham = self._probabilities(token)

        # If *token* appears in the message,
        # add the log probability of seeing it
        if token in text_tokens:
            log_prob_if_spam += math.log(prob_if_spam)
            log_prob_if_ham += math.log(prob_if_ham)

        # Otherwise add the log probability of _not_ seeing it,
        # which is log(1 - probability of seeing it)
        else:
            log_prob_if_spam += math.log(1.0 - prob_if_spam)
            log_prob_if_ham += math.log(1.0 - prob_if_ham)
```

```
    prob_if_spam = math.exp(log_prob_if_spam)
    prob_if_ham = math.exp(log_prob_if_ham)
    return prob_if_spam / (prob_if_spam + prob_if_ham)
```

And now we have a classifier.

Testing Our Model

Let's make sure our model works by writing some unit tests for it.

```
messages = [Message("spam rules", is_spam=True),
            Message("ham rules", is_spam=False),
            Message("hello ham", is_spam=False)]

model = NaiveBayesClassifier(k=0.5)
model.train(messages)
```

First, let's check that it got the counts right:

```
assert model.tokens == {"spam", "ham", "rules", "hello"}
assert model.spam_messages == 1
assert model.ham_messages == 2
assert model.token_spam_counts == {"spam": 1, "rules": 1}
assert model.token_ham_counts == {"ham": 2, "rules": 1, "hello": 1}
```

Now let's make a prediction. We'll also (laboriously) go through our Naive Bayes logic by hand, and make sure that we get the same result:

```
text = "hello spam"

probs_if_spam = [
    (1 + 0.5) / (1 + 2 * 0.5),      # "spam"  (present)
    1 - (0 + 0.5) / (1 + 2 * 0.5),  # "ham"   (not present)
    1 - (1 + 0.5) / (1 + 2 * 0.5),  # "rules" (not present)
    (0 + 0.5) / (1 + 2 * 0.5)       # "hello" (present)
]

probs_if_ham = [
    (0 + 0.5) / (2 + 2 * 0.5),      # "spam"  (present)
    1 - (2 + 0.5) / (2 + 2 * 0.5),  # "ham"   (not present)
    1 - (1 + 0.5) / (2 + 2 * 0.5),  # "rules" (not present)
    (1 + 0.5) / (2 + 2 * 0.5),      # "hello" (present)
]

p_if_spam = math.exp(sum(math.log(p) for p in probs_if_spam))
p_if_ham = math.exp(sum(math.log(p) for p in probs_if_ham))

# Should be about 0.83
assert model.predict(text) == p_if_spam / (p_if_spam + p_if_ham)
```

This test passes, so it seems like our model is doing what we think it is. If you look at the actual probabilities, the two big drivers are that our message contains *spam* (which our lone training spam message did) and that it doesn't contain *ham* (which both our training ham messages did).

Now let's try it on some real data.

Using Our Model

A popular (if somewhat old) dataset is the SpamAssassin public corpus (*https://spamassassin.apache.org/old/publiccorpus/*). We'll look at the files prefixed with *20021010*.

Here is a script that will download and unpack them to the directory of your choice (or you can do it manually):

```
from io import BytesIO  # So we can treat bytes as a file.
import requests         # To download the files, which
import tarfile          # are in .tar.bz format.

BASE_URL = "https://spamassassin.apache.org/old/publiccorpus"
FILES = ["20021010_easy_ham.tar.bz2",
         "20021010_hard_ham.tar.bz2",
         "20021010_spam.tar.bz2"]

# This is where the data will end up,
# in /spam, /easy_ham, and /hard_ham subdirectories.
# Change this to where you want the data.
OUTPUT_DIR = 'spam_data'

for filename in FILES:
    # Use requests to get the file contents at each URL.
    content = requests.get(f"{BASE_URL}/{filename}").content

    # Wrap the in-memory bytes so we can use them as a "file."
    fin = BytesIO(content)

    # And extract all the files to the specified output dir.
    with tarfile.open(fileobj=fin, mode='r:bz2') as tf:
        tf.extractall(OUTPUT_DIR)
```

It's possible the location of the files will change (this happened between the first and second editions of this book), in which case adjust the script accordingly.

After downloading the data you should have three folders: *spam*, *easy_ham*, and *hard_ham*. Each folder contains many emails, each contained in a single file. To keep things *really* simple, we'll just look at the subject lines of each email.

How do we identify the subject line? When we look through the files, they all seem to start with "Subject:". So we'll look for that:

```
import glob, re
```

```
# modify the path to wherever you've put the files
path = 'spam_data/*/*'

data: List[Message] = []

# glob.glob returns every filename that matches the wildcarded path
for filename in glob.glob(path):
    is_spam = "ham" not in filename

    # There are some garbage characters in the emails; the errors='ignore'
    # skips them instead of raising an exception.
    with open(filename, errors='ignore') as email_file:
        for line in email_file:
            if line.startswith("Subject:"):
                subject = line.lstrip("Subject: ")
                data.append(Message(subject, is_spam))
                break  # done with this file
```

Now we can split the data into training data and test data, and then we're ready to build a classifier:

```
import random
from scratch.machine_learning import split_data

random.seed(0)      # just so you get the same answers as me
train_messages, test_messages = split_data(data, 0.75)

model = NaiveBayesClassifier()
model.train(train_messages)
```

Let's generate some predictions and check how our model does:

```
from collections import Counter

predictions = [(message, model.predict(message.text))
               for message in test_messages]

# Assume that spam_probability > 0.5 corresponds to spam prediction
# and count the combinations of (actual is_spam, predicted is_spam)
confusion_matrix = Counter((message.is_spam, spam_probability > 0.5)
                           for message, spam_probability in predictions)

print(confusion_matrix)
```

This gives 84 true positives (spam classified as "spam"), 25 false positives (ham classified as "spam"), 703 true negatives (ham classified as "ham"), and 44 false negatives (spam classified as "ham"). This means our precision is 84 / (84 + 25) = 77%, and our recall is 84 / (84 + 44) = 65%, which are not bad numbers for such a simple model. (Presumably we'd do better if we looked at more than the subject lines.)

We can also inspect the model's innards to see which words are least and most indicative of spam:

```
def p_spam_given_token(token: str, model: NaiveBayesClassifier) -> float:
    # We probably shouldn't call private methods, but it's for a good cause.
    prob_if_spam, prob_if_ham = model._probabilities(token)

    return prob_if_spam / (prob_if_spam + prob_if_ham)

words = sorted(model.tokens, key=lambda t: p_spam_given_token(t, model))

print("spammiest_words", words[-10:])
print("hammiest_words", words[:10])
```

The spammiest words include things like *sale*, *mortgage*, *money*, and *rates*, whereas the hammiest words include things like *spambayes*, *users*, *apt*, and *perl*. So that also gives us some intuitive confidence that our model is basically doing the right thing.

How could we get better performance? One obvious way would be to get more data to train on. There are a number of ways to improve the model as well. Here are some possibilities that you might try:

- Look at the message content, not just the subject line. You'll have to be careful how you deal with the message headers.

- Our classifier takes into account every word that appears in the training set, even words that appear only once. Modify the classifier to accept an optional min_count threshold and ignore tokens that don't appear at least that many times.

- The tokenizer has no notion of similar words (e.g., *cheap* and *cheapest*). Modify the classifier to take an optional stemmer function that converts words to *equivalence classes* of words. For example, a really simple stemmer function might be:

  ```
  def drop_final_s(word):
      return re.sub("s$", "", word)
  ```

  Creating a good stemmer function is hard. People frequently use the Porter stemmer (*http://tartarus.org/martin/PorterStemmer/*).

- Although our features are all of the form "message contains word w_i," there's no reason why this has to be the case. In our implementation, we could add extra features like "message contains a number" by creating phony tokens like *contains:number* and modifying the tokenizer to emit them when appropriate.

For Further Exploration

- Paul Graham's articles "A Plan for Spam" (*http://www.paulgraham.com/spam.html*) and "Better Bayesian Filtering" (*http://www.paulgraham.com/better.html*) are interesting and give more insight into the ideas behind building spam filters.

- scikit-learn (*https://scikit-learn.org/stable/modules/naive_bayes.html*) contains a `BernoulliNB` model that implements the same Naive Bayes algorithm we implemented here, as well as other variations on the model.

## CHAPTER 14

Simple Linear Regression

Art, like morality, consists in drawing the line somewhere.
—G. K. Chesterton

In Chapter 5, we used the `correlation` function to measure the strength of the linear relationship between two variables. For most applications, knowing that such a linear relationship exists isn't enough. We'll want to understand the nature of the relationship. This is where we'll use simple linear regression.

The Model

Recall that we were investigating the relationship between a DataSciencester user's number of friends and the amount of time the user spends on the site each day. Let's assume that you've convinced yourself that having more friends *causes* people to spend more time on the site, rather than one of the alternative explanations we discussed.

The VP of Engagement asks you to build a model describing this relationship. Since you found a pretty strong linear relationship, a natural place to start is a linear model.

In particular, you hypothesize that there are constants α (alpha) and β (beta) such that:

$$y_i = \beta x_i + \alpha + \varepsilon_i$$

where y_i is the number of minutes user i spends on the site daily, x_i is the number of friends user i has, and ε is a (hopefully small) error term representing the fact that there are other factors not accounted for by this simple model.

Assuming we've determined such an `alpha` and `beta`, then we make predictions simply with:

```
def predict(alpha: float, beta: float, x_i: float) -> float:
    return beta * x_i + alpha
```

How do we choose `alpha` and `beta`? Well, any choice of `alpha` and `beta` gives us a predicted output for each input `x_i`. Since we know the actual output `y_i`, we can compute the error for each pair:

```
def error(alpha: float, beta: float, x_i: float, y_i: float) -> float:
    """
    The error from predicting beta * x_i + alpha
    when the actual value is y_i
    """
    return predict(alpha, beta, x_i) - y_i
```

What we'd really like to know is the total error over the entire dataset. But we don't want to just add the errors—if the prediction for `x_1` is too high and the prediction for `x_2` is too low, the errors may just cancel out.

So instead we add up the *squared* errors:

```
from scratch.linear_algebra import Vector

def sum_of_sqerrors(alpha: float, beta: float, x: Vector, y: Vector) -> float:
    return sum(error(alpha, beta, x_i, y_i) ** 2
               for x_i, y_i in zip(x, y))
```

The *least squares solution* is to choose the `alpha` and `beta` that make `sum_of_sqerrors` as small as possible.

Using calculus (or tedious algebra), the error-minimizing `alpha` and `beta` are given by:

```
from typing import Tuple
from scratch.linear_algebra import Vector
from scratch.statistics import correlation, standard_deviation, mean

def least_squares_fit(x: Vector, y: Vector) -> Tuple[float, float]:
    """
    Given two vectors x and y,
    find the least-squares values of alpha and beta
    """
    beta = correlation(x, y) * standard_deviation(y) / standard_deviation(x)
    alpha = mean(y) - beta * mean(x)
    return alpha, beta
```

Without going through the exact mathematics, let's think about why this might be a reasonable solution. The choice of `alpha` simply says that when we see the average value of the independent variable x, we predict the average value of the dependent variable y.

The choice of `beta` means that when the input value increases by `standard_devia`
`tion(x)`, the prediction then increases by `correlation(x, y)` * `standard_devia`
`tion(y)`. In the case where x and y are perfectly correlated, a one-standard-deviation
increase in x results in a one-standard-deviation-of-y increase in the prediction.
When they're perfectly anticorrelated, the increase in x results in a *decrease* in the
prediction. And when the correlation is 0, `beta` is 0, which means that changes in x
don't affect the prediction at all.

As usual, let's write a quick test for this:

```
x = [i for i in range(-100, 110, 10)]
y = [3 * i - 5 for i in x]

# Should find that y = 3x - 5
assert least_squares_fit(x, y) == (-5, 3)
```

Now it's easy to apply this to the outlierless data from Chapter 5:

```
from scratch.statistics import num_friends_good, daily_minutes_good

alpha, beta = least_squares_fit(num_friends_good, daily_minutes_good)
assert 22.9 < alpha < 23.0
assert 0.9 < beta < 0.905
```

This gives values of `alpha` = 22.95 and `beta` = 0.903. So our model says that we expect
a user with *n* friends to spend 22.95 + *n* * 0.903 minutes on the site each day. That is,
we predict that a user with no friends on DataSciencester would still spend about 23
minutes a day on the site. And for each additional friend, we expect a user to spend
almost a minute more on the site each day.

In Figure 14-1, we plot the prediction line to get a sense of how well the model fits the
observed data.

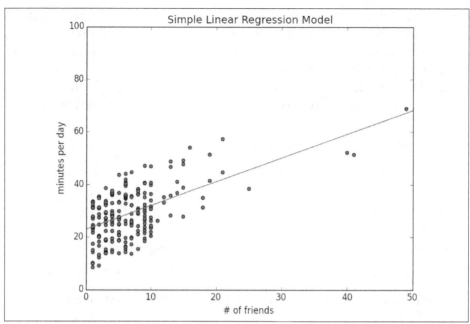

Figure 14-1. Our simple linear model

Of course, we need a better way to figure out how well we've fit the data than staring at the graph. A common measure is the *coefficient of determination* (or *R-squared*), which measures the fraction of the total variation in the dependent variable that is captured by the model:

```
from scratch.statistics import de_mean

def total_sum_of_squares(y: Vector) -> float:
    """the total squared variation of y_i's from their mean"""
    return sum(v ** 2 for v in de_mean(y))

def r_squared(alpha: float, beta: float, x: Vector, y: Vector) -> float:
    """
    the fraction of variation in y captured by the model, which equals
    1 - the fraction of variation in y not captured by the model
    """
    return 1.0 - (sum_of_sqerrors(alpha, beta, x, y) /
                      total_sum_of_squares(y))

rsq = r_squared(alpha, beta, num_friends_good, daily_minutes_good)
assert 0.328 < rsq < 0.330
```

Recall that we chose the `alpha` and `beta` that minimized the sum of the squared prediction errors. A linear model we could have chosen is "always predict `mean(y)`" (corresponding to `alpha` = mean(y) and `beta` = 0), whose sum of squared errors exactly equals its total sum of squares. This means an R-squared of 0, which indicates a model that (obviously, in this case) performs no better than just predicting the mean.

Clearly, the least squares model must be at least as good as that one, which means that the sum of the squared errors is *at most* the total sum of squares, which means that the R-squared must be at least 0. And the sum of squared errors must be at least 0, which means that the R-squared can be at most 1.

The higher the number, the better our model fits the data. Here we calculate an R-squared of 0.329, which tells us that our model is only sort of okay at fitting the data, and that clearly there are other factors at play.

Using Gradient Descent

If we write `theta = [alpha, beta]`, we can also solve this using gradient descent:

```
import random
import tqdm
from scratch.gradient_descent import gradient_step

num_epochs = 10000
random.seed(0)

guess = [random.random(), random.random()]  # choose random value to start

learning_rate = 0.00001

with tqdm.trange(num_epochs) as t:
    for _ in t:
        alpha, beta = guess

        # Partial derivative of loss with respect to alpha
        grad_a = sum(2 * error(alpha, beta, x_i, y_i)
                     for x_i, y_i in zip(num_friends_good,
                                         daily_minutes_good))

        # Partial derivative of loss with respect to beta
        grad_b = sum(2 * error(alpha, beta, x_i, y_i) * x_i
                     for x_i, y_i in zip(num_friends_good,
                                         daily_minutes_good))

        # Compute loss to stick in the tqdm description
        loss = sum_of_sqerrors(alpha, beta,
                               num_friends_good, daily_minutes_good)
        t.set_description(f"loss: {loss:.3f}")

        # Finally, update the guess
        guess = gradient_step(guess, [grad_a, grad_b], -learning_rate)

# We should get pretty much the same results:
```

```
    alpha, beta = guess
    assert 22.9 < alpha < 23.0
    assert 0.9 < beta < 0.905
```

If you run this you'll get the same values for `alpha` and `beta` as we did using the exact formula.

Maximum Likelihood Estimation

Why choose least squares? One justification involves *maximum likelihood estimation*. Imagine that we have a sample of data $v_1, ..., v_n$ that comes from a distribution that depends on some unknown parameter θ (theta):

$$p(v_1, ..., v_n | \theta)$$

If we didn't know θ, we could turn around and think of this quantity as the *likelihood* of θ given the sample:

$$L(\theta | v_1, ..., v_n)$$

Under this approach, the most likely θ is the value that maximizes this likelihood function—that is, the value that makes the observed data the most probable. In the case of a continuous distribution, in which we have a probability distribution function rather than a probability mass function, we can do the same thing.

Back to regression. One assumption that's often made about the simple regression model is that the regression errors are normally distributed with mean 0 and some (known) standard deviation σ. If that's the case, then the likelihood based on seeing a pair (x_i, y_i) is:

$$L(\alpha, \beta | x_i, y_i, \sigma) = \frac{1}{\sqrt{2\pi}\sigma} \exp\left(-(y_i - \alpha - \beta x_i)^2 / 2\sigma^2\right)$$

The likelihood based on the entire dataset is the product of the individual likelihoods, which is largest precisely when `alpha` and `beta` are chosen to minimize the sum of squared errors. That is, in this case (with these assumptions), minimizing the sum of squared errors is equivalent to maximizing the likelihood of the observed data.

For Further Exploration

Continue reading about multiple regression in Chapter 15!

Multiple Regression

I don't look at a problem and put variables in there that don't affect it.
—Bill Parcells

Although the VP is pretty impressed with your predictive model, she thinks you can do better. To that end, you've collected additional data: you know how many hours each of your users works each day, and whether they have a PhD. You'd like to use this additional data to improve your model.

Accordingly, you hypothesize a linear model with more independent variables:

$$\text{minutes} = \alpha + \beta_1 \text{friends} + \beta_2 \text{work hours} + \beta_3 \text{phd} + \varepsilon$$

Obviously, whether a user has a PhD is not a number—but, as we mentioned in Chapter 11, we can introduce a *dummy variable* that equals 1 for users with PhDs and 0 for users without, after which it's just as numeric as the other variables.

The Model

Recall that in Chapter 14 we fit a model of the form:

$$y_i = \alpha + \beta x_i + \varepsilon_i$$

Now imagine that each input x_i is not a single number but rather a vector of k numbers, $x_{i1}, ..., x_{ik}$. The multiple regression model assumes that:

$$y_i = \alpha + \beta_1 x_{i1} + \ldots + \beta_k x_{ik} + \varepsilon_i$$

In multiple regression the vector of parameters is usually called β. We'll want this to include the constant term as well, which we can achieve by adding a column of 1s to our data:

```
beta = [alpha, beta_1, ..., beta_k]
```

and:

```
x_i = [1, x_i1, ..., x_ik]
```

Then our model is just:

```
from scratch.linear_algebra import dot, Vector

def predict(x: Vector, beta: Vector) -> float:
    """assumes that the first element of x is 1"""
    return dot(x, beta)
```

In this particular case, our independent variable x will be a list of vectors, each of which looks like this:

```
[1,     # constant term
 49,    # number of friends
 4,     # work hours per day
 0]     # doesn't have PhD
```

Further Assumptions of the Least Squares Model

There are a couple of further assumptions that are required for this model (and our solution) to make sense.

The first is that the columns of *x* are *linearly independent*—that there's no way to write any one as a weighted sum of some of the others. If this assumption fails, it's impossible to estimate beta. To see this in an extreme case, imagine we had an extra field num_acquaintances in our data that for every user was exactly equal to num_friends.

Then, starting with any beta, if we add *any* amount to the num_friends coefficient and subtract that same amount from the num_acquaintances coefficient, the model's predictions will remain unchanged. This means that there's no way to find *the* coefficient for num_friends. (Usually violations of this assumption won't be so obvious.)

The second important assumption is that the columns of *x* are all uncorrelated with the errors ε. If this fails to be the case, our estimates of beta will be systematically wrong.

For instance, in Chapter 14, we built a model that predicted that each additional friend was associated with an extra 0.90 daily minutes on the site.

Imagine it's also the case that:

- People who work more hours spend less time on the site.

- People with more friends tend to work more hours.

That is, imagine that the "actual" model is:

$$minutes = \alpha + \beta_1 friends + \beta_2 work\ hours + \varepsilon$$

where β_2 is negative, and that work hours and friends are positively correlated. In that case, when we minimize the errors of the single-variable model:

$$minutes = \alpha + \beta_1 friends + \varepsilon$$

we will underestimate β_1.

Think about what would happen if we made predictions using the single-variable model with the "actual" value of β_1. (That is, the value that arises from minimizing the errors of what we called the "actual" model.) The predictions would tend to be way too large for users who work many hours and a little too large for users who work few hours, because $\beta_2 < 0$ and we "forgot" to include it. Because work hours is positively correlated with number of friends, this means the predictions tend to be way too large for users with many friends, and only slightly too large for users with few friends.

The result of this is that we can reduce the errors (in the single-variable model) by decreasing our estimate of β_1, which means that the error-minimizing β_1 is smaller than the "actual" value. That is, in this case the single-variable least squares solution is biased to underestimate β_1. And, in general, whenever the independent variables are correlated with the errors like this, our least squares solution will give us a biased estimate of β_1.

Fitting the Model

As we did in the simple linear model, we'll choose `beta` to minimize the sum of squared errors. Finding an exact solution is not simple to do by hand, which means we'll need to use gradient descent. Again we'll want to minimize the sum of the squared errors. The error function is almost identical to the one we used in Chapter 14, except that instead of expecting parameters [`alpha`, `beta`] it will take a vector of arbitrary length:

```
from typing import List

def error(x: Vector, y: float, beta: Vector) -> float:
    return predict(x, beta) - y
```

```
def squared_error(x: Vector, y: float, beta: Vector) -> float:
    return error(x, y, beta) ** 2

x = [1, 2, 3]
y = 30
beta = [4, 4, 4]  # so prediction = 4 + 8 + 12 = 24

assert error(x, y, beta) == -6
assert squared_error(x, y, beta) == 36
```

If you know calculus, it's easy to compute the gradient:

```
def sqerror_gradient(x: Vector, y: float, beta: Vector) -> Vector:
    err = error(x, y, beta)
    return [2 * err * x_i for x_i in x]

assert sqerror_gradient(x, y, beta) == [-12, -24, -36]
```

Otherwise, you'll need to take my word for it.

At this point, we're ready to find the optimal beta using gradient descent. Let's first write out a least_squares_fit function that can work with any dataset:

```
import random
import tqdm
from scratch.linear_algebra import vector_mean
from scratch.gradient_descent import gradient_step


def least_squares_fit(xs: List[Vector],
                      ys: List[float],
                      learning_rate: float = 0.001,
                      num_steps: int = 1000,
                      batch_size: int = 1) -> Vector:
    """
    Find the beta that minimizes the sum of squared errors
    assuming the model y = dot(x, beta).
    """
    # Start with a random guess
    guess = [random.random() for _ in xs[0]]

    for _ in tqdm.trange(num_steps, desc="least squares fit"):
        for start in range(0, len(xs), batch_size):
            batch_xs = xs[start:start+batch_size]
            batch_ys = ys[start:start+batch_size]

            gradient = vector_mean([sqerror_gradient(x, y, guess)
                                    for x, y in zip(batch_xs, batch_ys)])
            guess = gradient_step(guess, gradient, -learning_rate)

    return guess
```

We can then apply that to our data:

```
from scratch.statistics import daily_minutes_good
from scratch.gradient_descent import gradient_step

random.seed(0)
# I used trial and error to choose num_iters and step_size.
# This will run for a while.
learning_rate = 0.001

beta = least_squares_fit(inputs, daily_minutes_good, learning_rate, 5000, 25)
assert 30.50 < beta[0] < 30.70  # constant
assert  0.96 < beta[1] <  1.00  # num friends
assert -1.89 < beta[2] < -1.85  # work hours per day
assert  0.91 < beta[3] <  0.94  # has PhD
```

In practice, you wouldn't estimate a linear regression using gradient descent; you'd get the exact coefficients using linear algebra techniques that are beyond the scope of this book. If you did so, you'd find the equation:

$$\text{minutes} = 30.58 + 0.972 \text{ friends} - 1.87 \text{ work hours} + 0.923 \text{ phd}$$

which is pretty close to what we found.

Interpreting the Model

You should think of the coefficients of the model as representing all-else-being-equal estimates of the impacts of each factor. All else being equal, each additional friend corresponds to an extra minute spent on the site each day. All else being equal, each additional hour in a user's workday corresponds to about two fewer minutes spent on the site each day. All else being equal, having a PhD is associated with spending an extra minute on the site each day.

What this doesn't (directly) tell us is anything about the interactions among the variables. It's possible that the effect of work hours is different for people with many friends than it is for people with few friends. This model doesn't capture that. One way to handle this case is to introduce a new variable that is the *product* of "friends" and "work hours." This effectively allows the "work hours" coefficient to increase (or decrease) as the number of friends increases.

Or it's possible that the more friends you have, the more time you spend on the site *up to a point*, after which further friends cause you to spend less time on the site. (Perhaps with too many friends the experience is just too overwhelming?) We could try to capture this in our model by adding another variable that's the *square* of the number of friends.

Once we start adding variables, we need to worry about whether their coefficients "matter." There are no limits to the numbers of products, logs, squares, and higher powers we could add.

Goodness of Fit

Again we can look at the R-squared:

```
from scratch.simple_linear_regression import total_sum_of_squares

def multiple_r_squared(xs: List[Vector], ys: Vector, beta: Vector) -> float:
    sum_of_squared_errors = sum(error(x, y, beta) ** 2
                                for x, y in zip(xs, ys))
    return 1.0 - sum_of_squared_errors / total_sum_of_squares(ys)
```

which has now increased to 0.68:

```
assert 0.67 < multiple_r_squared(inputs, daily_minutes_good, beta) < 0.68
```

Keep in mind, however, that adding new variables to a regression will *necessarily* increase the R-squared. After all, the simple regression model is just the special case of the multiple regression model where the coefficients on "work hours" and "PhD" both equal 0. The optimal multiple regression model will necessarily have an error at least as small as that one.

Because of this, in a multiple regression, we also need to look at the *standard errors* of the coefficients, which measure how certain we are about our estimates of each β_i. The regression as a whole may fit our data very well, but if some of the independent variables are correlated (or irrelevant), their coefficients might not *mean* much.

The typical approach to measuring these errors starts with another assumption—that the errors ε_i are independent normal random variables with mean 0 and some shared (unknown) standard deviation σ. In that case, we (or, more likely, our statistical software) can use some linear algebra to find the standard error of each coefficient. The larger it is, the less sure our model is about that coefficient. Unfortunately, we're not set up to do that kind of linear algebra from scratch.

Digression: The Bootstrap

Imagine that we have a sample of n data points, generated by some (unknown to us) distribution:

```
data = get_sample(num_points=n)
```

In Chapter 5, we wrote a function that could compute the median of the sample, which we can use as an estimate of the median of the distribution itself.

But how confident can we be about our estimate? If all the data points in the sample are very close to 100, then it seems likely that the actual median is close to 100. If approximately half the data points in the sample are close to 0 and the other half are close to 200, then we can't be nearly as certain about the median.

If we could repeatedly get new samples, we could compute the medians of many samples and look at the distribution of those medians. Often we can't. In that case we can *bootstrap* new datasets by choosing *n* data points *with replacement* from our data. And then we can compute the medians of those synthetic datasets:

```
from typing import TypeVar, Callable

X = TypeVar('X')         # Generic type for data
Stat = TypeVar('Stat')   # Generic type for "statistic"

def bootstrap_sample(data: List[X]) -> List[X]:
    """randomly samples len(data) elements with replacement"""
    return [random.choice(data) for _ in data]

def bootstrap_statistic(data: List[X],
                        stats_fn: Callable[[List[X]], Stat],
                        num_samples: int) -> List[Stat]:
    """evaluates stats_fn on num_samples bootstrap samples from data"""
    return [stats_fn(bootstrap_sample(data)) for _ in range(num_samples)]
```

For example, consider the two following datasets:

```
# 101 points all very close to 100
close_to_100 = [99.5 + random.random() for _ in range(101)]

# 101 points, 50 of them near 0, 50 of them near 200
far_from_100 = ([99.5 + random.random()] +
                [random.random() for _ in range(50)] +
                [200 + random.random() for _ in range(50)])
```

If you compute the medians of the two datasets, both will be very close to 100. However, if you look at:

```
from scratch.statistics import median, standard_deviation

medians_close = bootstrap_statistic(close_to_100, median, 100)
```

you will mostly see numbers really close to 100. But if you look at:

```
medians_far = bootstrap_statistic(far_from_100, median, 100)
```

you will see a lot of numbers close to 0 and a lot of numbers close to 200.

The standard_deviation of the first set of medians is close to 0, while that of the second set of medians is close to 100:

```
assert standard_deviation(medians_close) < 1
assert standard_deviation(medians_far) > 90
```

(This extreme a case would be pretty easy to figure out by manually inspecting the data, but in general that won't be true.)

Standard Errors of Regression Coefficients

We can take the same approach to estimating the standard errors of our regression coefficients. We repeatedly take a `bootstrap_sample` of our data and estimate `beta` based on that sample. If the coefficient corresponding to one of the independent variables (say, `num_friends`) doesn't vary much across samples, then we can be confident that our estimate is relatively tight. If the coefficient varies greatly across samples, then we can't be at all confident in our estimate.

The only subtlety is that, before sampling, we'll need to `zip` our x data and y data to make sure that corresponding values of the independent and dependent variables are sampled together. This means that `bootstrap_sample` will return a list of pairs (`x_i`, `y_i`), which we'll need to reassemble into an `x_sample` and a `y_sample`:

```
from typing import Tuple

import datetime

def estimate_sample_beta(pairs: List[Tuple[Vector, float]]):
    x_sample = [x for x, _ in pairs]
    y_sample = [y for _, y in pairs]
    beta = least_squares_fit(x_sample, y_sample, learning_rate, 5000, 25)
    print("bootstrap sample", beta)
    return beta

random.seed(0) # so that you get the same results as me

# This will take a couple of minutes!
bootstrap_betas = bootstrap_statistic(list(zip(inputs, daily_minutes_good)),
                                      estimate_sample_beta,
                                      100)
```

After which we can estimate the standard deviation of each coefficient:

```
bootstrap_standard_errors = [
    standard_deviation([beta[i] for beta in bootstrap_betas])
    for i in range(4)]

print(bootstrap_standard_errors)

# [1.272,    # constant term, actual error = 1.19
#  0.103,    # num_friends,   actual error = 0.080
#  0.155,    # work_hours,    actual error = 0.127
#  1.249]    # phd,           actual error = 0.998
```

(We would likely get better estimates if we collected more than 100 samples and used more than 5,000 iterations to estimate each `beta`, but we don't have all day.)

We can use these to test hypotheses such as "does β_i equal 0?" Under the null hypothesis $\beta_i = 0$ (and with our other assumptions about the distribution of ε_i), the statistic:

$$t_j = \widehat{\beta_j}/\widehat{\sigma_j}$$

which is our estimate of β_j divided by our estimate of its standard error, follows a *Student's t-distribution* with "$n - k$ degrees of freedom."

If we had a `students_t_cdf` function, we could compute p-values for each least-squares coefficient to indicate how likely we would be to observe such a value if the actual coefficient were 0. Unfortunately, we don't have such a function. (Although we would if we weren't working from scratch.)

However, as the degrees of freedom get large, the t-distribution gets closer and closer to a standard normal. In a situation like this, where n is much larger than k, we can use `normal_cdf` and still feel good about ourselves:

```
from scratch.probability import normal_cdf

def p_value(beta_hat_j: float, sigma_hat_j: float) -> float:
    if beta_hat_j > 0:
        # if the coefficient is positive, we need to compute twice the
        # probability of seeing an even *larger* value
        return 2 * (1 - normal_cdf(beta_hat_j / sigma_hat_j))
    else:
        # otherwise twice the probability of seeing a *smaller* value
        return 2 * normal_cdf(beta_hat_j / sigma_hat_j)

assert p_value(30.58, 1.27)    < 0.001  # constant term
assert p_value(0.972, 0.103)   < 0.001  # num_friends
assert p_value(-1.865, 0.155) < 0.001  # work_hours
assert p_value(0.923, 1.249)  > 0.4     # phd
```

(In a situation *not* like this, we would probably be using statistical software that knows how to compute the t-distribution, as well as how to compute the exact standard errors.)

While most of the coefficients have very small p-values (suggesting that they are indeed nonzero), the coefficient for "PhD" is not "significantly" different from 0, which makes it likely that the coefficient for "PhD" is random rather than meaningful.

In more elaborate regression scenarios, you sometimes want to test more elaborate hypotheses about the data, such as "at least one of the β_j is nonzero" or "β_1 equals β_2 and β_3 equals β_4." You can do this with an *F-test*, but alas, that falls outside the scope of this book.

Regularization

In practice, you'd often like to apply linear regression to datasets with large numbers of variables. This creates a couple of extra wrinkles. First, the more variables you use, the more likely you are to overfit your model to the training set. And second, the more nonzero coefficients you have, the harder it is to make sense of them. If the goal is to *explain* some phenomenon, a sparse model with three factors might be more useful than a slightly better model with hundreds.

Regularization is an approach in which we add to the error term a penalty that gets larger as beta gets larger. We then minimize the combined error and penalty. The more importance we place on the penalty term, the more we discourage large coefficients.

For example, in *ridge regression*, we add a penalty proportional to the sum of the squares of the beta_i (except that typically we don't penalize beta_0, the constant term):

```python
# alpha is a *hyperparameter* controlling how harsh the penalty is.
# Sometimes it's called "lambda" but that already means something in Python.
def ridge_penalty(beta: Vector, alpha: float) -> float:
    return alpha * dot(beta[1:], beta[1:])

def squared_error_ridge(x: Vector,
                        y: float,
                        beta: Vector,
                        alpha: float) -> float:
    """estimate error plus ridge penalty on beta"""
    return error(x, y, beta) ** 2 + ridge_penalty(beta, alpha)
```

We can then plug this into gradient descent in the usual way:

```python
from scratch.linear_algebra import add

def ridge_penalty_gradient(beta: Vector, alpha: float) -> Vector:
    """gradient of just the ridge penalty"""
    return [0.] + [2 * alpha * beta_j for beta_j in beta[1:]]

def sqerror_ridge_gradient(x: Vector,
                           y: float,
                           beta: Vector,
                           alpha: float) -> Vector:
    """
    the gradient corresponding to the ith squared error term
    including the ridge penalty
    """
    return add(sqerror_gradient(x, y, beta),
               ridge_penalty_gradient(beta, alpha))
```

And then we just need to modify the `least_squares_fit` function to use the `sqerror_ridge_gradient` instead of `sqerror_gradient`. (I'm not going to repeat the code here.)

With `alpha` set to 0, there's no penalty at all and we get the same results as before:

```
random.seed(0)
beta_0 = least_squares_fit_ridge(inputs, daily_minutes_good, 0.0,  # alpha
                                 learning_rate, 5000, 25)
# [30.51, 0.97, -1.85, 0.91]
assert 5 < dot(beta_0[1:], beta_0[1:]) < 6
assert 0.67 < multiple_r_squared(inputs, daily_minutes_good, beta_0) < 0.69
```

As we increase `alpha`, the goodness of fit gets worse, but the size of `beta` gets smaller:

```
beta_0_1 = least_squares_fit_ridge(inputs, daily_minutes_good, 0.1,  # alpha
                                   learning_rate, 5000, 25)
# [30.8, 0.95, -1.83, 0.54]
assert 4 < dot(beta_0_1[1:], beta_0_1[1:]) < 5
assert 0.67 < multiple_r_squared(inputs, daily_minutes_good, beta_0_1) < 0.69

beta_1 = least_squares_fit_ridge(inputs, daily_minutes_good, 1,  # alpha
                                 learning_rate, 5000, 25)
# [30.6, 0.90, -1.68, 0.10]
assert 3 < dot(beta_1[1:], beta_1[1:]) < 4
assert 0.67 < multiple_r_squared(inputs, daily_minutes_good, beta_1) < 0.69

beta_10 = least_squares_fit_ridge(inputs, daily_minutes_good,10,  # alpha
                                  learning_rate, 5000, 25)
# [28.3, 0.67, -0.90, -0.01]
assert 1 < dot(beta_10[1:], beta_10[1:]) < 2
assert 0.5 < multiple_r_squared(inputs, daily_minutes_good, beta_10) < 0.6
```

In particular, the coefficient on "PhD" vanishes as we increase the penalty, which accords with our previous result that it wasn't significantly different from 0.

 Usually you'd want to rescale your data before using this approach. After all, if you changed years of experience to centuries of experience, its least squares coefficient would increase by a factor of 100 and suddenly get penalized much more, even though it's the same model.

Another approach is *lasso regression*, which uses the penalty:

```
def lasso_penalty(beta, alpha):
    return alpha * sum(abs(beta_i) for beta_i in beta[1:])
```

Whereas the ridge penalty shrank the coefficients overall, the lasso penalty tends to force coefficients to be 0, which makes it good for learning sparse models. Unfortunately, it's not amenable to gradient descent, which means that we won't be able to solve it from scratch.

For Further Exploration

- Regression has a rich and expansive theory behind it. This is another place where you should consider reading a textbook, or at least a lot of Wikipedia articles.

- scikit-learn has a `linear_model` module (*https://scikit-learn.org/stable/modules/linear_model.html*) that provides a `LinearRegression` model similar to ours, as well as ridge regression, lasso regression, and other types of regularization.

- Statsmodels (*https://www.statsmodels.org*) is another Python module that contains (among other things) linear regression models.

## CHAPTER 16

Logistic Regression

> *A lot of people say there's a fine line between genius and insanity. I don't think there's a fine line, I actually think there's a yawning gulf.*
>   —Bill Bailey

In Chapter 1, we briefly looked at the problem of trying to predict which DataSciencester users paid for premium accounts. Here we'll revisit that problem.

The Problem

We have an anonymized dataset of about 200 users, containing each user's salary, her years of experience as a data scientist, and whether she paid for a premium account (Figure 16-1). As is typical with categorical variables, we represent the dependent variable as either 0 (no premium account) or 1 (premium account).

As usual, our data is a list of rows [experience, salary, paid_account]. Let's turn it into the format we need:

```
xs = [[1.0] + row[:2] for row in data]   # [1, experience, salary]
ys = [row[2] for row in data]            # paid_account
```

An obvious first attempt is to use linear regression and find the best model:

$$\text{paid account} = \beta_0 + \beta_1 \text{experience} + \beta_2 \text{salary} + \varepsilon$$

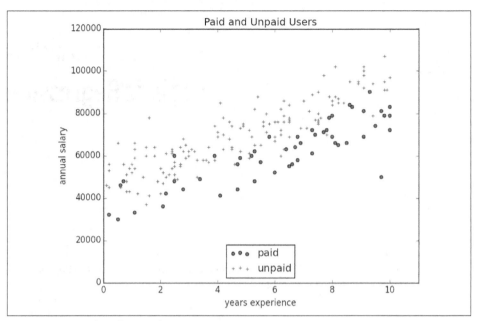

Figure 16-1. Paid and unpaid users

And certainly, there's nothing preventing us from modeling the problem this way. The results are shown in Figure 16-2:

```
from matplotlib import pyplot as plt
from scratch.working_with_data import rescale
from scratch.multiple_regression import least_squares_fit, predict
from scratch.gradient_descent import gradient_step

learning_rate = 0.001
rescaled_xs = rescale(xs)
beta = least_squares_fit(rescaled_xs, ys, learning_rate, 1000, 1)
# [0.26, 0.43, -0.43]
predictions = [predict(x_i, beta) for x_i in rescaled_xs]

plt.scatter(predictions, ys)
plt.xlabel("predicted")
plt.ylabel("actual")
plt.show()
```

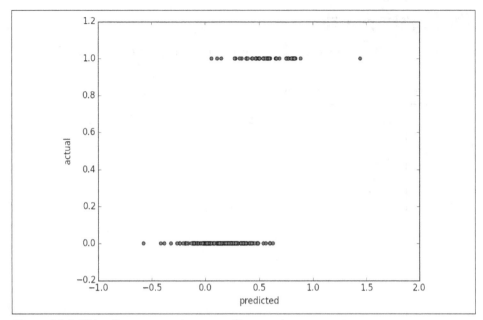

Figure 16-2. Using linear regression to predict premium accounts

But this approach leads to a couple of immediate problems:

- We'd like for our predicted outputs to be 0 or 1, to indicate class membership. It's fine if they're between 0 and 1, since we can interpret these as probabilities—an output of 0.25 could mean 25% chance of being a paid member. But the outputs of the linear model can be huge positive numbers or even negative numbers, which it's not clear how to interpret. Indeed, here a lot of our predictions were negative.

- The linear regression model assumed that the errors were uncorrelated with the columns of x. But here, the regression coefficient for `experience` is 0.43, indicating that more experience leads to a greater likelihood of a premium account. This means that our model outputs very large values for people with lots of experience. But we know that the actual values must be at most 1, which means that necessarily very large outputs (and therefore very large values of `experience`) correspond to very large negative values of the error term. Because this is the case, our estimate of `beta` is biased.

What we'd like instead is for large positive values of `dot(x_i, beta)` to correspond to probabilities close to 1, and for large negative values to correspond to probabilities close to 0. We can accomplish this by applying another function to the result.

The Logistic Function

In the case of logistic regression, we use the *logistic function*, pictured in Figure 16-3:

```python
def logistic(x: float) -> float:
    return 1.0 / (1 + math.exp(-x))
```

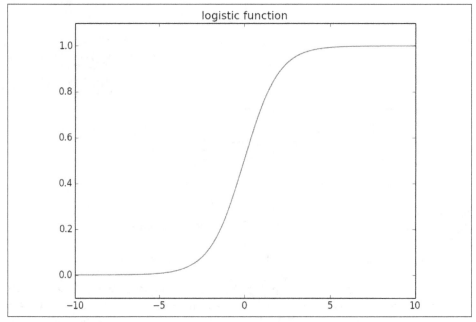

Figure 16-3. The logistic function

As its input gets large and positive, it gets closer and closer to 1. As its input gets large and negative, it gets closer and closer to 0. Additionally, it has the convenient property that its derivative is given by:

```python
def logistic_prime(x: float) -> float:
    y = logistic(x)
    return y * (1 - y)
```

which we'll make use of in a bit. We'll use this to fit a model:

$$y_i = f(x_i\beta) + \varepsilon_i$$

where *f* is the `logistic` function.

Recall that for linear regression we fit the model by minimizing the sum of squared errors, which ended up choosing the β that maximized the likelihood of the data.

Here the two aren't equivalent, so we'll use gradient descent to maximize the likelihood directly. This means we need to calculate the likelihood function and its gradient.

Given some β, our model says that each y_i should equal 1 with probability $f(x_i\beta)$ and 0 with probability $1 - f(x_i\beta)$.

In particular, the PDF for y_i can be written as:

$$p(y_i|x_i, \beta) = f(x_i\beta)^{y_i}(1 - f(x_i\beta))^{1-y_i}$$

since if y_i is 0, this equals:

$$1 - f(x_i\beta)$$

and if y_i is 1, it equals:

$$f(x_i\beta)$$

It turns out that it's actually simpler to maximize the *log likelihood*:

$$\log L(\beta|x_i, y_i) = y_i \log f(x_i\beta) + (1 - y_i) \log (1 - f(x_i\beta))$$

Because log is a strictly increasing function, any `beta` that maximizes the log likelihood also maximizes the likelihood, and vice versa. Because gradient descent minimizes things, we'll actually work with the *negative* log likelihood, since maximizing the likelihood is the same as minimizing its negative:

```python
import math
from scratch.linear_algebra import Vector, dot

def _negative_log_likelihood(x: Vector, y: float, beta: Vector) -> float:
    """The negative log likelihood for one data point"""
    if y == 1:
        return -math.log(logistic(dot(x, beta)))
    else:
        return -math.log(1 - logistic(dot(x, beta)))
```

If we assume different data points are independent from one another, the overall likelihood is just the product of the individual likelihoods. That means the overall log likelihood is the sum of the individual log likelihoods:

```python
from typing import List
```

```
def negative_log_likelihood(xs: List[Vector],
                            ys: List[float],
                            beta: Vector) -> float:
    return sum(_negative_log_likelihood(x, y, beta)
              for x, y in zip(xs, ys))
```

A little bit of calculus gives us the gradient:

```
from scratch.linear_algebra import vector_sum

def _negative_log_partial_j(x: Vector, y: float, beta: Vector, j: int) -> float:
    """
    The jth partial derivative for one data point.
    Here i is the index of the data point.
    """
    return -(y - logistic(dot(x, beta))) * x[j]

def _negative_log_gradient(x: Vector, y: float, beta: Vector) -> Vector:
    """
    The gradient for one data point.
    """
    return [_negative_log_partial_j(x, y, beta, j)
            for j in range(len(beta))]

def negative_log_gradient(xs: List[Vector],
                          ys: List[float],
                          beta: Vector) -> Vector:
    return vector_sum([_negative_log_gradient(x, y, beta)
                       for x, y in zip(xs, ys)])
```

at which point we have all the pieces we need.

Applying the Model

We'll want to split our data into a training set and a test set:

```
from scratch.machine_learning import train_test_split
import random
import tqdm

random.seed(0)
x_train, x_test, y_train, y_test = train_test_split(rescaled_xs, ys, 0.33)

learning_rate = 0.01

# pick a random starting point
beta = [random.random() for _ in range(3)]

with tqdm.trange(5000) as t:
    for epoch in t:
        gradient = negative_log_gradient(x_train, y_train, beta)
        beta = gradient_step(beta, gradient, -learning_rate)
```

```
loss = negative_log_likelihood(x_train, y_train, beta)
t.set_description(f"loss: {loss:.3f} beta: {beta}")
```

after which we find that `beta` is approximately:

```
[-2.0, 4.7, -4.5]
```

These are coefficients for the `rescaled` data, but we can transform them back to the original data as well:

```
from scratch.working_with_data import scale

means, stdevs = scale(xs)
beta_unscaled = [(beta[0]
                  - beta[1] * means[1] / stdevs[1]
                  - beta[2] * means[2] / stdevs[2]),
                 beta[1] / stdevs[1],
                 beta[2] / stdevs[2]]
# [8.9, 1.6, -0.000288]
```

Unfortunately, these are not as easy to interpret as linear regression coefficients. All else being equal, an extra year of experience adds 1.6 to the input of `logistic`. All else being equal, an extra $10,000 of salary subtracts 2.88 from the input of `logistic`.

The impact on the output, however, depends on the other inputs as well. If `dot(beta, x_i)` is already large (corresponding to a probability close to 1), increasing it even by a lot cannot affect the probability very much. If it's close to 0, increasing it just a little might increase the probability quite a bit.

What we can say is that—all else being equal—people with more experience are more likely to pay for accounts. And that—all else being equal—people with higher salaries are less likely to pay for accounts. (This was also somewhat apparent when we plotted the data.)

Goodness of Fit

We haven't yet used the test data that we held out. Let's see what happens if we predict *paid account* whenever the probability exceeds 0.5:

```
true_positives = false_positives = true_negatives = false_negatives = 0

for x_i, y_i in zip(x_test, y_test):
    prediction = logistic(dot(beta, x_i))

    if y_i == 1 and prediction >= 0.5:  # TP: paid and we predict paid
        true_positives += 1
    elif y_i == 1:                      # FN: paid and we predict unpaid
        false_negatives += 1
    elif prediction >= 0.5:            # FP: unpaid and we predict paid
        false_positives += 1
    else:                              # TN: unpaid and we predict unpaid
```

```
        true_negatives += 1

    precision = true_positives / (true_positives + false_positives)
    recall = true_positives / (true_positives + false_negatives)
```

This gives a precision of 75% ("when we predict *paid account* we're right 75% of the time") and a recall of 80% ("when a user has a paid account we predict *paid account* 80% of the time"), which is not terrible considering how little data we have.

We can also plot the predictions versus the actuals (Figure 16-4), which also shows that the model performs well:

```
predictions = [logistic(dot(beta, x_i)) for x_i in x_test]
plt.scatter(predictions, y_test, marker='+')
plt.xlabel("predicted probability")
plt.ylabel("actual outcome")
plt.title("Logistic Regression Predicted vs. Actual")
plt.show()
```

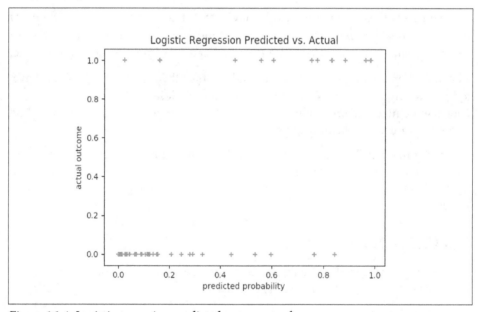

Figure 16-4. Logistic regression predicted versus actual

Support Vector Machines

The set of points where dot(beta, x_i) equals 0 is the boundary between our classes. We can plot this to see exactly what our model is doing (Figure 16-5).

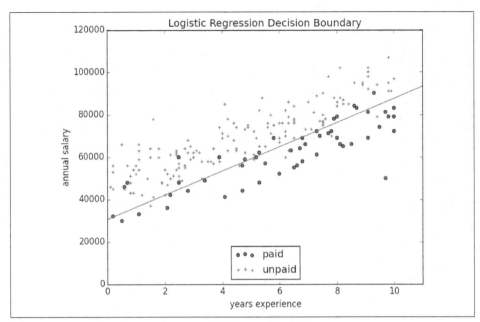

Figure 16-5. Paid and unpaid users with decision boundary

This boundary is a *hyperplane* that splits the parameter space into two half-spaces corresponding to *predict paid* and *predict unpaid*. We found it as a side effect of finding the most likely logistic model.

An alternative approach to classification is to just look for the hyperplane that "best" separates the classes in the training data. This is the idea behind the *support vector machine*, which finds the hyperplane that maximizes the distance to the nearest point in each class (Figure 16-6).

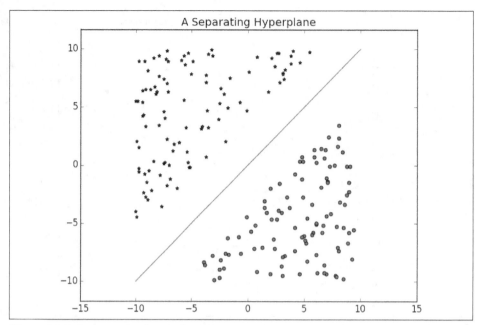

Figure 16-6. A separating hyperplane

Finding such a hyperplane is an optimization problem that involves techniques that are too advanced for us. A different problem is that a separating hyperplane might not exist at all. In our "who pays?" dataset there simply is no line that perfectly separates the paid users from the unpaid users.

We can sometimes get around this by transforming the data into a higher-dimensional space. For example, consider the simple one-dimensional dataset shown in Figure 16-7.

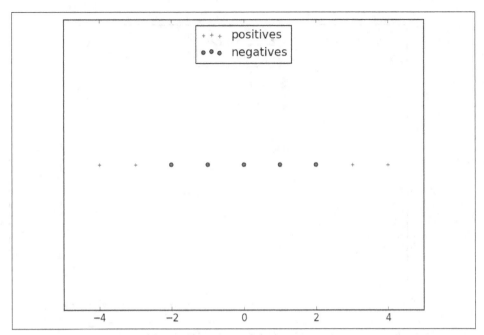

Figure 16-7. A nonseparable one-dimensional dataset

It's clear that there's no hyperplane that separates the positive examples from the negative ones. However, look at what happens when we map this dataset to two dimensions by sending the point x to (x, x**2). Suddenly it's possible to find a hyperplane that splits the data (Figure 16-8).

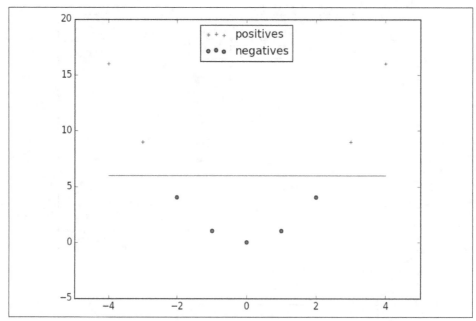

Figure 16-8. Dataset becomes separable in higher dimensions

This is usually called the *kernel trick* because rather than actually mapping the points into the higher-dimensional space (which could be expensive if there are a lot of points and the mapping is complicated), we can use a "kernel" function to compute dot products in the higher-dimensional space and use those to find a hyperplane.

It's hard (and probably not a good idea) to *use* support vector machines without relying on specialized optimization software written by people with the appropriate expertise, so we'll have to leave our treatment here.

For Further Investigation

- scikit-learn has modules for both logistic regression (*https://scikit-learn.org/ stable/modules/linear_model.html#logistic-regression*) and support vector machines (*https://scikit-learn.org/stable/modules/svm.html*).

- LIBSVM (*https://www.csie.ntu.edu.tw/~cjlin/libsvm/*) is the support vector machine implementation that scikit-learn is using behind the scenes. Its website has a variety of useful documentation about support vector machines.

## CHAPTER 17

Decision Trees

A tree is an incomprehensible mystery.
—Jim Woodring

DataSciencester's VP of Talent has interviewed a number of job candidates from the site, with varying degrees of success. He's collected a dataset consisting of several (qualitative) attributes of each candidate, as well as whether that candidate interviewed well or poorly. Could you, he asks, use this data to build a model identifying which candidates will interview well, so that he doesn't have to waste time conducting interviews?

This seems like a good fit for a *decision tree*, another predictive modeling tool in the data scientist's kit.

What Is a Decision Tree?

A decision tree uses a tree structure to represent a number of possible *decision paths* and an outcome for each path.

If you have ever played the game Twenty Questions (*http://en.wikipedia.org/wiki/ Twenty_Questions*), then you are familiar with decision trees. For example:

- "I am thinking of an animal."
- "Does it have more than five legs?"
- "No."
- "Is it delicious?"
- "No."
- "Does it appear on the back of the Australian five-cent coin?"

- "Yes."
- "Is it an echidna?"
- "Yes, it is!"

This corresponds to the path:

"Not more than 5 legs" → "Not delicious" → "On the 5-cent coin" → "Echidna!"

in an idiosyncratic (and not very comprehensive) "guess the animal" decision tree (Figure 17-1).

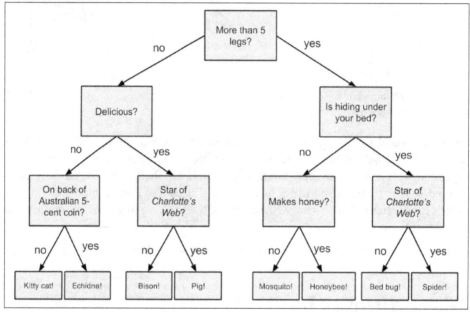

Figure 17-1. A "guess the animal" decision tree

Decision trees have a lot to recommend them. They're very easy to understand and interpret, and the process by which they reach a prediction is completely transparent. Unlike the other models we've looked at so far, decision trees can easily handle a mix of numeric (e.g., number of legs) and categorical (e.g., delicious/not delicious) attributes and can even classify data for which attributes are missing.

At the same time, finding an "optimal" decision tree for a set of training data is computationally a very hard problem. (We will get around this by trying to build a good-enough tree rather than an optimal one, although for large datasets this can still be a lot of work.) More important, it is very easy (and very bad) to build decision trees that are *overfitted* to the training data, and that don't generalize well to unseen data. We'll look at ways to address this.

Most people divide decision trees into *classification trees* (which produce categorical outputs) and *regression trees* (which produce numeric outputs). In this chapter, we'll focus on classification trees, and we'll work through the ID3 algorithm for learning a decision tree from a set of labeled data, which should help us understand how decision trees actually work. To make things simple, we'll restrict ourselves to problems with binary outputs like "Should I hire this candidate?" or "Should I show this website visitor advertisement A or advertisement B?" or "Will eating this food I found in the office fridge make me sick?"

Entropy

In order to build a decision tree, we will need to decide what questions to ask and in what order. At each stage of the tree there are some possibilities we've eliminated and some that we haven't. After learning that an animal doesn't have more than five legs, we've eliminated the possibility that it's a grasshopper. We haven't eliminated the possibility that it's a duck. Each possible question partitions the remaining possibilities according to its answer.

Ideally, we'd like to choose questions whose answers give a lot of information about what our tree should predict. If there's a single yes/no question for which "yes" answers always correspond to True outputs and "no" answers to False outputs (or vice versa), this would be an awesome question to pick. Conversely, a yes/no question for which neither answer gives you much new information about what the prediction should be is probably not a good choice.

We capture this notion of "how much information" with *entropy*. You have probably heard this term used to mean disorder. We use it to represent the uncertainty associated with data.

Imagine that we have a set S of data, each member of which is labeled as belonging to one of a finite number of classes $C_1, ..., C_n$. If all the data points belong to a single class, then there is no real uncertainty, which means we'd like there to be low entropy. If the data points are evenly spread across the classes, there is a lot of uncertainty and we'd like there to be high entropy.

In math terms, if p_i is the proportion of data labeled as class c_i, we define the entropy as:

$$H(S) = -p_1 \log_2 p_1 - ... - p_n \log_2 p_n$$

with the (standard) convention that $0 \log 0 = 0$.

Without worrying too much about the grisly details, each term $-p_i \log_2 p_i$ is non-negative and is close to 0 precisely when p_i is either close to 0 or close to 1 (Figure 17-2).

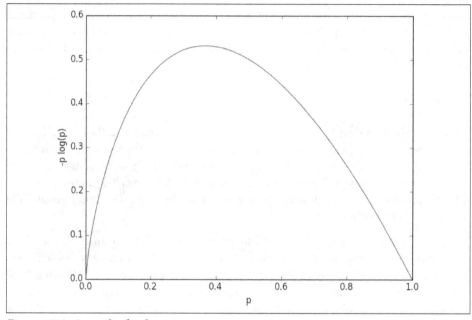

Figure 17-2. A graph of -p log p

This means the entropy will be small when every p_i is close to 0 or 1 (i.e., when most of the data is in a single class), and it will be larger when many of the p_i's are not close to 0 (i.e., when the data is spread across multiple classes). This is exactly the behavior we desire.

It is easy enough to roll all of this into a function:

```
from typing import List
import math

def entropy(class_probabilities: List[float]) -> float:
    """Given a list of class probabilities, compute the entropy"""
    return sum(-p * math.log(p, 2)
               for p in class_probabilities
               if p > 0)                        # ignore zero probabilities

assert entropy([1.0]) == 0
assert entropy([0.5, 0.5]) == 1
assert 0.81 < entropy([0.25, 0.75]) < 0.82
```

Our data will consist of pairs (input, label), which means that we'll need to compute the class probabilities ourselves. Notice that we don't actually care which label is associated with each probability, only what the probabilities are:

```
from typing import Any
from collections import Counter

def class_probabilities(labels: List[Any]) -> List[float]:
    total_count = len(labels)
    return [count / total_count
            for count in Counter(labels).values()]

def data_entropy(labels: List[Any]) -> float:
    return entropy(class_probabilities(labels))

assert data_entropy(['a']) == 0
assert data_entropy([True, False]) == 1
assert data_entropy([3, 4, 4, 4]) == entropy([0.25, 0.75])
```

The Entropy of a Partition

What we've done so far is compute the entropy (think "uncertainty") of a single set of labeled data. Now, each stage of a decision tree involves asking a question whose answer partitions data into one or (hopefully) more subsets. For instance, our "does it have more than five legs?" question partitions animals into those that have more than five legs (e.g., spiders) and those that don't (e.g., echidnas).

Correspondingly, we'd like some notion of the entropy that results from partitioning a set of data in a certain way. We want a partition to have low entropy if it splits the data into subsets that themselves have low entropy (i.e., are highly certain), and high entropy if it contains subsets that (are large and) have high entropy (i.e., are highly uncertain).

For example, my "Australian five-cent coin" question was pretty dumb (albeit pretty lucky!), as it partitioned the remaining animals at that point into S_1 = {echidna} and S_2 = {everything else}, where S_2 is both large and high-entropy. (S_1 has no entropy, but it represents a small fraction of the remaining "classes.")

Mathematically, if we partition our data S into subsets $S_1, ..., S_m$ containing proportions $q_1, ..., q_m$ of the data, then we compute the entropy of the partition as a weighted sum:

$$H = q_1 H(S_1) + ... + q_m H(S_m)$$

which we can implement as:

```
def partition_entropy(subsets: List[List[Any]]) -> float:
    """Returns the entropy from this partition of data into subsets"""
    total_count = sum(len(subset) for subset in subsets)

    return sum(data_entropy(subset) * len(subset) / total_count
               for subset in subsets)
```

 One problem with this approach is that partitioning by an attribute with many different values will result in a very low entropy due to overfitting. For example, imagine you work for a bank and are trying to build a decision tree to predict which of your customers are likely to default on their mortgages, using some historical data as your training set. Imagine further that the dataset contains each customer's Social Security number. Partitioning on SSN will produce one-person subsets, each of which necessarily has zero entropy. But a model that relies on SSN is *certain* not to generalize beyond the training set. For this reason, you should probably try to avoid (or bucket, if appropriate) attributes with large numbers of possible values when creating decision trees.

Creating a Decision Tree

The VP provides you with the interviewee data, consisting of (per your specification) a NamedTuple of the relevant attributes for each candidate—her level, her preferred language, whether she is active on Twitter, whether she has a PhD, and whether she interviewed well:

```
from typing import NamedTuple, Optional

class Candidate(NamedTuple):
    level: str
    lang: str
    tweets: bool
    phd: bool
    did_well: Optional[bool] = None  # allow unlabeled data

                  # level      lang     tweets   phd   did_well
inputs = [Candidate('Senior', 'Java',   False, False, False),
          Candidate('Senior', 'Java',   False, True,  False),
          Candidate('Mid',    'Python', False, False, True),
          Candidate('Junior', 'Python', False, False, True),
          Candidate('Junior', 'R',      True,  False, True),
          Candidate('Junior', 'R',      True,  True,  False),
          Candidate('Mid',    'R',      True,  True,  True),
          Candidate('Senior', 'Python', False, False, False),
          Candidate('Senior', 'R',      True,  False, True),
          Candidate('Junior', 'Python', True,  False, True),
          Candidate('Senior', 'Python', True,  True,  True),
          Candidate('Mid',    'Python', False, True,  True),
```

```
        Candidate('Mid',    'Java',   True,  False, True),
        Candidate('Junior', 'Python', False, True,  False)
    ]
```

Our tree will consist of *decision nodes* (which ask a question and direct us differently depending on the answer) and *leaf nodes* (which give us a prediction). We will build it using the relatively simple *ID3* algorithm, which operates in the following manner. Let's say we're given some labeled data, and a list of attributes to consider branching on:

- If the data all have the same label, create a leaf node that predicts that label and then stop.
- If the list of attributes is empty (i.e., there are no more possible questions to ask), create a leaf node that predicts the most common label and then stop.
- Otherwise, try partitioning the data by each of the attributes.
- Choose the partition with the lowest partition entropy.
- Add a decision node based on the chosen attribute.
- Recur on each partitioned subset using the remaining attributes.

This is what's known as a "greedy" algorithm because, at each step, it chooses the most immediately best option. Given a dataset, there may be a better tree with a worse-looking first move. If so, this algorithm won't find it. Nonetheless, it is relatively easy to understand and implement, which makes it a good place to begin exploring decision trees.

Let's manually go through these steps on the interviewee dataset. The dataset has both True and False labels, and we have four attributes we can split on. So our first step will be to find the partition with the least entropy. We'll start by writing a function that does the partitioning:

```
from typing import Dict, TypeVar
from collections import defaultdict

T = TypeVar('T')  # generic type for inputs

def partition_by(inputs: List[T], attribute: str) -> Dict[Any, List[T]]:
    """Partition the inputs into lists based on the specified attribute."""
    partitions: Dict[Any, List[T]] = defaultdict(list)
    for input in inputs:
        key = getattr(input, attribute)  # value of the specified attribute
        partitions[key].append(input)    # add input to the correct partition
    return partitions
```

and one that uses it to compute entropy:

```
def partition_entropy_by(inputs: List[Any],
                         attribute: str,
```

```
                      label_attribute: str) -> float:
    """Compute the entropy corresponding to the given partition"""
    # partitions consist of our inputs
    partitions = partition_by(inputs, attribute)

    # but partition_entropy needs just the class labels
    labels = [[getattr(input, label_attribute) for input in partition]
              for partition in partitions.values()]

    return partition_entropy(labels)
```

Then we just need to find the minimum-entropy partition for the whole dataset:

```
for key in ['level','lang','tweets','phd']:
    print(key, partition_entropy_by(inputs, key, 'did_well'))

assert 0.69 < partition_entropy_by(inputs, 'level', 'did_well')  < 0.70
assert 0.86 < partition_entropy_by(inputs, 'lang', 'did_well')   < 0.87
assert 0.78 < partition_entropy_by(inputs, 'tweets', 'did_well') < 0.79
assert 0.89 < partition_entropy_by(inputs, 'phd', 'did_well')    < 0.90
```

The lowest entropy comes from splitting on level, so we'll need to make a subtree
for each possible level value. Every Mid candidate is labeled True, which means that
the Mid subtree is simply a leaf node predicting True. For Senior candidates, we have
a mix of Trues and Falses, so we need to split again:

```
senior_inputs = [input for input in inputs if input.level == 'Senior']

assert 0.4 == partition_entropy_by(senior_inputs, 'lang', 'did_well')
assert 0.0 == partition_entropy_by(senior_inputs, 'tweets', 'did_well')
assert 0.95 < partition_entropy_by(senior_inputs, 'phd', 'did_well') < 0.96
```

This shows us that our next split should be on tweets, which results in a zero-
entropy partition. For these Senior-level candidates, "yes" tweets always result in
True while "no" tweets always result in False.

Finally, if we do the same thing for the Junior candidates, we end up splitting on phd,
after which we find that no PhD always results in True and PhD always results in
False.

Figure 17-3 shows the complete decision tree.

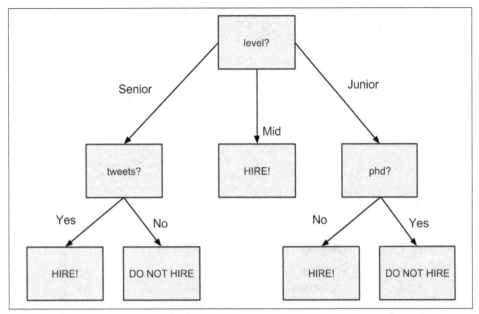

Figure 17-3. The decision tree for hiring

Putting It All Together

Now that we've seen how the algorithm works, we would like to implement it more generally. This means we need to decide how we want to represent trees. We'll use pretty much the most lightweight representation possible. We define a *tree* to be either:

- a Leaf (that predicts a single value), or
- a Split (containing an attribute to split on, subtrees for specific values of that attribute, and possibly a default value to use if we see an unknown value).

```python
from typing import NamedTuple, Union, Any

class Leaf(NamedTuple):
    value: Any

class Split(NamedTuple):
    attribute: str
    subtrees: dict
    default_value: Any = None

DecisionTree = Union[Leaf, Split]
```

With this representation, our hiring tree would look like:

```
hiring_tree = Split('level', {        # first, consider "level"
    'Junior': Split('phd', {          # if level is "Junior", next look at "phd"
        False: Leaf(True),            #   if "phd" is False, predict True
        True: Leaf(False)             #   if "phd" is True, predict False
    }),
    'Mid': Leaf(True),                # if level is "Mid", just predict True
    'Senior': Split('tweets', {       # if level is "Senior", look at "tweets"
        False: Leaf(False),           #   if "tweets" is False, predict False
        True: Leaf(True)              #   if "tweets" is True, predict True
    })
})
```

There's still the question of what to do if we encounter an unexpected (or missing) attribute value. What should our hiring tree do if it encounters a candidate whose level is Intern? We'll handle this case by populating the default_value attribute with the most common label.

Given such a representation, we can classify an input with:

```
def classify(tree: DecisionTree, input: Any) -> Any:
    """classify the input using the given decision tree"""

    # If this is a leaf node, return its value
    if isinstance(tree, Leaf):
        return tree.value

    # Otherwise this tree consists of an attribute to split on
    # and a dictionary whose keys are values of that attribute
    # and whose values are subtrees to consider next
    subtree_key = getattr(input, tree.attribute)

    if subtree_key not in tree.subtrees:    # If no subtree for key,
        return tree.default_value           # return the default value.

    subtree = tree.subtrees[subtree_key]    # Choose the appropriate subtree
    return classify(subtree, input)         # and use it to classify the input.
```

All that's left is to build the tree representation from our training data:

```
def build_tree_id3(inputs: List[Any],
                   split_attributes: List[str],
                   target_attribute: str) -> DecisionTree:
    # Count target labels
    label_counts = Counter(getattr(input, target_attribute)
                           for input in inputs)
    most_common_label = label_counts.most_common(1)[0][0]

    # If there's a unique label, predict it
    if len(label_counts) == 1:
        return Leaf(most_common_label)

    # If no split attributes left, return the majority label
    if not split_attributes:
```

```
        return Leaf(most_common_label)

    # Otherwise split by the best attribute

    def split_entropy(attribute: str) -> float:
        """Helper function for finding the best attribute"""
        return partition_entropy_by(inputs, attribute, target_attribute)

    best_attribute = min(split_attributes, key=split_entropy)

    partitions = partition_by(inputs, best_attribute)
    new_attributes = [a for a in split_attributes if a != best_attribute]

    # Recursively build the subtrees
    subtrees = {attribute_value : build_tree_id3(subset,
                                                 new_attributes,
                                                 target_attribute)
                for attribute_value, subset in partitions.items()}

    return Split(best_attribute, subtrees, default_value=most_common_label)
```

In the tree we built, every leaf consisted entirely of `True` inputs or entirely of `False` inputs. This means that the tree predicts perfectly on the training dataset. But we can also apply it to new data that wasn't in the training set:

```
tree = build_tree_id3(inputs,
                      ['level', 'lang', 'tweets', 'phd'],
                      'did_well')

# Should predict True
assert classify(tree, Candidate("Junior", "Java", True, False))

# Should predict False
assert not classify(tree, Candidate("Junior", "Java", True, True))
```

And also to data with unexpected values:

```
# Should predict True
assert classify(tree, Candidate("Intern", "Java", True, True))
```

 Since our goal was mainly to demonstrate *how* to build a tree, we built the tree using the entire dataset. As always, if we were really trying to create a good model for something, we would have collected more data and split it into train/validation/test subsets.

Random Forests

Given how closely decision trees can fit themselves to their training data, it's not surprising that they have a tendency to overfit. One way of avoiding this is a technique called *random forests*, in which we build multiple decision trees and combine their outputs. If they're classification trees, we might let them vote; if they're regression trees, we might average their predictions.

Our tree-building process was deterministic, so how do we get random trees?

One piece involves bootstrapping data (recall "Digression: The Bootstrap" on page 196). Rather than training each tree on all the inputs in the training set, we train each tree on the result of bootstrap_sample(inputs). Since each tree is built using different data, each tree will be different from every other tree. (A side benefit is that it's totally fair to use the nonsampled data to test each tree, which means you can get away with using all of your data as the training set if you are clever in how you measure performance.) This technique is known as *bootstrap aggregating* or *bagging*.

A second source of randomness involves changing the way we choose the best_attribute to split on. Rather than looking at all the remaining attributes, we first choose a random subset of them and then split on whichever of those is best:

```
# if there are already few enough split candidates, look at all of them
if len(split_candidates) <= self.num_split_candidates:
    sampled_split_candidates = split_candidates
# otherwise pick a random sample
else:
    sampled_split_candidates = random.sample(split_candidates,
                                             self.num_split_candidates)

# now choose the best attribute only from those candidates
best_attribute = min(sampled_split_candidates, key=split_entropy)

partitions = partition_by(inputs, best_attribute)
```

This is an example of a broader technique called *ensemble learning* in which we combine several *weak learners* (typically high-bias, low-variance models) in order to produce an overall strong model.

For Further Exploration

- scikit-learn has many decision tree (*https://scikit-learn.org/stable/modules/tree.html*) models. It also has an ensemble (*https://scikit-learn.org/stable/modules/classes.html#module-sklearn.ensemble*) module that includes a RandomForestClassifier as well as other ensemble methods.

- XGBoost (*https://xgboost.ai/*) is a library for training *gradient boosted* decision trees that tends to win a lot of Kaggle-style machine learning competitions.

- We've barely scratched the surface of decision trees and their algorithms. Wikipedia (*https://en.wikipedia.org/wiki/Decision_tree_learning*) is a good starting point for broader exploration.

## CHAPTER 18

Neural Networks

I like nonsense; it wakes up the brain cells.
—Dr. Seuss

An *artificial neural network* (or neural network for short) is a predictive model motivated by the way the brain operates. Think of the brain as a collection of neurons wired together. Each neuron looks at the outputs of the other neurons that feed into it, does a calculation, and then either fires (if the calculation exceeds some threshold) or doesn't (if it doesn't).

Accordingly, artificial neural networks consist of artificial neurons, which perform similar calculations over their inputs. Neural networks can solve a wide variety of problems like handwriting recognition and face detection, and they are used heavily in deep learning, one of the trendiest subfields of data science. However, most neural networks are "black boxes"—inspecting their details doesn't give you much understanding of *how* they're solving a problem. And large neural networks can be difficult to train. For most problems you'll encounter as a budding data scientist, they're probably not the right choice. Someday, when you're trying to build an artificial intelligence to bring about the Singularity, they very well might be.

Perceptrons

Pretty much the simplest neural network is the *perceptron*, which approximates a single neuron with n binary inputs. It computes a weighted sum of its inputs and "fires" if that weighted sum is 0 or greater:

```
from scratch.linear_algebra import Vector, dot

def step_function(x: float) -> float:
    return 1.0 if x >= 0 else 0.0
```

```
def perceptron_output(weights: Vector, bias: float, x: Vector) -> float:
    """Returns 1 if the perceptron 'fires', 0 if not"""
    calculation = dot(weights, x) + bias
    return step_function(calculation)
```

The perceptron is simply distinguishing between the half-spaces separated by the hyperplane of points x for which:

```
dot(weights, x) + bias == 0
```

With properly chosen weights, perceptrons can solve a number of simple problems (Figure 18-1). For example, we can create an *AND gate* (which returns 1 if both its inputs are 1 but returns 0 if one of its inputs is 0) with:

```
and_weights = [2., 2]
and_bias = -3.

assert perceptron_output(and_weights, and_bias, [1, 1]) == 1
assert perceptron_output(and_weights, and_bias, [0, 1]) == 0
assert perceptron_output(and_weights, and_bias, [1, 0]) == 0
assert perceptron_output(and_weights, and_bias, [0, 0]) == 0
```

If both inputs are 1, the calculation equals 2 + 2 – 3 = 1, and the output is 1. If only one of the inputs is 1, the calculation equals 2 + 0 – 3 = –1, and the output is 0. And if both of the inputs are 0, the calculation equals –3, and the output is 0.

Using similar reasoning, we could build an *OR gate* with:

```
or_weights = [2., 2]
or_bias = -1.

assert perceptron_output(or_weights, or_bias, [1, 1]) == 1
assert perceptron_output(or_weights, or_bias, [0, 1]) == 1
assert perceptron_output(or_weights, or_bias, [1, 0]) == 1
assert perceptron_output(or_weights, or_bias, [0, 0]) == 0
```

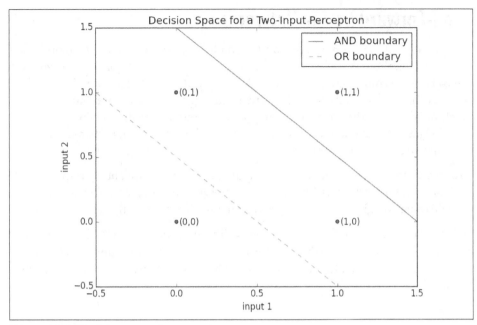

Figure 18-1. Decision space for a two-input perceptron

We could also build a *NOT gate* (which has one input and converts 1 to 0 and 0 to 1) with:

```
not_weights = [-2.]
not_bias = 1.

assert perceptron_output(not_weights, not_bias, [0]) == 1
assert perceptron_output(not_weights, not_bias, [1]) == 0
```

However, there are some problems that simply can't be solved by a single perceptron. For example, no matter how hard you try, you cannot use a perceptron to build an *XOR gate* that outputs 1 if exactly one of its inputs is 1 and 0 otherwise. This is where we start needing more complicated neural networks.

Of course, you don't need to approximate a neuron in order to build a logic gate:

```
and_gate = min
or_gate = max
xor_gate = lambda x, y: 0 if x == y else 1
```

Like real neurons, artificial neurons start getting more interesting when you start connecting them together.

Feed-Forward Neural Networks

The topology of the brain is enormously complicated, so it's common to approximate it with an idealized *feed-forward* neural network that consists of discrete *layers* of neurons, each connected to the next. This typically entails an input layer (which receives inputs and feeds them forward unchanged), one or more "hidden layers" (each of which consists of neurons that take the outputs of the previous layer, performs some calculation, and passes the result to the next layer), and an output layer (which produces the final outputs).

Just like in the perceptron, each (noninput) neuron has a weight corresponding to each of its inputs and a bias. To make our representation simpler, we'll add the bias to the end of our weights vector and give each neuron a *bias input* that always equals 1.

As with the perceptron, for each neuron we'll sum up the products of its inputs and its weights. But here, rather than outputting the `step_function` applied to that product, we'll output a smooth approximation of it. Here we'll use the `sigmoid` function (Figure 18-2):

```
import math

def sigmoid(t: float) -> float:
    return 1 / (1 + math.exp(-t))
```

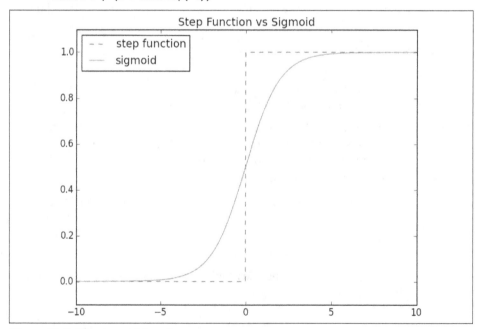

Figure 18-2. The sigmoid function

Why use `sigmoid` instead of the simpler `step_function`? In order to train a neural network, we need to use calculus, and in order to use calculus, we need *smooth* functions. `step_function` isn't even continuous, and `sigmoid` is a good smooth approximation of it.

 You may remember `sigmoid` from Chapter 16, where it was called `logistic`. Technically "sigmoid" refers to the *shape* of the function and "logistic" to this particular function, although people often use the terms interchangeably.

We then calculate the output as:

```
def neuron_output(weights: Vector, inputs: Vector) -> float:
    # weights includes the bias term, inputs includes a 1
    return sigmoid(dot(weights, inputs))
```

Given this function, we can represent a neuron simply as a vector of weights whose length is one more than the number of inputs to that neuron (because of the bias weight). Then we can represent a neural network as a list of (noninput) *layers*, where each layer is just a list of the neurons in that layer.

That is, we'll represent a neural network as a list (layers) of lists (neurons) of vectors (weights).

Given such a representation, using the neural network is quite simple:

```
from typing import List

def feed_forward(neural_network: List[List[Vector]],
                 input_vector: Vector) -> List[Vector]:
    """
    Feeds the input vector through the neural network.
    Returns the outputs of all layers (not just the last one).
    """
    outputs: List[Vector] = []

    for layer in neural_network:
        input_with_bias = input_vector + [1]              # Add a constant.
        output = [neuron_output(neuron, input_with_bias)  # Compute the output
                  for neuron in layer]                     # for each neuron.
        outputs.append(output)                             # Add to results.

        # Then the input to the next layer is the output of this one
        input_vector = output

    return outputs
```

Now it's easy to build the XOR gate that we couldn't build with a single perceptron. We just need to scale the weights up so that the neuron_outputs are either really close to 0 or really close to 1:

```
xor_network = [# hidden layer
              [[20., 20, -30],      # 'and' neuron
               [20., 20, -10]],     # 'or'  neuron
              # output layer
              [[-60., 60, -30]]]    # '2nd input but not 1st input' neuron

# feed_forward returns the outputs of all layers, so the [-1] gets the
# final output, and the [0] gets the value out of the resulting vector
assert 0.000 < feed_forward(xor_network, [0, 0])[-1][0] < 0.001
assert 0.999 < feed_forward(xor_network, [1, 0])[-1][0] < 1.000
assert 0.999 < feed_forward(xor_network, [0, 1])[-1][0] < 1.000
assert 0.000 < feed_forward(xor_network, [1, 1])[-1][0] < 0.001
```

For a given input (which is a two-dimensional vector), the hidden layer produces a two-dimensional vector consisting of the "and" of the two input values and the "or" of the two input values.

And the output layer takes a two-dimensional vector and computes "second element but not first element." The result is a network that performs "or, but not and," which is precisely XOR (Figure 18-3).

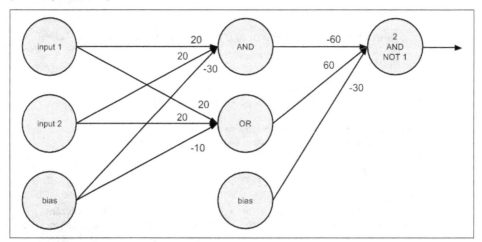

Figure 18-3. A neural network for XOR

One suggestive way of thinking about this is that the hidden layer is computing *features* of the input data (in this case "and" and "or") and the output layer is combining those features in a way that generates the desired output.

Backpropagation

Usually we don't build neural networks by hand. This is in part because we use them to solve much bigger problems—an image recognition problem might involve hundreds or thousands of neurons. And it's in part because we usually won't be able to "reason out" what the neurons should be.

Instead (as usual) we use data to *train* neural networks. The typical approach is an algorithm called *backpropagation*, which uses gradient descent or one of its variants.

Imagine we have a training set that consists of input vectors and corresponding target output vectors. For example, in our previous xor_network example, the input vector [1, 0] corresponded to the target output [1]. Imagine that our network has some set of weights. We then adjust the weights using the following algorithm:

1. Run feed_forward on an input vector to produce the outputs of all the neurons in the network.

2. We know the target output, so we can compute a *loss* that's the sum of the squared errors.

3. Compute the gradient of this loss as a function of the output neuron's weights.

4. "Propagate" the gradients and errors backward to compute the gradients with respect to the hidden neurons' weights.

5. Take a gradient descent step.

Typically we run this algorithm many times for our entire training set until the network converges.

To start with, let's write the function to compute the gradients:

```python
def sqerror_gradients(network: List[List[Vector]],
                      input_vector: Vector,
                      target_vector: Vector) -> List[List[Vector]]:
    """
    Given a neural network, an input vector, and a target vector,
    make a prediction and compute the gradient of the squared error
    loss with respect to the neuron weights.
    """
    # forward pass
    hidden_outputs, outputs = feed_forward(network, input_vector)

    # gradients with respect to output neuron pre-activation outputs
    output_deltas = [output * (1 - output) * (output - target)
                     for output, target in zip(outputs, target_vector)]

    # gradients with respect to output neuron weights
    output_grads = [[output_deltas[i] * hidden_output
                     for hidden_output in hidden_outputs + [1]]
```

```
                        for i, output_neuron in enumerate(network[-1])]

        # gradients with respect to hidden neuron pre-activation outputs
        hidden_deltas = [hidden_output * (1 - hidden_output) *
                            dot(output_deltas, [n[i] for n in network[-1]])
                         for i, hidden_output in enumerate(hidden_outputs)]

        # gradients with respect to hidden neuron weights
        hidden_grads = [[hidden_deltas[i] * input for input in input_vector + [1]]
                        for i, hidden_neuron in enumerate(network[0])]

        return [hidden_grads, output_grads]
```

The math behind the preceding calculations is not terribly difficult, but it involves some tedious calculus and careful attention to detail, so I'll leave it as an exercise for you.

Armed with the ability to compute gradients, we can now train neural networks. Let's try to learn the XOR network we previously designed by hand.

We'll start by generating the training data and initializing our neural network with random weights:

```
import random
random.seed(0)

# training data
xs = [[0., 0], [0., 1], [1., 0], [1., 1]]
ys = [[0.], [1.], [1.], [0.]]

# start with random weights
network = [ # hidden layer: 2 inputs -> 2 outputs
            [[random.random() for _ in range(2 + 1)],   # 1st hidden neuron
             [random.random() for _ in range(2 + 1)]],  # 2nd hidden neuron
            # output layer: 2 inputs -> 1 output
            [[random.random() for _ in range(2 + 1)]]   # 1st output neuron
          ]
```

As usual, we can train it using gradient descent. One difference from our previous examples is that here we have several parameter vectors, each with its own gradient, which means we'll have to call gradient_step for each of them.

```
from scratch.gradient_descent import gradient_step
import tqdm

learning_rate = 1.0

for epoch in tqdm.trange(20000, desc="neural net for xor"):
    for x, y in zip(xs, ys):
        gradients = sqerror_gradients(network, x, y)

        # Take a gradient step for each neuron in each layer
```

```
            network = [[gradient_step(neuron, grad, -learning_rate)
                        for neuron, grad in zip(layer, layer_grad)]
                      for layer, layer_grad in zip(network, gradients)]

    # check that it learned XOR
    assert feed_forward(network, [0, 0])[-1][0] < 0.01
    assert feed_forward(network, [0, 1])[-1][0] > 0.99
    assert feed_forward(network, [1, 0])[-1][0] > 0.99
    assert feed_forward(network, [1, 1])[-1][0] < 0.01
```

For me the resulting network has weights that look like:

```
[   # hidden layer
    [[7, 7, -3],      # computes OR
     [5, 5, -8]],     # computes AND
    # output layer
    [[11, -12, -5]]   # computes "first but not second"
]
```

which is conceptually pretty similar to our previous bespoke network.

Example: Fizz Buzz

The VP of Engineering wants to interview technical candidates by making them solve "Fizz Buzz," the following well-trod programming challenge:

> Print the numbers 1 to 100, except that if the number is divisible by 3, print "fizz"; if the number is divisible by 5, print "buzz"; and if the number is divisible by 15, print "fizzbuzz".

He thinks the ability to solve this demonstrates extreme programming skill. You think that this problem is so simple that a neural network could solve it.

Neural networks take vectors as inputs and produce vectors as outputs. As stated, the programming problem is to turn an integer into a string. So the first challenge is to come up with a way to recast it as a vector problem.

For the outputs it's not tough: there are basically four classes of outputs, so we can encode the output as a vector of four 0s and 1s:

```
def fizz_buzz_encode(x: int) -> Vector:
    if x % 15 == 0:
        return [0, 0, 0, 1]
    elif x % 5 == 0:
        return [0, 0, 1, 0]
    elif x % 3 == 0:
        return [0, 1, 0, 0]
    else:
        return [1, 0, 0, 0]

assert fizz_buzz_encode(2) == [1, 0, 0, 0]
assert fizz_buzz_encode(6) == [0, 1, 0, 0]
```

```
        assert fizz_buzz_encode(10) == [0, 0, 1, 0]
        assert fizz_buzz_encode(30) == [0, 0, 0, 1]
```

We'll use this to generate our target vectors. The input vectors are less obvious. You don't want to just use a one-dimensional vector containing the input number, for a couple of reasons. A single input captures an "intensity," but the fact that 2 is twice as much as 1, and that 4 is twice as much again, doesn't feel relevant to this problem. Additionally, with just one input the hidden layer wouldn't be able to compute very interesting features, which means it probably wouldn't be able to solve the problem.

It turns out that one thing that works reasonably well is to convert each number to its *binary* representation of 1s and 0s. (Don't worry, this isn't obvious—at least it wasn't to me.)

```
def binary_encode(x: int) -> Vector:
    binary: List[float] = []

    for i in range(10):
        binary.append(x % 2)
        x = x // 2

    return binary

#                             1  2  4  8  16 32 64 128 256 512
assert binary_encode(0)   == [0, 0, 0, 0, 0, 0, 0, 0,  0,  0]
assert binary_encode(1)   == [1, 0, 0, 0, 0, 0, 0, 0,  0,  0]
assert binary_encode(10)  == [0, 1, 0, 1, 0, 0, 0, 0,  0,  0]
assert binary_encode(101) == [1, 0, 1, 0, 0, 1, 1, 0,  0,  0]
assert binary_encode(999) == [1, 1, 1, 0, 0, 1, 1, 1,  1,  1]
```

As the goal is to construct the outputs for the numbers 1 to 100, it would be cheating to train on those numbers. Therefore, we'll train on the numbers 101 to 1,023 (which is the largest number we can represent with 10 binary digits):

```
xs = [binary_encode(n) for n in range(101, 1024)]
ys = [fizz_buzz_encode(n) for n in range(101, 1024)]
```

Next, let's create a neural network with random initial weights. It will have 10 input neurons (since we're representing our inputs as 10-dimensional vectors) and 4 output neurons (since we're representing our targets as 4-dimensional vectors). We'll give it 25 hidden units, but we'll use a variable for that so it's easy to change:

```
NUM_HIDDEN = 25

network = [
    # hidden layer: 10 inputs -> NUM_HIDDEN outputs
    [[random.random() for _ in range(10 + 1)] for _ in range(NUM_HIDDEN)],

    # output_layer: NUM_HIDDEN inputs -> 4 outputs
    [[random.random() for _ in range(NUM_HIDDEN + 1)] for _ in range(4)]
]
```

That's it. Now we're ready to train. Because this is a more involved problem (and there are a lot more things to mess up), we'd like to closely monitor the training process. In particular, for each epoch we'll track the sum of squared errors and print them out. We want to make sure they decrease:

```
from scratch.linear_algebra import squared_distance

learning_rate = 1.0

with tqdm.trange(500) as t:
    for epoch in t:
        epoch_loss = 0.0

        for x, y in zip(xs, ys):
            predicted = feed_forward(network, x)[-1]
            epoch_loss += squared_distance(predicted, y)
            gradients = sqerror_gradients(network, x, y)

            # Take a gradient step for each neuron in each layer
            network = [[gradient_step(neuron, grad, -learning_rate)
                        for neuron, grad in zip(layer, layer_grad)]
                       for layer, layer_grad in zip(network, gradients)]

        t.set_description(f"fizz buzz (loss: {epoch_loss:.2f})")
```

This will take a while to train, but eventually the loss should start to bottom out.

At last we're ready to solve our original problem. We have one remaining issue. Our network will produce a four-dimensional vector of numbers, but we want a single prediction. We'll do that by taking the argmax, which is the index of the largest value:

```
def argmax(xs: list) -> int:
    """Returns the index of the largest value"""
    return max(range(len(xs)), key=lambda i: xs[i])

assert argmax([0, -1]) == 0              # items[0] is largest
assert argmax([-1, 0]) == 1              # items[1] is largest
assert argmax([-1, 10, 5, 20, -3]) == 3  # items[3] is largest
```

Now we can finally solve "FizzBuzz":

```
num_correct = 0

for n in range(1, 101):
    x = binary_encode(n)
    predicted = argmax(feed_forward(network, x)[-1])
    actual = argmax(fizz_buzz_encode(n))
    labels = [str(n), "fizz", "buzz", "fizzbuzz"]
    print(n, labels[predicted], labels[actual])

    if predicted == actual:
        num_correct += 1
```

```
print(num_correct, "/", 100)
```

For me the trained network gets 96/100 correct, which is well above the VP of Engineering's hiring threshold. Faced with the evidence, he relents and changes the interview challenge to "Invert a Binary Tree."

For Further Exploration

- Keep reading: Chapter 19 will explore these topics in much more detail.
- My blog post on "Fizz Buzz in Tensorflow" (*http://joelgrus.com/2016/05/23/fizz-buzz-in-tensorflow/*) is pretty good.

Deep Learning

A little learning is a dangerous thing; Drink deep, or taste not the Pierian spring.
—Alexander Pope

Deep learning originally referred to the application of "deep" neural networks (that is, networks with more than one hidden layer), although in practice the term now encompasses a wide variety of neural architectures (including the "simple" neural networks we developed in Chapter 18).

In this chapter we'll build on our previous work and look at a wider variety of neural networks. To do so, we'll introduce a number of abstractions that allow us to think about neural networks in a more general way.

The Tensor

Previously, we made a distinction between vectors (one-dimensional arrays) and matrices (two-dimensional arrays). When we start working with more complicated neural networks, we'll need to use higher-dimensional arrays as well.

In many neural network libraries, *n*-dimensional arrays are referred to as *tensors*, which is what we'll call them too. (There are pedantic mathematical reasons not to refer to *n*-dimensional arrays as tensors; if you are such a pedant, your objection is noted.)

If I were writing an entire book about deep learning, I'd implement a full-featured Tensor class that overloaded Python's arithmetic operators and could handle a variety of other operations. Such an implementation would take an entire chapter on its own. Here we'll cheat and say that a Tensor is just a list. This is true in one direction—all of our vectors and matrices and higher-dimensional analogues *are* lists. It is certainly not true in the other direction—most Python lists are not *n*-dimensional arrays in our sense.

 Ideally you'd like to do something like:

```
# A Tensor is either a float, or a List of Tensors
Tensor = Union[float, List[Tensor]]
```

However, Python won't let you define recursive types like that. And even if it did that definition is still not right, as it allows for bad "tensors" like:

```
[[1.0, 2.0],
 [3.0]]
```

whose rows have different sizes, which makes it not an *n*-dimensional array.

So, like I said, we'll just cheat:

```
Tensor = list
```

And we'll write a helper function to find a tensor's *shape*:

```
from typing import List

def shape(tensor: Tensor) -> List[int]:
    sizes: List[int] = []
    while isinstance(tensor, list):
        sizes.append(len(tensor))
        tensor = tensor[0]
    return sizes

assert shape([1, 2, 3]) == [3]
assert shape([[1, 2], [3, 4], [5, 6]]) == [3, 2]
```

Because tensors can have any number of dimensions, we'll typically need to work with them recursively. We'll do one thing in the one-dimensional case and recurse in the higher-dimensional case:

```
def is_1d(tensor: Tensor) -> bool:
    """
    If tensor[0] is a list, it's a higher-order tensor.
    Otherwise, tensor is 1-dimensional (that is, a vector).
    """
    return not isinstance(tensor[0], list)

assert is_1d([1, 2, 3])
assert not is_1d([[1, 2], [3, 4]])
```

which we can use to write a recursive `tensor_sum` function:

```
def tensor_sum(tensor: Tensor) -> float:
    """Sums up all the values in the tensor"""
```

```
        if is_1d(tensor):
            return sum(tensor)  # just a list of floats, use Python sum
        else:
            return sum(tensor_sum(tensor_i)    # Call tensor_sum on each row
                       for tensor_i in tensor)  # and sum up those results.

    assert tensor_sum([1, 2, 3]) == 6
    assert tensor_sum([[1, 2], [3, 4]]) == 10
```

If you're not used to thinking recursively, you should ponder this until it makes sense, because we'll use the same logic throughout this chapter. However, we'll create a couple of helper functions so that we don't have to rewrite this logic everywhere. The first applies a function elementwise to a single tensor:

```
    from typing import Callable

    def tensor_apply(f: Callable[[float], float], tensor: Tensor) -> Tensor:
        """Applies f elementwise"""
        if is_1d(tensor):
            return [f(x) for x in tensor]
        else:
            return [tensor_apply(f, tensor_i) for tensor_i in tensor]

    assert tensor_apply(lambda x: x + 1, [1, 2, 3]) == [2, 3, 4]
    assert tensor_apply(lambda x: 2 * x, [[1, 2], [3, 4]]) == [[2, 4], [6, 8]]
```

We can use this to write a function that creates a zero tensor with the same shape as a given tensor:

```
    def zeros_like(tensor: Tensor) -> Tensor:
        return tensor_apply(lambda _: 0.0, tensor)

    assert zeros_like([1, 2, 3]) == [0, 0, 0]
    assert zeros_like([[1, 2], [3, 4]]) == [[0, 0], [0, 0]]
```

We'll also need to apply a function to corresponding elements from two tensors (which had better be the exact same shape, although we won't check that):

```
    def tensor_combine(f: Callable[[float, float], float],
                       t1: Tensor,
                       t2: Tensor) -> Tensor:
        """Applies f to corresponding elements of t1 and t2"""
        if is_1d(t1):
            return [f(x, y) for x, y in zip(t1, t2)]
        else:
            return [tensor_combine(f, t1_i, t2_i)
                    for t1_i, t2_i in zip(t1, t2)]

    import operator
    assert tensor_combine(operator.add, [1, 2, 3], [4, 5, 6]) == [5, 7, 9]
    assert tensor_combine(operator.mul, [1, 2, 3], [4, 5, 6]) == [4, 10, 18]
```

The Layer Abstraction

In the previous chapter we built a simple neural net that allowed us to stack two layers of neurons, each of which computed sigmoid(dot(weights, inputs)).

Although that's perhaps an idealized representation of what an actual neuron does, in practice we'd like to allow a wider variety of things. Perhaps we'd like the neurons to remember something about their previous inputs. Perhaps we'd like to use a different activation function than sigmoid. And frequently we'd like to use more than two layers. (Our feed_forward function actually handled any number of layers, but our gradient computations did not.)

In this chapter we'll build machinery for implementing such a variety of neural networks. Our fundamental abstraction will be the Layer, something that knows how to apply some function to its inputs and that knows how to backpropagate gradients.

One way of thinking about the neural networks we built in Chapter 18 is as a "linear" layer, followed by a "sigmoid" layer, then another linear layer and another sigmoid layer. We didn't distinguish them in these terms, but doing so will allow us to experiment with much more general structures:

```python
from typing import Iterable, Tuple

class Layer:
    """
    Our neural networks will be composed of Layers, each of which
    knows how to do some computation on its inputs in the "forward"
    direction and propagate gradients in the "backward" direction.
    """
    def forward(self, input):
        """
        Note the lack of types. We're not going to be prescriptive
        about what kinds of inputs layers can take and what kinds
        of outputs they can return.
        """
        raise NotImplementedError

    def backward(self, gradient):
        """
        Similarly, we're not going to be prescriptive about what the
        gradient looks like. It's up to you the user to make sure
        that you're doing things sensibly.
        """
        raise NotImplementedError

    def params(self) -> Iterable[Tensor]:
        """
        Returns the parameters of this layer. The default implementation
        returns nothing, so that if you have a layer with no parameters
        you don't have to implement this.
```

```
        """
        return ()

    def grads(self) -> Iterable[Tensor]:
        """
        Returns the gradients, in the same order as params().
        """
        return ()
```

The `forward` and `backward` methods will have to be implemented in our concrete subclasses. Once we build a neural net, we'll want to train it using gradient descent, which means we'll want to update each parameter in the network using its gradient. Accordingly, we insist that each layer be able to tell us its parameters and gradients.

Some layers (for example, a layer that applies `sigmoid` to each of its inputs) have no parameters to update, so we provide a default implementation that handles that case.

Let's look at that layer:

```
from scratch.neural_networks import sigmoid

class Sigmoid(Layer):
    def forward(self, input: Tensor) -> Tensor:
        """
        Apply sigmoid to each element of the input tensor,
        and save the results to use in backpropagation.
        """
        self.sigmoids = tensor_apply(sigmoid, input)
        return self.sigmoids

    def backward(self, gradient: Tensor) -> Tensor:
        return tensor_combine(lambda sig, grad: sig * (1 - sig) * grad,
                              self.sigmoids,
                              gradient)
```

There are a couple of things to notice here. One is that during the forward pass we saved the computed sigmoids so that we could use them later in the backward pass. Our layers will typically need to do this sort of thing.

Second, you may be wondering where the `sig * (1 - sig) * grad` comes from. This is just the chain rule from calculus and corresponds to the `output * (1 - output) * (output - target)` term in our previous neural networks.

Finally, you can see how we were able to make use of the `tensor_apply` and the `tensor_combine` functions. Most of our layers will use these functions similarly.

The Linear Layer

The other piece we'll need to duplicate the neural networks from Chapter 18 is a "linear" layer that represents the `dot(weights, inputs)` part of the neurons.

This layer will have parameters, which we'd like to initialize with random values.

It turns out that the initial parameter values can make a huge difference in how quickly (and sometimes *whether*) the network trains. If weights are too big, they may produce large outputs in a range where the activation function has near-zero gradients. And parts of the network that have zero gradients necessarily can't learn anything via gradient descent.

Accordingly, we'll implement three different schemes for randomly generating our weight tensors. The first is to choose each value from the random uniform distribution on [0, 1]—that is, as a random.random(). The second (and default) is to choose each value randomly from a standard normal distribution. And the third is to use *Xavier initialization*, where each weight is initialized with a random draw from a normal distribution with mean 0 and variance 2 / (num_inputs + num_outputs). It turns out this often works nicely for neural network weights. We'll implement these with a random_uniform function and a random_normal function:

```
import random

from scratch.probability import inverse_normal_cdf

def random_uniform(*dims: int) -> Tensor:
    if len(dims) == 1:
        return [random.random() for _ in range(dims[0])]
    else:
        return [random_uniform(*dims[1:]) for _ in range(dims[0])]

def random_normal(*dims: int,
                  mean: float = 0.0,
                  variance: float = 1.0) -> Tensor:
    if len(dims) == 1:
        return [mean + variance * inverse_normal_cdf(random.random())
                for _ in range(dims[0])]
    else:
        return [random_normal(*dims[1:], mean=mean, variance=variance)
                for _ in range(dims[0])]

assert shape(random_uniform(2, 3, 4)) == [2, 3, 4]
assert shape(random_normal(5, 6, mean=10)) == [5, 6]
```

And then wrap them all in a random_tensor function:

```
def random_tensor(*dims: int, init: str = 'normal') -> Tensor:
    if init == 'normal':
        return random_normal(*dims)
    elif init == 'uniform':
        return random_uniform(*dims)
    elif init == 'xavier':
        variance = len(dims) / sum(dims)
        return random_normal(*dims, variance=variance)
```

```
        else:
            raise ValueError(f"unknown init: {init}")
```

Now we can define our linear layer. We need to initialize it with the dimension of the inputs (which tells us how many weights each neuron needs), the dimension of the outputs (which tells us how many neurons we should have), and the initialization scheme we want:

```
from scratch.linear_algebra import dot

class Linear(Layer):
    def __init__(self,
                 input_dim: int,
                 output_dim: int,
                 init: str = 'xavier') -> None:
        """
        A layer of output_dim neurons, each with input_dim weights
        (and a bias).
        """
        self.input_dim = input_dim
        self.output_dim = output_dim

        # self.w[o] is the weights for the oth neuron
        self.w = random_tensor(output_dim, input_dim, init=init)

        # self.b[o] is the bias term for the oth neuron
        self.b = random_tensor(output_dim, init=init)
```

 In case you're wondering how important the initialization schemes are, some of the networks in this chapter I couldn't get to train at all with different initializations than the ones I used.

The `forward` method is easy to implement. We'll get one output per neuron, which we stick in a vector. And each neuron's output is just the `dot` of its weights with the input, plus its bias:

```
    def forward(self, input: Tensor) -> Tensor:
        # Save the input to use in the backward pass.
        self.input = input

        # Return the vector of neuron outputs.
        return [dot(input, self.w[o]) + self.b[o]
                for o in range(self.output_dim)]
```

The `backward` method is more involved, but if you know calculus it's not difficult:

```
    def backward(self, gradient: Tensor) -> Tensor:
        # Each b[o] gets added to output[o], which means
        # the gradient of b is the same as the output gradient.
```

```
        self.b_grad = gradient

        # Each w[o][i] multiplies input[i] and gets added to output[o].
        # So its gradient is input[i] * gradient[o].
        self.w_grad = [[self.input[i] * gradient[o]
                        for i in range(self.input_dim)]
                       for o in range(self.output_dim)]

        # Each input[i] multiplies every w[o][i] and gets added to every
        # output[o]. So its gradient is the sum of w[o][i] * gradient[o]
        # across all the outputs.
        return [sum(self.w[o][i] * gradient[o] for o in range(self.output_dim))
                for i in range(self.input_dim)]
```

 In a "real" tensor library, these (and many other) operations would be represented as matrix or tensor multiplications, which those libraries are designed to do very quickly. Our library is *very* slow.

Finally, here we do need to implement params and grads. We have two parameters and two corresponding gradients:

```
        def params(self) -> Iterable[Tensor]:
            return [self.w, self.b]

        def grads(self) -> Iterable[Tensor]:
            return [self.w_grad, self.b_grad]
```

Neural Networks as a Sequence of Layers

We'd like to think of neural networks as sequences of layers, so let's come up with a way to combine multiple layers into one. The resulting neural network is itself a layer, and it implements the Layer methods in the obvious ways:

```
from typing import List

class Sequential(Layer):
    """
    A layer consisting of a sequence of other layers.
    It's up to you to make sure that the output of each layer
    makes sense as the input to the next layer.
    """
    def __init__(self, layers: List[Layer]) -> None:
        self.layers = layers

    def forward(self, input):
        """Just forward the input through the layers in order."""
        for layer in self.layers:
            input = layer.forward(input)
```

```
        return input

    def backward(self, gradient):
        """Just backpropagate the gradient through the layers in reverse."""
        for layer in reversed(self.layers):
            gradient = layer.backward(gradient)
        return gradient

    def params(self) -> Iterable[Tensor]:
        """Just return the params from each layer."""
        return (param for layer in self.layers for param in layer.params())

    def grads(self) -> Iterable[Tensor]:
        """Just return the grads from each layer."""
        return (grad for layer in self.layers for grad in layer.grads())
```

So we could represent the neural network we used for XOR as:

```
xor_net = Sequential([
    Linear(input_dim=2, output_dim=2),
    Sigmoid(),
    Linear(input_dim=2, output_dim=1),
    Sigmoid()
])
```

But we still need a little more machinery to train it.

Loss and Optimization

Previously we wrote out individual loss functions and gradient functions for our
models. Here we'll want to experiment with different loss functions, so (as usual) we'll
introduce a new Loss abstraction that encapsulates both the loss computation and the
gradient computation:

```
class Loss:
    def loss(self, predicted: Tensor, actual: Tensor) -> float:
        """How good are our predictions? (Larger numbers are worse.)"""
        raise NotImplementedError

    def gradient(self, predicted: Tensor, actual: Tensor) -> Tensor:
        """How does the loss change as the predictions change?"""
        raise NotImplementedError
```

We've already worked many times with the loss that's the sum of the squared errors,
so we should have an easy time implementing that. The only trick is that we'll need to
use tensor_combine:

```
class SSE(Loss):
    """Loss function that computes the sum of the squared errors."""
    def loss(self, predicted: Tensor, actual: Tensor) -> float:
        # Compute the tensor of squared differences
        squared_errors = tensor_combine(
```

```
        lambda predicted, actual: (predicted - actual) ** 2,
        predicted,
        actual)

    # And just add them up
    return tensor_sum(squared_errors)

def gradient(self, predicted: Tensor, actual: Tensor) -> Tensor:
    return tensor_combine(
        lambda predicted, actual: 2 * (predicted - actual),
        predicted,
        actual)
```

(We'll look at a different loss function in a bit.)

The last piece to figure out is gradient descent. Throughout the book we've done all of our gradient descent manually by having a training loop that involves something like:

```
theta = gradient_step(theta, grad, -learning_rate)
```

Here that won't quite work for us, for a couple reasons. The first is that our neural nets will have many parameters, and we'll need to update all of them. The second is that we'd like to be able to use more clever variants of gradient descent, and we don't want to have to rewrite them each time.

Accordingly, we'll introduce a (you guessed it) `Optimizer` abstraction, of which gradient descent will be a specific instance:

```
class Optimizer:
    """
    An optimizer updates the weights of a layer (in place) using information
    known by either the layer or the optimizer (or by both).
    """
    def step(self, layer: Layer) -> None:
        raise NotImplementedError
```

After that it's easy to implement gradient descent, again using `tensor_combine`:

```
class GradientDescent(Optimizer):
    def __init__(self, learning_rate: float = 0.1) -> None:
        self.lr = learning_rate

    def step(self, layer: Layer) -> None:
        for param, grad in zip(layer.params(), layer.grads()):
            # Update param using a gradient step
            param[:] = tensor_combine(
                lambda param, grad: param - grad * self.lr,
                param,
                grad)
```

The only thing that's maybe surprising is the "slice assignment," which is a reflection of the fact that reassigning a list doesn't change its original value. That is, if you just did `param = tensor_combine(. . .)`, you would be redefining the local variable param, but you would not be affecting the original parameter tensor stored in the layer. If you assign to the slice [:], however, it actually changes the values inside the list.

Here's a simple example to demonstrate:

```
tensor = [[1, 2], [3, 4]]

for row in tensor:
    row = [0, 0]
assert tensor == [[1, 2], [3, 4]], "assignment doesn't update a list"

for row in tensor:
    row[:] = [0, 0]
assert tensor == [[0, 0], [0, 0]], "but slice assignment does"
```

If you are somewhat inexperienced in Python, this behavior may be surprising, so meditate on it and try examples yourself until it makes sense.

To demonstrate the value of this abstraction, let's implement another optimizer that uses *momentum*. The idea is that we don't want to overreact to each new gradient, and so we maintain a running average of the gradients we've seen, updating it with each new gradient and taking a step in the direction of the average:

```
class Momentum(Optimizer):
    def __init__(self,
                 learning_rate: float,
                 momentum: float = 0.9) -> None:
        self.lr = learning_rate
        self.mo = momentum
        self.updates: List[Tensor] = []  # running average

    def step(self, layer: Layer) -> None:
        # If we have no previous updates, start with all zeros
        if not self.updates:
            self.updates = [zeros_like(grad) for grad in layer.grads()]

        for update, param, grad in zip(self.updates,
                                       layer.params(),
                                       layer.grads()):
            # Apply momentum
            update[:] = tensor_combine(
                lambda u, g: self.mo * u + (1 - self.mo) * g,
                update,
                grad)

            # Then take a gradient step
            param[:] = tensor_combine(
                lambda p, u: p - self.lr * u,
                param,
                update)
```

Because we used an `Optimizer` abstraction, we can easily switch between our different optimizers.

Example: XOR Revisited

Let's see how easy it is to use our new framework to train a network that can compute XOR. We start by re-creating the training data:

```
# training data
xs = [[0., 0], [0., 1], [1., 0], [1., 1]]
ys = [[0.], [1.], [1.], [0.]]
```

and then we define the network, although now we can leave off the last sigmoid layer:

```
random.seed(0)

net = Sequential([
    Linear(input_dim=2, output_dim=2),
    Sigmoid(),
    Linear(input_dim=2, output_dim=1)
])
```

We can now write a simple training loop, except that now we can use the abstractions of `Optimizer` and `Loss`. This allows us to easily try different ones:

```
import tqdm

optimizer = GradientDescent(learning_rate=0.1)
loss = SSE()

with tqdm.trange(3000) as t:
    for epoch in t:
        epoch_loss = 0.0

        for x, y in zip(xs, ys):
            predicted = net.forward(x)
            epoch_loss += loss.loss(predicted, y)
            gradient = loss.gradient(predicted, y)
            net.backward(gradient)

            optimizer.step(net)

        t.set_description(f"xor loss {epoch_loss:.3f}")
```

This should train quickly, and you should see the loss go down. And now we can inspect the weights:

```
for param in net.params():
    print(param)
```

For my network I find roughly:

```
hidden1 = -2.6 * x1 + -2.7 * x2 + 0.2  # NOR
hidden2 =  2.1 * x1 +  2.1 * x2 - 3.4  # AND
output  = -3.1 * h1 + -2.6 * h2 + 1.8  # NOR
```

So `hidden1` activates if neither input is 1. `hidden2` activates if both inputs are 1. And `output` activates if neither hidden output is 1—that is, if it's not the case that neither input is 1 and it's also not the case that both inputs are 1. Indeed, this is exactly the logic of XOR.

Notice that this network learned different features than the one we trained in Chapter 18, but it still manages to do the same thing.

Other Activation Functions

The `sigmoid` function has fallen out of favor for a couple of reasons. One reason is that `sigmoid(0)` equals 1/2, which means that a neuron whose inputs sum to 0 has a positive output. Another is that its gradient is very close to 0 for very large and very small inputs, which means that its gradients can get "saturated" and its weights can get stuck.

One popular replacement is `tanh` ("hyperbolic tangent"), which is a different sigmoid-shaped function that ranges from –1 to 1 and outputs 0 if its input is 0. The derivative of `tanh(x)` is just `1 - tanh(x) ** 2`, which makes the layer easy to write:

```
import math

def tanh(x: float) -> float:
    # If x is very large or very small, tanh is (essentially) 1 or -1.
    # We check for this because, e.g., math.exp(1000) raises an error.
    if x < -100:  return -1
    elif x > 100: return 1

    em2x = math.exp(-2 * x)
    return (1 - em2x) / (1 + em2x)

class Tanh(Layer):
    def forward(self, input: Tensor) -> Tensor:
        # Save tanh output to use in backward pass.
        self.tanh = tensor_apply(tanh, input)
        return self.tanh

    def backward(self, gradient: Tensor) -> Tensor:
        return tensor_combine(
            lambda tanh, grad: (1 - tanh ** 2) * grad,
            self.tanh,
            gradient)
```

In larger networks another popular replacement is `Relu`, which is 0 for negative inputs and the identity for positive inputs:

```
class Relu(Layer):
    def forward(self, input: Tensor) -> Tensor:
        self.input = input
        return tensor_apply(lambda x: max(x, 0), input)

    def backward(self, gradient: Tensor) -> Tensor:
        return tensor_combine(lambda x, grad: grad if x > 0 else 0,
                              self.input,
                              gradient)
```

There are many others. I encourage you to play around with them in your networks.

Example: FizzBuzz Revisited

We can now use our "deep learning" framework to reproduce our solution from "Example: Fizz Buzz" on page 235. Let's set up the data:

```
from scratch.neural_networks import binary_encode, fizz_buzz_encode, argmax

xs = [binary_encode(n) for n in range(101, 1024)]
ys = [fizz_buzz_encode(n) for n in range(101, 1024)]
```

and create the network:

```
NUM_HIDDEN = 25

random.seed(0)

net = Sequential([
    Linear(input_dim=10, output_dim=NUM_HIDDEN, init='uniform'),
    Tanh(),
    Linear(input_dim=NUM_HIDDEN, output_dim=4, init='uniform'),
    Sigmoid()
])
```

As we're training, let's also track our accuracy on the training set:

```
def fizzbuzz_accuracy(low: int, hi: int, net: Layer) -> float:
    num_correct = 0
    for n in range(low, hi):
        x = binary_encode(n)
        predicted = argmax(net.forward(x))
        actual = argmax(fizz_buzz_encode(n))
        if predicted == actual:
            num_correct += 1

    return num_correct / (hi - low)

optimizer = Momentum(learning_rate=0.1, momentum=0.9)
loss = SSE()

with tqdm.trange(1000) as t:
    for epoch in t:
```

```
        epoch_loss = 0.0

        for x, y in zip(xs, ys):
            predicted = net.forward(x)
            epoch_loss += loss.loss(predicted, y)
            gradient = loss.gradient(predicted, y)
            net.backward(gradient)

            optimizer.step(net)

        accuracy = fizzbuzz_accuracy(101, 1024, net)
        t.set_description(f"fb loss: {epoch_loss:.2f} acc: {accuracy:.2f}")

    # Now check results on the test set
    print("test results", fizzbuzz_accuracy(1, 101, net))
```

After 1,000 training iterations, the model gets 90% accuracy on the test set; if you keep training it longer, it should do even better. (I don't think it's possible to train to 100% accuracy with only 25 hidden units, but it's definitely possible if you go up to 50 hidden units.)

Softmaxes and Cross-Entropy

The neural net we used in the previous section ended in a Sigmoid layer, which means that its output was a vector of numbers between 0 and 1. In particular, it could output a vector that was entirely 0s, or it could output a vector that was entirely 1s. Yet when we're doing classification problems, we'd like to output a 1 for the correct class and a 0 for all the incorrect classes. Generally our predictions will not be so perfect, but we'd at least like to predict an actual probability distribution over the classes.

For example, if we have two classes, and our model outputs [0, 0], it's hard to make much sense of that. It doesn't think the output belongs in either class?

But if our model outputs [0.4, 0.6], we can interpret it as a prediction that there's a probability of 0.4 that our input belongs to the first class and 0.6 that our input belongs to the second class.

In order to accomplish this, we typically forgo the final Sigmoid layer and instead use the softmax function, which converts a vector of real numbers to a vector of probabilities. We compute exp(x) for each number in the vector, which results in a vector of positive numbers. After that, we just divide each of those positive numbers by the sum, which gives us a bunch of positive numbers that add up to 1—that is, a vector of probabilities.

If we ever end up trying to compute, say, exp(1000) we will get a Python error, so before taking the exp we subtract off the largest value. This turns out to result in the same probabilities; it's just safer to compute in Python:

```
def softmax(tensor: Tensor) -> Tensor:
    """Softmax along the last dimension"""
    if is_1d(tensor):
        # Subtract largest value for numerical stability.
        largest = max(tensor)
        exps = [math.exp(x - largest) for x in tensor]

        sum_of_exps = sum(exps)               # This is the total "weight."
        return [exp_i / sum_of_exps           # Probability is the fraction
                    for exp_i in exps]        # of the total weight.
    else:
        return [softmax(tensor_i) for tensor_i in tensor]
```

Once our network produces probabilities, we often use a different loss function called *cross-entropy* (or sometimes "negative log likelihood").

You may recall that in "Maximum Likelihood Estimation" on page 190, we justified the use of least squares in linear regression by appealing to the fact that (under certain assumptions) the least squares coefficients maximized the likelihood of the observed data.

Here we can do something similar: if our network outputs are probabilities, the cross-entropy loss represents the negative log likelihood of the observed data, which means that minimizing that loss is the same as maximizing the log likelihood (and hence the likelihood) of the training data.

Typically we won't include the `softmax` function as part of the neural network itself. This is because it turns out that if `softmax` is part of your loss function but not part of the network itself, the gradients of the loss with respect to the network outputs are very easy to compute.

```
class SoftmaxCrossEntropy(Loss):
    """
    This is the negative-log-likelihood of the observed values, given the
    neural net model. So if we choose weights to minimize it, our model will
    be maximizing the likelihood of the observed data.
    """
    def loss(self, predicted: Tensor, actual: Tensor) -> float:
        # Apply softmax to get probabilities
        probabilities = softmax(predicted)

        # This will be log p_i for the actual class i and 0 for the other
        # classes. We add a tiny amount to p to avoid taking log(0).
        likelihoods = tensor_combine(lambda p, act: math.log(p + 1e-30) * act,
                                     probabilities,
                                     actual)

        # And then we just sum up the negatives.
        return -tensor_sum(likelihoods)

    def gradient(self, predicted: Tensor, actual: Tensor) -> Tensor:
```

```
    probabilities = softmax(predicted)

    # Isn't this a pleasant equation?
    return tensor_combine(lambda p, actual: p - actual,
                          probabilities,
                          actual)
```

If I now train the same Fizz Buzz network using SoftmaxCrossEntropy loss, I find that it typically trains much faster (that is, in many fewer epochs). Presumably this is because it is much easier to find weights that softmax to a given distribution than it is to find weights that sigmoid to a given distribution.

That is, if I need to predict class 0 (a vector with a 1 in the first position and 0s in the remaining positions), in the linear + sigmoid case I need the first output to be a large positive number and the remaining outputs to be large negative numbers. In the softmax case, however, I just need the first output to be *larger than* the remaining outputs. Clearly there are a lot more ways for the second case to happen, which suggests that it should be easier to find weights that make it so:

```
random.seed(0)

net = Sequential([
    Linear(input_dim=10, output_dim=NUM_HIDDEN, init='uniform'),
    Tanh(),
    Linear(input_dim=NUM_HIDDEN, output_dim=4, init='uniform')
    # No final sigmoid layer now
])

optimizer = Momentum(learning_rate=0.1, momentum=0.9)
loss = SoftmaxCrossEntropy()

with tqdm.trange(100) as t:
    for epoch in t:
        epoch_loss = 0.0

        for x, y in zip(xs, ys):
            predicted = net.forward(x)
            epoch_loss += loss.loss(predicted, y)
            gradient = loss.gradient(predicted, y)
            net.backward(gradient)

            optimizer.step(net)

        accuracy = fizzbuzz_accuracy(101, 1024, net)
        t.set_description(f"fb loss: {epoch_loss:.3f} acc: {accuracy:.2f}")

# Again check results on the test set
print("test results", fizzbuzz_accuracy(1, 101, net))
```

Dropout

Like most machine learning models, neural networks are prone to overfitting to their training data. We've previously seen ways to ameliorate this; for example, in "Regularization" on page 200 we penalized large weights and that helped prevent overfitting.

A common way of regularizing neural networks is using *dropout*. At training time, we randomly turn off each neuron (that is, replace its output with 0) with some fixed probability. This means that the network can't learn to depend on any individual neuron, which seems to help with overfitting.

At evaluation time, we don't want to dropout any neurons, so a `Dropout` layer will need to know whether it's training or not. In addition, at training time a `Dropout` layer only passes on some random fraction of its input. To make its output comparable during evaluation, we'll scale down the outputs (uniformly) using that same fraction:

```python
class Dropout(Layer):
    def __init__(self, p: float) -> None:
        self.p = p
        self.train = True

    def forward(self, input: Tensor) -> Tensor:
        if self.train:
            # Create a mask of 0s and 1s shaped like the input
            # using the specified probability.
            self.mask = tensor_apply(
                lambda _: 0 if random.random() < self.p else 1,
                input)
            # Multiply by the mask to dropout inputs.
            return tensor_combine(operator.mul, input, self.mask)
        else:
            # During evaluation just scale down the outputs uniformly.
            return tensor_apply(lambda x: x * (1 - self.p), input)

    def backward(self, gradient: Tensor) -> Tensor:
        if self.train:
            # Only propagate the gradients where mask == 1.
            return tensor_combine(operator.mul, gradient, self.mask)
        else:
            raise RuntimeError("don't call backward when not in train mode")
```

We'll use this to help prevent our deep learning models from overfitting.

Example: MNIST

MNIST (*http://yann.lecun.com/exdb/mnist/*) is a dataset of handwritten digits that everyone uses to learn deep learning.

It is available in a somewhat tricky binary format, so we'll install the mnist library to work with it. (Yes, this part is technically not "from scratch.")

```
python -m pip install mnist
```

And then we can load the data:

```
import mnist

# This will download the data; change this to where you want it.
# (Yes, it's a 0-argument function, that's what the library expects.)
# (Yes, I'm assigning a lambda to a variable, like I said never to do.)
mnist.temporary_dir = lambda: '/tmp'

# Each of these functions first downloads the data and returns a numpy array.
# We call .tolist() because our "tensors" are just lists.
train_images = mnist.train_images().tolist()
train_labels = mnist.train_labels().tolist()

assert shape(train_images) == [60000, 28, 28]
assert shape(train_labels) == [60000]
```

Let's plot the first 100 training images to see what they look like (Figure 19-1):

```
import matplotlib.pyplot as plt

fig, ax = plt.subplots(10, 10)

for i in range(10):
    for j in range(10):
        # Plot each image in black and white and hide the axes.
        ax[i][j].imshow(train_images[10 * i + j], cmap='Greys')
        ax[i][j].xaxis.set_visible(False)
        ax[i][j].yaxis.set_visible(False)

plt.show()
```

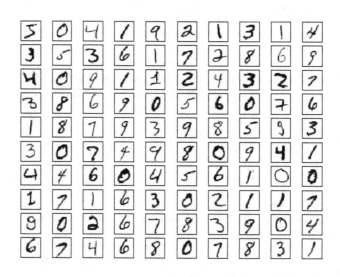

Figure 19-1. MNIST images

You can see that indeed they look like handwritten digits.

My first attempt at showing the images resulted in yellow numbers on black backgrounds. I am neither clever nor subtle enough to know that I needed to add `cmap=Greys` to get black-and-white images; I Googled it and found the solution on Stack Overflow. As a data scientist you will become quite adept at this workflow.

We also need to load the test images:

```
test_images = mnist.test_images().tolist()
test_labels = mnist.test_labels().tolist()

assert shape(test_images) == [10000, 28, 28]
assert shape(test_labels) == [10000]
```

Each image is 28 × 28 pixels, but our linear layers can only deal with one-dimensional inputs, so we'll just flatten them (and also divide by 256 to get them between 0 and 1). In addition, our neural net will train better if our inputs are 0 on average, so we'll subtract out the average value:

```
# Compute the average pixel value
avg = tensor_sum(train_images) / 60000 / 28 / 28

# Recenter, rescale, and flatten
train_images = [[(pixel - avg) / 256 for row in image for pixel in row]
```

```
              for image in train_images]
test_images = [[(pixel - avg) / 256 for row in image for pixel in row]
              for image in test_images]

assert shape(train_images) == [60000, 784], "images should be flattened"
assert shape(test_images) == [10000, 784], "images should be flattened"

# After centering, average pixel should be very close to 0
assert -0.0001 < tensor_sum(train_images) < 0.0001
```

We also want to one-hot-encode the targets, since we have 10 outputs. First let's write a one_hot_encode function:

```
def one_hot_encode(i: int, num_labels: int = 10) -> List[float]:
    return [1.0 if j == i else 0.0 for j in range(num_labels)]

assert one_hot_encode(3) == [0, 0, 0, 1, 0, 0, 0, 0, 0, 0]
assert one_hot_encode(2, num_labels=5) == [0, 0, 1, 0, 0]
```

and then apply it to our data:

```
train_labels = [one_hot_encode(label) for label in train_labels]
test_labels = [one_hot_encode(label) for label in test_labels]

assert shape(train_labels) == [60000, 10]
assert shape(test_labels) == [10000, 10]
```

One of the strengths of our abstractions is that we can use the same training/evaluation loop with a variety of models. So let's write that first. We'll pass it our model, the data, a loss function, and (if we're training) an optimizer.

It will make a pass through our data, track performance, and (if we passed in an optimizer) update our parameters:

```
import tqdm

def loop(model: Layer,
        images: List[Tensor],
        labels: List[Tensor],
        loss: Loss,
        optimizer: Optimizer = None) -> None:
    correct = 0        # Track number of correct predictions.
    total_loss = 0.0   # Track total loss.

    with tqdm.trange(len(images)) as t:
        for i in t:
            predicted = model.forward(images[i])           # Predict.
            if argmax(predicted) == argmax(labels[i]):     # Check for
                correct += 1                               # correctness.
            total_loss += loss.loss(predicted, labels[i])  # Compute loss.

            # If we're training, backpropagate gradient and update weights.
            if optimizer is not None:
```

```
                    gradient = loss.gradient(predicted, labels[i])
                    model.backward(gradient)
                    optimizer.step(model)

                # And update our metrics in the progress bar.
                avg_loss = total_loss / (i + 1)
                acc = correct / (i + 1)
                t.set_description(f"mnist loss: {avg_loss:.3f} acc: {acc:.3f}")
```

As a baseline, we can use our deep learning library to train a (multiclass) logistic regression model, which is just a single linear layer followed by a softmax. This model (in essence) just looks for 10 linear functions such that if the input represents, say, a 5, then the 5th linear function produces the largest output.

One pass through our 60,000 training examples should be enough to learn the model:

```
random.seed(0)

# Logistic regression is just a linear layer followed by softmax
model = Linear(784, 10)
loss = SoftmaxCrossEntropy()

# This optimizer seems to work
optimizer = Momentum(learning_rate=0.01, momentum=0.99)

# Train on the training data
loop(model, train_images, train_labels, loss, optimizer)

# Test on the test data (no optimizer means just evaluate)
loop(model, test_images, test_labels, loss)
```

This gets about 89% accuracy. Let's see if we can do better with a deep neural network. We'll use two hidden layers, the first with 30 neurons, and the second with 10 neurons. And we'll use our Tanh activation:

```
random.seed(0)

# Name them so we can turn train on and off
dropout1 = Dropout(0.1)
dropout2 = Dropout(0.1)

model = Sequential([
    Linear(784, 30),   # Hidden layer 1: size 30
    dropout1,
    Tanh(),
    Linear(30, 10),    # Hidden layer 2: size 10
    dropout2,
    Tanh(),
    Linear(10, 10)     # Output layer: size 10
])
```

And we can just use the same training loop!

```
optimizer = Momentum(learning_rate=0.01, momentum=0.99)
loss = SoftmaxCrossEntropy()

# Enable dropout and train (takes > 20 minutes on my laptop!)
dropout1.train = dropout2.train = True
loop(model, train_images, train_labels, loss, optimizer)

# Disable dropout and evaluate
dropout1.train = dropout2.train = False
loop(model, test_images, test_labels, loss)
```

Our deep model gets better than 92% accuracy on the test set, which is a nice improvement from the simple logistic model.

The MNIST website (*http://yann.lecun.com/exdb/mnist/*) describes a variety of models that outperform these. Many of them could be implemented using the machinery we've developed so far but would take an extremely long time to train in our lists-as-tensors framework. Some of the best models involve *convolutional* layers, which are important but unfortunately quite out of scope for an introductory book on data science.

Saving and Loading Models

These models take a long time to train, so it would be nice if we could save them so that we don't have to train them every time. Luckily, we can use the `json` module to easily serialize model weights to a file.

For saving, we can use `Layer.params` to collect the weights, stick them in a list, and use `json.dump` to save that list to a file:

```
import json

def save_weights(model: Layer, filename: str) -> None:
    weights = list(model.params())
    with open(filename, 'w') as f:
        json.dump(weights, f)
```

Loading the weights back is only a little more work. We just use `json.load` to get the list of weights back from the file and slice assignment to set the weights of our model.

(In particular, this means that we have to instantiate the model ourselves and *then* load the weights. An alternative approach would be to also save some representation of the model architecture and use that to instantiate the model. That's not a terrible idea, but it would require a lot more code and changes to all our `Layer`s, so we'll stick with the simpler way.)

Before we load the weights, we'd like to check that they have the same shapes as the model params we're loading them into. (This is a safeguard against, for example, trying to load the weights for a saved deep network into a shallow network, or similar issues.)

```
def load_weights(model: Layer, filename: str) -> None:
    with open(filename) as f:
        weights = json.load(f)

    # Check for consistency
    assert all(shape(param) == shape(weight)
               for param, weight in zip(model.params(), weights))

    # Then load using slice assignment
    for param, weight in zip(model.params(), weights):
        param[:] = weight
```

 JSON stores your data as text, which makes it an extremely inefficient representation. In real applications you'd probably use the `pickle` serialization library, which serializes things to a more efficient binary format. Here I decided to keep it simple and human-readable.

You can download the weights for the various networks we train from the book's GitHub repository (*https://github.com/joelgrus/data-science-from-scratch*).

For Further Exploration

Deep learning is really hot right now, and in this chapter we barely scratched its surface. There are many good books and blog posts (and many, many bad blog posts) about almost any aspect of deep learning you'd like to know about.

- The canonical textbook *Deep Learning* (*https://www.deeplearningbook.org/*), by Ian Goodfellow, Yoshua Bengio, and Aaron Courville (MIT Press), is freely available online. It is very good, but it involves quite a bit of mathematics.

- Francois Chollet's *Deep Learning with Python* (*https://www.manning.com/books/deep-learning-with-python*) (Manning) is a great introduction to the Keras library, after which our deep learning library is sort of patterned.

- I myself mostly use PyTorch (*https://pytorch.org/*) for deep learning. Its website has lots of documentation and tutorials.

## CHAPTER 20

Clustering

Where we such clusters had
As made us nobly wild, not mad
> —Robert Herrick

Most of the algorithms in this book are what's known as *supervised learning* algorithms, in that they start with a set of labeled data and use that as the basis for making predictions about new, unlabeled data. Clustering, however, is an example of *unsupervised learning*, in which we work with completely unlabeled data (or in which our data has labels but we ignore them).

The Idea

Whenever you look at some source of data, it's likely that the data will somehow form *clusters*. A dataset showing where millionaires live probably has clusters in places like Beverly Hills and Manhattan. A dataset showing how many hours people work each week probably has a cluster around 40 (and if it's taken from a state with laws mandating special benefits for people who work at least 20 hours a week, it probably has another cluster right around 19). A dataset of demographics of registered voters likely forms a variety of clusters (e.g., "soccer moms," "bored retirees," "unemployed millennials") that pollsters and political consultants consider relevant.

Unlike some of the problems we've looked at, there is generally no "correct" clustering. An alternative clustering scheme might group some of the "unemployed millennials" with "grad students," and others with "parents' basement dwellers." Neither scheme is necessarily more correct—instead, each is likely more optimal with respect to its own "how good are the clusters?" metric.

Furthermore, the clusters won't label themselves. You'll have to do that by looking at the data underlying each one.

The Model

For us, each `input` will be a vector in d-dimensional space, which, as usual, we will represent as a list of numbers. Our goal will be to identify clusters of similar inputs and (sometimes) to find a representative value for each cluster.

For example, each input could be a numeric vector that represents the title of a blog post, in which case the goal might be to find clusters of similar posts, perhaps in order to understand what our users are blogging about. Or imagine that we have a picture containing thousands of (`red`, `green`, `blue`) colors and that we need to screen-print a 10-color version of it. Clustering can help us choose 10 colors that will minimize the total "color error."

One of the simplest clustering methods is k-means, in which the number of clusters k is chosen in advance, after which the goal is to partition the inputs into sets $S_1, ..., S_k$ in a way that minimizes the total sum of squared distances from each point to the mean of its assigned cluster.

There are a lot of ways to assign n points to k clusters, which means that finding an optimal clustering is a very hard problem. We'll settle for an iterative algorithm that usually finds a good clustering:

1. Start with a set of k-means, which are points in d-dimensional space.
2. Assign each point to the mean to which it is closest.
3. If no point's assignment has changed, stop and keep the clusters.
4. If some point's assignment has changed, recompute the means and return to step 2.

Using the `vector_mean` function from Chapter 4, it's pretty simple to create a class that does this.

To start with, we'll create a helper function that measures how many coordinates two vectors differ in. We'll use this to track our training progress:

```
from scratch.linear_algebra import Vector

def num_differences(v1: Vector, v2: Vector) -> int:
    assert len(v1) == len(v2)
    return len([x1 for x1, x2 in zip(v1, v2) if x1 != x2])

assert num_differences([1, 2, 3], [2, 1, 3]) == 2
assert num_differences([1, 2], [1, 2]) == 0
```

We also need a function that, given some vectors and their assignments to clusters, computes the means of the clusters. It may be the case that some cluster has no points assigned to it. We can't take the mean of an empty collection, so in that case we'll just randomly pick one of the points to serve as the "mean" of that cluster:

```python
from typing import List
from scratch.linear_algebra import vector_mean

def cluster_means(k: int,
                  inputs: List[Vector],
                  assignments: List[int]) -> List[Vector]:
    # clusters[i] contains the inputs whose assignment is i
    clusters = [[] for i in range(k)]
    for input, assignment in zip(inputs, assignments):
        clusters[assignment].append(input)

    # if a cluster is empty, just use a random point
    return [vector_mean(cluster) if cluster else random.choice(inputs)
            for cluster in clusters]
```

And now we're ready to code up our clusterer. As usual, we'll use tqdm to track our progress, but here we don't know how many iterations it will take, so we then use itertools.count, which creates an infinite iterable, and we'll return out of it when we're done:

```python
import itertools
import random
import tqdm
from scratch.linear_algebra import squared_distance

class KMeans:
    def __init__(self, k: int) -> None:
        self.k = k                      # number of clusters
        self.means = None

    def classify(self, input: Vector) -> int:
        """return the index of the cluster closest to the input"""
        return min(range(self.k),
                   key=lambda i: squared_distance(input, self.means[i]))

    def train(self, inputs: List[Vector]) -> None:
        # Start with random assignments
        assignments = [random.randrange(self.k) for _ in inputs]

        with tqdm.tqdm(itertools.count()) as t:
            for _ in t:
                # Compute means and find new assignments
                self.means = cluster_means(self.k, inputs, assignments)
                new_assignments = [self.classify(input) for input in inputs]

                # Check how many assignments changed and if we're done
                num_changed = num_differences(assignments, new_assignments)
                if num_changed == 0:
                    return
```

```
# Otherwise keep the new assignments, and compute new means
assignments = new_assignments
self.means = cluster_means(self.k, inputs, assignments)
t.set_description(f"changed: {num_changed} / {len(inputs)}")
```

Let's take a look at how this works.

Example: Meetups

To celebrate DataSciencester's growth, your VP of User Rewards wants to organize several in-person meetups for your hometown users, complete with beer, pizza, and DataSciencester t-shirts. You know the locations of all your local users (Figure 20-1), and she'd like you to choose meetup locations that make it convenient for everyone to attend.

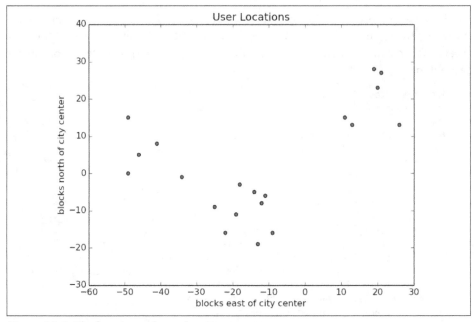

Figure 20-1. The locations of your hometown users

Depending on how you look at it, you probably see two or three clusters. (It's easy to do visually because the data is only two-dimensional. With more dimensions, it would be a lot harder to eyeball.)

Imagine first that she has enough budget for three meetups. You go to your computer and try this:

```
random.seed(12)                    # so you get the same results as me
clusterer = KMeans(k=3)
```

```
clusterer.train(inputs)
means = sorted(clusterer.means)    # sort for the unit test

assert len(means) == 3

# Check that the means are close to what we expect
assert squared_distance(means[0], [-44, 5]) < 1
assert squared_distance(means[1], [-16, -10]) < 1
assert squared_distance(means[2], [18, 20]) < 1
```

You find three clusters centered at [–44, 5], [–16, –10], and [18, 20], and you look for meetup venues near those locations (Figure 20-2).

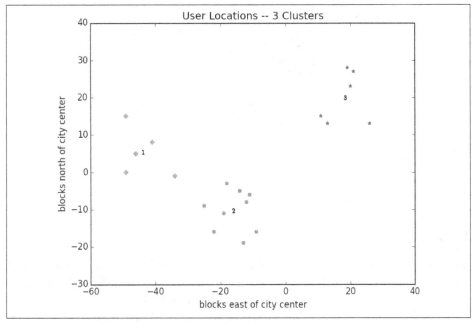

Figure 20-2. User locations grouped into three clusters

You show your results to the VP, who informs you that now she only has enough budgeted for *two* meetups.

"No problem," you say:

```
random.seed(0)
clusterer = KMeans(k=2)
clusterer.train(inputs)
means = sorted(clusterer.means)

assert len(means) == 2
assert squared_distance(means[0], [-26, -5]) < 1
assert squared_distance(means[1], [18, 20]) < 1
```

As shown in Figure 20-3, one meetup should still be near [18, 20], but now the other should be near [−26, −5].

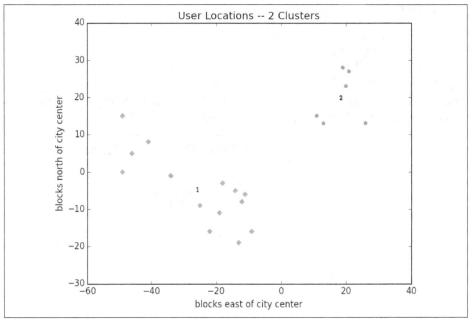

Figure 20-3. User locations grouped into two clusters

Choosing k

In the previous example, the choice of *k* was driven by factors outside of our control. In general, this won't be the case. There are various ways to choose a *k*. One that's reasonably easy to understand involves plotting the sum of squared errors (between each point and the mean of its cluster) as a function of *k* and looking at where the graph "bends":

```
from matplotlib import pyplot as plt

def squared_clustering_errors(inputs: List[Vector], k: int) -> float:
    """finds the total squared error from k-means clustering the inputs"""
    clusterer = KMeans(k)
    clusterer.train(inputs)
    means = clusterer.means
    assignments = [clusterer.classify(input) for input in inputs]

    return sum(squared_distance(input, means[cluster])
               for input, cluster in zip(inputs, assignments))
```

which we can apply to our previous example:

```
# now plot from 1 up to len(inputs) clusters

ks = range(1, len(inputs) + 1)
errors = [squared_clustering_errors(inputs, k) for k in ks]

plt.plot(ks, errors)
plt.xticks(ks)
plt.xlabel("k")
plt.ylabel("total squared error")
plt.title("Total Error vs. # of Clusters")
plt.show()
```

Looking at Figure 20-4, this method agrees with our original eyeballing that three is the "right" number of clusters.

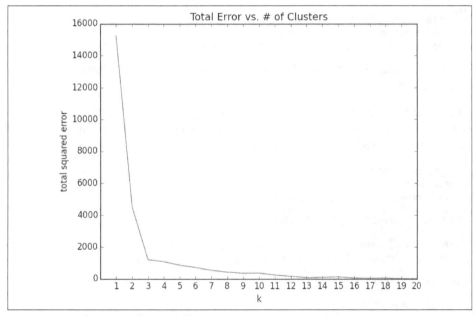

Figure 20-4. Choosing a k

Example: Clustering Colors

The VP of Swag has designed attractive DataSciencester stickers that he'd like you to hand out at meetups. Unfortunately, your sticker printer can print at most five colors per sticker. And since the VP of Art is on sabbatical, the VP of Swag asks if there's some way you can take his design and modify it so that it contains only five colors.

Computer images can be represented as two-dimensional arrays of pixels, where each pixel is itself a three-dimensional vector (red, green, blue) indicating its color.

Creating a five-color version of the image, then, entails:

1. Choosing five colors.

2. Assigning one of those colors to each pixel.

It turns out this is a great task for *k*-means clustering, which can partition the pixels into five clusters in red-green-blue space. If we then recolor the pixels in each cluster to the mean color, we're done.

To start with, we'll need a way to load an image into Python. We can do this with matplotlib, if we first install the pillow library:

```
python -m pip install pillow
```

Then we can just use `matplotlib.image.imread`:

```
image_path = r"girl_with_book.jpg"     # wherever your image is
import matplotlib.image as mpimg
img = mpimg.imread(image_path) / 256 # rescale to between 0 and 1
```

Behind the scenes `img` is a NumPy array, but for our purposes, we can treat it as a list of lists of lists.

`img[i][j]` is the pixel in the *i*th row and *j*th column, and each pixel is a list `[red, green, blue]` of numbers between 0 and 1 indicating the color of that pixel (*http://en.wikipedia.org/wiki/RGB_color_model*):

```
top_row = img[0]
top_left_pixel = top_row[0]
red, green, blue = top_left_pixel
```

In particular, we can get a flattened list of all the pixels as:

```
# .tolist() converts a NumPy array to a Python list
pixels = [pixel.tolist() for row in img for pixel in row]
```

and then feed them to our clusterer:

```
clusterer = KMeans(5)
clusterer.train(pixels)   # this might take a while
```

Once it finishes, we just construct a new image with the same format:

```
def recolor(pixel: Vector) -> Vector:
    cluster = clusterer.classify(pixel)     # index of the closest cluster
    return clusterer.means[cluster]         # mean of the closest cluster

new_img = [[recolor(pixel) for pixel in row]    # recolor this row of pixels
           for row in img]                      # for each row in the image
```

and display it, using `plt.imshow`:

```
plt.imshow(new_img)
plt.axis('off')
plt.show()
```

It is difficult to show color results in a black-and-white book, but Figure 20-5 shows grayscale versions of a full-color picture and the output of using this process to reduce it to five colors.

Figure 20-5. Original picture and its 5-means decoloring

Bottom-Up Hierarchical Clustering

An alternative approach to clustering is to "grow" clusters from the bottom up. We can do this in the following way:

1. Make each input its own cluster of one.

2. As long as there are multiple clusters remaining, find the two closest clusters and merge them.

At the end, we'll have one giant cluster containing all the inputs. If we keep track of the merge order, we can re-create any number of clusters by unmerging. For example, if we want three clusters, we can just undo the last two merges.

We'll use a really simple representation of clusters. Our values will live in *leaf* clusters, which we will represent as NamedTuples:

```python
from typing import NamedTuple, Union

class Leaf(NamedTuple):
    value: Vector

leaf1 = Leaf([10,  20])
leaf2 = Leaf([30, -15])
```

We'll use these to grow *merged* clusters, which we will also represent as NamedTuples:

```
class Merged(NamedTuple):
    children: tuple
    order: int

merged = Merged((leaf1, leaf2), order=1)

Cluster = Union[Leaf, Merged]
```

 This is another case where Python's type annotations have let us down. You'd like to type hint Merged.children as Tuple[Cluster, Cluster] but mypy doesn't allow recursive types like that.

We'll talk about merge order in a bit, but first let's create a helper function that recursively returns all the values contained in a (possibly merged) cluster:

```
def get_values(cluster: Cluster) -> List[Vector]:
    if isinstance(cluster, Leaf):
        return [cluster.value]
    else:
        return [value
                for child in cluster.children
                for value in get_values(child)]

assert get_values(merged) == [[10, 20], [30, -15]]
```

In order to merge the closest clusters, we need some notion of the distance between clusters. We'll use the *minimum* distance between elements of the two clusters, which merges the two clusters that are closest to touching (but will sometimes produce large chain-like clusters that aren't very tight). If we wanted tight spherical clusters, we might use the *maximum* distance instead, as it merges the two clusters that fit in the smallest ball. Both are common choices, as is the *average* distance:

```
from typing import Callable
from scratch.linear_algebra import distance

def cluster_distance(cluster1: Cluster,
                     cluster2: Cluster,
                     distance_agg: Callable = min) -> float:
    """
    compute all the pairwise distances between cluster1 and cluster2
    and apply the aggregation function _distance_agg_ to the resulting list
    """
    return distance_agg([distance(v1, v2)
                         for v1 in get_values(cluster1)
                         for v2 in get_values(cluster2)])
```

We'll use the merge order slot to track the order in which we did the merging. Smaller numbers will represent *later* merges. This means when we want to unmerge clusters, we do so from lowest merge order to highest. Since `Leaf` clusters were never merged, we'll assign them infinity, the highest possible value. And since they don't have an `.order` property, we'll create a helper function:

```python
def get_merge_order(cluster: Cluster) -> float:
    if isinstance(cluster, Leaf):
        return float('inf')  # was never merged
    else:
        return cluster.order
```

Similarly, since `Leaf` clusters don't have children, we'll create and add a helper function for that:

```python
from typing import Tuple

def get_children(cluster: Cluster):
    if isinstance(cluster, Leaf):
        raise TypeError("Leaf has no children")
    else:
        return cluster.children
```

Now we're ready to create the clustering algorithm:

```python
def bottom_up_cluster(inputs: List[Vector],
                      distance_agg: Callable = min) -> Cluster:
    # Start with all leaves
    clusters: List[Cluster] = [Leaf(input) for input in inputs]

    def pair_distance(pair: Tuple[Cluster, Cluster]) -> float:
        return cluster_distance(pair[0], pair[1], distance_agg)

    # as long as we have more than one cluster left...
    while len(clusters) > 1:
        # find the two closest clusters
        c1, c2 = min(((cluster1, cluster2)
                      for i, cluster1 in enumerate(clusters)
                      for cluster2 in clusters[:i]),
                     key=pair_distance)

        # remove them from the list of clusters
        clusters = [c for c in clusters if c != c1 and c != c2]

        # merge them, using merge_order = # of clusters left
        merged_cluster = Merged((c1, c2), order=len(clusters))

        # and add their merge
        clusters.append(merged_cluster)

    # when there's only one cluster left, return it
    return clusters[0]
```

Its use is very simple:

```
base_cluster = bottom_up_cluster(inputs)
```

This produces a clustering that looks as follows:

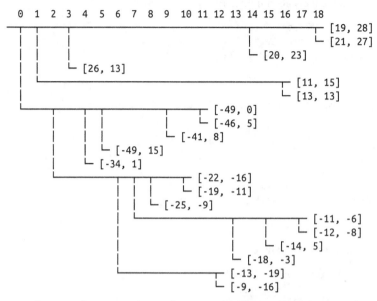

The numbers at the top indicate "merge order." Since we had 20 inputs, it took 19 merges to get to this one cluster. The first merge created cluster 18 by combining the leaves [19, 28] and [21, 27]. And the last merge created cluster 0.

If you wanted only two clusters, you'd split at the first fork ("0"), creating one cluster with six points and a second with the rest. For three clusters, you'd continue to the second fork ("1"), which indicates to split that first cluster into the cluster with ([19, 28], [21, 27], [20, 23], [26, 13]) and the cluster with ([11, 15], [13, 13]). And so on.

Generally, though, we don't want to be squinting at nasty text representations like this. Instead, let's write a function that generates any number of clusters by performing the appropriate number of unmerges:

```python
def generate_clusters(base_cluster: Cluster,
                      num_clusters: int) -> List[Cluster]:
    # start with a list with just the base cluster
    clusters = [base_cluster]

    # as long as we don't have enough clusters yet...
    while len(clusters) < num_clusters:
        # choose the last-merged of our clusters
        next_cluster = min(clusters, key=get_merge_order)
        # remove it from the list
        clusters = [c for c in clusters if c != next_cluster]

        # and add its children to the list (i.e., unmerge it)
```

```
        clusters.extend(get_children(next_cluster))

    # once we have enough clusters...
    return clusters
```

So, for example, if we want to generate three clusters, we can just do:

```
three_clusters = [get_values(cluster)
                  for cluster in generate_clusters(base_cluster, 3)]
```

which we can easily plot:

```
for i, cluster, marker, color in zip([1, 2, 3],
                                     three_clusters,
                                     ['D','o','*'],
                                     ['r','g','b']):
    xs, ys = zip(*cluster)  # magic unzipping trick
    plt.scatter(xs, ys, color=color, marker=marker)

    # put a number at the mean of the cluster
    x, y = vector_mean(cluster)
    plt.plot(x, y, marker='$' + str(i) + '$', color='black')

plt.title("User Locations -- 3 Bottom-Up Clusters, Min")
plt.xlabel("blocks east of city center")
plt.ylabel("blocks north of city center")
plt.show()
```

This gives very different results than k-means did, as shown in Figure 20-6.

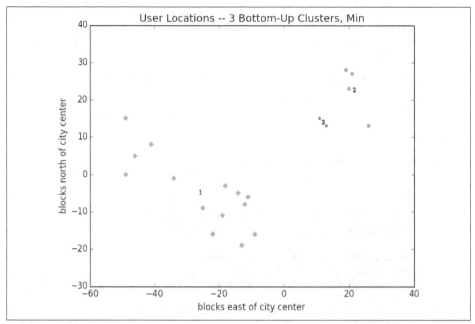

Figure 20-6. Three bottom-up clusters using min distance

As mentioned previously, this is because using `min` in `cluster_distance` tends to give chain-like clusters. If we instead use `max` (which gives tight clusters), it looks the same as the 3-means result (Figure 20-7).

The previous `bottom_up_clustering` implementation is relatively simple, but also shockingly inefficient. In particular, it recomputes the distance between each pair of inputs at every step. A more efficient implementation might instead precompute the distances between each pair of inputs and then perform a lookup inside `clus ter_distance`. A *really* efficient implementation would likely also remember the `cluster_distances` from the previous step.

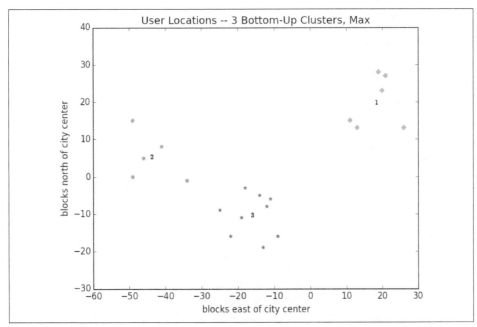

Figure 20-7. Three bottom-up clusters using max distance

For Further Exploration

- scikit-learn has an entire module, `sklearn.cluster` (*http://scikit-learn.org/stable/modules/clustering.html*), that contains several clustering algorithms including `KMeans` and the `Ward` hierarchical clustering algorithm (which uses a different criterion for merging clusters than ours did).

- SciPy (*http://www.scipy.org/*) has two clustering models: `scipy.cluster.vq`, which does *k*-means, and `scipy.cluster.hierarchy`, which has a variety of hierarchical clustering algorithms.

## CHAPTER 21

Natural Language Processing

They have been at a great feast of languages, and stolen the scraps.
—William Shakespeare

Natural language processing (NLP) refers to computational techniques involving language. It's a broad field, but we'll look at a few techniques, both simple and not simple.

Word Clouds

In Chapter 1, we computed word counts of users' interests. One approach to visualizing words and counts is *word clouds*, which artistically depict the words at sizes proportional to their counts.

Generally, though, data scientists don't think much of word clouds, in large part because the placement of the words doesn't mean anything other than "here's some space where I was able to fit a word."

If you ever are forced to create a word cloud, think about whether you can make the axes convey something. For example, imagine that, for each of some collection of data science–related buzzwords, you have two numbers between 0 and 100—the first representing how frequently it appears in job postings, and the second how frequently it appears on résumés:

```
data = [ ("big data", 100, 15), ("Hadoop", 95, 25), ("Python", 75, 50),
         ("R", 50, 40), ("machine learning", 80, 20), ("statistics", 20, 60),
         ("data science", 60, 70), ("analytics", 90, 3),
         ("team player", 85, 85), ("dynamic", 2, 90), ("synergies", 70, 0),
         ("actionable insights", 40, 30), ("think out of the box", 45, 10),
         ("self-starter", 30, 50), ("customer focus", 65, 15),
         ("thought leadership", 35, 35)]
```

The word cloud approach is just to arrange the words on a page in a cool-looking font (Figure 21-1).

Figure 21-1. Buzzword cloud

This looks neat but doesn't really tell us anything. A more interesting approach might be to scatter them so that horizontal position indicates posting popularity and vertical position indicates résumé popularity, which produces a visualization that conveys a few insights (Figure 21-2):

```
from matplotlib import pyplot as plt

def text_size(total: int) -> float:
    """equals 8 if total is 0, 28 if total is 200"""
    return 8 + total / 200 * 20

for word, job_popularity, resume_popularity in data:
    plt.text(job_popularity, resume_popularity, word,
             ha='center', va='center',
             size=text_size(job_popularity + resume_popularity))
plt.xlabel("Popularity on Job Postings")
plt.ylabel("Popularity on Resumes")
plt.axis([0, 100, 0, 100])
plt.xticks([])
plt.yticks([])
plt.show()
```

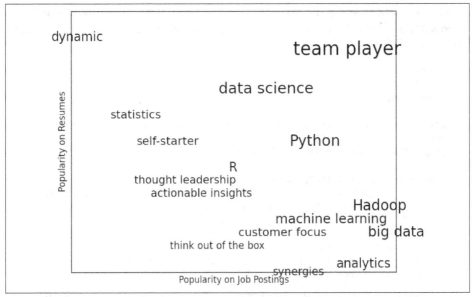

Figure 21-2. A more meaningful (if less attractive) word cloud

n-Gram Language Models

The DataSciencester VP of Search Engine Marketing wants to create thousands of web pages about data science so that your site will rank higher in search results for data science–related terms. (You attempt to explain to her that search engine algorithms are clever enough that this won't actually work, but she refuses to listen.)

Of course, she doesn't want to write thousands of web pages, nor does she want to pay a horde of "content strategists" to do so. Instead, she asks you whether you can somehow programmatically generate these web pages. To do this, we'll need some way of modeling language.

One approach is to start with a corpus of documents and learn a statistical model of language. In our case, we'll start with Mike Loukides's essay "What Is Data Science?" (*http://oreil.ly/1Cd6ykN*)

As in Chapter 9, we'll use the Requests and Beautiful Soup libraries to retrieve the data. There are a couple of issues worth calling attention to.

The first is that the apostrophes in the text are actually the Unicode character u"\u2019". We'll create a helper function to replace them with normal apostrophes:

```python
def fix_unicode(text: str) -> str:
    return text.replace(u"\u2019", "'")
```

The second issue is that once we get the text of the web page, we'll want to split it into a sequence of words and periods (so that we can tell where sentences end). We can do this using re.findall:

```
import re
from bs4 import BeautifulSoup
import requests

url = "https://www.oreilly.com/ideas/what-is-data-science"
html = requests.get(url).text
soup = BeautifulSoup(html, 'html5lib')

content = soup.find("div", "article-body")   # find article-body div
regex = r"[\w']+|[\.]"                        # matches a word or a period

document = []

for paragraph in content("p"):
    words = re.findall(regex, fix_unicode(paragraph.text))
    document.extend(words)
```

We certainly could (and likely should) clean this data further. There is still some amount of extraneous text in the document (for example, the first word is *Section*), and we've split on midsentence periods (for example, in *Web 2.0*), and there are a handful of captions and lists sprinkled throughout. Having said that, we'll work with the document as it is.

Now that we have the text as a sequence of words, we can model language in the following way: given some starting word (say, *book*) we look at all the words that follow it in the source document. We randomly choose one of these to be the next word, and we repeat the process until we get to a period, which signifies the end of the sentence. We call this a *bigram model*, as it is determined completely by the frequencies of the bigrams (word pairs) in the original data.

What about a starting word? We can just pick randomly from words that *follow* a period. To start, let's precompute the possible word transitions. Recall that zip stops when any of its inputs is done, so that zip(document, document[1:]) gives us precisely the pairs of consecutive elements of document:

```
from collections import defaultdict

transitions = defaultdict(list)
for prev, current in zip(document, document[1:]):
    transitions[prev].append(current)
```

Now we're ready to generate sentences:

```
def generate_using_bigrams() -> str:
    current = "."    # this means the next word will start a sentence
    result = []
    while True:
```

```
    next_word_candidates = transitions[current]      # bigrams (current, _)
    current = random.choice(next_word_candidates)    # choose one at random
    result.append(current)                           # append it to results
    if current == ".": return " ".join(result)       # if "." we're done
```

The sentences it produces are gibberish, but they're the kind of gibberish you might put on your website if you were trying to sound data-sciencey. For example:

> If you may know which are you want to data sort the data feeds web friend someone on trending topics as the data in Hadoop is the data science requires a book demonstrates why visualizations are but we do massive correlations across many commercial disk drives in Python language and creates more tractable form making connections then use and uses it to solve a data.
>
> —Bigram Model

We can make the sentences less gibberishy by looking at *trigrams*, triplets of consecutive words. (More generally, you might look at *n-grams* consisting of *n* consecutive words, but three will be plenty for us.) Now the transitions will depend on the previous *two* words:

```
trigram_transitions = defaultdict(list)
starts = []

for prev, current, next in zip(document, document[1:], document[2:]):

    if prev == ".":              # if the previous "word" was a period
        starts.append(current)   # then this is a start word

    trigram_transitions[(prev, current)].append(next)
```

Notice that now we have to track the starting words separately. We can generate sentences in pretty much the same way:

```
def generate_using_trigrams() -> str:
    current = random.choice(starts)    # choose a random starting word
    prev = "."                         # and precede it with a '.'
    result = [current]
    while True:
        next_word_candidates = trigram_transitions[(prev, current)]
        next_word = random.choice(next_word_candidates)

        prev, current = current, next_word
        result.append(current)

        if current == ".":
            return " ".join(result)
```

This produces better sentences like:

> In hindsight MapReduce seems like an epidemic and if so does that give us new insights into how economies work That's not a question we could even have asked a few years there has been instrumented.

Of course, they sound better because at each step the generation process has fewer choices, and at many steps only a single choice. This means that we frequently generate sentences (or at least long phrases) that were seen verbatim in the original data. Having more data would help; it would also work better if we collected *n*-grams from multiple essays about data science.

Grammars

A different approach to modeling language is with *grammars*, rules for generating acceptable sentences. In elementary school, you probably learned about parts of speech and how to combine them. For example, if you had a really bad English teacher, you might say that a sentence necessarily consists of a *noun* followed by a *verb*. If you then have a list of nouns and verbs, you can generate sentences according to the rule.

We'll define a slightly more complicated grammar:

```
from typing import List, Dict

# Type alias to refer to grammars later
Grammar = Dict[str, List[str]]

grammar = {
    "_S"  : ["_NP _VP"],
    "_NP" : ["_N",
             "_A _NP _P _A _N"],
    "_VP" : ["_V",
             "_V _NP"],
    "_N"  : ["data science", "Python", "regression"],
    "_A"  : ["big", "linear", "logistic"],
    "_P"  : ["about", "near"],
    "_V"  : ["learns", "trains", "tests", "is"]
}
```

I made up the convention that names starting with underscores refer to *rules* that need further expanding, and that other names are *terminals* that don't need further processing.

So, for example, "_S" is the "sentence" rule, which produces an "_NP" ("noun phrase") rule followed by a "_VP" ("verb phrase") rule.

The verb phrase rule can produce either the "_V" ("verb") rule, or the verb rule followed by the noun phrase rule.

Notice that the "_NP" rule contains itself in one of its productions. Grammars can be recursive, which allows even finite grammars like this to generate infinitely many different sentences.

How do we generate sentences from this grammar? We'll start with a list containing the sentence rule ["_S"]. And then we'll repeatedly expand each rule by replacing it with a randomly chosen one of its productions. We stop when we have a list consisting solely of terminals.

For example, one such progression might look like:

```
['_S']
['_NP','_VP']
['_N','_VP']
['Python','_VP']
['Python','_V','_NP']
['Python','trains','_NP']
['Python','trains','_A','_NP','_P','_A','_N']
['Python','trains','logistic','_NP','_P','_A','_N']
['Python','trains','logistic','_N','_P','_A','_N']
['Python','trains','logistic','data science','_P','_A','_N']
['Python','trains','logistic','data science','about','_A', '_N']
['Python','trains','logistic','data science','about','logistic','_N']
['Python','trains','logistic','data science','about','logistic','Python']
```

How do we implement this? Well, to start, we'll create a simple helper function to identify terminals:

```python
def is_terminal(token: str) -> bool:
    return token[0] != "_"
```

Next we need to write a function to turn a list of tokens into a sentence. We'll look for the first nonterminal token. If we can't find one, that means we have a completed sentence and we're done.

If we do find a nonterminal, then we randomly choose one of its productions. If that production is a terminal (i.e., a word), we simply replace the token with it. Otherwise, it's a sequence of space-separated nonterminal tokens that we need to split and then splice into the current tokens. Either way, we repeat the process on the new set of tokens.

Putting it all together, we get:

```python
def expand(grammar: Grammar, tokens: List[str]) -> List[str]:
    for i, token in enumerate(tokens):
        # If this is a terminal token, skip it.
        if is_terminal(token): continue

        # Otherwise, it's a nonterminal token,
        # so we need to choose a replacement at random.
        replacement = random.choice(grammar[token])

        if is_terminal(replacement):
            tokens[i] = replacement
        else:
            # Replacement could be, e.g., "_NP _VP", so we need to
```

```
            # split it on spaces and splice it in.
            tokens = tokens[:i] + replacement.split() + tokens[(i+1):]

        # Now call expand on the new list of tokens.
        return expand(grammar, tokens)

    # If we get here, we had all terminals and are done.
    return tokens
```

And now we can start generating sentences:

```
def generate_sentence(grammar: Grammar) -> List[str]:
    return expand(grammar, ["_S"])
```

Try changing the grammar—add more words, add more rules, add your own parts of speech—until you're ready to generate as many web pages as your company needs.

Grammars are actually more interesting when they're used in the other direction. Given a sentence, we can use a grammar to *parse* the sentence. This then allows us to identify subjects and verbs and helps us make sense of the sentence.

Using data science to generate text is a neat trick; using it to *understand* text is more magical. (See "For Further Exploration" on page 308 for libraries that you could use for this.)

An Aside: Gibbs Sampling

Generating samples from some distributions is easy. We can get uniform random variables with:

```
random.random()
```

and normal random variables with:

```
inverse_normal_cdf(random.random())
```

But some distributions are harder to sample from. *Gibbs sampling* is a technique for generating samples from multidimensional distributions when we only know some of the conditional distributions.

For example, imagine rolling two dice. Let x be the value of the first die and y be the sum of the dice, and imagine you wanted to generate lots of (x, y) pairs. In this case it's easy to generate the samples directly:

```
from typing import Tuple
import random

def roll_a_die() -> int:
    return random.choice([1, 2, 3, 4, 5, 6])

def direct_sample() -> Tuple[int, int]:
    d1 = roll_a_die()
```

```
    d2 = roll_a_die()
    return d1, d1 + d2
```

But imagine that you only knew the conditional distributions. The distribution of y conditional on x is easy—if you know the value of x, y is equally likely to be $x + 1$, $x + 2$, $x + 3$, $x + 4$, $x + 5$, or $x + 6$:

```
def random_y_given_x(x: int) -> int:
    """equally likely to be x + 1, x + 2, ... , x + 6"""
    return x + roll_a_die()
```

The other direction is more complicated. For example, if you know that y is 2, then necessarily x is 1 (since the only way two dice can sum to 2 is if both of them are 1). If you know y is 3, then x is equally likely to be 1 or 2. Similarly, if y is 11, then x has to be either 5 or 6:

```
def random_x_given_y(y: int) -> int:
    if y <= 7:
        # if the total is 7 or less, the first die is equally likely to be
        # 1, 2, ..., (total - 1)
        return random.randrange(1, y)
    else:
        # if the total is 7 or more, the first die is equally likely to be
        # (total - 6), (total - 5), ..., 6
        return random.randrange(y - 6, 7)
```

The way Gibbs sampling works is that we start with any (valid) values for x and y and then repeatedly alternate replacing x with a random value picked conditional on y and replacing y with a random value picked conditional on x. After a number of iterations, the resulting values of x and y will represent a sample from the unconditional joint distribution:

```
def gibbs_sample(num_iters: int = 100) -> Tuple[int, int]:
    x, y = 1, 2 # doesn't really matter
    for _ in range(num_iters):
        x = random_x_given_y(y)
        y = random_y_given_x(x)
    return x, y
```

You can check that this gives similar results to the direct sample:

```
def compare_distributions(num_samples: int = 1000) -> Dict[int, List[int]]:
    counts = defaultdict(lambda: [0, 0])
    for _ in range(num_samples):
        counts[gibbs_sample()][0] += 1
        counts[direct_sample()][1] += 1
    return counts
```

We'll use this technique in the next section.

Topic Modeling

When we built our "Data Scientists You May Know" recommender in Chapter 1, we simply looked for exact matches in people's stated interests.

A more sophisticated approach to understanding our users' interests might try to identify the *topics* that underlie those interests. A technique called *latent Dirichlet allocation* (LDA) is commonly used to identify common topics in a set of documents. We'll apply it to documents that consist of each user's interests.

LDA has some similarities to the Naive Bayes classifier we built in Chapter 13, in that it assumes a probabilistic model for documents. We'll gloss over the hairier mathematical details, but for our purposes the model assumes that:

- There is some fixed number K of topics.
- There is a random variable that assigns each topic an associated probability distribution over words. You should think of this distribution as the probability of seeing word w given topic k.
- There is another random variable that assigns each document a probability distribution over topics. You should think of this distribution as the mixture of topics in document d.
- Each word in a document was generated by first randomly picking a topic (from the document's distribution of topics) and then randomly picking a word (from the topic's distribution of words).

In particular, we have a collection of `documents`, each of which is a `list` of words. And we have a corresponding collection of `document_topics` that assigns a topic (here a number between 0 and $K - 1$) to each word in each document.

So, the fifth word in the fourth document is:

```
documents[3][4]
```

and the topic from which that word was chosen is:

```
document_topics[3][4]
```

This very explicitly defines each document's distribution over topics, and it implicitly defines each topic's distribution over words.

We can estimate the likelihood that topic 1 produces a certain word by comparing how many times topic 1 produces that word with how many times topic 1 produces *any* word. (Similarly, when we built a spam filter in Chapter 13, we compared how many times each word appeared in spams with the total number of words appearing in spams.)

Although these topics are just numbers, we can give them descriptive names by look-ing at the words on which they put the heaviest weight. We just have to somehow generate the document_topics. This is where Gibbs sampling comes into play.

We start by assigning every word in every document a topic completely at random. Now we go through each document one word at a time. For that word and document, we construct weights for each topic that depend on the (current) distribution of top-ics in that document and the (current) distribution of words for that topic. We then use those weights to sample a new topic for that word. If we iterate this process many times, we will end up with a joint sample from the topic–word distribution and the document–topic distribution.

To start with, we'll need a function to randomly choose an index based on an arbi-trary set of weights:

```python
def sample_from(weights: List[float]) -> int:
    """returns i with probability weights[i] / sum(weights)"""
    total = sum(weights)
    rnd = total * random.random()       # uniform between 0 and total
    for i, w in enumerate(weights):
        rnd -= w                        # return the smallest i such that
        if rnd <= 0: return i           # weights[0] + ... + weights[i] >= rnd
```

For instance, if you give it weights [1, 1, 3], then one-fifth of the time it will return 0, one-fifth of the time it will return 1, and three-fifths of the time it will return 2. Let's write a test:

```python
from collections import Counter

# Draw 1000 times and count
draws = Counter(sample_from([0.1, 0.1, 0.8]) for _ in range(1000))
assert 10 < draws[0] < 190   # should be ~10%, this is a really loose test
assert 10 < draws[1] < 190   # should be ~10%, this is a really loose test
assert 650 < draws[2] < 950  # should be ~80%, this is a really loose test
assert draws[0] + draws[1] + draws[2] == 1000
```

Our documents are our users' interests, which look like:

```python
documents = [
    ["Hadoop", "Big Data", "HBase", "Java", "Spark", "Storm", "Cassandra"],
    ["NoSQL", "MongoDB", "Cassandra", "HBase", "Postgres"],
    ["Python", "scikit-learn", "scipy", "numpy", "statsmodels", "pandas"],
    ["R", "Python", "statistics", "regression", "probability"],
    ["machine learning", "regression", "decision trees", "libsvm"],
    ["Python", "R", "Java", "C++", "Haskell", "programming languages"],
    ["statistics", "probability", "mathematics", "theory"],
    ["machine learning", "scikit-learn", "Mahout", "neural networks"],
    ["neural networks", "deep learning", "Big Data", "artificial intelligence"],
    ["Hadoop", "Java", "MapReduce", "Big Data"],
    ["statistics", "R", "statsmodels"],
    ["C++", "deep learning", "artificial intelligence", "probability"],
```

```
    ["pandas", "R", "Python"],
    ["databases", "HBase", "Postgres", "MySQL", "MongoDB"],
    ["libsvm", "regression", "support vector machines"]
]
```

And we'll try to find:

```
K = 4
```

topics. In order to calculate the sampling weights, we'll need to keep track of several counts. Let's first create the data structures for them.

- How many times each topic is assigned to each document:

```
# a list of Counters, one for each document
document_topic_counts = [Counter() for _ in documents]
```

- How many times each word is assigned to each topic:

```
# a list of Counters, one for each topic
topic_word_counts = [Counter() for _ in range(K)]
```

- The total number of words assigned to each topic:

```
# a list of numbers, one for each topic
topic_counts = [0 for _ in range(K)]
```

- The total number of words contained in each document:

```
# a list of numbers, one for each document
document_lengths = [len(document) for document in documents]
```

- The number of distinct words:

```
distinct_words = set(word for document in documents for word in document)
W = len(distinct_words)
```

- And the number of documents:

```
D = len(documents)
```

Once we populate these, we can find, for example, the number of words in docu ments[3] associated with topic 1 as follows:

```
document_topic_counts[3][1]
```

And we can find the number of times *nlp* is associated with topic 2 as follows:

```
topic_word_counts[2]["nlp"]
```

Now we're ready to define our conditional probability functions. As in Chapter 13, each has a smoothing term that ensures every topic has a nonzero chance of being chosen in any document and that every word has a nonzero chance of being chosen for any topic:

```
def p_topic_given_document(topic: int, d: int, alpha: float = 0.1) -> float:
    """
```

```
      The fraction of words in document 'd'
      that are assigned to 'topic' (plus some smoothing)
      """
      return ((document_topic_counts[d][topic] + alpha) /
              (document_lengths[d] + K * alpha))

  def p_word_given_topic(word: str, topic: int, beta: float = 0.1) -> float:
      """
      The fraction of words assigned to 'topic'
      that equal 'word' (plus some smoothing)
      """
      return ((topic_word_counts[topic][word] + beta) /
              (topic_counts[topic] + W * beta))
```

We'll use these to create the weights for updating topics:

```
  def topic_weight(d: int, word: str, k: int) -> float:
      """
      Given a document and a word in that document,
      return the weight for the kth topic
      """
      return p_word_given_topic(word, k) * p_topic_given_document(k, d)

  def choose_new_topic(d: int, word: str) -> int:
      return sample_from([topic_weight(d, word, k)
                          for k in range(K)])
```

There are solid mathematical reasons why topic_weight is defined the way it is, but their details would lead us too far afield. Hopefully it makes at least intuitive sense that—given a word and its document—the likelihood of any topic choice depends on both how likely that topic is for the document and how likely that word is for the topic.

This is all the machinery we need. We start by assigning every word to a random topic and populating our counters appropriately:

```
  random.seed(0)
  document_topics = [[random.randrange(K) for word in document]
                     for document in documents]

  for d in range(D):
      for word, topic in zip(documents[d], document_topics[d]):
          document_topic_counts[d][topic] += 1
          topic_word_counts[topic][word] += 1
          topic_counts[topic] += 1
```

Our goal is to get a joint sample of the topics–word distribution and the documents–topic distribution. We do this using a form of Gibbs sampling that uses the conditional probabilities defined previously:

```
  import tqdm

  for iter in tqdm.trange(1000):
```

```
for d in range(D):
    for i, (word, topic) in enumerate(zip(documents[d],
                                           document_topics[d])):

        # remove this word / topic from the counts
        # so that it doesn't influence the weights
        document_topic_counts[d][topic] -= 1
        topic_word_counts[topic][word] -= 1
        topic_counts[topic] -= 1
        document_lengths[d] -= 1

        # choose a new topic based on the weights
        new_topic = choose_new_topic(d, word)
        document_topics[d][i] = new_topic

        # and now add it back to the counts
        document_topic_counts[d][new_topic] += 1
        topic_word_counts[new_topic][word] += 1
        topic_counts[new_topic] += 1
        document_lengths[d] += 1
```

What are the topics? They're just numbers 0, 1, 2, and 3. If we want names for them, we have to do that ourselves. Let's look at the five most heavily weighted words for each (Table 21-1):

```
for k, word_counts in enumerate(topic_word_counts):
    for word, count in word_counts.most_common():
        if count > 0:
            print(k, word, count)
```

Table 21-1. Most common words per topic

Topic 0	Topic 1	Topic 2	Topic 3
Java	R	HBase	regression
Big Data	statistics	Postgres	libsvm
Hadoop	Python	MongoDB	scikit-learn
deep learning	probability	Cassandra	machine learning
artificial intelligence	pandas	NoSQL	neural networks

Based on these I'd probably assign topic names:

```
topic_names = ["Big Data and programming languages",
               "Python and statistics",
               "databases",
               "machine learning"]
```

at which point we can see how the model assigns topics to each user's interests:

```
for document, topic_counts in zip(documents, document_topic_counts):
    print(document)
    for topic, count in topic_counts.most_common():
```

```
        if count > 0:
            print(topic_names[topic], count)
    print()
```

which gives:

```
['Hadoop', 'Big Data', 'HBase', 'Java', 'Spark', 'Storm', 'Cassandra']
Big Data and programming languages 4 databases 3
['NoSQL', 'MongoDB', 'Cassandra', 'HBase', 'Postgres']
databases 5
['Python', 'scikit-learn', 'scipy', 'numpy', 'statsmodels', 'pandas']
Python and statistics 5 machine learning 1
```

and so on. Given the "ands" we needed in some of our topic names, it's possible we should use more topics, although most likely we don't have enough data to successfully learn them.

Word Vectors

A lot of recent advances in NLP involve deep learning. In the rest of this chapter we'll look at a couple of them using the machinery we developed in Chapter 19.

One important innovation involves representing words as low-dimensional vectors. These vectors can be compared, added together, fed into machine learning models, or anything else you want to do with them. They usually have nice properties; for example, similar words tend to have similar vectors. That is, typically the word vector for *big* is pretty close to the word vector for *large*, so that a model operating on word vectors can (to some degree) handle things like synonymy for free.

Frequently the vectors will exhibit delightful arithmetic properties as well. For instance, in some such models if you take the vector for *king*, subtract the vector for *man*, and add the vector for *woman*, you will end up with a vector that's very close to the vector for *queen*. It can be interesting to ponder what this means about what the word vectors actually "learn," although we won't spend time on that here.

Coming up with such vectors for a large vocabulary of words is a difficult undertaking, so typically we'll *learn* them from a corpus of text. There are a couple of different schemes, but at a high level the task typically looks something like this:

1. Get a bunch of text.
2. Create a dataset where the goal is to predict a word given nearby words (or alternatively, to predict nearby words given a word).
3. Train a neural net to do well on this task.
4. Take the internal states of the trained neural net as the word vectors.

In particular, because the task is to predict a word given nearby words, words that occur in similar contexts (and hence have similar nearby words) should have similar internal states and therefore similar word vectors.

Here we'll measure "similarity" using *cosine similarity*, which is a number between –1 and 1 that measures the degree to which two vectors point in the same direction:

```
from scratch.linear_algebra import dot, Vector
import math

def cosine_similarity(v1: Vector, v2: Vector) -> float:
    return dot(v1, v2) / math.sqrt(dot(v1, v1) * dot(v2, v2))

assert cosine_similarity([1., 1, 1], [2., 2, 2]) == 1,  "same direction"
assert cosine_similarity([-1., -1], [2., 2]) == -1,     "opposite direction"
assert cosine_similarity([1., 0], [0., 1]) == 0,        "orthogonal"
```

Let's learn some word vectors to see how this works.

To start with, we'll need a toy dataset. The commonly used word vectors are typically derived from training on millions or even billions of words. As our toy library can't cope with that much data, we'll create an artificial dataset with some structure to it:

```
colors = ["red", "green", "blue", "yellow", "black", ""]
nouns = ["bed", "car", "boat", "cat"]
verbs = ["is", "was", "seems"]
adverbs = ["very", "quite", "extremely", ""]
adjectives = ["slow", "fast", "soft", "hard"]

def make_sentence() -> str:
    return " ".join([
        "The",
        random.choice(colors),
        random.choice(nouns),
        random.choice(verbs),
        random.choice(adverbs),
        random.choice(adjectives),
        ".",
    ])

NUM_SENTENCES = 50

random.seed(0)
sentences = [make_sentence() for _ in range(NUM_SENTENCES)]
```

This will generate lots of sentences with similar structure but different words; for example, "The green boat seems quite slow." Given this setup, the colors will mostly appear in "similar" contexts, as will the nouns, and so on. So if we do a good job of assigning word vectors, the colors should get similar vectors, and so on.

In practical usage, you'd probably have a corpus of millions of sentences, in which case you'd get "enough" context from the sentences as they are. Here, with only 50 sentences, we have to make them somewhat artificial.

As mentioned earlier, we'll want to one-hot-encode our words, which means we'll need to convert them to IDs. We'll introduce a Vocabulary class to keep track of this mapping:

```python
from scratch.deep_learning import Tensor

class Vocabulary:
    def __init__(self, words: List[str] = None) -> None:
        self.w2i: Dict[str, int] = {}  # mapping word -> word_id
        self.i2w: Dict[int, str] = {}  # mapping word_id -> word

        for word in (words or []):     # If words were provided,
            self.add(word)             # add them.

    @property
    def size(self) -> int:
        """how many words are in the vocabulary"""
        return len(self.w2i)

    def add(self, word: str) -> None:
        if word not in self.w2i:          # If the word is new to us:
            word_id = len(self.w2i)       # Find the next id.
            self.w2i[word] = word_id      # Add to the word -> word_id map.
            self.i2w[word_id] = word      # Add to the word_id -> word map.

    def get_id(self, word: str) -> int:
        """return the id of the word (or None)"""
        return self.w2i.get(word)

    def get_word(self, word_id: int) -> str:
        """return the word with the given id (or None)"""
        return self.i2w.get(word_id)

    def one_hot_encode(self, word: str) -> Tensor:
        word_id = self.get_id(word)
        assert word_id is not None, f"unknown word {word}"

        return [1.0 if i == word_id else 0.0 for i in range(self.size)]
```

These are all things we could do manually, but it's handy to have it in a class. We should probably test it:

```python
vocab = Vocabulary(["a", "b", "c"])
assert vocab.size == 3,              "there are 3 words in the vocab"
assert vocab.get_id("b") == 1,       "b should have word_id 1"
assert vocab.one_hot_encode("b") == [0, 1, 0]
```

```
    assert vocab.get_id("z") is None,    "z is not in the vocab"
    assert vocab.get_word(2) == "c",     "word_id 2 should be c"
    vocab.add("z")
    assert vocab.size == 4,              "now there are 4 words in the vocab"
    assert vocab.get_id("z") == 3,       "now z should have id 3"
    assert vocab.one_hot_encode("z") == [0, 0, 0, 1]
```

We should also write simple helper functions to save and load a vocabulary, just as we have for our deep learning models:

```
import json

def save_vocab(vocab: Vocabulary, filename: str) -> None:
    with open(filename, 'w') as f:
        json.dump(vocab.w2i, f)        # Only need to save w2i

def load_vocab(filename: str) -> Vocabulary:
    vocab = Vocabulary()
    with open(filename) as f:
        # Load w2i and generate i2w from it
        vocab.w2i = json.load(f)
        vocab.i2w = {id: word for word, id in vocab.w2i.items()}
    return vocab
```

We'll be using a word vector model called *skip-gram* that takes as input a word and generates probabilities for what words are likely to be seen near it. We will feed it training pairs (`word, nearby_word`) and try to minimize the `SoftmaxCrossEntropy` loss.

 Another common model, *continuous bag-of-words* (CBOW), takes the nearby words as the inputs and tries to predict the original word.

Let's design our neural network. At its heart will be an *embedding* layer that takes as input a word ID and returns a word vector. Under the covers we can just use a lookup table for this.

We'll then pass the word vector to a `Linear` layer with the same number of outputs as we have words in our vocabulary. As before, we'll use `softmax` to convert these outputs to probabilities over nearby words. As we use gradient descent to train the model, we will be updating the vectors in the lookup table. Once we've finished training, that lookup table gives us our word vectors.

Let's create that embedding layer. In practice we might want to embed things other than words, so we'll construct a more general `Embedding` layer. (Later we'll write a `TextEmbedding` subclass that's specifically for word vectors.)

In its constructor we'll provide the number and dimension of our embedding vectors, so it can create the embeddings (which will be standard random normals, initially):

```
from typing import Iterable
from scratch.deep_learning import Layer, Tensor, random_tensor, zeros_like

class Embedding(Layer):
    def __init__(self, num_embeddings: int, embedding_dim: int) -> None:
        self.num_embeddings = num_embeddings
        self.embedding_dim = embedding_dim

        # One vector of size embedding_dim for each desired embedding
        self.embeddings = random_tensor(num_embeddings, embedding_dim)
        self.grad = zeros_like(self.embeddings)

        # Save last input id
        self.last_input_id = None
```

In our case we'll only be embedding one word at a time. However, in other models we might want to embed a sequence of words and get back a sequence of word vectors. (For example, if we wanted to train the CBOW model described earlier.) So an alternative design would take sequences of word IDs. We'll stick with one at a time, to make things simpler.

```
    def forward(self, input_id: int) -> Tensor:
        """"Just select the embedding vector corresponding to the input id"""
        self.input_id = input_id    # remember for use in backpropagation

        return self.embeddings[input_id]
```

For the backward pass we'll get a gradient corresponding to the chosen embedding vector, and we'll need to construct the corresponding gradient for self.embeddings, which is zero for every embedding other than the chosen one:

```
    def backward(self, gradient: Tensor) -> None:
        # Zero out the gradient corresponding to the last input.
        # This is way cheaper than creating a new all-zero tensor each time.
        if self.last_input_id is not None:
            zero_row = [0 for _ in range(self.embedding_dim)]
            self.grad[self.last_input_id] = zero_row

        self.last_input_id = self.input_id
        self.grad[self.input_id] = gradient
```

Because we have parameters and gradients, we need to override those methods:

```
    def params(self) -> Iterable[Tensor]:
        return [self.embeddings]

    def grads(self) -> Iterable[Tensor]:
        return [self.grad]
```

As mentioned earlier, we'll want a subclass specifically for word vectors. In that case our number of embeddings is determined by our vocabulary, so let's just pass that in instead:

```
class TextEmbedding(Embedding):
    def __init__(self, vocab: Vocabulary, embedding_dim: int) -> None:
        # Call the superclass constructor
        super().__init__(vocab.size, embedding_dim)

        # And hang onto the vocab
        self.vocab = vocab
```

The other built-in methods will all work as is, but we'll add a couple more methods specific to working with text. For example, we'd like to be able to retrieve the vector for a given word. (This is not part of the Layer interface, but we are always free to add extra methods to specific layers as we like.)

```
    def __getitem__(self, word: str) -> Tensor:
        word_id = self.vocab.get_id(word)
        if word_id is not None:
            return self.embeddings[word_id]
        else:
            return None
```

This dunder method will allow us to retrieve word vectors using indexing:

```
word_vector = embedding["black"]
```

And we'd also like the embedding layer to tell us the closest words to a given word:

```
    def closest(self, word: str, n: int = 5) -> List[Tuple[float, str]]:
        """Returns the n closest words based on cosine similarity"""
        vector = self[word]

        # Compute pairs (similarity, other_word), and sort most similar first
        scores = [(cosine_similarity(vector, self.embeddings[i]), other_word)
                     for other_word, i in self.vocab.w2i.items()]
        scores.sort(reverse=True)

        return scores[:n]
```

Our embedding layer just outputs vectors, which we can feed into a Linear layer.

Now we're ready to assemble our training data. For each input word, we'll choose as target words the two words to its left and the two words to its right.

Let's start by lowercasing the sentences and splitting them into words:

```
import re

# This is not a great regex, but it works on our data.
tokenized_sentences = [re.findall("[a-z]+|[.]", sentence.lower())
                          for sentence in sentences]
```

at which point we can construct a vocabulary:

```
# Create a vocabulary (that is, a mapping word -> word_id) based on our text.
vocab = Vocabulary(word
                   for sentence_words in tokenized_sentences
                   for word in sentence_words)
```

And now we can create training data:

```
from scratch.deep_learning import Tensor, one_hot_encode

inputs: List[int] = []
targets: List[Tensor] = []

for sentence in tokenized_sentences:
    for i, word in enumerate(sentence):      # For each word
        for j in [i - 2, i - 1, i + 1, i + 2]:   # take the nearby locations
            if 0 <= j < len(sentence):        # that aren't out of bounds
                nearby_word = sentence[j]     # and get those words.

                # Add an input that's the original word_id
                inputs.append(vocab.get_id(word))

                # Add a target that's the one-hot-encoded nearby word
                targets.append(vocab.one_hot_encode(nearby_word))
```

With the machinery we've built up, it's now easy to create our model:

```
from scratch.deep_learning import Sequential, Linear

random.seed(0)
EMBEDDING_DIM = 5  # seems like a good size

# Define the embedding layer separately, so we can reference it.
embedding = TextEmbedding(vocab=vocab, embedding_dim=EMBEDDING_DIM)

model = Sequential([
    # Given a word (as a vector of word_ids), look up its embedding.
    embedding,
    # And use a linear layer to compute scores for "nearby words."
    Linear(input_dim=EMBEDDING_DIM, output_dim=vocab.size)
])
```

Using the machinery from Chapter 19, it's easy to train our model:

```
from scratch.deep_learning import SoftmaxCrossEntropy, Momentum, GradientDescent

loss = SoftmaxCrossEntropy()
optimizer = GradientDescent(learning_rate=0.01)

for epoch in range(100):
    epoch_loss = 0.0
    for input, target in zip(inputs, targets):
        predicted = model.forward(input)
```

```
        epoch_loss += loss.loss(predicted, target)
        gradient = loss.gradient(predicted, target)
        model.backward(gradient)
        optimizer.step(model)
    print(epoch, epoch_loss)                 # Print the loss
    print(embedding.closest("black"))        # and also a few nearest words
    print(embedding.closest("slow"))         # so we can see what's being
    print(embedding.closest("car"))          # learned.
```

As you watch this train, you can see the colors getting closer to each other, the adjectives getting closer to each other, and the nouns getting closer to each other.

Once the model is trained, it's fun to explore the most similar words:

```
pairs = [(cosine_similarity(embedding[w1], embedding[w2]), w1, w2)
         for w1 in vocab.w2i
         for w2 in vocab.w2i
         if w1 < w2]
pairs.sort(reverse=True)
print(pairs[:5])
```

which (for me) results in:

```
[(0.9980283554864815, 'boat', 'car'),
 (0.9975147744587706, 'bed', 'cat'),
 (0.9953153441218054, 'seems', 'was'),
 (0.9927107440377975, 'extremely', 'quite'),
 (0.9836183658415987, 'bed', 'car')]
```

(Obviously *bed* and *cat* are not really similar, but in our training sentences they appear to be, and that's what the model is capturing.)

We can also extract the first two principal components and plot them:

```
from scratch.working_with_data import pca, transform
import matplotlib.pyplot as plt

# Extract the first two principal components and transform the word vectors
components = pca(embedding.embeddings, 2)
transformed = transform(embedding.embeddings, components)

# Scatter the points (and make them white so they're "invisible")
fig, ax = plt.subplots()
ax.scatter(*zip(*transformed), marker='.', color='w')

# Add annotations for each word at its transformed location
for word, idx in vocab.w2i.items():
    ax.annotate(word, transformed[idx])

# And hide the axes
ax.get_xaxis().set_visible(False)
ax.get_yaxis().set_visible(False)

plt.show()
```

which shows that similar words are indeed clustering together (Figure 21-3):

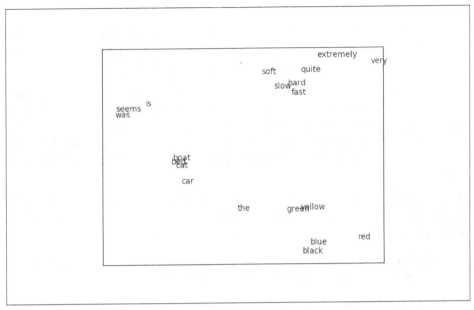

Figure 21-3. Word vectors

If you're interested, it's not hard to train CBOW word vectors. You'll have to do a little work. First, you'll need to modify the Embedding layer so that it takes as input a *list* of IDs and outputs a *list* of embedding vectors. Then you'll have to create a new layer (Sum?) that takes a list of vectors and returns their sum.

Each word represents a training example where the input is the word IDs for the surrounding words, and the target is the one-hot encoding of the word itself.

The modified Embedding layer turns the surrounding words into a list of vectors, the new Sum layer collapses the list of vectors down to a single vector, and then a Linear layer can produce scores that can be softmaxed to get a distribution representing "most likely words, given this context."

I found the CBOW model harder to train than the skip-gram one, but I encourage you to try it out.

Recurrent Neural Networks

The word vectors we developed in the previous section are often used as the inputs to neural networks. One challenge to doing this is that sentences have varying lengths: you could think of a 3-word sentence as a [3, embedding_dim] tensor and a 10-word sentence as a [10, embedding_dim] tensor. In order to, say, pass them to a Linear layer, we need to do something about that first variable-length dimension.

One option is to use a Sum layer (or a variant that takes the average); however, the *order* of the words in a sentence is usually important to its meaning. To take a common example, "dog bites man" and "man bites dog" are two very different stories!

Another way of handling this is using *recurrent neural networks* (RNNs), which have a *hidden state* they maintain between inputs. In the simplest case, each input is combined with the current hidden state to produce an output, which is then used as the new hidden state. This allows such networks to "remember" (in a sense) the inputs they've seen, and to build up to a final output that depends on all the inputs and their order.

We'll create pretty much the simplest possible RNN layer, which will accept a single input (corresponding to, e.g., a single word in a sentence, or a single character in a word), and which will maintain its hidden state between calls.

Recall that our Linear layer had some weights, w, and a bias, b. It took a vector input and produced a different vector as output using the logic:

```
output[o] = dot(w[o], input) + b[o]
```

Here we'll want to incorporate our hidden state, so we'll have *two* sets of weights—one to apply to the input and one to apply to the previous hidden state:

```
output[o] = dot(w[o], input) + dot(u[o], hidden) + b[o]
```

Next, we'll use the output vector as the new value of hidden. This isn't a huge change, but it will allow our networks to do wonderful things.

```python
from scratch.deep_learning import tensor_apply, tanh

class SimpleRnn(Layer):
    """Just about the simplest possible recurrent layer."""
    def __init__(self, input_dim: int, hidden_dim: int) -> None:
        self.input_dim = input_dim
        self.hidden_dim = hidden_dim

        self.w = random_tensor(hidden_dim, input_dim, init='xavier')
        self.u = random_tensor(hidden_dim, hidden_dim, init='xavier')
        self.b = random_tensor(hidden_dim)

        self.reset_hidden_state()

    def reset_hidden_state(self) -> None:
        self.hidden = [0 for _ in range(self.hidden_dim)]
```

You can see that we start out the hidden state as a vector of 0s, and we provide a function that people using the network can call to reset the hidden state.

Given this setup, the `forward` function is reasonably straightforward (at least, it is if you remember and understand how our `Linear` layer worked):

```
def forward(self, input: Tensor) -> Tensor:
    self.input = input                  # Save both input and previous
    self.prev_hidden = self.hidden      # hidden state to use in backprop.

    a = [(dot(self.w[h], input) +       # weights @ input
          dot(self.u[h], self.hidden) + # weights @ hidden
          self.b[h])                    # bias
         for h in range(self.hidden_dim)]

    self.hidden = tensor_apply(tanh, a)  # Apply tanh activation
    return self.hidden                   # and return the result.
```

The backward pass is similar to the one in our `Linear` layer, except that it needs to compute an additional set of gradients for the u weights:

```
def backward(self, gradient: Tensor):
    # Backpropagate through the tanh
    a_grad = [gradient[h] * (1 - self.hidden[h] ** 2)
              for h in range(self.hidden_dim)]

    # b has the same gradient as a
    self.b_grad = a_grad

    # Each w[h][i] is multiplied by input[i] and added to a[h],
    # so each w_grad[h][i] = a_grad[h] * input[i]
    self.w_grad = [[a_grad[h] * self.input[i]
                    for i in range(self.input_dim)]
                   for h in range(self.hidden_dim)]

    # Each u[h][h2] is multiplied by hidden[h2] and added to a[h],
    # so each u_grad[h][h2] = a_grad[h] * prev_hidden[h2]
    self.u_grad = [[a_grad[h] * self.prev_hidden[h2]
                    for h2 in range(self.hidden_dim)]
                   for h in range(self.hidden_dim)]

    # Each input[i] is multiplied by every w[h][i] and added to a[h],
    # so each input_grad[i] = sum(a_grad[h] * w[h][i] for h in ...)
    return [sum(a_grad[h] * self.w[h][i] for h in range(self.hidden_dim))
            for i in range(self.input_dim)]
```

And finally we need to override the `params` and `grads` methods:

```
def params(self) -> Iterable[Tensor]:
    return [self.w, self.u, self.b]

def grads(self) -> Iterable[Tensor]:
    return [self.w_grad, self.u_grad, self.b_grad]
```

This "simple" RNN is so simple that you probably shouldn't use it in practice.

Our SimpleRnn has a couple of undesirable features. One is that its entire hidden state is used to update the input every time you call it. The other is that the entire hidden state is overwritten every time you call it. Both of these make it difficult to train; in particular, they make it difficult for the model to learn long-range dependencies.

For this reason, almost no one uses this kind of simple RNN. Instead, they use more complicated variants like the LSTM ("long short-term memory") or the GRU ("gated recurrent unit"), which have many more parameters and use parameterized "gates" that allow only some of the state to be updated (and only some of the state to be used) at each timestep.

There is nothing particularly *difficult* about these variants; however, they involve a great deal more code, which would not be (in my opinion) correspondingly more edifying to read. The code for this chapter on GitHub (*https://github.com/joelgrus/data-science-from-scratch*) includes an LSTM implementation. I encourage you to check it out, but it's somewhat tedious and so we won't discuss it further here.

One other quirk of our implementation is that it takes only one "step" at a time and requires us to manually reset the hidden state. A more practical RNN implementation might accept sequences of inputs, set its hidden state to 0s at the beginning of each sequence, and produce sequences of outputs. Ours could certainly be modified to behave this way; again, this would require more code and complexity for little gain in understanding.

Example: Using a Character-Level RNN

The newly hired VP of Branding did not come up with the name *DataSciencester* himself, and (accordingly) he suspects that a better name might lead to more success for the company. He asks you to use data science to suggest candidates for replacement.

One "cute" application of RNNs involves using *characters* (rather than words) as their inputs, training them to learn the subtle language patterns in some dataset, and then using them to generate fictional instances from that dataset.

For example, you could train an RNN on the names of alternative bands, use the trained model to generate new names for fake alternative bands, and then hand-select the funniest ones and share them on Twitter. Hilarity!

Having seen this trick enough times to no longer consider it clever, you decide to give it a shot.

After some digging, you find that the startup accelerator Y Combinator has published a list of its top 100 (actually 101) most successful startups (*https://www.ycombina tor.com/topcompanies/*), which seems like a good starting point. Checking the page, you find that the company names all live inside `<b class="h4">` tags, which means it's easy to use your web scraping skills to retrieve them:

```
from bs4 import BeautifulSoup
import requests

url = "https://www.ycombinator.com/topcompanies/"
soup = BeautifulSoup(requests.get(url).text, 'html5lib')

# We get the companies twice, so use a set comprehension to deduplicate.
companies = list({b.text
                  for b in soup("b")
                  if "h4" in b.get("class", ())})
assert len(companies) == 101
```

As always, the page may change (or vanish), in which case this code won't work. If so, you can use your newly learned data science skills to fix it or just get the list from the book's GitHub site.

So what is our plan? We'll train a model to predict the next character of a name, given the current character *and* a hidden state representing all the characters we've seen so far.

As usual, we'll actually predict a probability distribution over characters and train our model to minimize the `SoftmaxCrossEntropy` loss.

Once our model is trained, we can use it to generate some probabilities, randomly sample a character according to those probabilities, and then feed that character as its next input. This will allow us to *generate* company names using the learned weights.

To start with, we should build a `Vocabulary` from the characters in the names:

```
vocab = Vocabulary([c for company in companies for c in company])
```

In addition, we'll use special tokens to signify the start and end of a company name. This allows the model to learn which characters should *begin* a company name and also to learn when a company name is *finished*.

We'll just use the regex characters for start and end, which (luckily) don't appear in our list of companies:

```
START = "^"
STOP = "$"

# We need to add them to the vocabulary too.
```

```
vocab.add(START)
vocab.add(STOP)
```

For our model, we'll one-hot-encode each character, pass it through two `SimpleRnns`, and then use a `Linear` layer to generate the scores for each possible next character:

```
HIDDEN_DIM = 32  # You should experiment with different sizes!

rnn1 = SimpleRnn(input_dim=vocab.size, hidden_dim=HIDDEN_DIM)
rnn2 = SimpleRnn(input_dim=HIDDEN_DIM, hidden_dim=HIDDEN_DIM)
linear = Linear(input_dim=HIDDEN_DIM, output_dim=vocab.size)

model = Sequential([
    rnn1,
    rnn2,
    linear
])
```

Imagine for the moment that we've trained this model. Let's write the function that uses it to generate new company names, using the `sample_from` function from "Topic Modeling" on page 288:

```
from scratch.deep_learning import softmax

def generate(seed: str = START, max_len: int = 50) -> str:
    rnn1.reset_hidden_state()  # Reset both hidden states
    rnn2.reset_hidden_state()
    output = [seed]            # Start the output with the specified seed

    # Keep going until we produce the STOP character or reach the max length
    while output[-1] != STOP and len(output) < max_len:
        # Use the last character as the input
        input = vocab.one_hot_encode(output[-1])

        # Generate scores using the model
        predicted = model.forward(input)

        # Convert them to probabilities and draw a random char_id
        probabilities = softmax(predicted)
        next_char_id = sample_from(probabilities)

        # Add the corresponding char to our output
        output.append(vocab.get_word(next_char_id))

    # Get rid of START and END characters and return the word
    return ''.join(output[1:-1])
```

At long last, we're ready to train our character-level RNN. It will take a while!

```
loss = SoftmaxCrossEntropy()
optimizer = Momentum(learning_rate=0.01, momentum=0.9)

for epoch in range(300):
```

```
random.shuffle(companies)  # Train in a different order each epoch.
epoch_loss = 0             # Track the loss.
for company in tqdm.tqdm(companies):
    rnn1.reset_hidden_state()  # Reset both hidden states.
    rnn2.reset_hidden_state()
    company = START + company + STOP   # Add START and STOP characters.

    # The rest is just our usual training loop, except that the inputs
    # and target are the one-hot-encoded previous and next characters.
    for prev, next in zip(company, company[1:]):
        input = vocab.one_hot_encode(prev)
        target = vocab.one_hot_encode(next)
        predicted = model.forward(input)
        epoch_loss += loss.loss(predicted, target)
        gradient = loss.gradient(predicted, target)
        model.backward(gradient)
        optimizer.step(model)

# Each epoch, print the loss and also generate a name.
print(epoch, epoch_loss, generate())

# Turn down the learning rate for the last 100 epochs.
# There's no principled reason for this, but it seems to work.
if epoch == 200:
    optimizer.lr *= 0.1
```

After training, the model generates some actual names from the list (which isn't surprising, since the model has a fair amount of capacity and not a lot of training data),
as well as names that are only slightly different from training names (Scripe, Loin-
bare, Pozium), names that seem genuinely creative (Benuus, Cletpo, Equite, Vivest),
and names that are garbage-y but still sort of word-like (SFitreasy, Sint ocanelp,
GliyOx, Doorboronelhav).

Unfortunately, like most character-level-RNN outputs, these are only mildly clever,
and the VP of Branding ends up unable to use them.

If I up the hidden dimension to 64, I get a lot more names verbatim from the list; if I
drop it to 8, I get mostly garbage. The vocabulary and final weights for all these
model sizes are available on the book's GitHub site (*https://github.com/joelgrus/data-
science-from-scratch*), and you can use load_weights and load_vocab to use them
yourself.

As mentioned previously, the GitHub code for this chapter also contains an implementation for an LSTM, which you should feel free to swap in as a replacement for
the SimpleRnns in our company name model.

For Further Exploration

- NLTK (*http://www.nltk.org/*) is a popular library of NLP tools for Python. It has its own entire book (*http://www.nltk.org/book/*), which is available to read online.

- gensim (*http://radimrehurek.com/gensim/*) is a Python library for topic modeling, which is a better bet than our from-scratch model.

- spaCy (*https://spacy.io/*) is a library for "Industrial Strength Natural Language Processing in Python" and is also quite popular.

- Andrej Karpathy has a famous blog post, "The Unreasonable Effectiveness of Recurrent Neural Networks" (*http://karpathy.github.io/2015/05/21/rnn-effectiveness/*), that's very much worth reading.

- My day job involves building AllenNLP (*https://allennlp.org/*), a Python library for doing NLP research. (At least, as of the time this book went to press, it did.) The library is quite beyond the scope of this book, but you might still find it interesting, and it has a cool interactive demo of many state-of-the-art NLP models.

## CHAPTER 22

Network Analysis

Your connections to all the things around you literally define who you are.
—Aaron O'Connell

Many interesting data problems can be fruitfully thought of in terms of *networks*, consisting of *nodes* of some type and the *edges* that join them.

For instance, your Facebook friends form the nodes of a network whose edges are friendship relations. A less obvious example is the World Wide Web itself, with each web page a node and each hyperlink from one page to another an edge.

Facebook friendship is mutual—if I am Facebook friends with you, then necessarily you are friends with me. In this case, we say that the edges are *undirected*. Hyperlinks are not—my website links to *whitehouse.gov*, but (for reasons inexplicable to me) *whitehouse.gov* refuses to link to my website. We call these types of edges *directed*. We'll look at both kinds of networks.

Betweenness Centrality

In Chapter 1, we computed the key connectors in the DataSciencester network by counting the number of friends each user had. Now we have enough machinery to take a look at other approaches. We will use the same network, but now we'll use NamedTuples for the data.

Recall that the network (Figure 22-1) comprised users:

```
from typing import NamedTuple

class User(NamedTuple):
    id: int
    name: str
```

```
users = [User(0, "Hero"), User(1, "Dunn"), User(2, "Sue"), User(3, "Chi"),
         User(4, "Thor"), User(5, "Clive"), User(6, "Hicks"),
         User(7, "Devin"), User(8, "Kate"), User(9, "Klein")]
```

and friendships:

```
friend_pairs = [(0, 1), (0, 2), (1, 2), (1, 3), (2, 3), (3, 4),
                (4, 5), (5, 6), (5, 7), (6, 8), (7, 8), (8, 9)]
```

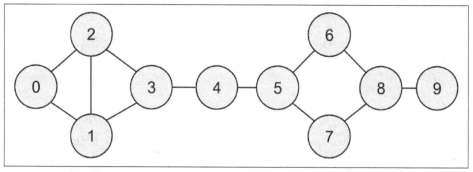

Figure 22-1. The DataSciencester network

The friendships will be easier to work with as a `dict`:

```
from typing import Dict, List

# type alias for keeping track of Friendships
Friendships = Dict[int, List[int]]

friendships: Friendships = {user.id: [] for user in users}

for i, j in friend_pairs:
    friendships[i].append(j)
    friendships[j].append(i)

assert friendships[4] == [3, 5]
assert friendships[8] == [6, 7, 9]
```

When we left off we were dissatisfied with our notion of *degree centrality*, which didn't really agree with our intuition about who the key connectors of the network were.

An alternative metric is *betweenness centrality*, which identifies people who frequently are on the shortest paths between pairs of other people. In particular, the betweenness centrality of node i is computed by adding up, for every other pair of nodes j and k, the proportion of shortest paths between node j and node k that pass through i.

That is, to figure out Thor's betweenness centrality, we'll need to compute all the shortest paths between all pairs of people who aren't Thor. And then we'll need to count how many of those shortest paths pass through Thor. For instance, the only shortest path between Chi (`id 3`) and Clive (`id 5`) passes through Thor, while neither of the two shortest paths between Hero (`id 0`) and Chi (`id 3`) does.

So, as a first step, we'll need to figure out the shortest paths between all pairs of people. There are some pretty sophisticated algorithms for doing so efficiently, but (as is almost always the case) we will use a less efficient, easier-to-understand algorithm.

This algorithm (an implementation of breadth-first search) is one of the more complicated ones in the book, so let's talk through it carefully:

1. Our goal is a function that takes a `from_user` and finds *all* shortest paths to every other user.

2. We'll represent a path as a `list` of user IDs. Since every path starts at `from_user`, we won't include her ID in the list. This means that the length of the list representing the path will be the length of the path itself.

3. We'll maintain a dictionary called `shortest_paths_to` where the keys are user IDs and the values are lists of paths that end at the user with the specified ID. If there is a unique shortest path, the list will just contain that one path. If there are multiple shortest paths, the list will contain all of them.

4. We'll also maintain a queue called `frontier` that contains the users we want to explore in the order we want to explore them. We'll store them as pairs (`prev_user, user`) so that we know how we got to each one. We initialize the queue with all the neighbors of `from_user`. (We haven't talked about queues, which are data structures optimized for "add to the end" and "remove from the front" operations. In Python, they are implemented as `collections.deque`, which is actually a double-ended queue.)

5. As we explore the graph, whenever we find new neighbors that we don't already know the shortest paths to, we add them to the end of the queue to explore later, with the current user as `prev_user`.

6. When we take a user off the queue, and we've never encountered that user before, we've definitely found one or more shortest paths to him—each of the shortest paths to `prev_user` with one extra step added.

7. When we take a user off the queue and we *have* encountered that user before, then either we've found another shortest path (in which case we should add it) or we've found a longer path (in which case we shouldn't).

8. When no more users are left on the queue, we've explored the whole graph (or, at least, the parts of it that are reachable from the starting user) and we're done.

We can put this all together into a (large) function:

```
from collections import deque
```

```
Path = List[int]

def shortest_paths_from(from_user_id: int,
                        friendships: Friendships) -> Dict[int, List[Path]]:
    # A dictionary from user_id to *all* shortest paths to that user.
    shortest_paths_to: Dict[int, List[Path]] = {from_user_id: [[]]}

    # A queue of (previous user, next user) that we need to check.
    # Starts out with all pairs (from_user, friend_of_from_user).
    frontier = deque((from_user_id, friend_id)
                     for friend_id in friendships[from_user_id])

    # Keep going until we empty the queue.
    while frontier:
        # Remove the pair that's next in the queue.
        prev_user_id, user_id = frontier.popleft()

        # Because of the way we're adding to the queue,
        # necessarily we already know some shortest paths to prev_user.
        paths_to_prev_user = shortest_paths_to[prev_user_id]
        new_paths_to_user = [path + [user_id] for path in paths_to_prev_user]

        # It's possible we already know a shortest path to user_id.
        old_paths_to_user = shortest_paths_to.get(user_id, [])

        # What's the shortest path to here that we've seen so far?
        if old_paths_to_user:
            min_path_length = len(old_paths_to_user[0])
        else:
            min_path_length = float('inf')

        # Only keep paths that aren't too long and are actually new.
        new_paths_to_user = [path
                             for path in new_paths_to_user
                             if len(path) <= min_path_length
                             and path not in old_paths_to_user]

        shortest_paths_to[user_id] = old_paths_to_user + new_paths_to_user

        # Add never-seen neighbors to the frontier.
        frontier.extend((user_id, friend_id)
                        for friend_id in friendships[user_id]
                        if friend_id not in shortest_paths_to)

    return shortest_paths_to
```

Now let's compute all the shortest paths:

```
# For each from_user, for each to_user, a list of shortest paths.
shortest_paths = {user.id: shortest_paths_from(user.id, friendships)
                  for user in users}
```

And we're finally ready to compute betweenness centrality. For every pair of nodes i and j, we know the n shortest paths from i to j. Then, for each of those paths, we just add 1/n to the centrality of each node on that path:

```
betweenness_centrality = {user.id: 0.0 for user in users}

for source in users:
    for target_id, paths in shortest_paths[source.id].items():
        if source.id < target_id:           # don't double count
            num_paths = len(paths)           # how many shortest paths?
            contrib = 1 / num_paths          # contribution to centrality
            for path in paths:
                for between_id in path:
                    if between_id not in [source.id, target_id]:
                        betweenness_centrality[between_id] += contrib
```

As shown in Figure 22-2, users 0 and 9 have centrality 0 (as neither is on any shortest path between other users), whereas 3, 4, and 5 all have high centralities (as all three lie on many shortest paths).

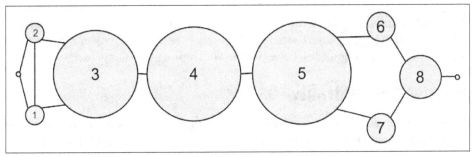

Figure 22-2. The DataSciencester network sized by betweenness centrality

> Generally the centrality numbers aren't that meaningful themselves. What we care about is how the numbers for each node compare to the numbers for other nodes.

Another measure we can look at is *closeness centrality*. First, for each user we compute her *farness*, which is the sum of the lengths of her shortest paths to each other user. Since we've already computed the shortest paths between each pair of nodes, it's easy to add their lengths. (If there are multiple shortest paths, they all have the same length, so we can just look at the first one.)

```
def farness(user_id: int) -> float:
    """the sum of the lengths of the shortest paths to each other user"""
    return sum(len(paths[0])
               for paths in shortest_paths[user_id].values())
```

after which it's very little work to compute closeness centrality (Figure 22-3):

```
closeness_centrality = {user.id: 1 / farness(user.id) for user in users}
```

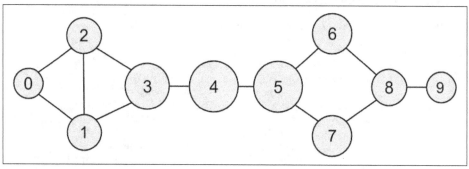

Figure 22-3. The DataSciencester network sized by closeness centrality

There is much less variation here—even the very central nodes are still pretty far from the nodes out on the periphery.

As we saw, computing shortest paths is kind of a pain. For this reason, betweenness and closeness centrality aren't often used on large networks. The less intuitive (but generally easier to compute) *eigenvector centrality* is more frequently used.

Eigenvector Centrality

In order to talk about eigenvector centrality, we have to talk about eigenvectors, and in order to talk about eigenvectors, we have to talk about matrix multiplication.

Matrix Multiplication

If A is an $n \times m$ matrix and B is an $m \times k$ matrix (notice that the second dimension of A is same as the first dimension of B), then their product AB is the $n \times k$ matrix whose (i,j)th entry is:

$$A_{i1}B_{1j} + A_{i2}B_{2j} + \cdots + A_{im}B_{mj}$$

which is just the dot product of the ith row of A (thought of as a vector) with the jth column of B (also thought of as a vector).

We can implement this using the `make_matrix` function from Chapter 4:

```
from scratch.linear_algebra import Matrix, make_matrix, shape

def matrix_times_matrix(m1: Matrix, m2: Matrix) -> Matrix:
    nr1, nc1 = shape(m1)
    nr2, nc2 = shape(m2)
```

```
        assert nc1 == nr2, "must have (# of columns in m1) == (# of rows in m2)"

        def entry_fn(i: int, j: int) -> float:
            """dot product of i-th row of m1 with j-th column of m2"""
            return sum(m1[i][k] * m2[k][j] for k in range(nc1))

        return make_matrix(nr1, nc2, entry_fn)
```

If we think of an *m*-dimensional vector as an (m, 1) matrix, we can multiply it by an (n, m) matrix to get an (n, 1) matrix, which we can then think of as an *n*-dimensional vector.

This means another way to think about an (n, m) matrix is as a linear mapping that transforms *m*-dimensional vectors into *n*-dimensional vectors:

```
from scratch.linear_algebra import Vector, dot

def matrix_times_vector(m: Matrix, v: Vector) -> Vector:
    nr, nc = shape(m)
    n = len(v)
    assert nc == n, "must have (# of cols in m) == (# of elements in v)"

    return [dot(row, v) for row in m]  # output has length nr
```

When *A* is a *square* matrix, this operation maps *n*-dimensional vectors to other *n*-dimensional vectors. It's possible that, for some matrix *A* and vector *v*, when *A* operates on *v* we get back a scalar multiple of *v*—that is, that the result is a vector that points in the same direction as *v*. When this happens (and when, in addition, *v* is not a vector of all zeros), we call *v* an *eigenvector* of *A*. And we call the multiplier an *eigenvalue*.

One possible way to find an eigenvector of *A* is by picking a starting vector *v*, applying matrix_times_vector, rescaling the result to have magnitude 1, and repeating until the process converges:

```
from typing import Tuple
import random
from scratch.linear_algebra import magnitude, distance

def find_eigenvector(m: Matrix,
                     tolerance: float = 0.00001) -> Tuple[Vector, float]:
    guess = [random.random() for _ in m]

    while True:
        result = matrix_times_vector(m, guess)    # transform guess
        norm = magnitude(result)                  # compute norm
        next_guess = [x / norm for x in result]   # rescale

        if distance(guess, next_guess) < tolerance:
            # convergence so return (eigenvector, eigenvalue)
            return next_guess, norm
```

```
guess = next_guess
```

By construction, the returned `guess` is a vector such that, when you apply `matrix_times_vector` to it and rescale it to have length 1, you get back a vector very close to itself—which means it's an eigenvector.

Not all matrices of real numbers have eigenvectors and eigenvalues. For example, the matrix:

```
rotate = [[ 0, 1],
          [-1, 0]]
```

rotates vectors 90 degrees clockwise, which means that the only vector it maps to a scalar multiple of itself is a vector of zeros. If you tried `find_eigenvector(rotate)` it would run forever. Even matrices that have eigenvectors can sometimes get stuck in cycles. Consider the matrix:

```
flip = [[0, 1],
        [1, 0]]
```

This matrix maps any vector [x, y] to [y, x]. This means that, for example, [1, 1] is an eigenvector with eigenvalue 1. However, if you start with a random vector with unequal coordinates, `find_eigenvector` will just repeatedly swap the coordinates forever. (Not-from-scratch libraries like NumPy use different methods that would work in this case.) Nonetheless, when `find_eigenvector` does return a result, that result is indeed an eigenvector.

Centrality

How does this help us understand the DataSciencester network? To start, we'll need to represent the connections in our network as an `adjacency_matrix`, whose (i,j)th entry is either 1 (if user i and user j are friends) or 0 (if they're not):

```
def entry_fn(i: int, j: int):
    return 1 if (i, j) in friend_pairs or (j, i) in friend_pairs else 0

n = len(users)
adjacency_matrix = make_matrix(n, n, entry_fn)
```

The eigenvector centrality for each user is then the entry corresponding to that user in the eigenvector returned by `find_eigenvector` (Figure 22-4).

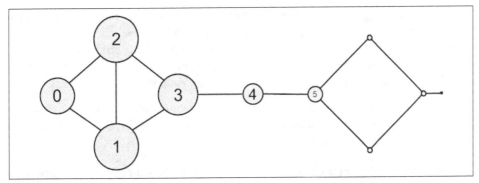

Figure 22-4. The DataSciencester network sized by eigenvector centrality

 For technical reasons that are way beyond the scope of this book, any nonzero adjacency matrix necessarily has an eigenvector, all of whose values are nonnegative. And fortunately for us, for this `adjacency_matrix` our `find_eigenvector` function finds it.

```
eigenvector_centralities, _ = find_eigenvector(adjacency_matrix)
```

Users with high eigenvector centrality should be those who have a lot of connections, and connections to people who themselves have high centrality.

Here users 1 and 2 are the most central, as they both have three connections to people who are themselves highly central. As we move away from them, people's centralities steadily drop off.

On a network this small, eigenvector centrality behaves somewhat erratically. If you try adding or subtracting links, you'll find that small changes in the network can dramatically change the centrality numbers. In a much larger network, this would not particularly be the case.

We still haven't motivated why an eigenvector might lead to a reasonable notion of centrality. Being an eigenvector means that if you compute:

```
matrix_times_vector(adjacency_matrix, eigenvector_centralities)
```

the result is a scalar multiple of `eigenvector_centralities`.

If you look at how matrix multiplication works, `matrix_times_vector` produces a vector whose *i*th element is:

```
dot(adjacency_matrix[i], eigenvector_centralities)
```

which is precisely the sum of the eigenvector centralities of the users connected to user *i*.

In other words, eigenvector centralities are numbers, one per user, such that each user's value is a constant multiple of the sum of his neighbors' values. In this case centrality means being connected to people who themselves are central. The more centrality you are directly connected to, the more central you are. This is of course a circular definition—eigenvectors are the way of breaking out of the circularity.

Another way of understanding this is by thinking about what find_eigenvector is doing here. It starts by assigning each node a random centrality. It then repeats the following two steps until the process converges:

1. Give each node a new centrality score that equals the sum of its neighbors' (old) centrality scores.

2. Rescale the vector of centralities to have magnitude 1.

Although the mathematics behind it may seem somewhat opaque at first, the calculation itself is relatively straightforward (unlike, say, betweenness centrality) and is pretty easy to perform on even very large graphs. (At least, if you use a real linear algebra library it's easy to perform on large graphs. If you used our matrices-as-lists implementation you'd struggle.)

Directed Graphs and PageRank

DataSciencester isn't getting much traction, so the VP of Revenue considers pivoting from a friendship model to an endorsement model. It turns out that no one particularly cares which data scientists are *friends* with one another, but tech recruiters care very much which data scientists are *respected* by other data scientists.

In this new model, we'll track endorsements (source, target) that no longer represent a reciprocal relationship, but rather that source endorses target as an awesome data scientist (Figure 22-5).

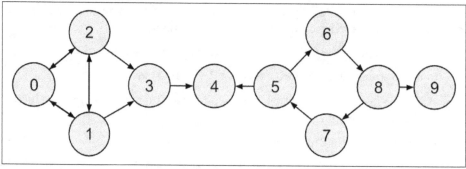

Figure 22-5. The DataSciencester network of endorsements

We'll need to account for this asymmetry:

```
endorsements = [(0, 1), (1, 0), (0, 2), (2, 0), (1, 2),
                (2, 1), (1, 3), (2, 3), (3, 4), (5, 4),
                (5, 6), (7, 5), (6, 8), (8, 7), (8, 9)]
```

after which we can easily find the most_endorsed data scientists and sell that information to recruiters:

```
from collections import Counter

endorsement_counts = Counter(target for source, target in endorsements)
```

However, "number of endorsements" is an easy metric to game. All you need to do is create phony accounts and have them endorse you. Or arrange with your friends to endorse each other. (As users 0, 1, and 2 seem to have done.)

A better metric would take into account *who* endorses you. Endorsements from people who have a lot of endorsements should somehow count more than endorsements from people with few endorsements. This is the essence of the PageRank algorithm, used by Google to rank websites based on which other websites link to them, which other websites link to those, and so on.

(If this sort of reminds you of the idea behind eigenvector centrality, it should.)

A simplified version looks like this:

1. There is a total of 1.0 (or 100%) PageRank in the network.
2. Initially this PageRank is equally distributed among nodes.
3. At each step, a large fraction of each node's PageRank is distributed evenly among its outgoing links.
4. At each step, the remainder of each node's PageRank is distributed evenly among all nodes.

```
import tqdm

def page_rank(users: List[User],
              endorsements: List[Tuple[int, int]],
              damping: float = 0.85,
              num_iters: int = 100) -> Dict[int, float]:
    # Compute how many people each person endorses
    outgoing_counts = Counter(target for source, target in endorsements)

    # Initially distribute PageRank evenly
    num_users = len(users)
    pr = {user.id : 1 / num_users for user in users}

    # Small fraction of PageRank that each node gets each iteration
    base_pr = (1 - damping) / num_users

    for iter in tqdm.trange(num_iters):
```

```
        next_pr = {user.id : base_pr for user in users}  # start with base_pr

    for source, target in endorsements:
        # Add damped fraction of source pr to target
        next_pr[target] += damping * pr[source] / outgoing_counts[source]

    pr = next_pr

    return pr
```

If we compute page ranks:

```
pr = page_rank(users, endorsements)

# Thor (user_id 4) has higher page rank than anyone else
assert pr[4] > max(page_rank
                    for user_id, page_rank in pr.items()
                    if user_id != 4)
```

PageRank (Figure 22-6) identifies user 4 (Thor) as the highest-ranked data scientist.

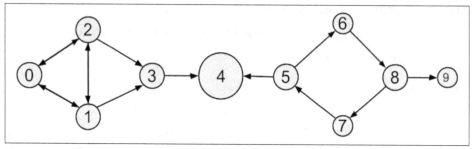

Figure 22-6. The DataSciencester network sized by PageRank

Even though Thor has fewer endorsements (two) than users 0, 1, and 2, his endorsements carry with them rank from their endorsements. Additionally, both of his endorsers endorsed only him, which means that he doesn't have to divide their rank with anyone else.

For Further Exploration

- There are many other notions of centrality (*http://en.wikipedia.org/wiki/Central ity*) besides the ones we used (although the ones we used are pretty much the most popular ones).

- NetworkX (*http://networkx.github.io/*) is a Python library for network analysis. It has functions for computing centralities and for visualizing graphs.

- Gephi (*https://gephi.org/*) is a love-it/hate-it GUI-based network visualization tool.

## CHAPTER 23

Recommender Systems

> *O nature, nature, why art thou so dishonest, as ever to send men with these false recommen-*
> *dations into the world!*
> —Henry Fielding

Another common data problem is producing *recommendations* of some sort. Netflix recommends movies you might want to watch. Amazon recommends products you might want to buy. Twitter recommends users you might want to follow. In this chapter, we'll look at several ways to use data to make recommendations.

In particular, we'll look at the dataset of `users_interests` that we've used before:

```
users_interests = [
    ["Hadoop", "Big Data", "HBase", "Java", "Spark", "Storm", "Cassandra"],
    ["NoSQL", "MongoDB", "Cassandra", "HBase", "Postgres"],
    ["Python", "scikit-learn", "scipy", "numpy", "statsmodels", "pandas"],
    ["R", "Python", "statistics", "regression", "probability"],
    ["machine learning", "regression", "decision trees", "libsvm"],
    ["Python", "R", "Java", "C++", "Haskell", "programming languages"],
    ["statistics", "probability", "mathematics", "theory"],
    ["machine learning", "scikit-learn", "Mahout", "neural networks"],
    ["neural networks", "deep learning", "Big Data", "artificial intelligence"],
    ["Hadoop", "Java", "MapReduce", "Big Data"],
    ["statistics", "R", "statsmodels"],
    ["C++", "deep learning", "artificial intelligence", "probability"],
    ["pandas", "R", "Python"],
    ["databases", "HBase", "Postgres", "MySQL", "MongoDB"],
    ["libsvm", "regression", "support vector machines"]
]
```

And we'll think about the problem of recommending new interests to a user based on her currently specified interests.

Manual Curation

Before the internet, when you needed book recommendations you would go to the library, where a librarian was available to suggest books that were relevant to your interests or similar to books you liked.

Given DataSciencester's limited number of users and interests, it would be easy for you to spend an afternoon manually recommending interests for each user. But this method doesn't scale particularly well, and it's limited by your personal knowledge and imagination. (Not that I'm suggesting that your personal knowledge and imagination are limited.) So let's think about what we can do with *data*.

Recommending What's Popular

One easy approach is to simply recommend what's popular:

```
from collections import Counter

popular_interests = Counter(interest
                            for user_interests in users_interests
                            for interest in user_interests)
```

which looks like:

```
[('Python', 4),
 ('R', 4),
 ('Java', 3),
 ('regression', 3),
 ('statistics', 3),
 ('probability', 3),
 # ...
]
```

Having computed this, we can just suggest to a user the most popular interests that he's not already interested in:

```
from typing import List, Tuple

def most_popular_new_interests(
        user_interests: List[str],
        max_results: int = 5) -> List[Tuple[str, int]]:
    suggestions = [(interest, frequency)
                   for interest, frequency in popular_interests.most_common()
                   if interest not in user_interests]
    return suggestions[:max_results]
```

So, if you are user 1, with interests:

```
["NoSQL", "MongoDB", "Cassandra", "HBase", "Postgres"]
```

then we'd recommend you:

```
[('Python', 4), ('R', 4), ('Java', 3), ('regression', 3), ('statistics', 3)]
```

If you are user 3, who's already interested in many of those things, you'd instead get:

```
[('Java', 3), ('HBase', 3), ('Big Data', 3),
 ('neural networks', 2), ('Hadoop', 2)]
```

Of course, "lots of people are interested in Python, so maybe you should be too" is not the most compelling sales pitch. If someone is brand new to our site and we don't know anything about them, that's possibly the best we can do. Let's see how we can do better by basing each user's recommendations on her existing interests.

User-Based Collaborative Filtering

One way of taking a user's interests into account is to look for users who are somehow *similar* to her, and then suggest the things that those users are interested in.

In order to do that, we'll need a way to measure how similar two users are. Here we'll use cosine similarity, which we used in Chapter 21 to measure how similar two word vectors were.

We'll apply this to vectors of 0s and 1s, each vector v representing one user's interests. v[i] will be 1 if the user specified the ith interest, and 0 otherwise. Accordingly, "similar users" will mean "users whose interest vectors most nearly point in the same direction." Users with identical interests will have similarity 1. Users with no identical interests will have similarity 0. Otherwise, the similarity will fall in between, with numbers closer to 1 indicating "very similar" and numbers closer to 0 indicating "not very similar."

A good place to start is collecting the known interests and (implicitly) assigning indices to them. We can do this by using a set comprehension to find the unique interests, and then sorting them into a list. The first interest in the resulting list will be interest 0, and so on:

```
unique_interests = sorted({interest
                           for user_interests in users_interests
                           for interest in user_interests})
```

This gives us a list that starts:

```
assert unique_interests[:6] == [
    'Big Data',
    'C++',
    'Cassandra',
    'HBase',
    'Hadoop',
    'Haskell',
    # ...
]
```

Next we want to produce an "interest" vector of 0s and 1s for each user. We just need to iterate over the unique_interests list, substituting a 1 if the user has each interest, and a 0 if not:

```
def make_user_interest_vector(user_interests: List[str]) -> List[int]:
    """
    Given a list of interests, produce a vector whose ith element is 1
    if unique_interests[i] is in the list, 0 otherwise
    """
    return [1 if interest in user_interests else 0
            for interest in unique_interests]
```

And now we can make a list of user interest vectors:

```
user_interest_vectors = [make_user_interest_vector(user_interests)
                         for user_interests in users_interests]
```

Now user_interest_vectors[i][j] equals 1 if user i specified interest j, and 0 otherwise.

Because we have a small dataset, it's no problem to compute the pairwise similarities between all of our users:

```
from scratch.nlp import cosine_similarity

user_similarities = [[cosine_similarity(interest_vector_i, interest_vector_j)
                      for interest_vector_j in user_interest_vectors]
                     for interest_vector_i in user_interest_vectors]
```

after which user_similarities[i][j] gives us the similarity between users i and j:

```
# Users 0 and 9 share interests in Hadoop, Java, and Big Data
assert 0.56 < user_similarities[0][9] < 0.58, "several shared interests"

# Users 0 and 8 share only one interest: Big Data
assert 0.18 < user_similarities[0][8] < 0.20, "only one shared interest"
```

In particular, user_similarities[i] is the vector of user i's similarities to every other user. We can use this to write a function that finds the most similar users to a given user. We'll make sure not to include the user herself, nor any users with zero similarity. And we'll sort the results from most similar to least similar:

```
def most_similar_users_to(user_id: int) -> List[Tuple[int, float]]:
    pairs = [(other_user_id, similarity)              # Find other
             for other_user_id, similarity in         # users with
                enumerate(user_similarities[user_id]) # nonzero
             if user_id != other_user_id and similarity > 0] # similarity.

    return sorted(pairs,                              # Sort them
                  key=lambda pair: pair[-1],          # most similar
                  reverse=True)                       # first.
```

For instance, if we call most_similar_users_to(0) we get:

```
[(9, 0.5669467095138409),
 (1, 0.3380617018914066),
 (8, 0.1889822365046136),
 (13, 0.1690308509457033),
 (5, 0.1543033499620919)]
```

How do we use this to suggest new interests to a user? For each interest, we can just add up the user similarities of the other users interested in it:

```
from collections import defaultdict

def user_based_suggestions(user_id: int,
                           include_current_interests: bool = False):
    # Sum up the similarities
    suggestions: Dict[str, float] = defaultdict(float)
    for other_user_id, similarity in most_similar_users_to(user_id):
        for interest in users_interests[other_user_id]:
            suggestions[interest] += similarity

    # Convert them to a sorted list
    suggestions = sorted(suggestions.items(),
                         key=lambda pair: pair[-1],  # weight
                         reverse=True)

    # And (maybe) exclude already interests
    if include_current_interests:
        return suggestions
    else:
        return [(suggestion, weight)
                for suggestion, weight in suggestions
                if suggestion not in users_interests[user_id]]
```

If we call user_based_suggestions(0), the first several suggested interests are:

```
[('MapReduce', 0.5669467095138409),
 ('MongoDB', 0.50709255283711),
 ('Postgres', 0.50709255283711),
 ('NoSQL', 0.3380617018914066),
 ('neural networks', 0.1889822365046136),
 ('deep learning', 0.1889822365046136),
 ('artificial intelligence', 0.1889822365046136),
 #...
]
```

These seem like pretty decent suggestions for someone whose stated interests are "Big Data" and database-related. (The weights aren't intrinsically meaningful; we just use them for ordering.)

This approach doesn't work as well when the number of items gets very large. Recall the curse of dimensionality from Chapter 12—in large-dimensional vector spaces most vectors are very far apart (and also point in very different directions). That is, when there are a large number of interests the "most similar users" to a given user might not be similar at all.

Imagine a site like Amazon.com, from which I've bought thousands of items over the last couple of decades. You could attempt to identify similar users to me based on buying patterns, but most likely in all the world there's no one whose purchase history looks even remotely like mine. Whoever my "most similar" shopper is, he's probably not similar to me at all, and his purchases would almost certainly make for lousy recommendations.

Item-Based Collaborative Filtering

An alternative approach is to compute similarities between interests directly. We can then generate suggestions for each user by aggregating interests that are similar to her current interests.

To start with, we'll want to *transpose* our user-interest matrix so that rows correspond to interests and columns correspond to users:

```
interest_user_matrix = [[user_interest_vector[j]
                         for user_interest_vector in user_interest_vectors]
                        for j, _ in enumerate(unique_interests)]
```

What does this look like? Row `j` of `interest_user_matrix` is column `j` of `user_interest_matrix`. That is, it has 1 for each user with that interest and 0 for each user without that interest.

For example, `unique_interests[0]` is Big Data, and so `interest_user_matrix[0]` is:

```
[1, 0, 0, 0, 0, 0, 0, 0, 1, 1, 0, 0, 0, 0, 0]
```

because users 0, 8, and 9 indicated interest in Big Data.

We can now use cosine similarity again. If precisely the same users are interested in two topics, their similarity will be 1. If no two users are interested in both topics, their similarity will be 0:

```
interest_similarities = [[cosine_similarity(user_vector_i, user_vector_j)
                          for user_vector_j in interest_user_matrix]
                         for user_vector_i in interest_user_matrix]
```

For example, we can find the interests most similar to Big Data (interest 0) using:

```
def most_similar_interests_to(interest_id: int):
    similarities = interest_similarities[interest_id]
    pairs = [(unique_interests[other_interest_id], similarity)
             for other_interest_id, similarity in enumerate(similarities)
             if interest_id != other_interest_id and similarity > 0]
    return sorted(pairs,
```

```
                key=lambda pair: pair[-1],
                reverse=True)
```

which suggests the following similar interests:

```
[('Hadoop', 0.8164965809277261),
 ('Java', 0.6666666666666666),
 ('MapReduce', 0.5773502691896258),
 ('Spark', 0.5773502691896258),
 ('Storm', 0.5773502691896258),
 ('Cassandra', 0.4082482904638631),
 ('artificial intelligence', 0.4082482904638631),
 ('deep learning', 0.4082482904638631),
 ('neural networks', 0.4082482904638631),
 ('HBase', 0.3333333333333333)]
```

Now we can create recommendations for a user by summing up the similarities of the interests similar to his:

```
def item_based_suggestions(user_id: int,
                           include_current_interests: bool = False):
    # Add up the similar interests
    suggestions = defaultdict(float)
    user_interest_vector = user_interest_vectors[user_id]
    for interest_id, is_interested in enumerate(user_interest_vector):
        if is_interested == 1:
            similar_interests = most_similar_interests_to(interest_id)
            for interest, similarity in similar_interests:
                suggestions[interest] += similarity

    # Sort them by weight
    suggestions = sorted(suggestions.items(),
                         key=lambda pair: pair[-1],
                         reverse=True)

    if include_current_interests:
        return suggestions
    else:
        return [(suggestion, weight)
                for suggestion, weight in suggestions
                if suggestion not in users_interests[user_id]]
```

For user 0, this generates the following (seemingly reasonable) recommendations:

```
[('MapReduce', 1.861807319565799),
 ('Postgres', 1.3164965809277263),
 ('MongoDB', 1.3164965809277263),
 ('NoSQL', 1.2844570503761732),
 ('programming languages', 0.5773502691896258),
 ('MySQL', 0.5773502691896258),
 ('Haskell', 0.5773502691896258),
 ('databases', 0.5773502691896258),
 ('neural networks', 0.4082482904638631),
 ('deep learning', 0.4082482904638631),
```

```
('C++', 0.4082482904638631),
('artificial intelligence', 0.4082482904638631),
('Python', 0.2886751345948129),
('R', 0.2886751345948129)]
```

Matrix Factorization

As we've seen, we can represent our users' preferences as a [num_users, num_items] matrix of 0s and 1s, where the 1s represent liked items and the 0s unliked items.

Sometimes you might actually have numeric *ratings*; for example, when you write an Amazon review you assign the item a score ranging from 1 to 5 stars. You could still represent these by numbers in a [num_users, num_items] matrix (ignoring for now the problem of what to do about unrated items).

In this section we'll assume we have such ratings data and try to learn a model that can predict the rating for a given user and item.

One way of approaching the problem is to assume that every user has some latent "type," which can be represented as a vector of numbers, and that each item similarly has some latent "type."

If the user types are represented as a [num_users, dim] matrix, and the transpose of the item types is represented as a [dim, num_items] matrix, their product is a [num_users, num_items] matrix. Accordingly, one way of building such a model is by "factoring" the preferences matrix into the product of a user matrix and an item matrix.

(Possibly this idea of latent types reminds you of the word embeddings we developed in Chapter 21. Hold on to that idea.)

Rather than working with our made-up 10-user dataset, we'll work with the Movie-Lens 100k dataset, which contains ratings from 0 to 5 for many movies from many users. Each user has only rated a small subset of the movies. We'll use this to try to build a system that can predict the rating for any given (user, movie) pair. We'll train it to predict well on the movies each user has rated; hopefully then it will generalize to movies the user hasn't rated.

To start with, let's acquire the dataset. You can download it from *http://files.group-lens.org/datasets/movielens/ml-100k.zip*.

Unzip it and extract the files; we'll only use two of them:

```
# This points to the current directory, modify if your files are elsewhere.
MOVIES = "u.item"    # pipe-delimited: movie_id|title|...
RATINGS = "u.data"   # tab-delimited: user_id, movie_id, rating, timestamp
```

As is often the case, we'll introduce a NamedTuple to make things easier to work with:

```
from typing import NamedTuple

class Rating(NamedTuple):
    user_id: str
    movie_id: str
    rating: float
```

 The movie ID and user IDs are actually integers, but they're not consecutive, which means if we worked with them as integers we'd end up with a lot of wasted dimensions (unless we renumbered everything). So to keep it simpler we'll just treat them as strings.

Now let's read in the data and explore it. The movies file is pipe-delimited and has many columns. We only care about the first two, which are the ID and the title:

```
import csv
# We specify this encoding to avoid a UnicodeDecodeError.
# See: https://stackoverflow.com/a/53136168/1076346.
with open(MOVIES, encoding="iso-8859-1") as f:
    reader = csv.reader(f, delimiter="|")
    movies = {movie_id: title for movie_id, title, *_ in reader}
```

The ratings file is tab-delimited and contains four columns for user_id, movie_id, rating (1 to 5), and timestamp. We'll ignore the timestamp, as we don't need it:

```
# Create a list of [Rating]
with open(RATINGS, encoding="iso-8859-1") as f:
    reader = csv.reader(f, delimiter="\t")
    ratings = [Rating(user_id, movie_id, float(rating))
               for user_id, movie_id, rating, _ in reader]


# 1682 movies rated by 943 users
assert len(movies) == 1682
assert len(list({rating.user_id for rating in ratings})) == 943
```

There's a lot of interesting exploratory analysis you can do on this data; for instance, you might be interested in the average ratings for *Star Wars* movies (the dataset is from 1998, which means it predates *The Phantom Menace* by a year):

```
import re

# Data structure for accumulating ratings by movie_id
star_wars_ratings = {movie_id: []
                     for movie_id, title in movies.items()
                     if re.search("Star Wars|Empire Strikes|Jedi", title)}

# Iterate over ratings, accumulating the Star Wars ones
for rating in ratings:
    if rating.movie_id in star_wars_ratings:
        star_wars_ratings[rating.movie_id].append(rating.rating)
```

```
# Compute the average rating for each movie
avg_ratings = [(sum(title_ratings) / len(title_ratings), movie_id)
               for movie_id, title_ratings in star_wars_ratings.items()]

# And then print them in order
for avg_rating, movie_id in sorted(avg_ratings, reverse=True):
    print(f"{avg_rating:.2f} {movies[movie_id]}")
```

They're all pretty highly rated:

```
4.36 Star Wars (1977)
4.20 Empire Strikes Back, The (1980)
4.01 Return of the Jedi (1983)
```

So let's try to come up with a model to predict these ratings. As a first step, let's split the ratings data into train, validation, and test sets:

```
import random
random.seed(0)
random.shuffle(ratings)

split1 = int(len(ratings) * 0.7)
split2 = int(len(ratings) * 0.85)

train = ratings[:split1]              # 70% of the data
validation = ratings[split1:split2]   # 15% of the data
test = ratings[split2:]               # 15% of the data
```

It's always good to have a simple baseline model and make sure that ours does better than that. Here a simple baseline model might be "predict the average rating." We'll be using mean squared error as our metric, so let's see how the baseline does on our test set:

```
avg_rating = sum(rating.rating for rating in train) / len(train)
baseline_error = sum((rating.rating - avg_rating) ** 2
                     for rating in test) / len(test)

# This is what we hope to do better than
assert 1.26 < baseline_error < 1.27
```

Given our embeddings, the predicted ratings are given by the matrix product of the user embeddings and the movie embeddings. For a given user and movie, that value is just the dot product of the corresponding embeddings.

So let's start by creating the embeddings. We'll represent them as dicts where the keys are IDs and the values are vectors, which will allow us to easily retrieve the embedding for a given ID:

```
from scratch.deep_learning import random_tensor

EMBEDDING_DIM = 2

# Find unique ids
```

```
user_ids = {rating.user_id for rating in ratings}
movie_ids = {rating.movie_id for rating in ratings}

# Then create a random vector per id
user_vectors = {user_id: random_tensor(EMBEDDING_DIM)
                for user_id in user_ids}
movie_vectors = {movie_id: random_tensor(EMBEDDING_DIM)
                 for movie_id in movie_ids}
```

By now we should be pretty expert at writing training loops:

```
from typing import List
import tqdm
from scratch.linear_algebra import dot

def loop(dataset: List[Rating],
         learning_rate: float = None) -> None:
    with tqdm.tqdm(dataset) as t:
        loss = 0.0
        for i, rating in enumerate(t):
            movie_vector = movie_vectors[rating.movie_id]
            user_vector = user_vectors[rating.user_id]
            predicted = dot(user_vector, movie_vector)
            error = predicted - rating.rating
            loss += error ** 2

            if learning_rate is not None:
                #     predicted = m_0 * u_0 + ... + m_k * u_k
                # So each u_j enters output with coefficent m_j
                # and each m_j enters output with coefficient u_j
                user_gradient = [error * m_j for m_j in movie_vector]
                movie_gradient = [error * u_j for u_j in user_vector]

                # Take gradient steps
                for j in range(EMBEDDING_DIM):
                    user_vector[j] -= learning_rate * user_gradient[j]
                    movie_vector[j] -= learning_rate * movie_gradient[j]

        t.set_description(f"avg loss: {loss / (i + 1)}")
```

And now we can train our model (that is, find the optimal embeddings). For me it worked best if I decreased the learning rate a little each epoch:

```
learning_rate = 0.05
for epoch in range(20):
    learning_rate *= 0.9
    print(epoch, learning_rate)
    loop(train, learning_rate=learning_rate)
    loop(validation)
loop(test)
```

This model is pretty apt to overfit the training set. I got the best results with EMBED DING_DIM=2, which got me an average loss on the test set of about 0.89.

If you wanted higher-dimensional embeddings, you could try regularization like we used in "Regularization" on page 200. In particular, at each gradient update you could shrink the weights toward 0. I was not able to get any better results that way.

Now, inspect the learned vectors. There's no reason to expect the two components to be particularly meaningful, so we'll use principal component analysis:

```
from scratch.working_with_data import pca, transform

original_vectors = [vector for vector in movie_vectors.values()]
components = pca(original_vectors, 2)
```

Let's transform our vectors to represent the principal components and join in the movie IDs and average ratings:

```
ratings_by_movie = defaultdict(list)
for rating in ratings:
    ratings_by_movie[rating.movie_id].append(rating.rating)

vectors = [
    (movie_id,
     sum(ratings_by_movie[movie_id]) / len(ratings_by_movie[movie_id]),
     movies[movie_id],
     vector)
    for movie_id, vector in zip(movie_vectors.keys(),
                                transform(original_vectors, components))
]

# Print top 25 and bottom 25 by first principal component
print(sorted(vectors, key=lambda v: v[-1][0])[:25])
print(sorted(vectors, key=lambda v: v[-1][0])[-25:])
```

The top 25 are all highly rated, while the bottom 25 are mostly low-rated (or unrated in the training data), which suggests that the first principal component is mostly capturing "how good is this movie?"

It's hard for me to make much sense of the second component; and, indeed the two-dimensional embeddings performed only slightly better than the one-dimensional embeddings, suggesting that whatever the second component captured is possibly very subtle. (Presumably one of the larger MovieLens datasets would have more interesting things going on.)

For Further Exploration

- Surprise (*http://surpriselib.com/*) is a Python library for "building and analyzing recommender systems" that seems reasonably popular and up-to-date.
- The Netflix Prize (*http://www.netflixprize.com*) was a somewhat famous competition to build a better system to recommend movies to Netflix users.

## CHAPTER 24

Databases and SQL

Memory is man's greatest friend and worst enemy.
—Gilbert Parker

The data you need will often live in *databases*, systems designed for efficiently storing and querying data. The bulk of these are *relational* databases, such as PostgreSQL, MySQL, and SQL Server, which store data in *tables* and are typically queried using Structured Query Language (SQL), a declarative language for manipulating data.

SQL is a pretty essential part of the data scientist's toolkit. In this chapter, we'll create NotQuiteABase, a Python implementation of something that's not quite a database. We'll also cover the basics of SQL while showing how they work in our not-quite database, which is the most "from scratch" way I could think of to help you understand what they're doing. My hope is that solving problems in NotQuiteABase will give you a good sense of how you might solve the same problems using SQL.

CREATE TABLE and INSERT

A relational database is a collection of tables, and of relationships among them. A table is simply a collection of rows, not unlike some of the matrices we've been working with. However, a table also has associated with it a fixed *schema* consisting of column names and column types.

For example, imagine a `users` dataset containing for each user her `user_id`, `name`, and `num_friends`:

```
users = [[0, "Hero", 0],
         [1, "Dunn", 2],
         [2, "Sue", 3],
         [3, "Chi", 3]]
```

In SQL, we might create this table with:

```
CREATE TABLE users (
    user_id INT NOT NULL,
    name VARCHAR(200),
    num_friends INT);
```

Notice that we specified that the user_id and num_friends must be integers (and that user_id isn't allowed to be NULL, which indicates a missing value and is sort of like our None) and that the name should be a string of length 200 or less. We'll use Python types in a similar way.

 SQL is almost completely case and indentation insensitive. The capitalization and indentation style here is my preferred style. If you start learning SQL, you will surely encounter other examples styled differently.

You can insert the rows with INSERT statements:

```
INSERT INTO users (user_id, name, num_friends) VALUES (0, 'Hero', 0);
```

Notice also that SQL statements need to end with semicolons, and that SQL requires single quotes for its strings.

In NotQuiteABase, you'll create a Table by specifying a similar schema. Then to insert a row, you'll use the table's insert method, which takes a list of row values that need to be in the same order as the table's column names.

Behind the scenes, we'll store each row as a dict from column names to values. A real database would never use such a space-wasting representation, but doing so will make NotQuiteABase much easier to work with.

We'll implement the NotQuiteABase Table as a giant class, which we'll implement one method at a time. Let's start by getting out of the way some imports and type aliases:

```
from typing import Tuple, Sequence, List, Any, Callable, Dict, Iterator
from collections import defaultdict

# A few type aliases we'll use later
Row = Dict[str, Any]                        # A database row
WhereClause = Callable[[Row], bool]         # Predicate for a single row
HavingClause = Callable[[List[Row]], bool]  # Predicate over multiple rows
```

Let's start with the constructor. To create a NotQuiteABase table, we'll need to pass in a list of column names, and a list of column types, just as you would if you were creating a table in a SQL database:

```
class Table:
    def __init__(self, columns: List[str], types: List[type]) -> None:
        assert len(columns) == len(types), "# of columns must == # of types"

        self.columns = columns      # Names of columns
        self.types = types          # Data types of columns
        self.rows: List[Row] = []    # (no data yet)
```

We'll add a helper method to get the type of a column:

```
    def col2type(self, col: str) -> type:
        idx = self.columns.index(col)      # Find the index of the column,
        return self.types[idx]             # and return its type.
```

And we'll add an `insert` method that checks that the values you're inserting are valid. In particular, you have to provide the correct number of values, and each has to be the correct type (or None):

```
    def insert(self, values: list) -> None:
        # Check for right # of values
        if len(values) != len(self.types):
            raise ValueError(f"You need to provide {len(self.types)} values")

        # Check for right types of values
        for value, typ3 in zip(values, self.types):
            if not isinstance(value, typ3) and value is not None:
                raise TypeError(f"Expected type {typ3} but got {value}")

        # Add the corresponding dict as a "row"
        self.rows.append(dict(zip(self.columns, values)))
```

In an actual SQL database you'd explicitly specify whether any given column was allowed to contain null (None) values; to make our lives simpler we'll just say that any column can.

We'll also introduce a few dunder methods that allow us to treat a table like a `List[Row]`, which we'll mostly use for testing our code:

```
    def __getitem__(self, idx: int) -> Row:
        return self.rows[idx]

    def __iter__(self) -> Iterator[Row]:
        return iter(self.rows)

    def __len__(self) -> int:
        return len(self.rows)
```

And we'll add a method to pretty-print our table:

```
    def __repr__(self):
        """Pretty representation of the table: columns then rows"""
        rows = "\n".join(str(row) for row in self.rows)
```

```
        return f"{self.columns}\n{rows}"
```

Now we can create our `Users` table:

```
# Constructor requires column names and types
users = Table(['user_id', 'name', 'num_friends'], [int, str, int])
users.insert([0, "Hero", 0])
users.insert([1, "Dunn", 2])
users.insert([2, "Sue", 3])
users.insert([3, "Chi", 3])
users.insert([4, "Thor", 3])
users.insert([5, "Clive", 2])
users.insert([6, "Hicks", 3])
users.insert([7, "Devin", 2])
users.insert([8, "Kate", 2])
users.insert([9, "Klein", 3])
users.insert([10, "Jen", 1])
```

If you now `print(users)`, you'll see:

```
['user_id', 'name', 'num_friends']
{'user_id': 0, 'name': 'Hero', 'num_friends': 0}
{'user_id': 1, 'name': 'Dunn', 'num_friends': 2}
{'user_id': 2, 'name': 'Sue', 'num_friends': 3}
...
```

The list-like API makes it easy to write tests:

```
assert len(users) == 11
assert users[1]['name'] == 'Dunn'
```

We've got a lot more functionality to add.

UPDATE

Sometimes you need to update the data that's already in the database. For instance, if Dunn acquires another friend, you might need to do this:

```
UPDATE users
SET num_friends = 3
WHERE user_id = 1;
```

The key features are:

- What table to update
- Which rows to update
- Which fields to update
- What their new values should be

We'll add a similar `update` method to NotQuiteABase. Its first argument will be a `dict` whose keys are the columns to update and whose values are the new values for those fields. Its second (optional) argument should be a `predicate` that returns `True` for rows that should be updated, and `False` otherwise:

```
def update(self,
           updates: Dict[str, Any],
           predicate: WhereClause = lambda row: True):
    # First make sure the updates have valid names and types
    for column, new_value in updates.items():
        if column not in self.columns:
            raise ValueError(f"invalid column: {column}")

        typ3 = self.col2type(column)
        if not isinstance(new_value, typ3) and new_value is not None:
            raise TypeError(f"expected type {typ3}, but got {new_value}")

    # Now update
    for row in self.rows:
        if predicate(row):
            for column, new_value in updates.items():
                row[column] = new_value
```

after which we can simply do this:

```
assert users[1]['num_friends'] == 2          # Original value

users.update({'num_friends' : 3},            # Set num_friends = 3
             lambda row: row['user_id'] == 1)  # in rows where user_id == 1

assert users[1]['num_friends'] == 3          # Updated value
```

DELETE

There are two ways to delete rows from a table in SQL. The dangerous way deletes every row from a table:

```
DELETE FROM users;
```

The less dangerous way adds a `WHERE` clause and deletes only rows that match a certain condition:

```
DELETE FROM users WHERE user_id = 1;
```

It's easy to add this functionality to our `Table`:

```
def delete(self, predicate: WhereClause = lambda row: True) -> None:
    """Delete all rows matching predicate"""
    self.rows = [row for row in self.rows if not predicate(row)]
```

If you supply a `predicate` function (i.e., a WHERE clause), this deletes only the rows that satisfy it. If you don't supply one, the default `predicate` always returns `True`, and you will delete every row.

For example:

```
# We're not actually going to run these
users.delete(lambda row: row["user_id"] == 1)  # Deletes rows with user_id == 1
users.delete()                                  # Deletes every row
```

SELECT

Typically you don't inspect SQL tables directly. Instead you query them with a SELECT statement:

```
SELECT * FROM users;                          -- get the entire contents
SELECT * FROM users LIMIT 2;                   -- get the first two rows
SELECT user_id FROM users;                     -- only get specific columns
SELECT user_id FROM users WHERE name = 'Dunn'; -- only get specific rows
```

You can also use SELECT statements to calculate fields:

```
SELECT LENGTH(name) AS name_length FROM users;
```

We'll give our `Table` class a `select` method that returns a new `Table`. The method accepts two optional arguments:

- `keep_columns` specifies the names of the columns you want to keep in the result. If you don't supply it, the result contains all the columns.

- `additional_columns` is a dictionary whose keys are new column names and whose values are functions specifying how to compute the values of the new columns. We'll peek at the type annotations of those functions to figure out the types of the new columns, so the functions will need to have annotated return types.

If you were to supply neither of them, you'd simply get back a copy of the table:

```
def select(self,
           keep_columns: List[str] = None,
           additional_columns: Dict[str, Callable] = None) -> 'Table':

    if keep_columns is None:          # If no columns specified,
        keep_columns = self.columns   # return all columns

    if additional_columns is None:
        additional_columns = {}

    # New column names and types
    new_columns = keep_columns + list(additional_columns.keys())
    keep_types = [self.col2type(col) for col in keep_columns]
```

```
# This is how to get the return type from a type annotation.
# It will crash if `calculation` doesn't have a return type.
add_types = [calculation.__annotations__['return']
             for calculation in additional_columns.values()]

# Create a new table for results
new_table = Table(new_columns, keep_types + add_types)

for row in self.rows:
    new_row = [row[column] for column in keep_columns]
    for column_name, calculation in additional_columns.items():
        new_row.append(calculation(row))
    new_table.insert(new_row)

return new_table
```

 Remember way back in Chapter 2 when we said that type annotations don't actually do anything? Well, here's the counterexample. But look at the convoluted procedure we have to go through to get at them.

Our `select` returns a new `Table`, while the typical SQL SELECT just produces some sort of transient result set (unless you explicitly insert the results into a table).

We'll also need `where` and `limit` methods. Both are pretty simple:

```
def where(self, predicate: WhereClause = lambda row: True) -> 'Table':
    """Return only the rows that satisfy the supplied predicate"""
    where_table = Table(self.columns, self.types)
    for row in self.rows:
        if predicate(row):
            values = [row[column] for column in self.columns]
            where_table.insert(values)
    return where_table

def limit(self, num_rows: int) -> 'Table':
    """Return only the first `num_rows` rows"""
    limit_table = Table(self.columns, self.types)
    for i, row in enumerate(self.rows):
        if i >= num_rows:
            break
        values = [row[column] for column in self.columns]
        limit_table.insert(values)
    return limit_table
```

after which we can easily construct NotQuiteABase equivalents to the preceding SQL statements:

```
# SELECT * FROM users;
all_users = users.select()
```

```
assert len(all_users) == 11

# SELECT * FROM users LIMIT 2;
two_users = users.limit(2)
assert len(two_users) == 2

# SELECT user_id FROM users;
just_ids = users.select(keep_columns=["user_id"])
assert just_ids.columns == ['user_id']

# SELECT user_id FROM users WHERE name = 'Dunn';
dunn_ids = (
    users
    .where(lambda row: row["name"] == "Dunn")
    .select(keep_columns=["user_id"])
)
assert len(dunn_ids) == 1
assert dunn_ids[0] == {"user_id": 1}

# SELECT LENGTH(name) AS name_length FROM users;
def name_length(row) -> int: return len(row["name"])

name_lengths = users.select(keep_columns=[],
                            additional_columns = {"name_length": name_length})
assert name_lengths[0]['name_length'] == len("Hero")
```

Notice that for the multiline "fluent" queries we have to wrap the whole query in parentheses.

GROUP BY

Another common SQL operation is GROUP BY, which groups together rows with identical values in specified columns and produces aggregate values like MIN and MAX and COUNT and SUM.

For example, you might want to find the number of users and the smallest user_id for each possible name length:

```
SELECT LENGTH(name) as name_length,
  MIN(user_id) AS min_user_id,
  COUNT(*) AS num_users
FROM users
GROUP BY LENGTH(name);
```

Every field we SELECT needs to be either in the GROUP BY clause (which name_length is) or an aggregate computation (which min_user_id and num_users are).

SQL also supports a HAVING clause that behaves similarly to a WHERE clause, except that its filter is applied to the aggregates (whereas a WHERE would filter out rows before aggregation even took place).

You might want to know the average number of friends for users whose names start with specific letters but see only the results for letters whose corresponding average is greater than 1. (Yes, some of these examples are contrived.)

```
SELECT SUBSTR(name, 1, 1) AS first_letter,
 AVG(num_friends) AS avg_num_friends
FROM users
GROUP BY SUBSTR(name, 1, 1)
HAVING AVG(num_friends) > 1;
```

 Functions for working with strings vary across SQL implementations; some databases might instead use SUBSTRING or something else.

You can also compute overall aggregates. In that case, you leave off the GROUP BY:

```
SELECT SUM(user_id) as user_id_sum
FROM users
WHERE user_id > 1;
```

To add this functionality to NotQuiteABase Tables, we'll add a group_by method. It takes the names of the columns you want to group by, a dictionary of the aggregation functions you want to run over each group, and an optional predicate called having that operates on multiple rows.

Then it does the following steps:

1. Creates a defaultdict to map tuples (of the group-by values) to rows (containing the group-by values). Recall that you can't use lists as dict keys; you have to use tuples.

2. Iterates over the rows of the table, populating the defaultdict.

3. Creates a new table with the correct output columns.

4. Iterates over the defaultdict and populates the output table, applying the having filter, if any.

```
def group_by(self,
             group_by_columns: List[str],
             aggregates: Dict[str, Callable],
             having: HavingClause = lambda group: True) -> 'Table':

    grouped_rows = defaultdict(list)

    # Populate groups
    for row in self.rows:
        key = tuple(row[column] for column in group_by_columns)
        grouped_rows[key].append(row)
```

```
    # Result table consists of group_by columns and aggregates
    new_columns = group_by_columns + list(aggregates.keys())
    group_by_types = [self.col2type(col) for col in group_by_columns]
    aggregate_types = [agg.__annotations__['return']
                       for agg in aggregates.values()]
    result_table = Table(new_columns, group_by_types + aggregate_types)

    for key, rows in grouped_rows.items():
        if having(rows):
            new_row = list(key)
            for aggregate_name, aggregate_fn in aggregates.items():
                new_row.append(aggregate_fn(rows))
            result_table.insert(new_row)

    return result_table
```

 An actual database would almost certainly do this in a more efficient manner.)

Again, let's see how we would do the equivalent of the preceding SQL statements. The
name_length metrics are:

```
def min_user_id(rows) -> int:
    return min(row["user_id"] for row in rows)

def length(rows) -> int:
    return len(rows)

stats_by_length = (
    users
    .select(additional_columns={"name_length" : name_length})
    .group_by(group_by_columns=["name_length"],
              aggregates={"min_user_id" : min_user_id,
                          "num_users" : length})
)
```

The first_letter metrics:

```
def first_letter_of_name(row: Row) -> str:
    return row["name"][0] if row["name"] else ""

def average_num_friends(rows: List[Row]) -> float:
    return sum(row["num_friends"] for row in rows) / len(rows)

def enough_friends(rows: List[Row]) -> bool:
    return average_num_friends(rows) > 1

avg_friends_by_letter = (
```

```
    users
    .select(additional_columns={'first_letter' : first_letter_of_name})
    .group_by(group_by_columns=['first_letter'],
              aggregates={"avg_num_friends" : average_num_friends},
              having=enough_friends)
)
```

and the user_id_sum is:

```
def sum_user_ids(rows: List[Row]) -> int:
    return sum(row["user_id"] for row in rows)

user_id_sum = (
    users
    .where(lambda row: row["user_id"] > 1)
    .group_by(group_by_columns=[],
              aggregates={ "user_id_sum" : sum_user_ids })
)
```

ORDER BY

Frequently, you'll want to sort your results. For example, you might want to know the (alphabetically) first two names of your users:

```
SELECT * FROM users
ORDER BY name
LIMIT 2;
```

This is easy to implement by giving our Table an order_by method that takes an order function:

```
def order_by(self, order: Callable[[Row], Any]) -> 'Table':
    new_table = self.select()        # make a copy
    new_table.rows.sort(key=order)
    return new_table
```

which we can then use as follows:

```
friendliest_letters = (
    avg_friends_by_letter
    .order_by(lambda row: -row["avg_num_friends"])
    .limit(4)
)
```

The SQL ORDER BY lets you specify ASC (ascending) or DESC (descending) for each sort field; here we'd have to bake that into our order function.

JOIN

Relational database tables are often *normalized*, which means that they're organized to minimize redundancy. For example, when we work with our users' interests in Python, we can just give each user a list containing his interests.

SQL tables can't typically contain lists, so the typical solution is to create a second table called `user_interests` containing the one-to-many relationship between `user_ids` and `interests`. In SQL you might do:

```
CREATE TABLE user_interests (
    user_id INT NOT NULL,
    interest VARCHAR(100) NOT NULL
);
```

whereas in NotQuiteABase you'd create the table:

```
user_interests = Table(['user_id', 'interest'], [int, str])
user_interests.insert([0, "SQL"])
user_interests.insert([0, "NoSQL"])
user_interests.insert([2, "SQL"])
user_interests.insert([2, "MySQL"])
```

There's still plenty of redundancy—the interest "SQL" is stored in two different places. In a real database you might store `user_id` and `interest_id` in the `user_interests` table and then create a third table, `interests`, mapping `interest_id` to `interest` so you could store the interest names only once each. Here that would just make our examples more complicated than they need to be.

When our data lives across different tables, how do we analyze it? By JOINing the tables together. A JOIN combines rows in the left table with corresponding rows in the right table, where the meaning of "corresponding" is based on how we specify the join.

For example, to find the users interested in SQL you'd query:

```
SELECT users.name
FROM users
JOIN user_interests
ON users.user_id = user_interests.user_id
WHERE user_interests.interest = 'SQL'
```

The JOIN says that, for each row in `users`, we should look at the `user_id` and associate that row with every row in `user_interests` containing the same `user_id`.

Notice we had to specify which tables to JOIN and also which columns to join ON. This is an INNER JOIN, which returns the combinations of rows (and only the combinations of rows) that match according to the specified join criteria.

There is also a LEFT JOIN, which—in addition to the combinations of matching rows —returns a row for each left-table row with no matching rows (in which case, the fields that would have come from the right table are all NULL).

Using a LEFT JOIN, it's easy to count the number of interests each user has:

```
SELECT users.id, COUNT(user_interests.interest) AS num_interests
FROM users
LEFT JOIN user_interests
ON users.user_id = user_interests.user_id
```

The LEFT JOIN ensures that users with no interests will still have rows in the joined dataset (with NULL values for the fields coming from user_interests), and COUNT counts only values that are non-NULL.

The NotQuiteABase join implementation will be more restrictive—it simply joins two tables on whatever columns they have in common. Even so, it's not trivial to write:

```
def join(self, other_table: 'Table', left_join: bool = False) -> 'Table':

    join_on_columns = [c for c in self.columns        # columns in
                       if c in other_table.columns]   # both tables

    additional_columns = [c for c in other_table.columns # columns only
                          if c not in join_on_columns]   # in right table

    # all columns from left table + additional_columns from right table
    new_columns = self.columns + additional_columns
    new_types = self.types + [other_table.col2type(col)
                              for col in additional_columns]

    join_table = Table(new_columns, new_types)

    for row in self.rows:
        def is_join(other_row):
            return all(other_row[c] == row[c] for c in join_on_columns)

        other_rows = other_table.where(is_join).rows

        # Each other row that matches this one produces a result row.
        for other_row in other_rows:
            join_table.insert([row[c] for c in self.columns] +
                              [other_row[c] for c in additional_columns])

        # If no rows match and it's a left join, output with Nones.
        if left_join and not other_rows:
            join_table.insert([row[c] for c in self.columns] +
                              [None for c in additional_columns])

    return join_table
```

So, we could find users interested in SQL with:

```
sql_users = (
    users
    .join(user_interests)
    .where(lambda row: row["interest"] == "SQL")
    .select(keep_columns=["name"])
)
```

And we could get the interest counts with:

```
def count_interests(rows: List[Row]) -> int:
    """counts how many rows have non-None interests"""
    return len([row for row in rows if row["interest"] is not None])

user_interest_counts = (
    users
    .join(user_interests, left_join=True)
    .group_by(group_by_columns=["user_id"],
              aggregates={"num_interests" : count_interests })
)
```

In SQL, there is also a `RIGHT JOIN`, which keeps rows from the right table that have no matches, and a `FULL OUTER JOIN`, which keeps rows from both tables that have no matches. We won't implement either of those.

Subqueries

In SQL, you can `SELECT` from (and `JOIN`) the results of queries as if they were tables. So, if you wanted to find the smallest `user_id` of anyone interested in SQL, you could use a subquery. (Of course, you could do the same calculation using a `JOIN`, but that wouldn't illustrate subqueries.)

```
SELECT MIN(user_id) AS min_user_id FROM
(SELECT user_id FROM user_interests WHERE interest = 'SQL') sql_interests;
```

Given the way we've designed NotQuiteABase, we get this for free. (Our query results are actual tables.)

```
likes_sql_user_ids = (
    user_interests
    .where(lambda row: row["interest"] == "SQL")
    .select(keep_columns=['user_id'])
)

likes_sql_user_ids.group_by(group_by_columns=[],
                            aggregates={ "min_user_id" : min_user_id })
```

Indexes

To find rows containing a specific value (say, where name is "Hero"), NotQuiteABase has to inspect every row in the table. If the table has a lot of rows, this can take a very long time.

Similarly, our join algorithm is extremely inefficient. For each row in the left table, it inspects every row in the right table to see if it's a match. With two large tables this could take approximately forever.

Also, you'd often like to apply constraints to some of your columns. For example, in your users table you probably don't want to allow two different users to have the same user_id.

Indexes solve all these problems. If the user_interests table had an index on user_id, a smart join algorithm could find matches directly rather than scanning the whole table. If the users table had a "unique" index on user_id, you'd get an error if you tried to insert a duplicate.

Each table in a database can have one or more indexes, which allow you to quickly look up rows by key columns, efficiently join tables together, and enforce unique constraints on columns or combinations of columns.

Designing and using indexes well is something of a black art (which varies somewhat depending on the specific database), but if you end up doing a lot of database work it's worth learning about.

Query Optimization

Recall the query to find all users who are interested in SQL:

```
SELECT users.name
FROM users
JOIN user_interests
ON users.user_id = user_interests.user_id
WHERE user_interests.interest = 'SQL'
```

In NotQuiteABase there are (at least) two different ways to write this query. You could filter the user_interests table before performing the join:

```
(
    user_interests
    .where(lambda row: row["interest"] == "SQL")
    .join(users)
    .select(["name"])
)
```

Or you could filter the results of the join:

```
(
    user_interests
    .join(users)
    .where(lambda row: row["interest"] == "SQL")
    .select(["name"])
)
```

You'll end up with the same results either way, but filter-before-join is almost certainly more efficient, since in that case join has many fewer rows to operate on.

In SQL, you generally wouldn't worry about this. You "declare" the results you want and leave it up to the query engine to execute them (and use indexes efficiently).

NoSQL

A recent trend in databases is toward nonrelational "NoSQL" databases, which don't represent data in tables. For instance, MongoDB is a popular schemaless database whose elements are arbitrarily complex JSON documents rather than rows.

There are column databases that store data in columns instead of rows (good when data has many columns but queries need few of them), key/value stores that are optimized for retrieving single (complex) values by their keys, databases for storing and traversing graphs, databases that are optimized to run across multiple datacenters, databases that are designed to run in memory, databases for storing time-series data, and hundreds more.

Tomorrow's flavor of the day might not even exist now, so I can't do much more than let you know that NoSQL is a thing. So now you know. It's a thing.

For Further Exploration

- If you'd like to download a relational database to play with, SQLite (*http://www.sqlite.org*) is fast and tiny, while MySQL (*http://www.mysql.com*) and PostgreSQL (*http://www.postgresql.org*) are larger and featureful. All are free and have lots of documentation.

- If you want to explore NoSQL, MongoDB (*http://www.mongodb.org*) is very simple to get started with, which can be both a blessing and somewhat of a curse. It also has pretty good documentation.

- The Wikipedia article on NoSQL (*http://en.wikipedia.org/wiki/NoSQL*) almost certainly now contains links to databases that didn't even exist when this book was written.

## CHAPTER 25

MapReduce

The future has already arrived. It's just not evenly distributed yet.
  —William Gibson

MapReduce is a programming model for performing parallel processing on large datasets. Although it is a powerful technique, its basics are relatively simple.

Imagine we have a collection of items we'd like to process somehow. For instance, the items might be website logs, the texts of various books, image files, or anything else. A basic version of the MapReduce algorithm consists of the following steps:

1. Use a `mapper` function to turn each item into zero or more key/value pairs. (Often this is called the `map` function, but there is already a Python function called `map` and we don't need to confuse the two.)

2. Collect together all the pairs with identical keys.

3. Use a `reducer` function on each collection of grouped values to produce output values for the corresponding key.

MapReduce is sort of passé, so much so that I considered removing this chapter from the second edition. But I decided it's still an interesting topic, so I ended up leaving it in (obviously).

This is all sort of abstract, so let's look at a specific example. There are few absolute rules of data science, but one of them is that your first MapReduce example has to involve counting words.

Example: Word Count

DataSciencester has grown to millions of users! This is great for your job security, but it makes routine analyses slightly more difficult.

For example, your VP of Content wants to know what sorts of things people are talking about in their status updates. As a first attempt, you decide to count the words that appear, so that you can prepare a report on the most frequent ones.

When you had a few hundred users, this was simple to do:

```python
from typing import List
from collections import Counter

def tokenize(document: str) -> List[str]:
    """Just split on whitespace"""
    return document.split()

def word_count_old(documents: List[str]):
    """Word count not using MapReduce"""
    return Counter(word
        for document in documents
        for word in tokenize(document))
```

With millions of users the set of documents (status updates) is suddenly too big to fit on your computer. If you can just fit this into the MapReduce model, you can use some "big data" infrastructure that your engineers have implemented.

First, we need a function that turns a document into a sequence of key/value pairs. We'll want our output to be grouped by word, which means that the keys should be words. And for each word, we'll just emit the value 1 to indicate that this pair corresponds to one occurrence of the word:

```python
from typing import Iterator, Tuple

def wc_mapper(document: str) -> Iterator[Tuple[str, int]]:
    """For each word in the document, emit (word, 1)"""
    for word in tokenize(document):
        yield (word, 1)
```

Skipping the "plumbing" step 2 for the moment, imagine that for some word we've collected a list of the corresponding counts we emitted. To produce the overall count for that word, then, we just need:

```python
from typing import Iterable

def wc_reducer(word: str,
               counts: Iterable[int]) -> Iterator[Tuple[str, int]]:
    """Sum up the counts for a word"""
    yield (word, sum(counts))
```

Returning to step 2, we now need to collect the results from wc_mapper and feed them to wc_reducer. Let's think about how we would do this on just one computer:

```
from collections import defaultdict

def word_count(documents: List[str]) -> List[Tuple[str, int]]:
    """Count the words in the input documents using MapReduce"""

    collector = defaultdict(list)  # To store grouped values

    for document in documents:
        for word, count in wc_mapper(document):
            collector[word].append(count)

    return [output
            for word, counts in collector.items()
            for output in wc_reducer(word, counts)]
```

Imagine that we have three documents ["data science", "big data", "science fiction"].

Then wc_mapper applied to the first document yields the two pairs ("data", 1) and ("science", 1). After we've gone through all three documents, the collector contains:

```
{"data" : [1, 1],
 "science" : [1, 1],
 "big" : [1],
 "fiction" : [1]}
```

Then wc_reducer produces the counts for each word:

```
[("data", 2), ("science", 2), ("big", 1), ("fiction", 1)]
```

Why MapReduce?

As mentioned earlier, the primary benefit of MapReduce is that it allows us to distribute computations by moving the processing to the data. Imagine we want to word-count across billions of documents.

Our original (non-MapReduce) approach requires the machine doing the processing to have access to every document. This means that the documents all need to either live on that machine or else be transferred to it during processing. More important, it means that the machine can process only one document at a time.

Possibly it can process up to a few at a time if it has multiple cores and if the code is rewritten to take advantage of them. But even so, all the documents still have to *get to* that machine.

Imagine now that our billions of documents are scattered across 100 machines. With the right infrastructure (and glossing over some of the details), we can do the following:

- Have each machine run the mapper on its documents, producing lots of key/value pairs.
- Distribute those key/value pairs to a number of "reducing" machines, making sure that the pairs corresponding to any given key all end up on the same machine.
- Have each reducing machine group the pairs by key and then run the reducer on each set of values.
- Return each (key, output) pair.

What is amazing about this is that it scales horizontally. If we double the number of machines, then (ignoring certain fixed costs of running a MapReduce system) our computation should run approximately twice as fast. Each mapper machine will only need to do half as much work, and (assuming there are enough distinct keys to further distribute the reducer work) the same is true for the reducer machines.

MapReduce More Generally

If you think about it for a minute, all of the word count–specific code in the previous example is contained in the wc_mapper and wc_reducer functions. This means that with a couple of changes we have a much more general framework (that still runs on a single machine).

We could use generic types to fully type-annotate our map_reduce function, but it would end up being kind of a mess pedagogically, so in this chapter we'll be much more casual about our type annotations:

```
from typing import Callable, Iterable, Any, Tuple

# A key/value pair is just a 2-tuple
KV = Tuple[Any, Any]

# A Mapper is a function that returns an Iterable of key/value pairs
Mapper = Callable[..., Iterable[KV]]

# A Reducer is a function that takes a key and an iterable of values
# and returns a key/value pair
Reducer = Callable[[Any, Iterable], KV]
```

Now we can write a general map_reduce function:

```
def map_reduce(inputs: Iterable,
               mapper: Mapper,
```

```
                reducer: Reducer) -> List[KV]:
    """Run MapReduce on the inputs using mapper and reducer"""
    collector = defaultdict(list)

    for input in inputs:
        for key, value in mapper(input):
            collector[key].append(value)

    return [output
            for key, values in collector.items()
            for output in reducer(key, values)]
```

Then we can count words simply by using:

```
word_counts = map_reduce(documents, wc_mapper, wc_reducer)
```

This gives us the flexibility to solve a wide variety of problems.

Before we proceed, notice that `wc_reducer` is just summing the values corresponding to each key. This kind of aggregation is common enough that it's worth abstracting it out:

```
def values_reducer(values_fn: Callable) -> Reducer:
    """Return a reducer that just applies values_fn to its values"""
    def reduce(key, values: Iterable) -> KV:
        return (key, values_fn(values))

    return reduce
```

After which we can easily create:

```
sum_reducer = values_reducer(sum)
max_reducer = values_reducer(max)
min_reducer = values_reducer(min)
count_distinct_reducer = values_reducer(lambda values: len(set(values)))

assert sum_reducer("key", [1, 2, 3, 3]) == ("key", 9)
assert min_reducer("key", [1, 2, 3, 3]) == ("key", 1)
assert max_reducer("key", [1, 2, 3, 3]) == ("key", 3)
assert count_distinct_reducer("key", [1, 2, 3, 3]) == ("key", 3)
```

and so on.

Example: Analyzing Status Updates

The content VP was impressed with the word counts and asks what else you can learn from people's status updates. You manage to extract a dataset of status updates that look like:

```
status_updates = [
    {"id": 2,
     "username" : "joelgrus",
     "text" : "Should I write a second edition of my data science book?",
```

```
        "created_at" : datetime.datetime(2018, 2, 21, 11, 47, 0),
        "liked_by" : ["data_guy", "data_gal", "mike"] },
    # ...
]
```

Let's say we need to figure out which day of the week people talk the most about data science. In order to find this, we'll just count how many data science updates there are on each day of the week. This means we'll need to group by the day of week, so that's our key. And if we emit a value of 1 for each update that contains "data science," we can simply get the total number using sum:

```
def data_science_day_mapper(status_update: dict) -> Iterable:
    """Yields (day_of_week, 1) if status_update contains "data science" """
    if "data science" in status_update["text"].lower():
        day_of_week = status_update["created_at"].weekday()
        yield (day_of_week, 1)

data_science_days = map_reduce(status_updates,
                               data_science_day_mapper,
                               sum_reducer)
```

As a slightly more complicated example, imagine we need to find out for each user the most common word that she puts in her status updates. There are three possible approaches that spring to mind for the mapper:

- Put the username in the key; put the words and counts in the values.
- Put the word in the key; put the usernames and counts in the values.
- Put the username and word in the key; put the counts in the values.

If you think about it a bit more, we definitely want to group by username, because we want to consider each person's words separately. And we don't want to group by word, since our reducer will need to see all the words for each person to find out which is the most popular. This means that the first option is the right choice:

```
def words_per_user_mapper(status_update: dict):
    user = status_update["username"]
    for word in tokenize(status_update["text"]):
        yield (user, (word, 1))

def most_popular_word_reducer(user: str,
                              words_and_counts: Iterable[KV]):
    """
    Given a sequence of (word, count) pairs,
    return the word with the highest total count
    """
    word_counts = Counter()
    for word, count in words_and_counts:
        word_counts[word] += count
```

```
    word, count = word_counts.most_common(1)[0]

    yield (user, (word, count))

user_words = map_reduce(status_updates,
                        words_per_user_mapper,
                        most_popular_word_reducer)
```

Or we could find out the number of distinct status-likers for each user:

```
def liker_mapper(status_update: dict):
    user = status_update["username"]
    for liker in status_update["liked_by"]:
        yield (user, liker)

distinct_likers_per_user = map_reduce(status_updates,
                                      liker_mapper,
                                      count_distinct_reducer)
```

Example: Matrix Multiplication

Recall from "Matrix Multiplication" on page 314 that given an [n, m] matrix A and an [m, k] matrix B, we can multiply them to form an [n, k] matrix C, where the element of C in row i and column j is given by:

```
C[i][j] = sum(A[i][x] * B[x][j] for x in range(m))
```

This works if we represent our matrices as lists of lists, as we've been doing.

But large matrices are sometimes *sparse*, which means that most of their elements equal 0. For large sparse matrices, a list of lists can be a very wasteful representation. A more compact representation stores only the locations with nonzero values:

```
from typing import NamedTuple

class Entry(NamedTuple):
    name: str
    i: int
    j: int
    value: float
```

For example, a 1 billion × 1 billion matrix has 1 *quintillion* entries, which would not be easy to store on a computer. But if there are only a few nonzero entries in each row, this alternative representation is many orders of magnitude smaller.

Given this sort of representation, it turns out that we can use MapReduce to perform matrix multiplication in a distributed manner.

To motivate our algorithm, notice that each element A[i][j] is only used to compute the elements of C in row i, and each element B[i][j] is only used to compute the elements of C in column j. Our goal will be for each output of our reducer to be a single entry of C, which means we'll need our mapper to emit keys identifying a single entry of C. This suggests the following:

```python
def matrix_multiply_mapper(num_rows_a: int, num_cols_b: int) -> Mapper:
    # C[x][y] = A[x][0] * B[0][y] + ... + A[x][m] * B[m][y]
    #
    # so an element A[i][j] goes into every C[i][y] with coef B[j][y]
    # and an element B[i][j] goes into every C[x][j] with coef A[x][i]
    def mapper(entry: Entry):
        if entry.name == "A":
            for y in range(num_cols_b):
                key = (entry.i, y)           # which element of C
                value = (entry.j, entry.value) # which entry in the sum
                yield (key, value)
        else:
            for x in range(num_rows_a):
                key = (x, entry.j)           # which element of C
                value = (entry.i, entry.value) # which entry in the sum
                yield (key, value)

    return mapper
```

And then:

```python
def matrix_multiply_reducer(key: Tuple[int, int],
                            indexed_values: Iterable[Tuple[int, int]]):
    results_by_index = defaultdict(list)

    for index, value in indexed_values:
        results_by_index[index].append(value)

    # Multiply the values for positions with two values
    # (one from A, and one from B) and sum them up.
    sumproduct = sum(values[0] * values[1]
                     for values in results_by_index.values()
                     if len(values) == 2)

    if sumproduct != 0.0:
        yield (key, sumproduct)
```

For example, if you had these two matrices:

```
A = [[3, 2, 0],
     [0, 0, 0]]

B = [[4, -1, 0],
     [10, 0, 0],
     [0, 0, 0]]
```

you could rewrite them as tuples:

```
entries = [Entry("A", 0, 0, 3), Entry("A", 0, 1,  2), Entry("B", 0, 0, 4),
           Entry("B", 0, 1, -1), Entry("B", 1, 0, 10)]
```

```
mapper = matrix_multiply_mapper(num_rows_a=2, num_cols_b=3)
reducer = matrix_multiply_reducer

# Product should be [[32, -3, 0], [0, 0, 0]].
# So it should have two entries.
assert (set(map_reduce(entries, mapper, reducer)) ==
        {((0, 1), -3), ((0, 0), 32)})
```

This isn't terribly interesting on such small matrices, but if you had millions of rows and millions of columns, it could help you a lot.

An Aside: Combiners

One thing you have probably noticed is that many of our mappers seem to include a bunch of extra information. For example, when counting words, rather than emitting (word, 1) and summing over the values, we could have emitted (word, None) and just taken the length.

One reason we didn't do this is that, in the distributed setting, we sometimes want to use *combiners* to reduce the amount of data that has to be transferred around from machine to machine. If one of our mapper machines sees the word *data* 500 times, we can tell it to combine the 500 instances of ("data", 1) into a single ("data", 500) before handing off to the reducing machine. This results in a lot less data getting moved around, which can make our algorithm substantially faster still.

Because of the way we wrote our reducer, it would handle this combined data correctly. (If we'd written it using len, it would not have.)

For Further Exploration

- Like I said, MapReduce feels a lot less popular now than it did when I wrote the first edition. It's probably not worth investing a ton of your time.

- That said, the most widely used MapReduce system is Hadoop (*http://hadoop.apache.org*). There are various commercial and noncommercial distributions and a huge ecosystem of Hadoop-related tools.

- Amazon.com offers an Elastic MapReduce (*http://aws.amazon.com/elasticmapreduce/*) service that's probably easier than setting up your own cluster.

- Hadoop jobs are typically high-latency, which makes them a poor choice for "real-time" analytics. A popular choice for these workloads is Spark (*http://spark.apache.org/*), which can be MapReduce-y.

## CHAPTER 26

Data Ethics

Grub first, then ethics.
—Bertolt Brecht

What Is Data Ethics?

With the use of data comes the misuse of data. This has pretty much always been the case, but recently this idea has been reified as "data ethics" and has featured somewhat prominently in the news.

For instance, in the 2016 election, a company called Cambridge Analytica improperly accessed Facebook data (*https://en.wikipedia.org/wiki/Facebook%E2%80%93Cambridge_Analytica_data_scandal*) and used that for political ad targeting.

In 2018, an autonomous car being tested by Uber struck and killed a pedestrian (*https://www.nytimes.com/2018/05/24/technology/uber-autonomous-car-ntsb-investigation.html*) (there was a "safety driver" in the car, but apparently she was not paying attention at the time).

Algorithms are used to predict the risk that criminals will reoffend (*https://www.themarshallproject.org/2015/08/04/the-new-science-of-sentencing*) and to sentence them accordingly. Is this more or less fair than allowing judges to determine the same?

Some airlines assign families separate seats (*https://twitter.com/ShelkeGaneshB/status/1066161967105216512*), forcing them to pay extra to sit together. Should a data scientist have stepped in to prevent this? (Many data scientists in the linked thread seem to believe so.)

"Data ethics" purports to provide answers to these questions, or at least a framework for wrestling with them. I'm not so arrogant as to tell you *how* to think about these things (and "these things" are changing quickly), so in this chapter we'll just take a quick tour of some of the most relevant issues and (hopefully) inspire you to think about them further. (Alas, I am not a good enough philosopher to do ethics *from scratch*.)

No, Really, What Is Data Ethics?

Well, let's start with "what is ethics?" If you take the average of every definition you can find, you end up with something like *ethics* is a framework for thinking about "right" and "wrong" behavior. *Data* ethics, then, is a framework for thinking about right and wrong behavior involving data.

Some people talk as if "data ethics" is (perhaps implicitly) a set of commandments about what you may and may not do. Some of them are hard at work creating manifestos, others crafting mandatory pledges to which they hope to make you swear. Still others are campaigning for data ethics to be made a mandatory part of the data science curriculum—hence this chapter, as a means of hedging my bets in case they succeed.

 Curiously, there is not much data suggesting that ethics courses lead to ethical behavior (*https://www.washingtonpost.com/news/on-leadership/wp/2014/01/13/can-you-teach-businessmen-to-be-ethical*), in which case perhaps this campaign is itself data-unethical!

Other people (for example, yours truly) think that reasonable people will frequently disagree over subtle matters of right and wrong, and that the important part of data ethics is committing to *consider* the ethical consequences of your behaviors. This requires *understanding* the sorts of things that many "data ethics" advocates don't approve of, but it doesn't necessarily require agreeing with their disapproval.

Should I Care About Data Ethics?

You should care about ethics whatever your job. If your job involves data, you are free to characterize your caring as "data ethics," but you should care just as much about ethics in the nondata parts of your job.

Perhaps what's different about technology jobs is that technology *scales*, and that decisions made by individuals working on technology problems (whether data-related or not) have potentially wide-reaching effects.

A tiny change to a news discovery algorithm could be the difference between millions of people reading an article and no one reading it.

A single flawed algorithm for granting parole that's used all over the country systematically affects millions of people, whereas a flawed-in-its-own-way parole board affects only the people who come before it.

So yes, in general, you should care about what effects your work has on the world. And the broader the effects of your work, the more you need to worry about these things.

Unfortunately, some of the discourse around data ethics involves people trying to force their ethical conclusions on you. Whether you should care about the same things *they* care about is really up to you.

Building Bad Data Products

Some "data ethics" issues are the result of building *bad products*.

For example, Microsoft released a chat bot named Tay (*https://en.wikipedia.org/wiki/Tay_(bot)*) that parroted back things tweeted to it, which the internet quickly discovered enabled them to get Tay to tweet all sorts of offensive things. It seems unlikely that anyone at Microsoft debated the ethicality of releasing a "racist" bot; most likely they simply built a bot and failed to think through how it could be abused. This is perhaps a low bar, but let's agree that you should think about how the things you build could be abused.

Another example is that Google Photos at one point used an image recognition algorithm that would sometimes classify pictures of black people as "gorillas" (*https://www.theverge.com/2018/1/12/16882408/google-racist-gorillas-photo-recognition-algorithm-ai*). Again, it is extremely unlikely that anyone at Google *explicitly decided* to ship this feature (let alone grappled with the "ethics" of it). Here it seems likely the problem is some combination of bad training data, model inaccuracy, and the gross offensiveness of the mistake (if the model had occasionally categorized mailboxes as fire trucks, probably no one would have cared).

In this case the solution is less obvious: how can you ensure that your trained model won't make predictions that are in some way offensive? Of course you should train (and test) your model on a diverse range of inputs, but can you ever be sure that there isn't *some* input somewhere out there that will make your model behave in a way that embarrasses you? This is a hard problem. (Google seems to have "solved" it by simply refusing to ever predict "gorilla.")

Trading Off Accuracy and Fairness

Imagine you are building a model that predicts how likely people are to take some action. You do a pretty good job (Table 26-1).

Table 26-1. A pretty good job

Prediction	People	Actions	%
Unlikely	125	25	20%
Likely	125	75	60%

Of the people you predict are unlikely to take the action, only 20% of them do. Of the people you predict are likely to take the action, 60% of them do. Seems not terrible.

Now imagine that the people can be split into two groups: A and B. Some of your colleagues are concerned that your model is *unfair* to one of the groups. Although the model does not take group membership into account, it does consider various other factors that correlate in complicated ways with group membership.

Indeed, when you break down the predictions by group, you discover surprising statistics (Table 26-2).

Table 26-2. Surprising statistics

Group	Prediction	People	Actions	%
A	Unlikely	100	20	20%
A	Likely	25	15	60%
B	Unlikely	25	5	20%
B	Likely	100	60	60%

Is your model unfair? The data scientists on your team make a variety of arguments:

Argument 1

Your model classifies 80% of group A as "unlikely" but 80% of group B as "likely." This data scientist complains that the model is treating the two groups unfairly in the sense that it is generating vastly different predictions across the two groups.

Argument 2

Regardless of group membership, if we predict "unlikely" you have a 20% chance of action, and if we predict "likely" you have a 60% chance of action. This data scientist insists that the model is "accurate" in the sense that its predictions seem to *mean* the same things no matter which group you belong to.

Argument 3

> 40/125 = 32% of group B were falsely labeled "likely," whereas only 10/125 = 8% of group A were falsely labeled "likely." This data scientist (who considers a "likely" prediction to be a bad thing) insists that the model unfairly stigmatizes group B.

Argument 4

> 20/125 = 16% of group A were falsely labeled "unlikely," whereas only 5/125 = 4% of group B were falsely labeled "unlikely." This data scientist (who considers an "unlikely" prediction to be a bad thing) insists that the model unfairly stigmatizes group A.

Which of these data scientists is correct? Are any of them correct? Perhaps it depends on the context.

Possibly you feel one way if the two groups are "men" and "women" and another way if the two groups are "R users" and "Python users." Or possibly not if it turns out that Python users skew male and R users skew female?

Possibly you feel one way if the model is for predicting whether a DataSciencester user will *apply* for a job through the DataSciencester job board and another way if the model is predicting whether a user will *pass* such an interview.

Possibly your opinion depends on the model itself, what features it takes into account, and what data it was trained on.

In any event, my point is to impress upon you that there can be a tradeoff between "accuracy" and "fairness" (depending, of course, on how you define them) and that these tradeoffs don't always have obvious "right" solutions.

Collaboration

A repressive (by your standards) country's government officials have finally decided to allow citizens to join DataSciencester. However, they insist that the users from their country not be allowed to discuss deep learning. Furthermore, they want you to report to them the names of any users who even *try* to seek out information on deep learning.

Are this country's data scientists better off with access to the topic-limited (and surveilled) DataSciencester that you'd be allowed to offer? Or are the proposed restrictions so awful that they'd be better off with no access at all?

Interpretability

The DataSciencester HR department asks you to develop a model predicting which employees are most at risk of leaving the company, so that it can intervene and try to make them happier. (Attrition rate is an important component of the "10 Happiest Workplaces" magazine feature that your CEO aspires to appear in.)

You've collected an assortment of historical data and are considering three models:

- A decision tree
- A neural network
- A high-priced "retention expert"

One of your data scientists insists that you should just use whichever model performs best.

A second insists that you not use the neural network model, as only the other two can explain their predictions, and that only explanation of the predictions can help HR institute widespread changes (as opposed to one-off interventions).

A third says that while the "expert" can offer *an* explanation for her predictions, there's no reason to take her at her word that it describes the *real* reasons she predicted the way she did.

As with our other examples, there is no absolute best choice here. In some circumstances (possibly for legal reasons or if your predictions are somehow life-changing) you might prefer a model that performs worse but whose predictions can be explained. In others, you might just want the model that predicts best. In still others, perhaps there is no interpretable model that performs well.

Recommendations

As we discussed in Chapter 23, a common data science application involves recommending things to people. When someone watches a YouTube video, YouTube recommends videos they should watch next.

YouTube makes money through advertising and (presumably) wants to recommend videos that you are more likely to watch, so that they can show you more advertisements. However, it turns out that people like to watch videos about conspiracy theories, which tend to feature in the recommendations.

 At the time I wrote this chapter, if you searched YouTube for "saturn" the third result was "Something Is Happening On Saturn… Are THEY Hiding It?" which maybe gives you a sense of the kinds of videos I'm talking about.

Does YouTube have an obligation not to recommend conspiracy videos? Even if that's what lots of people seem to want to watch?

A different example is that if you go to google.com (or bing.com) and start typing a search, the search engine will offer suggestions to autocomplete your search. These suggestions are based (at least in part) on other people's searches; in particular, if other people are searching for unsavory things this may be reflected in your suggestions.

Should a search engine try to affirmatively filter out suggestions it doesn't like? Google (for whatever reason) seems intent on not suggesting things related to people's religion. For example, if you type "mitt romney m" into Bing, the first suggestion is "mitt romney mormon" (which is what I would have expected), whereas Google refuses to provide that suggestion.

Indeed, Google explicitly filters out autosuggestions that it considers "offensive or disparaging" (*https://blog.google/products/search/google-search-autocomplete/*). (How it decides what's offensive or disparaging is left vague.) And yet sometimes the truth is offensive. Is protecting people from those suggestions the ethical thing to do? Or is it an unethical thing to do? Or is it not a question of ethics at all?

Biased Data

In "Word Vectors" on page 293 we used a corpus of documents to learn vector embeddings for words. These vectors were designed to exhibit *distributional similarity*. That is, words that appear in similar contexts should have similar vectors. In particular, any biases that exist in the training data will be reflected in the word vectors themselves.

For example, if our documents are all about how R users are moral reprobates and how Python users are paragons of virtue, most likely the model will learn such associations for "Python" and "R."

More commonly, word vectors are based on some combination of Google News articles, Wikipedia, books, and crawled web pages. This means that they'll learn whatever distributional patterns are present in those sources.

For example, if the majority of news articles about software engineers are about *male* software engineers, then the learned vector for "software" might lie closer to vectors for other "male" words than to the vectors for "female" words.

At that point any downstream applications you build using these vectors might also exhibit this closeness. Depending on the application, this may or may not be a problem for you. In that case there are various techniques that you can try to "remove" specific biases, although you'll probably never get all of them. But it's something you should be aware of.

Similarly, as in the "photos" example in "Building Bad Data Products" on page 363, if you train a model on nonrepresentative data, there's a strong possibility it will perform poorly in the real world, possibly in ways that are offensive or embarrassing.

Along different lines, it's also possible that your algorithms might codify actual biases that exist out in the world. For example, your parole model may do a perfect job of predicting which released criminals get rearrested, but if those rearrests are themselves the result of biased real-world processes, then your model might be perpetuating that bias.

Data Protection

You know a lot about the DataSciencester users. You know what technologies they like, who their data scientist friends are, where they work, how much they earn, how much time they spend on the site, which job postings they click on, and so forth.

The VP of Monetization wants to sell this data to advertisers, who are eager to market their various "big data" solutions to your users. The Chief Scientist wants to share this data with academic researchers, who are keen to publish papers about who becomes a data scientist. The VP of Electioneering has plans to provide this data to political campaigns, most of whom are eager to recruit their own data science organizations. And the VP of Government Affairs would like to use this data to answer questions from law enforcement.

Thanks to a forward-thinking VP of Contracts, your users agreed to terms of service that guarantee you the right to do pretty much whatever you want with their data.

However (as you have now come to expect), various of the data scientists on your team raise various objections to these various uses. One thinks it's wrong to hand the data over to advertisers; another worries that academics can't be trusted to safeguard the data responsibly. A third thinks that the company should stay out of politics, while the last insists that police can't be trusted and that collaborating with law enforcement will harm innocent people.

Do any of these data scientists have a point?

In Summary

These are a lot of things to worry about! And there are countless more we haven't mentioned, and still more that will come up in the future but that would never occur to us today.

For Further Exploration

- There is no shortage of people professing important thoughts about data ethics. Searching on Twitter (or your favorite news site) is probably the best way to find out about the most current data ethics controversy.

- If you want something slightly more practical, Mike Loukides, Hilary Mason, and DJ Patil have written a short ebook, *Ethics and Data Science* (*https://www.oreilly.com/library/view/ethics-and-data/9781492043898/*), on putting data ethics into practice, which I am honor-bound to recommend on account of Mike being the person who agreed to publish *Data Science from Scratch* way back in 2014. (Exercise: is this ethical of me?)

## CHAPTER 27

Go Forth and Do Data Science

And now, once again, I bid my hideous progeny go forth and prosper.
—Mary Shelley

Where do you go from here? Assuming I haven't scared you off of data science, there are a number of things you should learn next.

IPython

I mentioned IPython (*http://ipython.org/*) earlier in the book. It provides a shell with far more functionality than the standard Python shell, and it adds "magic functions" that allow you to (among other things) easily copy and paste code (which is normally complicated by the combination of blank lines and whitespace formatting) and run scripts from within the shell.

Mastering IPython will make your life far easier. (Even learning just a little bit of IPython will make your life a lot easier.)

In the first edition, I also recommended that you learn about the IPython (now Jupyter) Notebook, a computational environment that allows you to combine text, live Python code, and visualizations.

I've since become a notebook skeptic (*https://twitter.com/joelgrus/status/1033035196428378113*), as I find that they confuse beginners and encourage bad coding practices. (I have many other reasons too.) You will surely receive plenty of encouragement to use them from people who aren't me, so just remember that I'm the dissenting voice.

Mathematics

Throughout this book, we dabbled in linear algebra (Chapter 4), statistics (Chapter 5), probability (Chapter 6), and various aspects of machine learning.

To be a good data scientist, you should know much more about these topics, and I encourage you to give each of them a more in-depth study, using the textbooks recommended at the ends of the chapters, your own preferred textbooks, online courses, or even real-life courses.

Not from Scratch

Implementing things "from scratch" is great for understanding how they work. But it's generally not great for performance (unless you're implementing them specifically with performance in mind), ease of use, rapid prototyping, or error handling.

In practice, you'll want to use well-designed libraries that solidly implement the fundamentals. My original proposal for this book involved a second "now let's learn the libraries" half that O'Reilly, thankfully, vetoed. Since the first edition came out, Jake VanderPlas has written the *Python Data Science Handbook* (*http://shop.oreilly.com/product/0636920034919.do*) (O'Reilly), which is a good introduction to the relevant libraries and would be a good book for you to read next.

NumPy

NumPy (*http://www.numpy.org*) (for "Numeric Python") provides facilities for doing "real" scientific computing. It features arrays that perform better than our `list`-vectors, matrices that perform better than our `list-of-list`-matrices, and lots of numeric functions for working with them.

NumPy is a building block for many other libraries, which makes it especially valuable to know.

pandas

pandas (*http://pandas.pydata.org*) provides additional data structures for working with datasets in Python. Its primary abstraction is the `DataFrame`, which is conceptually similar to the NotQuiteABase `Table` class we constructed in Chapter 24, but with much more functionality and better performance.

If you're going to use Python to munge, slice, group, and manipulate datasets, pandas is an invaluable tool.

scikit-learn

scikit-learn (*http://scikit-learn.org*) is probably the most popular library for doing machine learning in Python. It contains all the models we've implemented and many more that we haven't. On a real problem, you'd never build a decision tree from scratch; you'd let scikit-learn do the heavy lifting. On a real problem, you'd never write an optimization algorithm by hand; you'd count on scikit-learn to already be using a really good one.

Its documentation contains many, many examples (*http://scikit-learn.org/stable/auto_examples/*) of what it can do (and, more generally, what machine learning can do).

Visualization

The matplotlib charts we've been creating have been clean and functional but not particularly stylish (and not at all interactive). If you want to get deeper into data visualization, you have several options.

The first is to further explore matplotlib, only a handful of whose features we've actually covered. Its website contains many examples (*http://matplotlib.org/examples/*) of its functionality and a gallery (*http://matplotlib.org/gallery.html*) of some of the more interesting ones. If you want to create static visualizations (say, for printing in a book), this is probably your best next step.

You should also check out seaborn (*https://seaborn.pydata.org/*), which is a library that (among other things) makes matplotlib more attractive.

If you'd like to create *interactive* visualizations that you can share on the web, the obvious choice is probably D3.js (*http://d3js.org*), a JavaScript library for creating "data-driven documents" (those are the three Ds). Even if you don't know much JavaScript, it's often possible to crib examples from the D3 gallery (*https://github.com/mbostock/d3/wiki/Gallery*) and tweak them to work with your data. (Good data scientists copy from the D3 gallery; great data scientists *steal* from the D3 gallery.)

Even if you have no interest in D3, just browsing the gallery is itself a pretty incredible education in data visualization.

Bokeh (*http://bokeh.pydata.org*) is a project that brings D3-style functionality into Python.

R

Although you can totally get away with not learning R (*http://www.r-project.org*), a lot of data scientists and data science projects use it, so it's worth getting at least familiar with it.

In part, this is so that you can understand people's R-based blog posts and examples and code; in part, this is to help you better appreciate the (comparatively) clean elegance of Python; and in part, this is to help you be a more informed participant in the never-ending "R versus Python" flamewars.

Deep Learning

You can be a data scientist without doing deep learning, but you can't be a *trendy* data scientist without doing deep learning.

The two most popular deep learning frameworks for Python are TensorFlow (*https://www.tensorflow.org/*) (created by Google) and PyTorch (*https://pytorch.org/*) (created by Facebook). The internet is full of tutorials for them that range from wonderful to awful.

TensorFlow is older and more widely used, but PyTorch is (in my opinion) much easier to use and (in particular) much more beginner-friendly. I prefer (and recommend) PyTorch, but—as they say—no one ever got fired for choosing TensorFlow.

Find Data

If you're doing data science as part of your job, you'll most likely get the data as part of your job (although not necessarily). What if you're doing data science for fun? Data is everywhere, but here are some starting points:

- Data.gov (*http://www.data.gov*) is the government's open data portal. If you want data on anything that has to do with the government (which seems to be most things these days), it's a good place to start.
- Reddit has a couple of forums, r/datasets (*http://www.reddit.com/r/datasets*) and r/data (*http://www.reddit.com/r/data*), that are places to both ask for and discover data.
- Amazon.com maintains a collection of public datasets (*http://aws.amazon.com/public-data-sets/*) that they'd like you to analyze using their products (but that you can analyze with whatever products you want).
- Robb Seaton has a quirky list of curated datasets on his blog (*http://rs.io/100-interesting-data-sets-for-statistics/*).
- Kaggle (*https://www.kaggle.com/*) is a site that holds data science competitions. I never managed to get into it (I don't have much of a competitive nature when it comes to data science), but you might. They host a lot of datasets.
- Google has a newish Dataset Search (*https://toolbox.google.com/datasetsearch*) that lets you (you guessed it) search for datasets.

Do Data Science

Looking through data catalogs is fine, but the best projects (and products) are ones that tickle some sort of itch. Here are a few that I've done.

Hacker News

Hacker News (*https://news.ycombinator.com/news*) is a news aggregation and discussion site for technology-related news. It collects lots and lots of articles, many of which aren't interesting to me.

Accordingly, several years ago, I set out to build a Hacker News story classifier (*https://github.com/joelgrus/hackernews*) to predict whether I would or would not be interested in any given story. This did not go over so well with the users of Hacker News, who resented the idea that someone might not be interested in every story on the site.

This involved hand-labeling a lot of stories (in order to have a training set), choosing story features (for example, words in the title, and domains of the links), and training a Naive Bayes classifier not unlike our spam filter.

For reasons now lost to history, I built it in Ruby. Learn from my mistakes.

Fire Trucks

For many years I lived on a major street in downtown Seattle, halfway between a fire station and most of the city's fires (or so it seemed). Accordingly, I developed a recreational interest in the Seattle Fire Department.

Luckily (from a data perspective), they maintain a Real-Time 911 site (*http://www2.seattle.gov/fire/realtime911/getDatePubTab.asp*) that lists every fire alarm along with the fire trucks involved.

And so, to indulge my interest, I scraped many years' worth of fire alarm data and performed a social network analysis (*https://github.com/joelgrus/fire*) of the fire trucks. Among other things, this required me to invent a fire-truck-specific notion of centrality, which I called TruckRank.

T-Shirts

I have a young daughter, and an incessant source of frustration to me throughout her childhood has been that most "girls' shirts" are quite boring, while many "boys' shirts" are a lot of fun.

In particular, it felt clear to me that there was a distinct difference between the shirts marketed to toddler boys and toddler girls. And so I asked myself if I could train a model to recognize these differences.

Spoiler: I could (*https://github.com/joelgrus/shirts*).

This involved downloading the images of hundreds of shirts, shrinking them all to the same size, turning them into vectors of pixel colors, and using logistic regression to build a classifier.

One approach looked simply at which colors were present in each shirt; a second found the first 10 principal components of the shirt image vectors and classified each shirt using its projections into the 10-dimensional space spanned by the "eigenshirts" (Figure 27-1).

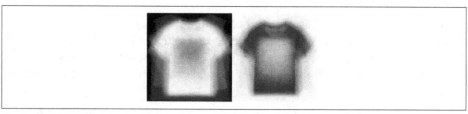

Figure 27-1. Eigenshirts corresponding to the first principal component

Tweets on a Globe

For many years I'd wanted to build a "spinning globe" visualization. During the 2016 election, I built a small web app (*https://twitter.com/voxdotcom/status/1069427256580284416*) that listened for geotagged tweets matching some search (I used "Trump," as it appeared in lots of tweets at that time), displayed them, and spun a globe to their location as they appeared.

This was entirely a JavaScript data project, so maybe learn some JavaScript.

And You?

What interests you? What questions keep you up at night? Look for a dataset (or scrape some websites) and do some data science.

Let me know what you find! Email me at *joelgrus@gmail.com* or find me on Twitter at *@joelgrus* (*https://twitter.com/joelgrus/*).

Index

A

A/B tests, 94
accuracy, 158
activation functions, 251
AllenNLP, 308
Altair library, 52
Anaconda Python distribution, 16
args, 37
argument unpacking, 36
arithmetic operations, 56
arrays, 22
artificial neural networks, 227
assert statements, 30
automated testing, 30
average (mean), 65

B

backpropagation, 233
bagging, 226
bar charts, 45-49
batch gradient descent, 109
Bayesian inference, 95
Bayes's theorem, 78
Beautiful Soup library, 117
bell-shaped curve, 81
BernoulliNB model, 184
Beta distributions, 96
betweenness centrality, 309-314
bias input, 230
bias-variance tradeoff, 160
biased data, 367
bigram models, 282
binary judgments, 158
Binomial distributions, 97

binomial random variables, 84
Bokeh library, 53, 373
Booleans, 28
bootstrap aggregating, 226
bootstrapping, 196
bottom-up hierarchical clustering, 271-276
breadth-first search, 311
business models, 153
Buzzword clouds, 280

C

causation, 73
central limit theorem, 84
central tendencies, 65
centrality
    betweenness, 309-314
    closeness, 313
    degree, 5
    eigenvector, 314-318
    other types of, 320
character-level RNNs, 304
charts
    bar charts, 45-49
    line charts, 44, 49
    scatterplots, 50-52
classes, 31
classification trees, 217
cleaning data, 138
closeness centrality, 313
clustering
    bottom-up hierarchical clustering, 271-276
    choosing k, 268
    clustering colors example, 269
    concept of, 263

statistics
  correlation, 68-71
    causation and, 73
    correlational caveats, 72
    Simpson's paradox, 71
  describing single sets of data, 63-68
  resources for learning, 74
  tools for, 73
StatsModels, 73
statsmodels, 202
status updates, analyzing, 355
stemmer functions, 183
stochastic gradient descent, 109
stride, 22
strings, 21, 121
Structured Query Language (SQL), 335 (see
  also databases and SQL)
Student's t-distribution, 199
Sum layer, 302
sum of squares, computing, 58
supervised models, 154
support vector machines, 210
Surprise, 333
sys.stdin, 111
sys.stdout, 111

T

tab-separated files, 115
tanh function, 251
TensorFlow, 374
tensors, 239
ternerary operators, 27
test sets, 157
text files, 113, 121
topic modeling, 288-293
tqdm library, 144
training sets, 157
trigrams, 283
true positives/true negatives, 158
truthiness, 28
tuples, 23, 135
Twitter APIs, 124-128
two-dimensional datasets, 131
Twython library, 124-128
type 1/type 2 errors, 89, 158
type annotations, 38-42

U

unauthenticated APIs, 122
underfitting and overfitting, 155
underflow, 177
undirected edges, 309
uniform distributions, 80
unit tests, 180
unpacking lists, 23
unsupervised learning, 263
unsupervised models, 154
UPDATE statement, 338
user-based collaborative filtering, 323

V

validation sets, 157
variables
  binomial random variables, 84
  confounding variables, 71
  random variables, 79
variance, 67, 160
vectors, 55-59
virtual environments, 16

W

weak learners, 226
web scraping
  HTML parsing, 117
  press release data example, 118
  using APIs, 121
weight tensors, randomly generating, 244
while loops, 27
whitespace formatting, 17
word clouds, 279
word counting, 26, 352
word vectors, 293-301

X

Xavier initialization, 244
XGBoost, 226
XOR example, 250

Z

Zen of Python, 15
zip function, 36

About the Author

Joel Grus is a research engineer at the Allen Institute for Artificial Intelligence. Previously he worked as a software engineer at Google and a data scientist at several start-ups. He lives in Seattle, where he regularly attends data science happy hours. He blogs infrequently at *joelgrus.com* and tweets all day long at *@joelgrus* (*https://twitter.com/ joelgrus/*).

Colophon

The animal on the cover of *Data Science from Scratch*, Second Edition, is a rock ptarmigan (*Lagopus muta*). This hardy, chicken-sized member of the grouse family inhabits the tundra environments of the northern hemisphere, living in the arctic and subarctic regions of Eurasia and North America. A ground feeder, it forages across these grasslands on its well-feathered feet, eating birch and willow buds, as well as seeds, flowers, leaves, and berries. Rock ptarmigan chicks also eat insects.

Rock ptarmigan are best known for the striking annual changes in their cryptic camouflage, having evolved to molt and regrow white and brownish-colored feathers a few times over the course of a year to best match the changing seasonal colors of their environment. In winter they have white feathers; in spring and fall, as snow cover mixes with open grassland, their feathers mix white and brown; and in summer, their patterned brown feathers match the varied coloring of the tundra. With this camouflage female ptarmigan can near-invisibly incubate their eggs, which are laid in nests on the ground.

Mature male rock ptarmigan also have a fringed, red comb structure over their eyes. During breeding season this is used for courtship display as well as signaling between contending males (studies have shown a correlation between comb size and male testosterone levels).

Ptarmigan populations are currently declining, though in their range they remain common (albeit difficult to spot). Ptarmigan have many predators, including arctic foxes, gyrfalcons, gulls, and jaegers. Also, in time, climate change may make their seasonal color changes a liability.

Many of the animals on O'Reilly covers are endangered; all of them are important to the world.

The cover image is from *Cassell's Book of Birds* (1875), by Thomas Rymer Jones. The cover fonts are Gilroy and Guardian Sans. The text font is Adobe Minion Pro; the heading font is Adobe Myriad Condensed; and the code font is Dalton Maag's Ubuntu Mono.